D1480078

TESTING WARS IN THE PUBLIC SCHOOLS

William J. Reese

Testing Wars in the Public Schools

A Forgotten History

HARVARD UNIVERSITY PRESS

Cambridge, Massachusetts, and London, England   2013

Library of Congress Cataloging-in-Publication Data

Reese, William J., 1951–
  Testing wars in the public schools : a forgotten history / William J. Reese.
    p. cm.
  Includes bibliographical references and index.
  ISBN 978-0-674-07304-3
  1. Educational tests and measurements—United States—History—19th
century. 2. Public schools—United States—History—19th century. I. Title.
  LB3051.R3553 2013
    371.26097309034   2012033665

To the memory of Lil and Ike Blemker

Contents

Introduction   *1*

1   Festivals of Learning   *8*

2   A-Putting Down Sin   *38*

3   Screwing Machines   *69*

4   A Pile of Thunder-Bolts   *98*

5   Thanatopsis and Square Roots   *127*

6   Chewing Pencil Tops   *158*

7   The Culture of Testing   *188*

Epilogue   *221*

Notes   *235*

Acknowledgments   *291*

Index   *293*

TESTING WARS IN THE PUBLIC SCHOOLS

Introduction

"This is a paper on examinations," the speaker warned his audience, "so, after you have heard it read, and have duly considered it, of course you will mark it—it may be zero—it may be infinity: and, after all, what's the difference?" For time would still pass, the stars still "sparkle, the sun still shine, figures still lie," pupils and teachers still tremble. "This is an age of examinations," he added. "Is it not a wonder that so many of our American boys and girls survive the almost continual examinations to which they are subjected? There are oral examinations, written examinations, daily examinations, weekly examinations, monthly examinations, quarterly examinations, yearly examinations, examinations for admission, examinations for promotion, examinations for graduation, competitive examinations. County Superintendent's examinations, School Board examinations, State examinations, legal examinations, medical examinations, spiritual examinations; in short, there is no end of examinations in this life and so thoroughly do we carry out the system that we even give a mortgage on the next by introducing a post mortem."[1]

An experienced administrator and current high school principal in Hyde Park, then a Chicago suburb, Charles I. Parker knew what he was talking about. In 1878, he had been invited to speak at the State Teachers' Association convention in Springfield. His audience consisted of superintendents, principals, and teachers, all of whom worked in a profession becoming transformed by the power and authority of written tests, especially in urban areas. Over the last few decades, villages, towns, and cities in the northern states had grouped children into classes and grades, an effort to build a more sequenced curriculum from the ABCs and the

1

basics extending to the high school. Implementing these forms of classroom organization faced considerable obstacles, since they challenged traditional practices. Moreover, most children lived in sparsely populated rural areas and attended ungraded one-room schools. But towns and cities were the future, where school innovation was greatest and written test scores became the dominant measure of student achievement.[2]

While not opposed to testing in reasonable doses, Parker believed America was gripped by "examination mania," turning pupils into "walking encyclopedias" and threatening to send teachers to an early grave or "insane asylum." School administrators spent countless hours preparing tests, calculating numbers, and compiling tables to track the academic progress of pupils and hold teachers accountable. Schools were being converted into "a statistical bureau." Without tenure or high status, teachers drilled, crammed, and coached their students, telling them to love knowledge for its own sake while dutifully recording marks and percentages for report cards and posterity. As examination days approached, students memorized the lengths of rivers and lists of words and definitions, the succession of American presidents and English monarchs, and countless historical dates, grammatical rules, and mathematical formulas. As written tests grew more common and influential, some ambitious scholars purchased "quiz books" with thousands of questions and answers on every school subject to game the new system.

An educational revolution occurred in the nineteenth century whose story remains untold. Unlike today, pupils in 1800 did not compete in timed, standardized, written examinations. As in previous centuries, the reputation of a school rested upon impressions. Did a teacher have an orderly school? Had pupils behaved and performed well when parents and community members visited a classroom? Most schools held annual exhibitions, popular community events. There the village elders might pose some questions to a few pupils, prepped for weeks by their teacher; other students memorized speeches to recite or entertained the audience with songs and religious hymns. The words "examination" and "exhibition" were often used synonymously. By the end of the nineteenth century, however, no respectable educator regarded a public performance as an examination. A real exam happened not in public but in class, tested everyone simultaneously, followed standard procedures, compared pupils, and produced results in black-and-white.

The history of this striking transformation is the focus of the *Testing Wars in the Public Schools: A Forgotten History.* Many scholars have explored various aspects of the evolution of testing, whose modern foundation rested upon nineteenth-century developments. Concentrating on later periods, historians have demonstrated that in the early decades of the twentieth century "examination mania" was alive and well, exemplified by the invention of intelligence, achievement, college admission, occupational, and every other imaginable kind of test. The triumph of testing in an age enamored of scientific management and governance by experts seemed to trump the rival ideals of child-centered educators inspired by Francis Parker, John Dewey, and other progressives. By 1930, the overbearing influence of psychometrics caused one educationist to describe an "orgy of testing" in the public schools. After World War II, more sophisticated statistical methods and recurrent demands by politicians and the public for accountability ensured that testing proliferated and high scores became the hallmark of a successful school.[3]

Testing is now a multibillion dollar enterprise. Test prep companies abound, and reformers try to link teachers' salaries to student scores. Charter school advocates promise better measurable results than regular schools. States compete for lucrative federal grants in a frantic "race to the top," an educational Mount Olympus ruled by school innovators, high-priced consultants, and the testing gods. Policy-makers and politicians routinely debate how to lift scores among the poor and racial minorities, and the media regularly report America's low performance on international tests in mathematics and science. When conservative Republicans joined hands with liberal Democrats such as Senator Ted Kennedy to pass *No Child Left Behind* (2002), accelerating federal authority in education, they assumed that more testing would raise standards throughout the school system. According to the law, every child would be proficient in the basics by 2014.[4]

While humorist Garrison Keillor reminds us that all of the children in mythical Lake Wobegon are "above average," the hard facts of life, never mind basic statistics, suggest otherwise everywhere else. Tests at school assume many forms and serve high stakes or low, but they typically document differences expressed in percentiles, standard deviations, and similar language alien to everyday speech. Tests are so familiar and seemingly natural that it requires imagination to remember that, like every other social activity, they have a history, in their case a fascinating one. In England, Cambridge University first adopted written tests in the eighteenth century to identify candidates for honours degrees. But as Charles Parker recognized, the nineteenth century was the age of examinations. It was when reformers first applied principles from a young science called statistics to America's public schools and our national obsession with testing originated.[5]

To understand why testing became so important means stepping back in time. This book revises the familiar narrative of the history of testing, insisting that competitive examinations were central to the very establishment of public school systems in the pre-Civil War era. By the 1840s, some of America's leading educational reformers advanced what later became known as standardized tests. Moreover, while modern critics routinely condemn testing as an enabler of sterile pedagogy, its most prominent and influential champions in the antebellum period believed it would advance the cause of progressive pedagogy. They were horrified at contemporary classroom practices that included heavy doses of memorization and occasional tanning of the hide. Reformers believed that competitive testing, enlightened pedagogy, and humane forms of discipline were fully compatible and mutually reinforcing.

Infatuated with statistics, reformers were awestruck by the potential value of written examinations. They confidently assumed that the proliferation of competitive tests through newly conceived pencil-and-paper formats would help revolutionize instruction. Testing was integrally bound with other far-reaching, interlocking reforms: more centralized authority, the setting of academic standards by elected officials or administrators, better age-graded classes taught by women, and more uniform textbooks and curricula. Test scores promised to document student achievement and to identify lazy and incompetent as well as effective and inspiring teachers. Abolitionists within educational reform circles also believed that tests could document the failure of public schools to lift the achievement of African-Americans and underscore the need for racially integrated classrooms.

To raise standards across the board and ensure accountability, antebellum reformers were the first to rank urban teachers, students, and schools based on quantitative scores, to shame the worst and honor the best. By the end of the nineteenth century, these reformers helped change how parents, taxpayers, and the public measured a school's worth. In the process, they set the basic parameters for debates about competitive tests and their meaning that echo—eerily so—to this very day.

The *Testing Wars in the Public Schools* begins with a panoramic view of a world that has disappeared, when Americans judged schools on the basis of public performances. It then centers on dramatic developments in Boston, where a handful of activists secretly crafted America's first big written test in 1845. Convinced that local schools were in a state of decline, these reformers faced formidable opposition from local and neighborhood interests as they tried to use test scores to transform educational practices from top to bottom, from how schools were organized to how teachers taught. Enjoying the benefits of college, professional training in law or medicine, and travel abroad, the leading reformers saw themselves as sophisticated, cosmopolitan people whose innovative ideas about teaching and classroom practices would improve and forever change American education. Their opponents regarded them as arrogant and pompous, disrespectful of the time-tested ways that communities judged schools. Heavily shaped by personal vendettas and political intrigue, Boston's experiment led to the first searching inquiries into the meaning, potential, and limitations of tests as reformers labored to document what children learned at school.

What reformers wrought in Boston was only the beginning. Less than a generation after Boston's controversial experiment, competitive exams were commonplace. By the 1870s and 1880s, testing was so widespread in America's cities that it generated a backlash. Critics complained that testing narrowed the curriculum, undermined the broad purposes of schooling, ruined children's health, and made teachers automatons, forcing them to teach to the test. But written, timed, in-class exams and statistical measures were here to stay, as traditional means of assessing schools lost their legitimacy. By 1900, their influence seemed unassailable. In subsequent decades, high school and college enrollments boomed, academic credentials grew in importance, and tests helped place pupils in ability groups, vocational tracks, and other pathways to adulthood.

Competitive testing, however, originated in the early decades of the nineteenth century, long before standardized exams became big business and corporations dominated American life. While a more visible federal regulatory state emerged in the early 1900s in areas such as banking, transportation, food and drugs, and even the consumption—and prohibition—of alcohol, government in different guises already shaped many aspects of American society. Since the nation's founding, political parties quarreled over the appropriate boundaries of local, state, and federal authority, but both elected officials and (male) voters assumed that government and its institutions would help shape fundamental aspects of daily life. State and federal aid, for example, helped entrepreneurs and private interests build the canals, turnpikes, and railroads that stimulated commerce and trade; tariff policies set in Washington, DC, affected the price of goods everywhere; and a national postal system enabled newspapers, the publishing industry, and a reading public to thrive. Government coffers thus stimulated the "invisible hand" of the market as advances in technology, communication, and transportation allowed ideas as well as goods to travel more cheaply and efficiently over ever-expanding national boundaries.[6]

New ideas about assessing schools and measuring academic merit could not have spread so rapidly after the 1840s without such public and private investments in internal improvements. They lowered the costs of printing common tests and textbooks and accelerated the distribution of periodicals and reports that chronicled innovative ways to teach, discipline, and evaluate teachers and pupils. Absent a strong federal agency to direct educational change—the U.S. Bureau of Education, founded in 1867, was tiny and toothless—innovations such as testing attracted attention through the correspondence, speeches, and writings of key reformers and the official publications of nascent professional groups dedicated to educational improvement. By mid-century, statistics provided Americans with a new way to perceive reality, whether the subject was poverty, insanity, or what exactly children mastered at school. Through trial and error, imitation and duplication, city schools in particular literally became a testing ground for novel educational ideas and practices.[7]

By the late nineteenth century, competitive written examinations were so ubiquitous that, in his speech in Springfield, Principal Parker accused testing zealots of vanity and arrogance and urged a little modesty among educators mesmerized by test scores. He quoted Isabella's sobering words in *Measure for Measure*. If every "pelting petty officer" possessed the power of Jove, she warned, they "would use his heaven for thunder: nothing but thunder.—Merciful heaven!"

. . . Man, proud man!
Dressed in a little brief authority,
Most ignorant of what he's most assured,
His glassy essence, like an angry ape,
Plays such fantastic tricks before high heaven
As make the angels weep. . . .[8]

The angels may weep, like a student who fails, but the authority of tests
has endured.

CHAPTER 1

Festivals of Learning

Mr. Spoutsound had a diminutive frame but a booming voice, impressing the villagers, who wondered why he had not become a preacher. On the Sabbath he drowned out fellow congregants honoring the Lord. A single term at an academy, where he cultivated public speaking, enabled him to land a teaching position for the winter term at a one-room school in rural New Hampshire. A former pupil described him as nothing less than "an enthusiastic votary to the Ciceronian art." Men filled most teaching positions in the early nineteenth century, and college students often taught between terms to help pay their tuition and prepare for the more prestigious and lucrative professions. Spoutsound was also just passing through, heading west and destined to practice law, where his oratorical skills might impress judge and jury. Before leaving New England, however, he made sure his pupils showcased their learning before the community. Pupils everywhere spent their days memorizing facts from textbooks and reciting them to their teachers. So a public exhibition "was a pleasant relief to the dullness of the old-fashioned routine," recalled the Reverend Warren Burton, who recounted his school days in *The District School As It Was.*[1]

Burton was born in Wilton, New Hampshire, in 1800. First published in Boston in 1833, his book became hugely popular, excerpted in newspapers and magazines and given flattering reviews. While disguising the name of his teacher, Burton recreated a familiar world and tapped the nostalgia of his readers. Like Burton, who graduated from Harvard and lived in greater Boston, most people grew up on farms or in rural areas. If formally educated, they attended ungraded one-room schools, where a single teacher usually taught pupils of all ages. School exhibitions were among the basic ways parents and taxpayers judged the fitness of teachers and accomplishments of students. Once Spoutsound announced the date of the exhibition, pupils searched in their school books for dialogues, poems, and speeches, everyone eager to impress parents and friends. For a week or two, he prepped his scholars, helping them calm their nerves while instructing them in the standard elocutionary rules on posture, gesture, breathing, and articulation. Even with his guidance, Burton recalled, "the old school-house" reminded him of "a little Babel in the confusion of tongues."[2]

Parents, too, helped their children, some barely past their ABCs, master their material, which they would "screech . . . out with most ear-splitting execution." On the last day of school the minister and committee that hired Spoutsound quizzed some scholars in an oral exam. The big event came later. As Burton explained, "the people of the district all intended to be at the exhibition in the evening, and examination was 'just nothing at all' with that in prospect." By half past six, the community huddled into the school to appraise the "oratorical gifts and accomplishments" of the pupils, all nicely attired and assembled on a makeshift stage. Some students entertained the audience with their musical instruments. Spoutsound then spoke, confirming his reputation for eloquence. As rehearsed, the pupils took their places. Several dramatists dressed in revolutionary garb proclaimed the grandeur of the nation and commitment to liberty. Eleven-year-old Memorus Wordwell "yelped forth" a stirring speech by William Pitt. Nearly every pupil had a turn, each rewarded with a rousing applause. The ritual completed, the crowd dispersed and the master moved on, soon replaced by another itinerant.[3]

Like modern pupils facing a high-stakes test, students departed from their usual classroom routines—memorizing subject matter and reciting to their teacher—to focus on the task at hand: doing well before Spoutsound, the school committee, and the community at large. Burton complained that the exhibition "swallowed up very much of the time that should have been devoted to the really important branches of education." Critical of dilapidated schoolhouses and tiresome pedagogical methods, he well described the traditional way that citizens at home and abroad evaluated a school: by impressions, not empirical evidence. Impressions could rest upon a public performance as well as the teacher's demeanor, appearance, ability to govern pupils, or willingness to accept a paltry salary of $8 a month.[4]

Within a decade of the publication of Burton's reminiscence, a new and controversial way to measure academic performance—through statistics generated by pupil scores on common written tests—attracted heightened attention in the northern seaboard cities. Written examinations did not transform the world of schooling overnight, but an educational revolution had begun, its importance better appreciated by understanding the traditional world of values and practices it ultimately supplanted.

While evaluating school achievement apart from standardized tests and statistics seems inconceivable today, everyone in the early nineteenth century evaluated schools on the basis of what they saw and heard. Familiar ways to identify, celebrate, and honor educational achievement had tradition on their side. Historically, oral presentations such as recitations, orations, and dialogues enabled adults to form opinions about students and teachers. Other forms of public display also mattered. Whenever pupils marched in school processions and parades, adults watched attentively to see how well they behaved, another marker of educational success. These ingrained ways of thinking about schools and how to assess them stood as a mighty fortress against the forces of change. Observations and hearsay counted for more than answers on slate or paper.

By the 1840s, reformers doubted that oral presentations and public exhibitions provided reliable evidence on how to judge a school. In the late eighteenth and early nineteenth centuries, however, it mattered not whether pupils attended all-male colleges or Latin grammar schools, charity schools or tuition-charging academies that admitted boys and girls alike, or racially segregated institutions. Competition on the public stage, said most adults, ensured that all children would strive for improvement and a few would excel.

I

"If other countries have their festivals for Saints, we have ours for patriotism and learning," wrote the editor of the *Boston Commercial Gazette* in the summer of 1825, following the annual dinner honoring the medal winners at the local grammar schools. "There is scarcely a village around us, but has some parade of a school examination, or an academic exhibition, in the course of a season." Festivals and celebrations of learning abounded. "Every muse is invoked for the occasion, and the names of the bards and orators of Greece and Rome become familiar to every infant ear. These are," the editor continued, "the holy-days of intellect, and the pledges for the diffusion of knowledge." Parades, festivals, processions, and exhibitions revealed what teachers taught and pupils learned not only to "animate the youthful" but also to awaken "the recollections of the aged." Reverend Burton could not have said it better.[5]

Parading and exhibiting children was very common in America's villages and urban centers by the late eighteenth century and drew upon considerable historical precedent. These practices were adapted from Catholic Europe by way of Protestant England. Orations and disputations were distinctive features of colleges and universities since their founding in the twelfth century. These and other aspects of the higher learning filtered down to every manner of school. In medieval Europe, children and adults also participated in ancient pagan festivals such as May Day and traditional feast and harvest days. Catholics added numerous religious holidays, some specifically for children. St. Nicholas Day honored the patron saint of children, while the Slaughter of the Innocents evoked memories of evil King Herod. These special days gave children and adolescents a break from routine and license to reverse social roles temporarily; they insisted on tribute in the form of money, food, or public recognition. In Reformation Britain, church and state either banned or discouraged most Catholic-inspired celebrations, replacing them with patriotic holidays and symbols of national unity such as Elizabeth I's birthday and Guy Fawkes Day, which commemorated the foiled attempt by Catholics to destroy the Houses of Parliament and assassinate James I in 1605.[6]

In the American colonies, Puritan leaders usually opposed traditional religious holidays, condemning them as pagan or (worse yet) Catholic in origin. Widely dispersed settlement, especially in the South, also led to fewer public celebrations than in the mother country. Children nevertheless often enjoyed May Day festivals as well as harvest day feasts. They frequently lined the streets whenever the local militia mustered or the judge arrived in town on court day, important dates on the civic calendar. By the 1730s, Bostonians celebrated Guy Fawkes Day (known locally as Pope Day), a raucous event that pulled many young men and rival gangs of youth into its orbit.[7]

In seventeenth- and eighteenth-century England, schools commonly celebrated student achievement publicly, setting important precedents for its colonies. Poor children attending charity schools marched in processions en route to church to hear the annual fund-raising sermon delivered on their behalf. In gratitude, pupils often sang religious hymns to thank their benefactors. At the opposite end of the educational and social scale, the male graduates at Oxford and Cambridge, the ancient universities, marked their rite of passage with pomp and circumstance on graduation day. While students, especially at collegiate festivities, sometimes misbehaved, decorum usually prevailed at these events, which commemorated learning and achievement.[8]

Similar celebrations took place on this side of the Atlantic, especially as more schools were built in the eighteenth century, particularly in New England. Depending on their age, ambition, social background, and geographical location, students attended a remarkable variety of institutions, many of which preserved familiar rituals. Literacy rates for whites were especially high in New England, where clerics and legislators had long promoted reading to enhance access to the Bible. In the 1630s, the Puritans of Boston established a Latin grammar school for boys as a feeder to Harvard, and similar schools formed elsewhere as demand merited. Drawing upon English examples, Protestant elites in the mid- to late eighteenth century in the eastern port cities added to the educational mix by funding free charity schools for the children of the unchurched poor. In addition to the nine colleges in existence on the eve of American independence, an array of academies for young and older pupils alike and common district schools such as the one memorialized by Burton also served countless students in subsequent decades. So did Sunday schools and infant schools in the early nineteenth century. They too honored academic achievement at community events.[9]

Schools, therefore, multiplied, reflecting ongoing Protestant support for religious and moral instruction and a growing belief over the course of the eighteenth century that literacy and numeracy enhanced trade, commerce, and good citizenship. Schools that closed during the Revolutionary period reopened and new ones were soon established. Many citizens in the 1780s also debated the role of education in a republic and its relationship to freedom, opportunity, and social order, which remained perennial concerns. Moreover, the spread of newspapers and magazines ensured that articles, advertisements, and commentary on schools, exhibitions, and graduation ceremonies proliferated.[10]

Contemporary writers often commented on the growing visibility of teachers and school celebrations after the American Revolution. An anonymous contributor to Connecticut's *Norwich Packet* explained in 1791 that something dramatic had occurred after political freedom (for the white citizenry) was secured.

> In our contest for freedom each honest Whig,
>   Was sure to be ap'd, by all those who'd look big;
> By coxcombs, by jockies, and each pedagogue;
>   For liberty! liberty, then was the Vogue.
> To defend our just rights, the use of our arms
>   Soon must be learnt, to secure us from alarms;
> Artill'rys and trainings, then serv'd as prologue
>   To what follow'd; for arms! 'twas arms led the Vogue.
> But when peace was obtain'd, then learning run high,
>   Each school, in each science, with others did vie;
> Led on by the mode, was each pedagogue,
>   Exhibitions, and plays, run highly in Vogue.[11]

Enthusiasm for schooling inspired satirists to poke fun at the nation's rising, exaggerated faith in education. Reminiscent of Jonathan Swift's parody of the Grand Academy of Lagado in *Gulliver's Travels* (1726), "Limping Lingo" published an "Advertisement Extraordinary" in the *New-York Journal, & Patriotic Register* in 1792. It publicized an upcoming exhibition at the Grand Academy of Muckinghteragogus. The "grand master" and the teaching staff ("man and boy") planned to examine the scholars "in the various branches of learning" and "in the presence of all of the governors, the lawgivers, the judges, and overseers of that institution." The exhibition would demonstrate that the pupils were making "wonderful progress," indeed "unparalleled proficiency" in Latin and Greek thanks to the newly appointed master, "the like of whom is not to be found among all the teachers, in all the seminaries of learning in Europe." Guests were even invited to "cross-examine the students" to document both their brilliance and the academy's contribution to the "rising glory of America."[12]

Despite the occasional send-up of schools and the learned, exhibitions, processions, and festivals remained popular events. Judging schools by impressions seemed natural, comforting, and unassailable, as reformers would discover.

II

Traditions passed down through generations ensured that school events shared similar characteristics. Teachers replicated rituals from their student days. Rituals might be altered, of course, depending on local preferences or circumstances, but deviation from basic norms was rare. Newspaper advertisements announcing a school exhibition were therefore brief, indicating the time and place and urging a good turnout. The audience that showed up at a public event at a college, charity school, academy, or district school did not need more details; they knew what to expect. Newspaper and magazine descriptions of exhibitions, processions, and graduation ceremonies focused on their well-known features, as the community gathered together to assess the quality of a teacher and school. Public performance was everything.

The experiences of Caleb Bingham aptly demonstrate the enduring place of rituals at school. Bingham became a prominent teacher in Boston and author of school readers that reprinted classic and modern speeches, dialogues, and Biblical stories that pupils studied and recited at many exhibitions. His best-selling textbooks drew upon his own schooling, where public presentations and oral culture were fundamental. Born to a farming family in Salisbury, Connecticut, in 1757, Bingham was taught at home and coached for college through tutorials from a local minister. Graduating as class valedictorian in 1782 from Dartmouth College, where memorization and recitation were the norm (as at most schools of all kinds) and commencement the event of the year, he began teaching at the local charity school for Native Americans. Like the college, the school emphasized student competition to foster academic achievement. It also held exhibitions to prove the native pupils were becoming "civilized." Bingham soon returned to the other side of the desk and in 1785 strode across the public stage in Hanover to receive his master's degree. The ritual was as old as higher education.[13]

The *Massachusetts Spy*, published in Worcester, provided a detailed description of the ceremony. According to the paper, various clergy and "other gentlemen of learning" from New Hampshire and "neighboring states" attended. At ten in the morning, undergraduates "formed themselves into a double line" that stretched from the "President's gate to the College Hall." Like a medieval procession, where different social orders assumed their places, the students, dressed in cap and gown, awaited the president's appearance, since he stood first in the scholastic parade, followed by the trustees, professors, college librarian, local ministers, and the graduating class. At College Hall, the president opened the ceremony with a prayer. Then came a Latin oration, introducing a "syllogistic disputation" that posed the question of whether war ultimately had an unsettling effect on the happiness of society. Students also debated (in English) whether citizens should stop trading with Europe, heard a "very pathetic dialogue" on the loyalists and the American Revolution and another one in "the Greek language" and, following a "Hebrew Oration," listened to some "vocal and instrumental music, which concluded the exhibitions of the forenoon."[14]

After a luncheon break came more orations and dialogues, a debate on whether nations with established churches were happiest, and finally the awarding of degrees to the collegians and to honorary guests. One of the graduates, Alfred Johnson, delivered "an elegant valedictory oration, and in tender and affecting terms took leave of the University and his fellow students." After another prayer, everyone reassembled for the final procession, ending at the president's residence, each group "in the same order in which it passed from thence in the morning." As the news reporter stated, "if we may judge by the attention and affection manifest in the countenances of a numerous and brilliant assembly of gentlemen and ladies, as well as from the audience, it may be safely pronounced that Commencement exhibitions have very rarely been managed, in any University, in a manner that has done more honour to the institution— reflected greater lustre on the candidates—or given higher evidence of the abilities and fidelity of the instructors, than those of this day."[15]

Hyperbolic descriptions of commencements were common. Numerous observers noted the orderly marching and uniform dress among students, the alignment of prayers, orations, dialogues, presentation of degrees, farewells, and more prayers. Caleb Bingham's experiences as a student were hardly out of the ordinary, whether reciting speeches he memorized, performing at exhibitions, or marching in line and crossing the stage. As a pupil he affirmed the longevity of these rituals and as a teacher and author helped ensure their survival.

Different types of schools adapted these rituals to the age and social background of pupils. Colleges and Latin grammar schools, given their classical orientation, honored centuries of tradition through presenta-tions in Latin, Greek, and occasionally Hebrew, though public ceremo-nies were mostly conducted in English. The lines separating academies and colleges were blurry, so classically oriented academies, which did not offer collegiate degrees, often had ceremonies indistinguishable from higher status schools. Academies that emphasized modern subjects usu-ally downplayed or dropped ancient languages from events, as did charity schools for the urban poor and rural district schools of the sort Reverend Burton described in his warm-hearted reminiscence.[16]

By the early nineteenth century, public rituals that contemporaries knew existed since "ancient" times, or as one writer claimed, "time out of mind," were familiar aspects of local schools. That was true of the lower as well as higher echelons of learning. For example, reflecting their English origins, charity schools in New York City, Philadelphia, and other urban areas held parades and exhibitions to publicize their good works. Aiming to "rescue" pupils from the squalor, poverty, and presumed immorality of their parents or guardians, these schools depended upon voluntary con-tributions for their survival. As in England, ministers preached annual sermons to raise money to educate and thus lift the poor above their degraded, impoverished station. They often appealed to the generosity of elites to help the downtrodden and to enhance law and order. In 1788, a contributor to Philadelphia's *Federal Gazette* typically urged citizens to help Episcopalians fund a charity school to steer the poor along a righ-teous path. "Then our streets will be no more crowded with the votaries of ignorance or vice, nor our persons endangered by the midnight robber or assassin; but knowledge more and more prevailing, industry and the useful arts, will follow in her train." As cities began providing tax support for charity schools, public favor remained essential as the number of poor children and educational budgets mushroomed.[17]

The public expected to see—literally *see*—the fruits of education. Fund-raising and the display of school children went hand-in-hand. In New York City in the 1790s, the Masons, the followers of Tammany, and vari-ous church sponsors organized parades and fund-raising events to sustain their charities. Tammany's members, with their trademark bucktails in their caps, marched on the Fourth of July to support the cause. Like the rituals at a Dartmouth or Harvard, processions of young indigents fol-lowed a set pattern. The charity pupils—the boys dressed in blue, the girls in white—marched through the city streets in a yearly procession led by their teachers, who insisted on order and propriety. On parade were well-scrubbed and well-groomed orphans, ragamuffins, "street arabs," and abandoned children of alcoholics, prostitutes, and other outcasts who, said the founders of charity schools, were being saved from perdition and lives of crime, even the gallows. As in other cities, spectators in the coming decades filled "every nook and avenue," often hooting and shouting, gawking and staring.[18]

Processions usually wound their way to a chapel or hall, where pupils dutifully filed into their assigned pews or seats, sang religious hymns, responded to previously assigned questions, and listened to sermons on sin and salvation and uplifting speeches by laymen. Six hundred pupils from one school marched in 1810. "Thousands of our Citizens crowded forward," said one New York City resident, "to view the little train . . . gathered by the hand of charity from the cells of penury and ignorance." In 1815 the *New-York Herald* described an exhibition of nine hundred students who heard an address by John Vanderbilt, a school trustee. The reporter said the "exhibition of the scholars far exceeded the expectations of the audience" so he praised their proficiency in "reading and writing," adding that "their improvement confers the greatest praise on the teachers." Vanderbilt told the audience that nothing was more important than helping the poor. He asked adults to open their wallets and purses and told pupils to obey their teachers, attend school punctually and church regularly, admire their benefactors, and use their education to improve themselves and enjoy life's blessings while preparing for Judgement Day.[19]

Throughout the first half of the nineteenth century, the heyday of urban charity schools, public presentations served multiple functions: demonstrating student achievement, teacher competence, and the generosity of philanthropists. The Baltimore *Sun* regularly reported on exhibitions and other school activities. As in many cities, boys and girls enrolled in separate male and female "departments," often sequestered on different floors in the same building. The boys and girls also had separate exhibitions, and the *Sun* usually praised their ability to answer questions posed by teachers or school officials. Appearances mattered greatly, proving whether schools had made a visible difference. At one school, "the sight of three hundred and fifty boys nearly of similar size, well dressed, and behaving themselves with the utmost decorum," said the *Sun* in 1842, "was itself a matter of no little interest." And the girls, who generally behaved better, also shined. Thousands of spectators and students turned out for elaborate May Day celebrations. There the guardians of the poor and champions of newly established high schools, which helped attract the middle classes to an expanding public system, lectured everyone on the value of hard work, respect for authority, and republican virtue. Who could doubt that public education deserved generous support?[20]

Not far away, in Georgetown and Washington, DC, the children of the poor also participated in popular exhibitions and parades. Lined up behind their own school's banner, the pupils marched past the White House, where President Zachary Taylor greeted them in 1849. "The procession then moved on," school by school, the children "waving their hats and handkerchiefs and cheering most heartily." A year later, two thousand pupils again braved the summer heat, offering a "public display of the schools." "Thousands upon thousands of people thronged the streets through which the procession was to pass, and accompanied it to the beautiful grounds east of the Capitol." There the pupils encountered a huge platform for a great exhibition attended by the school trustees, Common Council, legislators, and President Millard Fillmore, who distributed prizes for meritorious achievement. As one observer wrote, "the boys were gaily decked with the regalia of their respective districts, generally in uniform; the girls were in white, and wore flowers as their appropriate adornment, in many instances wreaths upon their heads, while the Teachers stood in the midst of the scholars to control and protect them."[21]

Performance at exhibitions held special importance for African-Americans. Frequently isolated in segregated charity or other public schools in the North, where classes were often held in dank basements, black children suffered the greatest indignities, so their parents, guardians, and supporters were especially proud of their achievements. Doing well on the public stage was not only, as for white children, essential, but also countered widespread doubts regarding their intellectual and moral worth. Hundreds of people flocked to charity school exhibitions in New York, Philadelphia, and other towns and cities to hear pupils sing religious hymns, deliver stirring orations, and engage in witty dialogues. Visitors often penned letters to the editor or essays on how the children, dressed in their best clothes, learned as much as anyone when given a chance. Describing a performance in New York City in 1823, one white observer typically said that the children "were neatly clad and arranged in the most perfect order," that the girls' needlework was impressive, and that the children answered promptly and accurately. Some children read original poetry, and there was no evidence "that the intellects of this unfortunate race are in any respect inferior to those of white children, or that they are incapable of the same attainments in knowledge."[22]

Frederick Douglass's *North Star* as well as other African-American newspapers and magazines frequently applauded school exhibitions and public displays of black achievement. Douglass stressed the importance of literacy and education in his remarkable transit from slavery to freedom and, in a century noted for its orators, became one of its most eloquent. As a child, he secured a copy of Caleb Bingham's *Columbian Orator*, where he read moving dialogues on slavery and Catholic emancipation. In his autobiography, published in 1845, Douglass said the experience made him a determined foe of racial oppression. The *North Star*, published in Rochester, New York, often stressed the value of education. Succeeding academically did not markedly change the labor market and black opportunity, but it enhanced one's dignity, pride, and sense of accomplishment. Describing an exhibition at a local "colored school," one citizen said it "afforded a lively proof of the capabilities of the colored race. Some of the recitations were really excellent. . . . No better refutation than this exhibition afforded, could be wished of the oft-repeated slanders of negro incapacity."[23]

How pupils collectively appeared, in an exhibition or parade, or how well some pupils declaimed, answered questions, or behaved at a fundraising event or May Day celebration: these signified how well schools, teachers, and pupils were doing. They revealed what was otherwise hidden from view when pupils left home and teachers locked the classroom door. Most but not all people liked what they saw.

III

School exhibitions were a familiar part of community life by the late eighteenth century, and they hardly disappeared once reformers crowned written examinations as the gold standard of education. Americans had long valued oral culture, the art of communication never limited to the printed page. In 1791, a visitor from Nova Scotia, after visiting Boston and greater New England, observed that "the habits of the people here are very favorable to oratory. Declamation is taught in every school. . . . It is a custom to call on some citizen to make a public oration on the anniversary of independence, and other interesting occasions." Countless articles on student orations, declamations, and other seemingly timeless traditions appeared in newspapers and magazines in the post-Revolutionary era. Reverend Burton's imaginative recounting of exhibitions as a schoolboy thus naturally appealed to the many readers who had personally experienced the ritual, as student or observer. "To the eye, ear, and heart, of an American parent," said one Bostonian in 1842, "the common school exhibitions . . . present scenes and subjects of surpassing interest."[24]

Helping to strengthen parental and public support, exhibitions were often well attended and enormously popular. While educators and other citizens sometimes complained about parental apathy and disinterest, the press often boasted about local achievements on the public stage, which boosted community pride. Lacking the rituals of an established national church or powerful centralized government, Americans funded a diverse range of schools that drew upon European traditions but affirmed what were presumably widely shared, homegrown values. Schools, said many commentators, were a miniature society, enabling the nation's "infant Ciceros" and rising talents to gain public recognition. Young orators routinely invoked universal ideals such as liberty, opportunity, and patriotism that resonated with the audience. Occasionally, they even brought attention, as did Caleb Bingham in his textbooks, to the mistreatment of American Indians or the injustice of slavery.[25]

When schools were too small, exhibitions were held in churches, town halls, rented rooms, even taverns, entertaining audiences and honoring the diligence and merits of teachers and pupils. In villages and big cities alike, parades, exhibitions, and commencement often attracted many people. An overflow crowd at an exhibition caused the school building to collapse in Malden, Massachusetts, in 1802, a mishap that also occurred in Norristown, Pennsylvania. Another widely reported accident took place in one Maryland community in 1826, when an exhibition drew so many people that the venue shifted to a tannery; the floor gave way and many in the audience dropped into vats in the cellar below. Tickets were sometimes required to attend a school exhibition to ensure public

safety and to exclude the rowdies and hecklers who had undermined the
event the year before. In some cities, policemen worked the night shift to
control the mob and mischief-makers.[26]

In different times and places, examiners included teachers, members
of the school committee, invited clergy and politicians, and occasionally the audience. "We the undersigned feel a pleasure in thus expressing our satisfaction of the progress made by our children in Spelling,
Writing and Arithmetic," wrote a committee of local worthies, which
included a merchant and a hatter, after attending an exhibition in Hagerstown, Maryland, in 1804. Ministers, among the most educated people
in many communities, commonly served on "visiting committees" along
with prominent merchants, lawyers, and physicians. In a scene repeated throughout the land at all types of schools, the visitors of the First
School Society of New Haven, Connecticut, were pleased to say in 1827
that an impressive gathering of "respectable citizens of both sexes" had
watched them quiz pupils at a local charity school. Esteemed guests along
with family members, neighbors, and friends made exhibitions and other
school-related ceremonies memorable.[27]

Old age had not dimmed the memories of a former schoolgirl in Boston, who remembered the excitement at the Hawes School.

> [T]he crowning glory of all the year
> Was the exhibition day,
> When the school-room doors were unclosed to all,
> And the parents, in brave array,
> Came fully expecting to hear the pith
> Of all that their children knew,
> When the girls were dressed in simple white,
> And sashes of pink or blue.
> A dialogue followed the lesson course,
> As sweets to a full repast,
> And medals awarded a faithful few.[28]

While parents and the public at large generally delighted in these
festivities, some people thought they were a sham and tried to expose
their deceptive nature. Throughout the late eighteenth and early nineteenth century, quite a few naysayers dismissed the value of exhibitions.
They said too many of them resembled the theater, whose reputation

for vulgarity was hardly worth imitating. They pointed out that teachers often hand-picked and coached their best pupils, who did not necessarily understand what they recited. Judging an entire school on the performance of a few scholars was illogical and misleading. The accolades bestowed upon the chosen few—in the form of prizes, honors, and a spotlight on stage—lacked merit, fed the vanity of pupils, and hoodwinked the public. Most offensive, said the most high-minded moralists, exhibitions honored the worst values, especially emulation, or the desire to surpass others.

That pupils obsessed more over their appearance on stage than what they knew was a common lament. A "Fable" published in Connecticut in 1785 said that girls at an exhibition focused on their "finery," not their intellectual improvement; in this instance, the would-be actresses received their comeuppance and were hissed off the stage. In 1791, a father in New York City, one "Publicus," condemned the theatricality at so many exhibitions. Learning to speak clearly and confidently in public was praiseworthy, but the approach being taught was an abomination. Did teachers aim to "educate our sons to be strolling actors? Good God! Our daughters too!" Aspiring thespians who spoke the loudest seemed to win the most plaudits. Soon after, a "Correspondent" to the *Salem Gazette* in Massachusetts similarly attacked "the rage for *Theatrical Exhibitions, &* speaking, or rather spouting, at present so prevalent in one of our neighboring schools." It was "farcical to see twenty or thirty scholars . . . from the raw, overgrown dunce of eighteen, down to the lisping youth of ten, all classed together, and engaged in the same fruitless pursuit." Critics were not shy to point out when the line between theater and school had been crossed. In 1828, the *Connecticut Herald* said the charity school pupil in New Haven who played Othello used too much boot-black.[29]

Spouting students became a stock figure in many satires, long before Reverend Burton introduced readers to Mr. Spoutsound in 1832. "Of all the plans which are adopted to wheedle a credulous community out of their money and their children out of their precious time, public exhibitions or plays are the most fascinating and deceptive." So claimed a critic in New York City in 1812 who said that teachers spent weeks prepping the pupils while ignoring instruction in assigned subjects. Why did this occur? "The answer is, that children may be taught the art of spouting." To impress parents and help raise funds, teachers forced pupils to learn "by *rote*, pieces which are far above their comprehension, and with the meaning of which, little or no pains are taken to make them acquainted." Burton and numerous contemporaries repeated the complaint. As one observer in Macon, Georgia, concluded, "school exhibitions, generally speaking, have no other effect, perhaps no other purpose, than to gratify the vanity of doting mamas, who may there see their little prodigies chattering like magpies, of things they do not understand."[30]

The southern states had a well-earned reputation for conversation, public speaking, and oral culture, and the region generated some of the most caustic criticisms. Like several northern writers, a contributor to the *Southern Literary Messenger* in 1836 accused parents of overestimating their children's talents, always placing them at the head of the class. Hyperbolic descriptions of their achievements did not help. "Little else is ever accomplished by these truly delusive spectacles," it seemed, "unless it be most injuriously to inflate the vanity of the poor pupils. The desire to be puffed in the newspapers, and talked about in public, is substituted for the love of learning for its own sake." Moreover, pupils resembled parrots, mindlessly repeating arcane knowledge. The *Southern Quarterly Review* later concluded that pupils without a clue about a subject impressed listeners with "grandiloquent and polysyllabic learning" so "cheaply yet brilliantly" choreographed by the teacher. "The public, however, not getting behind the curtain," relished the deception, delighting in "editorial puffs" that identified the many geniuses in their midst.[31]

As P. T. Barnum well knew, Americans were no innocents when it came to humbug.

IV

Clever students sometimes shot back at the critics. Tired of hearing the complaints, a classical pupil in Salem returned some blows at an exhibition near the turn of the nineteenth century. He reminded listeners of the incivility of politicians and other adults, who should look in the mirror.

> Perhaps you think it wond'rous weak in
> Our master to put us to speaking,
> "When raise'd to college, 'tis, no doubt,
> Quite soon enough to hear boys *spout*."

> But know, good folks, we, from our natures,
> Of men are servile imitators;
> Schools are of men the pictures true;
> And we are miniatures of you. . . .
> Since, then, good folks, in us you view
> The state and individuals too;
> Let us in *speaking* learn the graces,
> And *spout*, like those in higher places,
> As well as fight, and spit in faces.[32]

That teachers spent many hours preparing pupils for their performance was nevertheless often condemned. In 1818, a disgruntled citizen in New York City wrote that the usual "mode of school examinations" was fraudulent. Most exhibitions did not reveal "the actual knowledge of the pupils," since teachers "grind their pupils just before an examination, and thus enable each scholar to answer, with great promptness, a certain number of questions, thus palming them upon the audience." "Science, history, and the other important branches," added a resident of Maine in 1827, "are severe tasks, which, when learned by rote to pass examination at school, are never more thought of." But "showy accomplishments" seemed to satisfy most people. Even Reverend Burton, who wrote affectionately about schools, agreed that teachers wasted considerable time. Burton realized that parents wanted and expected children to do well at an exhibition. Even if they had an exaggerated sense of their children's talents, no one favored public humiliation. Usually pupils were named in print only if they performed well. Girls who spoke too softly or boys who forgot their lines were spared further embarrassment. But the superficiality of exams and excessive prepping for the "show," as critics called it, annoyed many observers.[33]

Poorly developed reading and elocutionary skills attracted considerable notice. "The art of reading or speaking with propriety, is undoubtedly one of the most useful and interesting accomplishments," wrote a contributor to an educational magazine in 1812. But it seemed "questionable, whether the learning children to *jabber* over the elevated and sublime compositions of Addison, Milton, Shakespeare, Pope, Burke, &c., before they are able to read and understand plain and simple narrative, or before they are acquainted with the first principles of English Grammar, will contribute much to the knowledge of elocution." After witnessing a local performance in 1825, another writer added that when asked to read aloud, pupils did so abominably, "galloping from page to page" at breakneck speed.[34]

Reciting famous speeches on the grand themes of life—honor, bravery, duty, loyalty, freedom, and justice—pupils tried their best but through nervousness, inexperience, or inability sometimes failed to modulate their voices or accent the right word, inadvertently turning tragedy into comedy. Even the brightest, best-coached pupils occasionally lost their composure. Like their teachers, students bungled assignments, leading to embarrassment while lightening the heavy atmosphere of some events. Student bloopers became fodder for those who thought the schools cultivated the memory above understanding. Pupils blurted answers out of turn and tripped over their words. Sometimes a teacher posed the wrong question to Johnny, who replied that that question was Harry's, who had skipped school. The audience usually applauded anyway as the curtain fell.

Humorous stories about such mix-ups appeared in newspapers across the nation, and they were often reprinted to amuse readers far and wide. Tales of country bumpkins mumbling and stumbling on stage brought laughs to urban readers, who could feel superior or recall their own school days. Whether the events ever occurred as reported or remembered was immaterial. Anyone familiar with the conventions of exhibitions recognized the underlying truth of a comical if fabricated tale. The pupils at Eastern Female High School of Baltimore performed a skit in 1849 on a country school examination, causing a pundit to remark that "there was as much truth as poetry in the affair. As a general rule school examinations are—school examinations." They were easily parodied.[35]

In 1839, a resident of Brattleboro, Vermont, published a favorable review of the local high school in the *Vermont Phoenix*, where he claimed that "the examination was conducted on right principles, to exhibit the actual knowledge of the pupils; no preparation was made other than what was proceeding during the whole term." While offering no hard evidence that the exam revealed the "actual knowledge of the pupils," writing about the secondary school jogged his memory. "We remember that, in our youthful days, we knew a week before hand every question that would be asked us on examination day, and shone accordingly. Such

a procedure is well fitted to make a show, but evidently affords no crite-
rion of the real advancement of the scholars."[36]

If exhibitions "evidently" failed to show the "real advancement" of
pupils and rested on questionable behavior, how could one justify them
ethically? By allegedly promoting theatricality, vanity, and elevating one
student over another, did they undermine Christian values? Some outspoken critics thought so, insisting that competition at school—the basis
for prizes, honors, and public recognition at exhibitions or commencement—rewarded unethical behavior. These criticisms intensified in the
late eighteenth century, when exhibitions grew ever popular, and hardly
disappeared in the first half of the nineteenth century. As one observer
lamented in 1832, however, emulation was "a principle almost universally employed" in all kinds of schools.[37]

Opponents of emulation frequently quoted the eighteenth-century
English poet William Cowper, whose poem *Tirocinium* (1785) became a
popular indictment against the practice.

> A principle, whose proud pretensions pass
> Unquestion'd, though the jewel be but glass—
> That with a world, not often over-nice,
> Ranks as a virtue, and is yet a vice;
> Or rather a gross compound, justly tried,
> Of envy, hatred, jealousy, and pride—
> Contributes most perhaps t' enhance their fame,
> And emulation is its specious name.

Cowper went on to say that pupils embraced emulation "less for improvement than to tickle spite," watching other students fail. He agreed that
"the spur is powerful, and I grant its force/It pricks the genius forward in
its course," while advancing everyone. "But judge, where so much evil
intervenes/The end, though plausible, not worth the means."[38]

Critics of emulation were often ministers or pious Protestants who
believed that students should study because it was the right thing to do,
the love of learning the most sublime motive to excel. The Anglican *Christian Observer*, published in London but reprinted in Boston and New York,
pilloried the competitive principle as unchristian; it bred schadenfreude
and placed pupils in the company of "wrestlers, racers, jockeys, buffoons,
boxers, and such-like persons." Critics also doubted whether emulation

actually motivated the vast majority of pupils to excel, since most pupils knew from the start they would never wear an academic laurel. As the head of a normal school in Massachusetts and former charity school teacher succinctly explained, "the longer the struggle, and the more distant the prize, the fewer will engage, the more will give out in its progress, and the greater will be the exhaustion of those who persevere."[39]

In 1831 Philadelphia's *Episcopal Recorder* attacked emulation for "its *effects on moral character*. Who can deny, that it is a copious source of jealousy; that it generally inflates the successful aspirant with pride, and fills his disappointed rival with envy?" Samuel R. Hall, the author of the leading primer on teaching in the antebellum period, felt ashamed that, as a teacher, he had forced pupils to compete; he told his readers to avoid his errors and characterized prize winners as the least meritorious pupils, since they sought honors. Hall's arguments did not go unchallenged. While High Church ministers and recovering advocates of competition and prizes especially condemned emulation, ministers representing a variety of congregations, Quakers and opponents of corporal punishment, and deeply religious laymen defended the practice. Invoking the Bible did not settle the matter, for both sides quoted scripture to buttress their position. Champions of emulation said it was preferable to threatening pupils with the ferule, since pupils were kept busy, idleness long recognized by pagans and believers alike as the Devil's workshop. Moreover, said a host of educators and ministers, God instilled a competitive ethos and desire for honor in all people, which prevented lazy and plodding students from setting the tone in a classroom.[40]

That competition promoted better deportment and student achievement seemed self-evident to many teachers, parents, and prize-winning students. Bingham's readers and those of his competitors reprinted speeches and stories that condemned sloth and praised the nobility of hard work and high achievement, epitomized by the success of Benjamin Franklin and other eminent individuals. *The American Preceptor* (1811), already in its forty-second edition, typically reminded students that "knowledge will not be acquired without pains and application." The competitive ideal was unshakeable in charity schools, academies, and district schools as well as in colleges, exemplified by the awarding of prizes, honors, and other forms of public recognition. Defenders of the practice cited the well-known writings of Quintilian, the first-century Roman rhetorician, who thought emulation rightly encouraged pupils to excel. Others cited the English essayist Francis Bacon or Scotsman Adam Smith, the most influential contemporary theorist of marketplace competition.[41]

Given the spread of market values in the early republic, it is not surprising that emulation largely triumphed at school. Even Cowper admitted that it worked, forcing pupils to achieve more, which proved difficult to argue with. As the *Weekly Wanderer* in Randolph, Vermont, concluded in 1802, "if a child seems inclined to sauntering and idleness, emulation is the proper cure." Was it not sensible, said charity school leaders, to teach the poor to excel and reward them accordingly? A Latin School pupil, speaking at an exhibition in 1831, recognized that the quest for classroom excellence was invaluable: "O'er indolence he gains the mastery/Rises by slow gradations to the first/And feels for early fame a generous thirst."[42]

Defenders of competition insisted that as long as teachers kept emulation within proper bounds, it was a healthy, natural, and fruitful basis for sound instruction. They favored only a "generous," "laudable," or "honest" emulation, nurturing a proper regard for mutual advancement, even if only a few scholars wore an academic crown upon graduation. Approbation and the love of distinction, said the editor of the Whig *North American Review* in 1836, was "natural to man," and "he who labors to suppress or eradicate them will not be likely very soon to be out of employment." These virtues had been honored since the ancient Olympic games; common sense also dictated that industry, frugality, and achievement should be rewarded and honored, at school as in the larger society. As another Whig, Daniel Webster, said at a school festival in 1838, "emulation is a passion implanted in man, to which it is his duty to attend." How else improve and excel? A contributor to the *Massachusetts Teacher* in 1848 reluctantly admitted that after decades of debate, most teachers still gave grades, honors, prizes, or other forms of recognition for achievement. They knew that emulation was "an inducement to labor easily offered, readily received and understood, and quick in its results."[43]

Despite recurrent complaints about competition, then, traditional practices endured. Reformers who favored written examinations recognized that traditional means of assessing schools and preparing pupils to excel in public performances had stood the test of time. So-called examinations of pupils at exhibitions remained popular ways to judge pupil achievement

and teacher competence. Persuading the public that academic achievement could only be measured reliably through statistics generated on
standard written tests would not be easy.

V

Critics were not just imagining that the audience at an exhibition loved
a good show. Hearty rounds of applause were part of the ritual. Descriptions of the public event always mentioned how many people attended,
which dialogues or orations received the most applause, and how well
particular pupils answered questions. Everyone noticed good or bad
behavior or if the mayor or some "literary friends" showed up, adding
status to the affair. Just as the demeanor and dress of children at processions and parades caught the public eye, so did their ability to answer
questions quickly and accurately.[44]

Students played on the good will of the audience, exemplified by a
clever nine-year-old girl who opened the festivities in Sterling, Massachusetts, in 1810:

> Our Master says, a prologue we must have,
> To usher in our little exhibition.
> How to begin? O! First your pardon crave,
> Lest I should make a blunder, or omission. . . .
> [W]hat's to come next you shall presently see;
> You shall not be detain'd any longer by me:
> With this I retire—should you see many blunders,
> I pray you forgive them—they cannot be wonders.[45]

Absent standardized test scores, a weighing of blunders and wonders
helped determine whether pupils had done well and teachers deserved
another contract.

When citizens assessed oral performance, they did not expect examiners to ask every child a question but always praised ready responses.
In 1786, the *New Jersey Gazette* covered the quarterly examination at an
academy in Trenton. The school enjoyed a good turnout of "respectable
characters, who expressed their approbation of the manner in which
the students in general performed their parts, and particularly of the
spirit of emulation which appeared conspicuously in a number of them."

Most impressive was the "readiness of the answers, from a very large class, to a variety of critical questions" in English grammar. Similarly, like women at various institutions, the graduates of the well-regarded Young Ladies' Academy of Philadelphia always earned high praise by acting appropriately while showing a "laudable ambition to excel each other" and by "promptly spelling and defining words, and . . . answering with facility, to questions in Orthography, Grammar, Composition" and other subjects.[46]

The public always focused carefully on the appearance and performance of charity school pupils, all drawn from the lower ranks of society, where crime, dissipation, and immorality ostensibly lurked. A good showing indicated money well spent. Joseph Lancaster, an English Quaker and influential founder and theorist of charity schools, emphasized emulation, military-style discipline (though not corporal punishment), and a hierarchically organized and tightly run school. Although charity schools had their share of detractors, few institutions enjoyed as much favorable press. Lancaster's ideas on pedagogy and school organization often received fawning praise, since his system promised to deliver superior instruction for the masses, and cheaply too.[47]

Charity school children in New York City and other communities were often taught in large halls, where pupils were "classed" into smaller groups on the basis of proficiency in reading and arithmetic; superior students were then appointed as unpaid or poorly paid teachers or "monitors," who taught most of the student body and were supervised by head teachers. Lancaster's elaborate system of prizes and rewards—books, toys, medals, and the like, awarded for good behavior, academic achievement, and class promotion—was central to his educational scheme. So was his rejection of corporal punishment. Emulation and public display took a special turn in charity schools. Lancaster and his followers believed that if children were kept busy and in a constant state of competition for prizes and approval, achievement would rise and physical punishment become superfluous. Children who were lazy, tardy, or disrespectful merited not physical pain but public humiliation and the withholding of tickets redeemable for trinkets and prizes. Painted signs in classrooms reminded pupils that "Emulation is Laudable." Disobedient pupils wore labels or sandwich-boards identifying their misdeeds—such as "Idle," "Noisy," "Suck Finger Baby"—but usually escaped the switch.[48]

As charity schools spread to various towns and cities after the 1790s, their superiority almost seemed self-evident. In 1813, a devotee of Lancaster in Albany, New York, said monitorial schools were without peer in educating the masses. No other system had *greater success,* for in every case in which a school of this kind has been properly taught, the proficiency of the scholars in learning their letters, in spelling, reading, writing, and cyphering, has been much more rapid, than in any schools taught in the ordinary way." A spokesman for the Lancasterian schools in New York City similarly proclaimed that "a child can learn in one month . . . what would take two or three months" elsewhere. In Poughkeepsie, New York, three examiners testified that at a local charity school, emulation, the key to academic achievement, enabled some children to memorize large portions of the Bible, proof that the system was literally a godsend. News reports throughout New England, the Ohio Valley, and the South repeatedly stated that pupils were "better instructed than under the old system," as one champion of monitorial education from Portsmouth, New Hampshire, wrote in 1821.[49]

High marks resulted for charity school pupils when they marched and behaved dutifully and answered questions without pause. The "air of military order" at a school in Lexington, Kentucky, as elsewhere, impressed contemporaries, amid fears that the poor lacked self-discipline and respect for authority. In Baltimore, charity school pupils recited in classrooms and at exhibitions in unison. A female teacher in 1842 asked "Little Mary Jane Crauthers," who was standing before a large map, to point "with a slender cane stalk" to particular locations. She did so promptly, whereupon "the whole class" joined in, providing "the name of the mountain, river, cape, sea, or isthmus, etc., with a rapidity perfectly amazing." When a school committee questioned pupils at an exhibition at a charity school established by New England missionaries in Oahu, "the scholars spoke with promptness and distinctness, and rarely was the teacher obliged to say, 'louder,' 'louder the gentlemen cannot hear.'"[50]

To say that children learned more rapidly in any particular system of instruction only seemed to require a few examples of successful students to seal the case. Relying on impressions to persuade donors, taxpayers, or skeptical parents to support a particular school was common and hardly restricted to institutions that only taught the poor. Claims about the superiority of Lancasterian schools were largely asserted without much evidence beyond rhetorical appeals and anecdote. Stories were written and retold about guttersnipes saved from a life of crime and sin and about ten-year-olds who recited an incredible amount of scripture on command.

Tall tales of pedagogical approaches that were cheaper or superior proliferated. Just as the attendee at Caleb Bingham's college graduation said the proceedings "reflected greater lustre" than ever on the students and gave "higher evidence of the abilities and fidelity of the instructors," other observers let the rhetoric fly after the cheering stopped at exhibitions. Puffing about schools and pupil performance was rampant. After listening to questions and answers at exhibitions, committeemen, teachers, and other adults felt confident they knew whether a school had stagnated, improved, fallen behind, or exceeded expectations. That they did so without much empirical evidence reflects the ease with which quantitative statements about school performance still rested mostly upon qualitative judgments.

High levels of literacy among the white citizenry in the half-century after the American Revolution generated a rising demand for newspapers, magazines, books, and reading materials, which became cheaper thanks to technological advances in publishing. The proliferation of schools, in turn, reinforced and boosted already impressive literacy rates. But what one saw, heard, and observed remained decisive in shaping opinions about teachers, pupils, and schools. School was still part of a face-to-face world. No one thought it odd when a handful of pupils answered pre-assigned questions or a whole class chimed in when Little Mary Jane took center stage and led the chorus. The public display provided sufficient evidence to assess any school.

Exhibitions sometimes provided more than recitations and student performances in plays or dialogues to impress the audience about school quality. To prove that children's writing skills were up to par, teachers might display student copy books, in which children imitated models from textbooks. After participating in the annual visitation of the Salem, Massachusetts, common schools in 1797, a local resident typically said that "correct reading, the clean copy book, and the ready answers at an examination, are proofs of real attainments," only found at the "best schools." When Senator Henry Clay surprised some students in New Orleans in 1846 by attending their exhibition, which focused on science, he was delighted to find blackboards covered with their drawings. In addition to promoting literacy and nondenominational Protestant values, charity schools sometimes taught boys basic carpentry; girls received lessons in sewing and weaving to help prepare them for jobs as domestics and seamstresses. Charity schools frequently featured their handiwork to impress visitors. In 1848, the *New York Herald* thus praised the girls in one school for their embroidery and boys for the quality of the "200 or 300 drawings and maps" on display, which "sufficiently proved that writing, connected with drawing, was taught . . . effectively." The quality of instruction and achievement was there for all to see.[51]

Impressions also enabled citizens to compare schools, to determine whether a particular institution improved or declined, or was better than competitors. A visitor to the Newark Academy in New Jersey in the late 1790s was convinced that academics there had improved, thanks to a heartier embrace of emulation. Saying this seemed enough to prove the case. At one East Coast charity school, two boys performed so well in 1820 that a correspondent urged anyone who doubted the claim to visit the school and judge for themselves! Obviously, so much puffing occurred that even puffers recognized that skeptics might dismiss the predictable over-the-top appraisals. Some assessments showed more restraint. School visitors in Concord, Vermont, admitted that it was difficult to judge the "relative merits" of schools but still concluded that the town system overall showed "general improvement."[52]

Hearsay and secondhand knowledge sustained many assertions about academic performance. In 1818, a citizen in Providence, Rhode Island, commenting on the local examinations, explained that citizens generally viewed Mr. Taft's public school as "better than any in the town." None of Taft's pupils were asked to spell, "but, it is believed, they can generally spell very well." The editor of the *American Repertory* in Burlington, Vermont, regretted that he had missed a local exhibition in 1822 but "as far as our inquiries have extended . . . the manifest improvement of the classes in the different branches of their studies, was not only very honorable to themselves and complimentary to their instructors, but perfectly satisfactory to those attending the examination." Similarly absent from an event, a contributor to the *Barre Gazette* in Massachusetts was "informed" that the pupils studying the "higher branches . . . exhibited great improvement in their various studies." Spectators crammed into the meetinghouse "to witness the Exhibition, which was got up in very good style, and we believe met the high [and] raised expectations of all present."[53]

Sometimes local pride and civic boosting made pens drip with purply praise. Apparently quite a few schools in America were without peer. In 1792, Charleston, South Carolina, had a female seminary "not inferior to any school on the continent." More modestly—but not to be outdone by neighboring Boston—the visiting committee of Salem's Latin School announced in 1823 that it "knew of no school, public or private, within this county, in which their children could enjoy greater advantage for acquiring a classical education." A single visit to an exhibition at the newly established Germantown Academy in Pennsylvania convinced one attendee that "the best schools of Europe, have seldom produced scholars adequate to such an exercise after an instruction of only two years." In a world where assessments about schools rested on criteria other than quantitative evidence, many people confidently asserted that their best students matched those in any high school, academy, or college. Without blushing, a writer in the *Connecticut Mirror* simply stated "without exaggeration" that Hartford's Central School was the best of its kind in the nation. A visitor at an annual citywide celebration in Albany, New York, in 1848, thought that even if pupils were a bit theatrical, "it would be difficult to find in any city in the State ten schools better disciplined, better looking, or giving better promise."[54]

For some pupils, whatever their looks or promise, the exhibition was stressful. Minds went blank. Pupils froze on stage. In her closing address, "Examination Day," at the Girls' High School in Portsmouth, New Hampshire, a pupil thanked the audience for their understanding.

> The day is now past, and the setting sun
> Tells us the hour of trial is done.
> Here's a sovereign balm for our every grief,
> To know it is over—how great the relief.
> Our senses in sleep, soon will Morpheus bind,
> For we're fairly fagged out, both in body and mind.
> By our efforts to show off, in tolerable dress,
> The little of knowledge we chance to possess,
> If you happen to think we did not succeed,
> Then good people all, take the word for the deed.[55]

Critics of exhibitions seemed immune to Morpheus and stardust, and complaints about traditional ways of judging schools grew louder during the antebellum period. Confident that written tests and statistics were superior tools in evaluating students and teachers, reformers insisted that exhibitions and examinations were not one-and-the-same thing.

VI

The majority of people who wrote about schools in the first half of the nineteenth century often treated the words "exhibition" and "examination" as synonyms and frequently used them interchangeably. Reformers seeking to elevate the importance of written, competitive examinations wanted to distinguish one from the other, which was easier said than done. After all, examinations (which were mostly oral) and exhibitions often happened at the same time. While students regularly recited to teachers and the school committee might question them prior to an evening show, some pupils were usually quizzed at exhibitions; there the public might also note the demeanor and behavior of teachers and pupils, examine copy books, drawings, and embroidery, and listen to young Ciceros, all part of the diverse criteria used to assess schools.

Practically speaking, then, exhibitions and examinations seemed inseparable, hindering efforts to gather reliable statistics to compare pupils and schools. Complaints by prominent educators and reform-minded citizens were plentiful. As late as 1857, the editor of the *Connecticut Common School Journal and Annals of Education* explained that "there are scarcely any subjects . . . on which there prevails so great a diversity of opinion and action, as on examinations and exhibitions." Written examinations had become more popular, but recitations and oral performance in rural schools especially remained the bread and butter of daily instruction and exhibitions. Like most leading educators by midcentury, the editor believed that examinations measured the mental acquirements of pupils in assigned subjects, while exhibitions were largely social events, more entertainment than a means to determine academic achievement rigorously.[56]

Although confusion over nomenclature persisted, some educators and citizens since the beginning of the century had increasingly made clearer distinctions between examinations and exhibitions. This was especially true in New England, a region with the strongest interest in schools. For example, in 1803, the school committee in Salem, Massachusetts, well aware that Boston held examinations on one day in each school to determine medal winners and conventional exhibitions for the community's benefit on another, proposed an experiment. The pupils at Salem's four public schools were told to appear at the courthouse for an examination. The committeemen wanted to force teachers and pupils alike to work more diligently to raise achievement, that is, through the "invisible hand" of emulation. As in Boston, the examinations were not written but oral. But the majority of pupils simply skipped the test, wrecking the experiment.[57]

The notion that examinations were strictly academic and should not be confused with the mishmash of activities at an exhibition nevertheless gained traction in a few places. A resident of New Haven, Connecticut, commented in 1825 that "school examinations are generally mere exhibitions" and urged citizens to find a more "impartial mode of investigating the progress of the pupils in the different branches." By the 1840s, other observers urged testing pupils in a "critical" manner, "more like an examination than a simple exhibition." To counter the widespread charge that pupils did not understand what they memorized and recited, some examiners told pupils to explain their answers fully "to completely convince the spectators that *their* examination was *no humbug.*" In the language of the day, scholars should not recite like parrots but master the "'whys' and 'wherefores' of their studies."[58]

A few cities on the East Coast also began requiring applicants to public high schools, which first opened in the 1820s, to take written admission exams, which generated numerical scores, not impressions. Test items were drawn from textbooks assigned in the top grammar grades, focusing on the Three R's, history, and geography, and requiring short written responses. While the pool of prospective pupils was small, their test scores provided educators for the first time with numerical scores that compared their performance, leading to speculation but never any consensus about why some candidates or pupils from different schools performed better than others. Moreover, educators concluded that raising admission standards could shape academic quality for everyone in the grades below, including the majority who never completed grammar school. In theory, academic expectations would rise across the board if secondary schools enhanced their scholastic profile.[59]

Admission standards were set locally, varied from year to year, and in practice shaped by the number of available seats in any particular secondary school. Aiming to attract the best scholars to enhance the status of the fledgling public system, high schools tried to set a reasonably high bar while remaining accessible to the majority of applicants. A few institutions became renowned for their selectivity. To enter Philadelphia's prestigious, all-male Central High School, which opened its doors in 1838, meant not only passing a rigorous entrance test but also a regimen of searching examinations once enrolled. Pupils faced a barrage of written tests from their classroom teachers as well as from external examiners, as the spirit of emulation soared. In 1846, pupils sat for eight-hour exams for three consecutive days. In 1850, Cincinnati's pupils prepped for a three-day entrance exam in seven subjects. Few high schools had such rigorous standards for entrance or exit but some educators increasingly recognized the superiority of written over oral tests.[60]

As midcentury approached, developments in Massachusetts, with its long record of investment in schooling, proved especially important in the history of testing. Pencil-and-paper exams soon touched the lives of far more pupils than the select group aspiring to high school. Complaints accelerated in the Bay State about the sorry state of its public schools, often taught by poorly educated teachers in ramshackle buildings. Old-fashioned exhibitions were still ubiquitous but increasingly ridiculed. Numerous towns reported that whenever school committees tried to raise standards, many pupils simply "dodged" the tests. In 1840, frustrated committeemen in Medfield threatened to publish the names of every no-show. But events came to a head in 1845 in a place everyone assumed had America's best schools.[61]

CHAPTER 2

A-Putting Down Sin

"The Public Schools of Boston are justly the pride and glory of the city."
So claimed Henry Barnard, one of America's leading champions of public education, in 1842. History seemed to justify his boast. Soon after migrating from England in 1629, the Puritan settlers had distinguished themselves by establishing a Latin grammar school, Harvard University at Cambridge, and other means of education and enlightenment. The commitment to schooling was impressive. In 1789, Boston created a separate committee to govern its various schools, including English grammar schools in which students pursued a non-classical education. By 1818, after lengthy debate, citizens approved funding for a system of primary schools, governed by a different board, and the nation's first public high school opened three years later. Praise for these institutions abounded in national magazines and locally in newspapers, official reports, Fourth of July addresses, and at the annual school festival, which honored the best scholars at a banquet at Faneuil Hall. Every summer the festival attracted local dignitaries and usually the governor, state officials, U.S. senators, and occasionally the president of the United States. Bostonians gushed that they outspent every city on public schools.[1]

Pride may anticipate a fall, but it was a long time coming to Boston. According to numerous observers, every year the schools were still the best, and getting better. When reformers in the 1820s promoted the charity school system then employed to teach poor children in rival New York City, the *Evening Gazette* recoiled at the idea, warning it would lower standards. "We are creditably informed," it said, "that the best scholars, in the highest classes, in the New York schools, which are now thought worthy of imitation, are not to be compared with those of the *second classes* of the Boston Grammar School[s]." Even citizens who favored school improvements—whether better textbooks, personnel, curricula, or organization—reflexively engaged in hyperbole. In 1832, many poor children were still not attending any primary school, complained one citizen in the *Courier*, who nevertheless agreed that "it has long been the pride and boast of Bostonians that their system of public instruction, professing to extend to all of every rank and condition of society, is of a higher character, better adapted to the wants of an enlightened community, than is to be found anywhere else in a large city or town in the United States, or even in the civilized world."[2]

Despite such alleged superiority, citizens periodically grumbled about tyrannical school masters, overcrowded classrooms, and high taxes. By the 1830s and 1840s, antislavery activists also denounced the schools for racism and segregation. For decades, however, visiting committees generally praised teachers and pupils, as did local newspapers and magazines. Examiners visited schools periodically to hear recitations, examine copy books, and determine if everything appeared orderly. The *Boston Weekly Messenger* often applauded the schools, concluding in 1824 that they "have been and still are proceeding in a continual course of improvement." After the annual exhibition of the city's fourteen English grammar schools in 1839, the *Daily Advertiser* similarly declared that "the condition of the schools is improving from year to year, and their efficiency increasing in a proportion fully equal to the increase in number, and in the number of pupils." In 1844, the *Christian Register*, the prominent weekly magazine of the Unitarians, typically announced that "all is well . . . our schools are in a healthy and prosperous condition."[3]

Emulation ruled in the Boston schools. On "visitation day" in 1789, master Charles Williams Windship told listeners at the South Grammar School that his male pupils properly sought the "expectation of reward suitable to [their] merit" and "to *surpass*" peers in "every laudable pursuit." Without competition and the hope of "honor," achievement would decline. Soon after, Bostonians learned that a famous native son, who had run away from an apprenticeship to find his fortune in Philadelphia, had bequeathed money for medals for the most meritorious school boys. The Franklin medals became the highest prize in the English grammar schools, and by the 1820s the most meritorious girls received "city medals" to encourage competition and high achievement. By then, the scramble for honors was so great that a critic sounded an alarm. "Perhaps the system of animating the pupils to industry by the principle of emulation, and rewarding them by medals, cards, &c. of which the object is to distinguish them from their fellows, is carried too far. Emulation," he concluded, "easily becomes envy," when pupils should only be encouraged to do well for its own sake. But few children seemed to heed the advice and Bostonians generally reveled in the glorious progress of their schools.[4]

Perhaps, however, the perennially good news was mistaken, based on nothing more than hubris and less than self-evident truths. Like citizens elsewhere, Bostonians based their judgments about schools on impressions more than anything else. How did anyone really know if Boston's pupils performed better than those in New York City? Or that the schools were "improving from year to year" and were "healthy and prosperous"? In the summer of 1845, a handful of reformers on the Boston School Committee, charged with examining the local English grammar schools, tried to answer these questions.

No one knew it at the time, but Boston was about to make history. The testing wars had begun.

I

It all began innocently enough. Or so it seemed. Every spring the School Committee appointed six colleagues to conduct its annual school examinations. The English grammar schools were typically divided into separate "reading" and "writing" schools, which were inspected by separate committees. On May 6, 1845, S. F. McCleary, longtime city clerk, recorded the following about the reading committee: "Ordered That Mssrs. Parsons, Howe and Neale be a Committee to make the annual examination of the several Grammar Schools, and report at the quarterly meeting in August next." This bland statement contrasts sharply with the backstage maneuvers that led to the appointments and the political controversies that raged after these three men, with an eye on the wholesale reform of the system, presented their report to the full school committee. Critics believed that Parsons, Howe, and Neale were part of a larger conspiracy that had intentionally smeared the fair name of the Boston schools. Like the writing committee, a more politically moderate group, they had broken with precedent and without warning given a common written test to the pupils of the first, or highest, classes. They then ranked the schools from best to worst, embarrassing many teachers and pupils alike.[5]

The reading and writing committees set in motion ideas about schools that ultimately changed the lives of every teacher and pupil in modern society. Today statistical measurements are the central means of pupil assessment, but that was hardly true in antebellum Boston or anywhere else. To understand the explosive events of 1845 and the revolutionary import of written examinations requires knowledge about the evolution of the grammar schools, their exalted place in the system, and the political context. Only then will the motives and behavior of the protagonists in the local drama of testing become clear.

Between the 1790s and the 1840s, Boston's grammar schools had developed an enviable reputation. The head teachers, known locally as masters, were often college graduates and men of distinction. Appointed annually every August, they hailed from Harvard, Brown, Dartmouth, and other New England colleges. Like their former classmates, they were often active in church groups, literary societies, and civic associations. Many had labored as ushers (teachers) and worked their way up the ladder. Masters often held their posts for many years and usually had friends on the School Committee, which had representatives from every ward; masters as well as some board members (themselves sometimes former teachers) often wrote the textbooks assigned locally. To supplement their income, the masters also made a profit on books and supplies, which they sold to the pupils. Before the 1820s, they even taught private lessons on the side, during a midday break, right in the local school house. Unlike the women who labored in the primary and grammar schools, they were very well paid, high status, and accustomed to deference and praise. The grammar schools taught children between the ages of seven and sixteen, many of them from prominent families. Boys could attend until fourteen, when they either graduated, left empty-handed, or applied to the all-male Latin School or English High. Girls could stay until sixteen, an effort to compensate them for the closure in 1828 of a short-lived Girls' High School, which the School Committee said was too costly.[6]

The English grammar schools were expensive to operate due to their growing numbers, unusual organization, and high administrative costs. Initially separate institutions, the reading and writing schools were united into one building in the 1820s, each usually occupying one large room in the same building (basically a long hall) on a separate floor. Pupils spent the morning in one "school," the afternoon in the other. In 1820, enrollment stood at 2,456 pupils but had more than tripled to 8,115 by the summer of 1845. There were nineteen grammar schools in 1845, and all but three of them had two masters, one for the reading, the other for the writing school. This understandably caused critics to complain about the exorbitant costs of the "double-headed" system. The masters, male ushers, and female teachers in the reading schools taught the "liberal arts," including history, geography, grammar, spelling, and reading; the reading masters, usually college graduates, had higher status than their counterparts in the writing schools who, along with their staff, taught the more "practical," commercially oriented subjects such as arithmetic, penmanship, and sometimes bookkeeping. By 1845, each grammar school enrolled approximately 430 pupils. Boys and girls were taught and recited separately, and every classroom held several ungraded classes of mixed ages, taught by the male masters or ushers, or female teachers, who spent the day listening to pupils recite their lessons one by one and maintaining order among the rest. A former student thus remembered a constant "humming noise" in the room, since pupils in the different classes often stood near the various instructors' desks reciting.[7]

The School Committee's regulations in 1823 affirmed that the masters had "priority of rank," full control of their schools. In 1845, they were paid generously: from $1,000 to $1,500 per year compared to $600 to the ushers and $300 to the female teachers. Little wonder that the masters fiercely protected their domain and resisted outside interference. They alone determined who matriculated from the primary schools, whose governing committee had no say in the matter. Controversially, they held pupils back at their discretion, not allowing some boys to graduate, for example, who seemed ready for the admission exam to the Latin or English high school. The masters retained some over-achievers for a simple reason: it helped them maintain their privileged status. While the masters taught the first and thus smallest classes, with the oldest and most accomplished scholars, male ushers and the lowly-paid female assistants taught everyone else. The first class—those examined by the reformers in the summer of 1845—symbolized all that was excellent in the system.[8]

Local newspapers and magazines frequently lauded the schools, and editors and reporters who attended the annual summer exhibitions, largely oral exams, offered a steady stream of compliments. In 1791, less than two years after Boston established its "System of Publick Education," the School Committee highlighted "the extraordinary proficiency of the youth in the several branches of their instruction." School visitors routinely identified "pleasing specimens of improvements in all the branches of instruction. The influential Federalist newspaper, the *Columbian Centinel*, thus commented in 1820 that examiners found the pupils well behaved, hardworking, and morally upright, with "improvement conspicuous in them all." One observer in 1826 remarked that the pupils responded well when "interrogated in Grammar, Geography, and Arithmetic. The specimens of Chirography, in many instances, were superior, and generally good. The upper classes also read with much propriety." In 1844, the year before the testing controversy pricked the congratulatory bubble, a local magazine applauded the grammar schools for their "highly satisfactory" performance, pupils and teachers alike. That every master was reappointed in August indicated "somewhat conclusively," it said, that the schools remained excellent.[9]

While the depth of the anger generated in 1845 between the masters and the examiners, and their supporters, was unprecedented, Bostonians occasionally found the schools wanting. Eminent community figures, the masters often enjoyed a cozy relationship with the School Committee, whose members were well-educated clergymen, professionals, and businessmen. Some masters and committeemen had attended college together or had family or other personal ties; at the least they shared the status of the well schooled and often well born. As enrollments grew along with expenditures, especially with the addition of primary schools after 1818, the favored position of the grammar schools attracted more critical attention. The spread of schools across the growing city meant that no one person or committee knew well what transpired in every building, despite concerted efforts by various examining committees. School masters enjoyed relative autonomy, a source of complaint whenever anything went awry. In addition to the annual inspection by the reading and writing committees, every grammar school had its own visiting committee, which always included a School Committee member from the local ward. This committee (in theory) visited its assigned school at least once a month and, to get its full flavor, for longer periods, usually a full day or two every quarter. It inspected the building, documented the "deportment and progress of the scholars, in order to commend good conduct and improvement, and to discourage negligence and vice," and every summer helped the master determine who deserved academic medals.[10]

Citizens sometimes tweaked the various examining committees for not living up to expectations. The *Boston Commercial Gazette* and other local newspapers complained about the superficiality of the annual exhibitions in 1825. In response, one examiner explained that yes, the summer exhibitions, held in every school before the celebration to honor the medal winners at Faneuil Hall, were often for show; despite other obligations, however, he had spent many days visiting schools, asking pupils questions, and attending to his duties in his ward. Citizens, he said, should not confuse an *exhibition* with an *examination*, a distinction confusing to many and sometimes lost on everyone since, as we have learned, contemporaries often used the terms synonymously. An examination, said the committeeman, was privately conducted and might consume a day or two of labor on the part of the examiners, while an exhibition was public and much less rigorous. Prior to the annual public exhibition, where parents wanted to see the pupils shine, the local visiting committees had already examined enough students orally for a day or two to appraise the school overall and help choose the medal winners. How many people, he asked, had either the "leisure or inclination" to do more than show up for the annual exhibition? Anything more than a superficial exhibition—asking a handful of pupils a few questions was the norm—was tedious and unappealing to everyone.[11]

The individuals recruited for the annual examinations of all of the grammar schools faced a more daunting responsibility, many refusing to serve more than once, or ever. Since the 1790s, the committeemen visited every school in May or June to "critically . . . examine the pupils in all the branches therein, in order to ascertain the condition of the schools and their comparative merit," and then report to the School Committee before reappointments and hiring decisions were made in August. Unlike colleagues on the local visiting committees, summer examiners had to rearrange their professional or business schedules to accommodate every master and then travel the breadth of the city to assess every school. Since the exams (like the public exhibitions later in the summer) were mostly oral, committeemen struggled to ascertain "comparative merit," since they could not possibly examine everyone. And, as enrollments expanded in the 1830s and 1840s, they often only examined the first class, taught by the master himself.[12]

In anticipation of the annual events, every master prepped his pupils for weeks beginning in early spring. "When the committee or any visitors were in the school," one former pupil recalled, the master demanded silence and "members of the first class were called upon to recite." A strong performance by the trophy pupils always impressed the examiners and enhanced the reputation of the schools. Year after year, the local press dutifully complimented the star students and the masters, who helped make "the free schools of this city . . . among its proudest distinctions." Few people questioned the assumption that the achievements of the top students should stand as a proxy for the whole school. After witnessing several exhibitions in the summer of 1818, however, one citizen did exactly that in a letter to the *Boston Patriot and Daily Chronicle.* "It is true there were specimens of good reading and writing exhibited at the English Schools; but the real state of the Schools is not to be learned from hearing the reading of a few elites of the upper class; and seeing the writing of those few only who have prepared themselves to exhibit."[13]

Events would prove that criticizing a school system so certain of its excellence and so proud of its past and present invited responses ranging from indifference to censure.

II

While the grammar schools were the pride of many citizens, several committeemen beginning in the 1820s tried to eliminate the double-headed system and institute other reforms. In 1828, Mayor Josiah Quincy, who took a keen interest in school policy, called for the appointment of a single master for each building. The masters rallied their supporters on the School Committee and the proposal went nowhere. Samuel A. Wells, a key figure in the creation of the non-classical English high school in 1821, headed a committee in 1830 that produced an impressive report on the local schools. The committee recommended better ways to classify and group students. A practical-minded and successful merchant, he spoke the language of good business practices and utilitarianism, seeking "the greatest good to the greatest number." Sharing the fact-finding instincts of many contemporary reformers, he wrote to the masters and asked them basic questions about their schools. Their responses convinced him that Boston did not have any school "system" at all. Every school had its own unwritten rules, dictated by the whims of the masters. "The organization and management of each school being on different plans, it is difficult, if not impractical," Wells concluded, "to judge of the comparative degree of excellence of the schools, or merit of the respective instructers." Visiting and examining committees, therefore, lacked reliable facts to judge how well any one school did from year to year, or how to compare them.[14]

Wells's committee reasoned that the teacher was the key to academic success, a foundational assumption in the emerging ethos of testing. What worked best in one school seemed attributable to teacher competence and effectiveness, and these characteristics should be identified and widely imitated. How to better measure educational outcomes, compare schools, and determine the best practices, however, seemed impossible unless the grammar schools were reorganized. The solution? More age-graded instruction, with pupils in separate rooms, wishful thinking given current realities. The whole system had to change and the parts seamlessly stitched together.

At the time, every primary school had one teacher, like those in the countryside, some with more than sixty pupils. The reading and writing schools often had four "classes" in each, and these classes were subdivided into "sections" similar to modern ability groups. Both the classes and their sections had children of different ages. Wells dreamed of a uniform, smoothly functioning school system, where pupils roughly the same age "in each and every school in the city" would enroll in comparable "classes and sections." They would take an annual exam "on the same day" to determine academic success or failure. Those who passed the exam would advance to the next level, but those who faltered would "remain in their sections, until the next term, or until they may be." Silent on the specific details of the proposed exam, Wells regarded uniform assessment central to his ideal system.[15]

Implementing such ideas was another matter. Subsequent attempts by blue-ribbon committees to change the organization of the schools faced stiff opposition. In an effort to concentrate authority exclusively with the reading masters, the School Committee in 1830 fired several ushers and writing masters, replacing them with less expensive female teachers in the girls' schools, while those retained received demotions and lower salaries. The female instructors, who generally governed children more gently than men, won the approval of most parents, but influential citizens complained about the shabby treatment of the writing masters, whose salary and autonomy were restored within a few years. Undeterred, another group of committeemen in 1836 urged colleagues to eliminate the double-headed system. The author of this report, a former usher, called the system an anachronism, "beaten" and "worn-out," inefficient and expensive. If having two schools in one was so ideal, he asked, why not build history and arithmetic schools, and spelling and geography schools, too?[16]

The sarcasm did not win many votes. The overall high reputation of Boston's grammar schools usually protected the masters, who basked in their glow. They reigned and ruled in their bailiwick, shaping the course of study and meting out discipline, though abuses of power generated recurrent complaints. Leah Nichols-Wellington, who became an art teacher at Wellesley College, was a pupil at the Bowdoin Grammar School between 1839 and 1846. In a memoir of her school days, she accurately recalled that the masters did not always teach the required full range of subjects. That enabled some to be effective, even inspiring, teachers, say, of history or penmanship. Critics, of course, countered that instructors should not be paid to teach their favorite hobbies. And the autocratic behavior of some masters, reflecting their accustomed independence, occasionally incensed parents. Nichols-Wellington remembered singing a song written by Lowell Mason, a nationally prominent composer who taught music in the Boston system.

> Rapidly the time passed,
>   Studies blent with play;
> Gladly performed each task,
>   Teachers to obey.[17]

Unfortunately, pupils were not always obedient. The two masters at Bowdoin, a girls' school, eschewed physical punishment; they preferred sarcasm and humiliation to control miscreants, often making offenders stand on their own desks. Nichols-Wellington never forgot Master Abraham Andrews. A Dartmouth graduate, he "wore a brown wig and gold-bowed spectacles" and "his word was law and his laws like those of the

Medes and Persians." He was known to escort offenders to "the very large coal hod, kept near the fire-place," right in front "of the highest-class girls." Being shamed in front of the master's prize pupils was embarrassing enough. Girls commonly wore white pantalettes, leg coverings of cotton or linen, so arriving home with sooty garments also alerted parents to trouble at school. Decades after attending the Hawes School, another girl remembered the disciplinary methods of her writing master, John Harris, who excelled at teaching mathematics. "How well I remember Master Harris's gray coat, that always hung by his desk," she recalled. "Sometimes to punish a girl he would stand her under it or set her under his desk." Harris had a "rough saltiness" and tagged unruly lads with rude nicknames but rarely used the rattan.[18]

Corporal punishment was common in the grammar schools. As one wag quipped, "Boston is a great city—great in science, great in literature, great in philosophy, and—great in flogging." Since the 1790s, Bostonians often debated the utility and morality of hitting children. The School Committee enjoined the masters to rule, whenever possible, without physical punishment. The earliest regulations forbade them from striking pupils "on the head, either with the hand or any instrument" or appointing any scholar "to inflict any corporal punishment on another." Recurrent complaints about over-zealous floggers always generated a defense of the system. As early as 1791, a contributor to the *Columbian Centinel* warned that governing youth without the threat of corporal punishment was a delusion and a rejection of Biblical truths and common sense. Throughout history the birch subdued "stubborn tempers" and turned idlers into productive adults. "We have seen the rod excite to diligence the lazy; to sprightliness the dull; to spirit the stupid; we have seen it produce order and method, where once was confusion and hubbub; and we are resolved to continue the use, so long as good effects follow from it."[19]

Some masters developed fearsome reputations as they meted out punishments to obstreperous boys in particular: tanning hides, rapping knuckles, boxing ears. An alumnus from the Boylston School of the 1820s reminisced decades later that the masters and ushers "seemed to think that order could be maintained only by severity." In some schools, a master without a rattan resembled a drum major without a baton. Adults occasionally made light of this, especially at the annual celebration at Faneuil Hall. In 1826 there were toasts to the health of the schools, to the future of the republic, and to "The Tree of Knowledge—May there be no serpent at its root, and no devil's apples on its branches." Another toast rang out on "Ancient School Discipline. A long oblivion to the old practice of treating intellect as though it were a blister, to be raised by applying a cow's hide to a boy's skin." At the festivities in 1833, pupils entertained the audience with a song filled with allusions to "Master Birch" and the "usher's scowl," indignities presumably forgotten as the medal scholars feasted with the masters, mayor, and other dignitaries.[20]

Irate parents nevertheless found physical punishment abhorrent, out of step with the romantic feelings and humanitarianism of the age, which emphasized childhood innocence and gentle childrearing. The School Committee told the masters to exhaust every means before using force, and then only to suit the crime. While more educators by the 1830s condemned corporal punishment, the masters generally dismissed such notions as pie in the sky. The male pupils at the Mayhew School dubbed that very era "The Reign of Terror." Time did not heal all wounds, as one alumnus of another grammar school revealed. His school resembled the fictional accounts that Charles Dickens immortalized in *Nicholas Nickleby* (1839) and *Hard Times* (1854). "About three times a week," he remembered, "a ferruling was administered me for 'doing nothing.'" The master—who combined the "qualities of the brute and the pedagogue"—thrashed about twenty to thirty boys daily and predicted a bleak future for the poor Irish immigrant pupils among them. Not surprisingly, the author of this reminiscence was regularly truant and regarded his school as nightmarish; classmates, he thought, rightly hooted when the masters announced the medal winners (toadies and "tale-bearers") after the summer exhibition. He then gratefully left that school forever but not before he and a friend exacted some revenge. After the August ceremony, they waited outside the school "until the appearance of our late master, when, joining his hated name to epithets there would be an impropriety in introducing in print, we raised our voices against him and fled."[21]

Between the 1790s and early 1840s, the grammar masters generally fended off their critics, preserved their autonomy, and enjoyed the perquisites of office. They even formed their own "association of masters" to discuss issues of mutual interest from pedagogy to politics and to respond collectively to criticisms about the double-headed system, high salaries, disciplinary methods, and their refusal to better articulate their schools with those above and below them. In 1838, one citizen rightly noted that the grammar masters "have, to a wide extent, been permitted to indulge their taste and to adopt their own plans. Hence it has happened that no fair comparison could be made by the examining committee between different schools, on account of the diversity in their classifications." The masters kept their first classes with the very best scholars as small as they wished to impress everyone when the examiners visited.[22]

By 1844, however, the masters had chosen to tangle with a new wave of reformers who were well organized and persistent. More trouble was brewing, and the masters knew it.

III

The substitution of written for oral tests by the annual examining committees in the summer of 1845 was momentous and controversial. Each side of the testing controversy accused the other of the worst motives. That neither masters nor pupils were informed about the change in format fueled endless speculation about the motives of the examiners. Since the arrogance of the masters was a staple of educational commentary, the key examiners also deserve scrutiny, before assuming that "reformers" had a monopoly on virtuous intentions. Why did they decide to use written tests at that moment in history and in stealth fashion? Why did they not confide in anyone outside of their small circle?

While their partisanship varied, everyone on the Boston School Committee was linked to party politics. Each member had won nomination for office at political conventions held in every ward and run on a political ticket. Newspapers might champion their favorites for their intelligence and devotion to the common good, but politics was the coin of the educational realm. The men on the two examining committees in 1845 were all newly elected. It was a burdensome, time-consuming task, often saddled on new members. The leading examiners in 1845 represented a long line of people who favored centralizing authority to make schools more efficient and uniform, which meant weakening the autonomy of the masters. As Samuel Wells had explained in his report of 1830, tests could measure the achievement of pupils as well as the quality of their instruction. Discerning the private thoughts of every examiner in 1845 is impossible, but some clearly believed that the test results would both discredit the masters and demonstrate a superior way to measure school quality.

Only the examiners and a few confidants knew the exact nature of the upcoming test. But the masters had good reasons to worry without knowing exactly what the reformers were planning. In 1842, a different group of examiners had criticized them for lax teaching methods; moreover, the state's leading school periodical published excerpts of their report, adding to their embarrassment. So the masters knew that membership on committees mattered, and neither they nor the new crop of examiners were political innocents. Testing was indeed incomprehensible apart from the charged political climate that then existed in the city. Traditionally, the mayor was an ex-officio member of the School Committee, over which he formally presided and made committee assignments. In early May of 1845, Josiah Quincy, Jr., the Whig mayor of Boston, dutifully appointed three members each to the reading and writing committee, setting the wheels of educational change in motion.[23]

Quincy was no ordinary person. Decades later, eulogists still remembered him as "a worthy scion of the old stock." Like his father, an activist mayor of the same name, he regarded government as an active agent in promoting the greater good, whether improving roads, the water supply, or schools. While serving in the legislature in the late 1830s, he and other Whigs had championed the establishment of a state board of education and state-funded normal schools, despite opposition from Democrats and some dissenting Whigs who saw them as expensive, centralizing institutions that weakened community control. In 1837, Quincy's allies helped persuade his old friend, fellow lawyer, and Whig colleague in the legislature, Horace Mann, to become secretary (or head) of the new state board, which soon advocated reforms such as age-graded classrooms and teacher training. As legislators both Quincy and Mann supported railroads and other internal improvements. Mann became a pivotal if sometimes shadowy figure in every aspect of the summer exams.[24]

Quincy neither shied from his duties on the School Committee nor hid his partisanship. Like other Whigs he believed that schools promoted progress, spreading literacy and moral values appropriate to a growing city and the republic. He named three prominent Whigs to the reading committee and two others, including William Brigham, to the writing committee. Some were among Mann's closest friends. Brigham, for example, had served with Mann in the legislature and was a fellow lawyer, teetotaler, and antislavery activist. The fact that these men were even on the School Committee resulted directly from Mann's behind-the-scenes politicking, since he had persistently lobbied them in the fall of 1844 to stand for office. Ever the politician, Mann had some unfinished business to conclude with the grammar masters. Though not all of the new committeemen were openly aligned with Mann, the masters understandably felt threatened and smelled a conspiracy.[25]

The nominal head of the reading committee, which became the center of the storm, was Theophilus Parsons, son of a famous judge and himself a well-regarded lawyer and classical scholar. The elder Parsons was chief justice of the Massachusetts court system in the early 1800s and an influential Federalist. Like his father a Harvard alumnus, the younger Parsons was professionally and socially prominent, one of the "gentleman founders," as one magazine described him, of the Boston Natural History Society. In 1844 he served as a delegate to the Whig state convention, the same year he stood for election to the School Committee. He and Mann were no strangers; their law offices in Boston in the 1830s were in the same building. A prolific author—of legal treatises especially, but also of works on religious mysticism—Parsons was appointed to the Harvard law faculty in 1847.[26]

Joining the forty-seven-year-old Parsons on the committee was the Reverend Rollin H. Neale, a Baptist minister. Born in Connecticut in 1808, he traveled a different path to local prominence. A religious conversion as a teenager directed his life toward soul saving, and he attended college in Washington, DC, and then the Newton Divinity School, a central training ground for Baptists. By 1833 he was minister of Boston's South Baptist church and soon began a forty-year tenure at prestigious First Baptist. Active in Sabbath schools and young men's Christian associations, he led religious revivals, signed antislavery petitions, and was persuaded to run for the School Committee. Like Parsons, he served a few terms despite taking more heat than comfortable in the summer of 1845.[27]

The prime mover on the reading committee was Samuel Gridley Howe. Though not the actual chairman, he did the lion's share of work and colluded with his dear friend, Horace Mann, who was tethered to him politically and emotionally. Like several other Whig reformers, he swept into office in the December 1844 elections. Contemporaries referred to the reading examiners' report as "Howe's report," since he wrote most of it, edited it in response to criticisms, and took most of the praise or blame for its contents.

Howe was born in Boston in 1801, the son of a prosperous businessman who fell on hard times during the War of 1812. Young Howe nevertheless attended Boston's famous Latin School, where a master disciplined him so severely that his "poor little hand was beaten almost to jelly." However much the story was embellished with the retelling, the incident made Howe a critic of corporal punishment, one of many issues on which he and Mann agreed. Their paths crossed early in life, laying the foundation of an enduring friendship. Howe attended Brown University, graduating in 1821; Mann had graduated two years earlier and remained in Providence for two years as a college tutor, when they likely first met. After studying medicine at Harvard, Howe fought in the Greek Wars of Independence, becoming a national celebrity both here and in Greece, and then traveled throughout Europe to study the education of the blind, opening a school back home that made him famous.[28]

Before the December 1844 elections, Howe and Mann were convinced that the grammar masters needed a comeuppance, or more. What had the masters done to stir them up? How did written tests become central to school reform?

IV

Howe's comrade-in-arms, Horace Mann, had precious little experience as an educator, certainly nothing like those who worked in the trenches in Boston or became a master after years of trial in the classroom. Born in Franklin, Massachusetts, in 1796, Mann was a son of Puritans who embraced Unitarianism, abandoning Calvinist views such as infant damnation and predestination while retaining a bipolar view of a world of good and evil. After tutoring at Brown, he attended law school, served in both houses of the Massachusetts legislature, and became a prominent Whig, ultimately heading the senate. After opening a law office in Boston in the early 1830s, Howe and Mann, fellow Unitarians, saw each other frequently. To say that the two men, central to the 1845 exams, were tightly knit is an understatement. Their mutual admiration seemed boundless, whether in private letters or in a public forum. Mann served as a Visitor at Howe's school for the blind and extolled his accomplishments in his annual reports as secretary of the state board and in his influential *Common School Journal*. Howe in turn assailed Mann's opponents in letters to the editor, legislative hearings, and testimonials. Both men soaked up and contributed to Boston's cosmopolitan intellectual and cultural life, and by the early 1840s together targeted the grammar masters as the source of every problem in the local schools.[29]

Residence in Boston gave both men extraordinary access to the latest trans-Atlantic proposals for educational and social reform. Since the colonial period, the seaport town was a major port of entry for books, periodicals, and reports from Europe, especially England. Like other eastern seaboard cities, Boston was deeply affected by the print revolution sweeping the nation. Once a largely Federalist and then, by the 1830s and 1840s, Whig stronghold, it was home to numerous newspapers, often owned and edited by leading figures in the dominant party. A preeminent educational center, Boston housed printing and publishing houses, book shops, and a famed university in nearby Cambridge, where local notables such as Mann served as examiners. Its leaders viewed the city as the nation's intellectual epicenter, "the Athens of America." Government documents, domestic and foreign, crossed the desks of officials and incipient reformers interested in modern approaches to crime, poverty, and education. Mann and Howe feasted on a steady diet of them, deepening their friendship as they considered new perspectives, often emanating from Europe, on how children learned and how to measure schools quantitatively.[30]

Mann and Howe were not only active in the Whig party but also embraced similar causes, especially educational reform and the new science of phrenology, a European import. Mann claimed in 1844 that Howe's school for the blind was the greatest innovation of its kind in the world, and he viewed schools generally as a panacea for the ills of society. In the midst of the examination controversy, Howe characteristically told his friend that "if the country and the race can be speeded on its great work of progress and improvement it must be by the education of the young." Later viewed as bogus science, phrenology was for a time enormously popular—especially among newly trained physicians and liberal clerics and educators—and seen as a handmaiden to reform. It offered an alternative to orthodox Christian metaphysics: a secular, empirical basis for understanding the mind and human behavior. If the brain, as phrenologists claimed, indeed comprised discrete faculties, proper cultivation could improve it: proof that people had free will and that education could contribute to human perfectibility.[31]

Seeking a more scientific and systematic approach to teaching and learning, both Mann and Howe corresponded with the leading phrenologists here and abroad. Mann became extremely close friends with the famous Scottish proponent George Combe, and he fretted about his children's head shapes. Howe in turn was a founding member and recording secretary of the Boston Phrenological Society. In 1836 Howe claimed that "what the discovery of the mariner's compass has been to navigators, will be the philosophy of Phrenology to education and legislation." "No one was safe from Howe's searching gaze," wrote one biographer, for "he always looked at people's heads trying to judge their character, especially those of famous men." For years, at his school for the blind, he stored the skull of Joseph Spurzheim, the German physician and phrenologist who died in 1832 during a lecture tour in Boston. Local professors of medicine also championed phrenology, which became so popular it invited skepticism and caricature. In 1834, a speaker at the Boston meetings of the American Institute of Instruction, an appropriately high-browed educational association that Howe helped create, joked that "the craniological fever is on, and will have its run. Blessed is the man now, who has a fine skull."[32]

Phrenology was no laughing matter to Howe. In a speech before the Boston group in 1837, he drew upon knowledge about the mind and education gained through study and travels in Europe as he searched for new ways to teach the blind. Teachers nearly everywhere, he feared, crammed students with knowledge without ensuring that pupils actually understood what they memorized and recited. Drill and excessive study ruined pupils' health, of obvious concern to this fully trained physician. Phrenology taught the importance of teaching children to analyze, reason, and think by strengthening certain faculties; too much memorization weakened the mind and body. Like many Whigs, Howe favored more professional training for teachers and more harmonious physical and intellectual development, and he told his audience that European schools were far in advance of America's. "The boys of the English, Scotch, and German high schools," Howe believed, "are better scholars than the titled graduates of our colleges; the members of all the learned professions in Europe, though they have less of the *savior faire* of ours, are better scholars, and more learned men. Our youth, while yet in all their greenness, are dubbed doctors, lawyers, and divines; and they begin to get knowledge by practicing upon the people; for, like the barber's apprentice, they must perforce learn to shave on the public chin, having no beards on their own."[33]

Other ideas with distant origins also circulated among Boston's educational elite to influence the 1845 exams. Chief among them was a new attentiveness to statistics. By the early nineteenth century, many European governments established standard weights and measures to better integrate their economies and sought more quantitative information on mortality, trade, and population growth, all part of nation building. By the 1830s and 1840s, statistical societies were increasingly common in European and American cities, further stimulating interest among elected officials, government employees, and the reading public with quantifiable knowledge, often expressed in charts and ranked lists. As more people in the Western world became numerate, new ways of understanding reality became possible. Precision even became popular in soul saving. Reverend Rollin H. Neale, Howe's colleague on the examining committee, announced in 1842 that he had baptized exactly 185 individuals— no more, no less—during a recent revival. Greater facility with numbers meant more citizens in all walks of life could better measure, count, compare, and determine trends over time. That was precisely what written exams aimed to do, and they were thus a creature of their times.[34]

By the 1820s, newspapers and magazines on the East Coast proliferated and not only described European educational innovations and trends but also provided a surfeit of statistical information on schools, from enrollment figures to graduation lists to per capita expenditures. That numbers provided an "authentic," "real," and "factual" basis for comprehending reality undergirded the widespread appeal of statistics. Boston established America's first statistical society in 1839, and Howe, Mann, and William Brigham (of the writing committee) were virtually charter members. Statistics were often deployed in other proposals for social innovation. In a speech before the Boston Phrenological Society in 1836, Howe claimed that comparative statistics revealed that America's frantic competitiveness produced more insanity per capita than England.

He called for more facts on every conceivable subject, including the number of blind, deaf, and dumb in Massachusetts, soon the nation's leading sponsor of statistical studies. Horace Mann helped initiate that trend. As a young legislator, Mann successfully led a movement in 1830 to establish a state lunatic asylum and dutifully gathered statistics to buttress his arguments. As secretary of the State Board of Education, Mann regularly published statistical abstracts from hundreds of school districts and in his very first report called for better record keeping. The *Christian Register and Boston Observer* praised Mann's *Fourth Report* in 1841 for providing so many interesting statistics on schools, "from which every one may form an independent judgement as to their actual state."[35]

Whether fascinated by skull shapes or student scores, Mann and Howe promised to overturn traditional ways of understanding education and schooling. The reformers lived in Boston but were inspired by Europe.

V

By the early 1840s, Howe and Mann were inseparable, corresponding regularly, visiting frequently, and providing moral support when necessary. In 1843, the men were such intimates that they traveled with their respective brides on a honeymoon to Europe. Travel had long been central to elite education. Howe's colleagues on the reading committee, too, had traveled to Europe, adding to their bank of knowledge and sophistication. Theophilus Parsons made his grand tour in 1817, two years after graduating from Harvard, then returned for law school. Reverend Neale journeyed to London, Rome, and other cities on the Continent in 1843, visiting historical sites, attending Baptist revivals, and keeping his brethren informed about his pilgrimage in the *Christian Watchman*.[36]

For Mann and Howe, the honeymoon trip, whatever its other virtues, proved decisive in their upcoming battles against the grammar masters. The newlyweds (at least the men) read the latest publications and reports on pedagogy, school inspection, and written tests. Howe's talented wife, Julia Ward Howe, who later wrote the "Battle Hymn of the Republic," recalled the period in her memoirs: "Upon arriving in England, [the couples] occupied for a time the same lodgings, and many of their visits were made in company. I remember among these workhouses, schools, and prisons." Her husband, she bitterly recalled, was a "Comet-Apostle"

who flitted from reform to reform and sometimes neglected his fatherly
duties. Resentful, she penned a bittersweet song:

> Rero, rero, riddlety rad
> This morning my baby caught sight of her Dad,
> Quote she, "Oh, Daddy, where have you been?"
> "With Mann and [Charles] Sumner a-putting down sin."[37]

In times of crisis or conflict, both men usually assumed the moral high
ground, imputing the worst of intentions to their adversaries. Whether
the cause was education, temperance, or antislavery, Howe did nothing
by half measures and neither did Mann.[38]

The grammar masters were in their crosshairs by the early 1840s, since
they publicly ridiculed Mann's various proposals for school reform. By
then, Mann was the risen star of the educational world. Since assuming his new position in 1837, he had stumped the state on behalf of
educational improvement, become a popular lecturer on school reform
throughout the North, and authored annual reports that brought him
national and international renown. His writings reflected the Whig belief
that government investment in school and society was the best guarantor
of a morally strong and prosperous republic. Along with other educational leaders, he urged schools to become more modern and accountable by adopting better grading practices, assigning uniform textbooks,
hiring professionally trained teachers, and appointing superintendents to
supervise instruction.[39]

Hostile to perceived abuses of centralized power, Democrats assailed
Mann's attempt to reform local schools from the top down and had generally opposed the creation of the State Board of Education. Mann had
also enraged some orthodox Congregationalist ministers in the late 1830s
by refusing to place their favored texts on a state-approved school library
list, saying they were sectarian, leading to charges that he favored Godless
education. Building nonsectarian (but broadly Christian) public schools
offended some ministers, and his adamant defense of professional training for teachers and related reforms also angered groups such as Boston's
grammar masters. Often college graduates, they mocked the notion that
teachers needed normal school training or that, as Mann and his circle of
friends believed, Boston needed to hire a superintendent, which clearly
threatened their authority. What did some upstart such as Mann know

about education? Writing to Howe in the spring of 1842, Mann called the masters "poor wretches" whom he would "grant a general amnesty . . . if I were sure the rascals, on being forgiven the old debt of sins, wouldn't begin immediately to run up a new score." Mann and Howe never forgot a slight, and they favored martial and religiously inspired metaphors for their rhetorical fire and brimstone. As Mann predicted, the masters soon committed a mortal sin in September of 1844, when thirty-one of them, on behalf of their "association," signed a long published attack on his latest report, based on his travels abroad.[40]

The battles between Mann and the grammar masters became personal, professional, and political, lethal combinations that shaped every aspect of the 1845 exams. The worldviews shared by Mann and his allies contrasted sharply with that of the masters; none of the latter belonged to the local statistical society, and they also ridiculed phrenology. But exactly what had the Secretary said in his latest publication to provoke them so? Mann's *Seventh Report* revealed that the grand honeymoon tour had broadened his repertoire of knowledge about education and school practices in different cultural settings. It opened his eyes wider on issues such as classroom discipline and instruction, teacher training, and examinations. It also confirmed much of what he already knew and believed.

Even before the trip, Mann had praised written tests in official reports and in editorials in the *Common School Journal.* Such tests were sometimes used to screen prospective teachers in Europe and some American cities and to vet pupils for the nation's fledgling high schools. After additional reading and conversations with educators during their travels, Mann and Howe recognized broader uses for written examinations. By yielding numerical scores, tests could help measure both teacher proficiency and pupil achievement, allowing comparisons within and between schools. Fortuitously, the honeymoon couples arrived in England at a time when reformers earnestly debated the merits of competitive testing, which soon led to civil service reform and the appointment of inspectors to examine primary schools. The former mother country was a cultural reference point for Bostonians, and the adoption of English innovations such as Sunday schools and charity schools in various American cities testified to its influence. In the eighteenth century, Cambridge University had also pioneered the use of competitive written tests in mathematics and for honours degrees and added similar exams in various university subjects

by the 1830s and 1840s. All of these well-publicized developments con-
stituted a blow against tradition and educational business as usual.[41]

After a whirlwind visit to schools in England, Scotland, and on the
Continent, most notably Prussia—well known for its autocratic government but also its high-quality schools—Mann returned home, studied his
extensive notes, began writing in November of 1843, and by January had
completed his report.

The *Seventh Report* applauded Prussian schoolmasters for teaching reading more creatively than in America. It applauded them not only for
their command of subject matter but also for employing the latest child-
friendly pedagogy. Sounding a theme that Howe regularly advanced
about teaching, Mann applauded Prussian educators for insisting that
children understand what they were taught and not simply memorize
facts and principles from textbooks. Textbooks, in fact, were absent in
the classrooms he visited. After observing schools in Prussia and Saxony,
Mann also noticed that, in contrast to prevailing practices back home, "I
never saw a teacher hearing a lesson of any kind, (excepting a reading
or spelling lesson,) *with a book in his hand"* or *"sitting." "I never saw one
child receiving punishment, or arraigned for misconduct. I never saw one child
in tears from having been punished, or from fear of being punished."* Prussia
had not banned corporal punishment, but Mann said it was rarely used.
State-financed normal schools, professional inspection and supervision,
and age-grouped classrooms—suspiciously identical to his favored innovations before heading to Europe—ensured the maintenance of rigorous
standards. The implication was clear: America's schools were slipping,
behind the times.[42]

For many years, reformers had publicized promising European innovations, but Mann's implicit warning about educational declension attracted
considerable attention. The *Niles' National Register,* published in Baltimore,
believed that Mann had persuasively shown that America's schools had
lost "the *front place"* to Prussia, which now set the "standard" for Western
nations. If left alone, it added, institutions inevitably ossified. In the early
months of 1844, letters arrived from various states congratulating Mann
on his latest report, and local newspapers and periodicals trumpeted its
virtues. The *Monthly Religious Magazine,* a Unitarian organ, praised Mann
and hoped his latest contribution gained a "wide circulation." The *Seventh
Report* was "full of instruction, even beyond any other similar document

from the same pen." Despite some nitpicking, the *North American Review* called it "excellent in manner and matter." Even the Democratic *Boston Post* touted the *Seventh Report* as "a most excellent production" whose "narratives are as interesting as they are instructive."[43]

Other reviewers, however, highlighted the implied comparison between what Mann saw abroad and conditions at home. The grammar masters must have cringed when Boston's highbrow *Athenaeum* said teachers could learn from Mann and identify "the principal deficiencies, as well as merits, of their rule." By April, the Secretary told a friend that despite the accolades, the *Report* had upset religious sectarians and certain teachers who felt "driven out of the paradise which their own self-esteem had erected for them."[44]

In May, George B. Emerson, an influential ally of Mann's, added to the masters' displeasure. Emerson had been the first principal of the English high school and likely nursed some old grievances against them for preventing some of their best pupils from taking its entrance exam. In 1836 he and other leaders of the American Institute of Instruction had lobbied the legislature to create the office of state superintendent of education, essentially the post filled by Mann a year later. Their petition noted that the German states, especially Prussia, had appointed special school officers to raise teaching and academic standards. Now Emerson applauded Mann's latest publication in a long essay in Boston's liberal *Christian Examiner and Religious Miscellany.* After extolling Mann for his inspired leadership, Emerson seconded the Secretary's views on Prussia's enlightened approach to pedagogy and the benefits of assigning one teacher for every grade, in separate classrooms, a direct knock on the double-headed system. Then Emerson bluntly asked "whether it is possible, in any part of Massachusetts,—in Boston, for example,—to manage the schools" along such progressive lines. In another potshot at the masters, Emerson wondered whether those lacking normal school training should be hired to teach.[45]

The grammar and writing masters, whose schools were not mentioned in the *Seventh Report,* had occasionally groused about Mann's commentaries and grandiose plans for reform. But they usually suffered in silence and had not complained or protested collectively. For years, Mann and his associates had waxed enthusiastically about age grading, statistics, and supervision and condemned emulation. The *Common School Journal* applauded the child-centered teaching methods of Swiss innovators such as Johann Pestalozzi, who treated children kindly and criticized rote instruction. Mann called him the "wisest of schoolmasters." Both Howe and Emerson had lobbied for state normal schools in the 1830s and helped sustain them when Democrats and some dissenting Whigs demanded their closure. Howe even insisted in Mann's journal that the Lexington normal school was "the best school I ever saw, in this or any other country." By 1844, the masters had long endured complaints about their labors and also feared that the tide was turning in favor of hiring a superintendent. This had already occurred elsewhere, so how long could Boston resist the trend? Instead of persuading the School Committee that the schools were doing fine, their usual default, they decided to take on the Secretary. An observer writing in the Whig *North American Review*, published in Boston, tried to explain why. While Mann had rarely spoken of the metropolis in his reports, his general calls for reform encouraged like-minded citizens "to ask, if the teachers and guardians of the Boston schools were not asleep," resting on their laurels. As for the masters, "the flame was pent up in their bosoms, but it was gathering strength there, and was ready to burst forth when the hour should come." Accumulated grievances exploded when Mann's *Seventh Report* appeared.[46]

By the summer of 1844, William B. Fowle, a prolific author of schoolbooks and the publisher of the *Common School Journal*, alerted Mann to trouble on the horizon. A native Bostonian, child prodigy, and Latin School alumnus, Fowle was an antislavery Whig, fellow Unitarian, and devotee of phrenology who had criticized the double-headed system since the 1820s. Apprenticed as an adolescent to none other than Caleb Bingham, he later ran the famous author's bookshop before teaching in a celebrated girls' monitorial school. Returning to the publishing business, Fowle became the eyes and ears of the Secretary in the early 1840s. His store often patronized by teachers and prominent Bostonians, he seemed to know every educator in the city. The white master of the segregated Smith School, Abner Forbes, stopped by Fowle's office in mid-July, seeking information. Under attack by anti-segregationists, Forbes was convinced that Emerson had turned Howe against him. He felt persecuted and knew his reputation and job were endangered. Regarding the *Seventh Report*, Forbes said the masters were working on a retort and aimed to "strike hard" though respectfully. After questioning one of the aggrieved masters, Fowle confirmed that they were coordinating "'a defense of the Schools' against some unjust aspersions" by the Secretary. Fowle told Mann not to worry: "I think the combined wisdom of the Boston craft will not do anything that needs excite any uneasiness. If they do not *lie* they are nothing, and if they *do* lie they are less than nothing. God help them."[47]

A few days later, Emerson tried to get to the bottom of everything. Fowle had heard that the masters specifically opposed Mann's views on reading instruction, and Emerson learned that they were generally upset at his favorable views on Prussia. Emerson regarded some of the masters as "absurdly conceited" and told Mann nothing could stop their proposed critique of his report. Some masters, he speculated, "are probably moved by a strong personal feeling of resentment at not having received due honor at your hands; others desire to be unprejudiced. I am told that no personal feelings will be allowed to appear in this review. They say they seek only to find out the truth and make it appear, to vindicate the Boston Schools from unfair implications."[48]

A geographically compact city, Boston was thus a fish bowl where the printed word and personal communication thrived, ensuring that rumors and innuendo flourished. By August, Mann was so anxious that he confided in Howe. "I have been in perpetual conflict, the whole season,— slept in my armor, I have been waked by the war whoop. The Cossacks are still after me, & whether I shall survive them is quite uncertain. My last Report," he added, "has wakened every form of opposition, & the assailants will doubtless find a leader." Feeling aggrieved and exhibiting self-pity, Mann believed "there are not half a dozen men in the state who *really & truly* care, what becomes of me, or are ready to lift a finger in my behalf. But, I would not trouble you with these despondencies."[49]

Howe took the less-than-subtle hint that Mann needed help. After the masters' report appeared in September, they began talking to their numerous friends about how to respond.

VI

Signed by thirty-one grammar masters, *Remarks on the Seventh Annual Report of the Hon. Horace Mann* was no small effort. It was 144 pages long and attacked every major claim in Mann's report. Contrary to what

Mann's friends anticipated, the masters' criticisms appeared personal. They called Mann an amateur whose minimal teaching experience made him susceptible to fads such as phrenology and various "hot-bed theories." His dream of eliminating corporal punishment reflected a "mawkish sentimentalism" and naïveté about children's nature, which was sinful and necessitated their obedience to adult authority. The masters doubted whether Mann had visited as many schools, at home or abroad, as he boasted, or stayed long enough to comprehend their nature. They read Mann's report as an affront. They repeatedly claimed that Mann knew nothing about Boston's schools and insisted, erroneously, that he had never visited them. Moreover, the grammar schools were excellent and always improving. "It may well be believed," claimed the masters, "that the schools of the metropolis of New England have long been under the guardianship of those, whose benevolence and care have increased in proportion to the number of the children." They obviously hoped to turn the School Committee against the Secretary. Dripping with sarcasm, the *Remarks* allowed the masters to defend the teaching profession against Mann's calumnies. "The Prussian and Scotch teachers seem to be all Newtons, Melancthons, Oberlins, and Mozarts," in the Secretary's warped view, "when compared with the David Gamuts, Dominie Sampsons, Ichabod Cranes, and old Squeerses, that the secretary had seen in Massachusetts." For good measure, the masters also zinged Howe for his "peculiar views."[50]

Mann rarely took professional disagreements in stride. Charles Sumner, a longtime friend to Howe and Mann, recognized this combativeness. He and Mann once had law offices in the same building, and he admired both men enormously. A Boston Latin and Harvard graduate, Sumner rallied around the Secretary when critics came near but perceived a vindictive nature and tendency to demonize others. Sumner was out of town when the local controversies heated up in late summer. On September 11, he wrote to Howe, urging both men to calm down. "I am very sorry," he wrote, "that the pedagogues of Boston have assailed Mann, and wish I could have joined in your counsels for his defense. To you and to Mann, I should say, *Moderation!* I honor, almost revere, the zeal of the latter, and the ability to which it is sustained; but I sometimes doubt his judgment and taste." Neither friend followed Sumner's advice, and he found himself entangled in the local intrigue after returning to Boston.[51]

After reading the masters' *Remarks,* Mann told Howe in late September that "the foe think the [State] Board of Education already destroyed, & that it only remains to record the sentence." Drawing upon the Book of Esther in the Old Testament, Mann added that "we will see who shall be Mordecai & who Haman." The gallows intended for Mann, as for Mordecai, might be used on the masters, and he imagined all thirty-one of them "hung on the same shaft . . . like a string of onions." Mann, Howe, and numerous friends clearly sought revenge, best achieved, Mann suggested, by electing reform-minded men to the School Committee. By October 8, Mann already had replacements in mind for the masters who would be fired if everything fell into place. A day later, Howe assured the Secretary that "I am doing all I can to procure some amelioration of the School Committee here. . . . I feel that now is the time for your friends to come to your aid, and I for one will do what little I can—would it were more: heretofore I have cheered you only in words: now if you will show me how to work I will do it." Grateful to Howe for agreeing to run for office, Mann told his dear friend, "A thousand thanks for your kind proffers of assistance to take me out of the hands of the Philistines." Unwilling to let his friends alone do the fighting, Mann told Howe he had nearly completed a long reply to the masters.[52]

The anger generated by the masters among Mann's coterie of associates did not dissipate. In addition, on October 1, Orestes Brownson, a former Transcendentalist undergoing a conversion to Catholicism, wrote a scathing attack on Mann, saying his policies promoted moral degeneration throughout the region. While emphasizing that he was not necessarily aligned with the grammar masters, Brownson did not mince words. "Mr. Mann knows nothing of the philosophy of education, for he knows nothing of the philosophy of human nature, and nothing of Christian morals and theology. His theory is derived from German quacks, and can only rear up a generation of infidels." Within a week, Mann wrote to Howe, asking if he had seen Brownson's tirade, "where he flings the javelin across my frontier?" Had he seen the slurs against him by an orthodox minister in the *Mercantile Journal?* But a solution was possible if "a majority of the right kind of men could be elected on the school committee this year," the Secretary's enemies removed, and a superintendent appointed to rein in the masters.[53]

Mann told Howe that he felt "desperate" but "determined." "Troubles thicken," he told another friend, "but that only makes me stiffen." He heard that a prominent master and that an ally on the School Committee planned to attack him and his ideas for school reform at an upcoming professional conference. Friends circled around Mann as his anxieties rose. Emerson tried to console him, writing on October 19 to say "I am very sorry to hear that the devil is abroad." But Emerson, who had helped agitate the masters, added more fuel to the fire that very month. He published an inflammatory pamphlet aimed directly at them, calling them smug and backward. "Could they really expect," he wrote, "that a person who had seen the best schools abroad, would come home prepared to pronounce panegyrics upon the Grammar Schools of Boston?" Did the masters "still suppose their schools the best in the world? And are they really disappointed that Mr. Mann did not pronounce them such?" That same month, Mann's acid pen finished a 176-page *Reply to the "Remarks"*. . . , which appeared in print a month later and endeavored to refute the masters, point by point. He defended his credentials as a teacher and educator and accused the masters of knowingly inflicting pain upon him, not surprising given their reputation as floggers. He promised another reply if the masters persisted.[54]

By early November, John Odin, Jr., a physician and leader on the Primary School Committee, joined the phalanx of people offended by the masters. To discredit the novel ideas on reading proposed by Mann, which rejected the traditional practice of memorizing the alphabet before learning words, the masters in their *Remarks* claimed that this approach had produced poor readers in the lower grades, weakening pupils' chances for admission to the grammar schools. Odin and his colleagues viewed the charges as false and gratuitous, and they accused the masters of maligning their schools because of their disdain for Mann. Odin pointed out that very few pupils were ignorant of their ABCs. Soon after, Odin decided to seek election to the Grammar School Committee.[55]

Watching these fireworks from a safe distance, the editor of the *Boston Daily Atlas* attempted a truce in late November between Mann and the masters. "It is, we are well aware, a thankless task, to attempt to take part in family quarrels, and this one certainly bears a strong similitude to one; a person is very apt to receive some hard knocks for his pains, from either party." A truce seemed unlikely since the Whig editor urged the masters to soften their tone and learn from their critics. While the masters in their *Reply* ridiculed the growing popularity of statistics, the editor embraced the utilitarian spirit of the times. "This is emphatically the age of *facts*," he insisted, and new theories about discipline and pedagogy and novel means of measurement might undermine everything the masters held dear. Smearing Mann, Howe, and their allies, warned the editor, could backfire.[56]

Mann could barely contain himself as the December elections approached. Throughout the fall, Howe urged Mann to lie low. "Of one thing be sure, that although your enemies may for the moment make a triumphant appeal to the prejudice and bigotry of the day, it will only be for the moment. . . . There never was and never will be a reformer, a man ahead of his generation, who had not a host of difficulties and enemies to encounter." On November 26, he again assured the Secretary that their "selfish and Devilish" adversaries would pay the price on election day. "You ask me what is going on: I can tell you what is going *off*—that is the reputation of the Boston School masters. Oh! Horace! You have a heavy debt to pay in good deeds from the qualifications you have given to all the sons and daughters of Cain by your flagellation of these old tyrants. I thought you disapproved of public executions, & never supposed you would turn hangman."[57]

A few days later, Mann wrote to George Combe, the Scottish phrenologist, about his recurrent battles with orthodox ministers and accelerating conflicts with the grammar masters. As usual, he saw the world in stark terms. "The very things in the [Seventh] Report," he wrote, "which made it acceptable to others made it hateful to them. The general reader was delighted with the idea of intelligent, gentlemanly teachers; of a mind-expanding education" and of children governed not by the ferrule but "moral means." But the "leading" grammar masters—guided by an "evil spirit"—"saw their own condemnation in this description of their European contemporaries." Mann cautiously believed Bostonians would vote for "better schools and less flogging" in the upcoming elections. His personal friend Quincy, running for reelection as mayor, stood for reform, and "things were coming to a crisis. The prevailing party will probably be left in possession of the field for some time to come."[58]

Bare knuckles indeed prevailed as election day drew near. On December 7, Howe, his usual combative self, published a letter in the *Atlas* that defended Mann and berated the grammar masters and their supporters, who wrote in "the very spirit of Judas." The next day, two grammar masters, fearing the situation might spin out of control, wrote to Mann to assure him that, while their names appeared on the *Remarks*, they meant no personal disrespect. Joshua Bates, Jr., newly appointed at the Brimmer School, feared that the *Seventh Report* had the *"unintentional"* effect of weakening respect for teachers throughout the commonwealth. Both men agreed to overlook their differences and remain friends. Master William J. Adams of the Hancock School, who publicly withdrew his name from the *Remarks* after it was published, similarly assured Mann that their disagreements were strictly professional.[59]

The real news came a few days later, when voters elected thirteen new individuals to the twenty-four member School Committee. In a few months, six of the newcomers, including some of Mann's friends, found themselves on the summer examination committees. In the meantime, the war of words between Mann and the masters remained the talk of the town. The Baptist *Christian Watchman* found their behavior shameful. "It is much to be regretted that the teachers should have descended to what looks so like lurking insinuations and ungentlemanly thrusts; and still more that an officer of the Commonwealth of Massachusetts, holding not only a highly dignified civil station, but an elevated moral position, should have felt it necessary to call to his aid the power of biting sarcasm and retort." The Boston correspondent to the *New York Observer*, a conservative Presbyterian publication, reported that passions were running high and "very possibly, the discussion is but just begun."[60]

CHAPTER 3

Screwing Machines

"The first meeting of the new Board was held on Thursday afternoon," the *Boston Daily Atlas* reported on January 18, 1845. A handful of reform-minded Whigs had swept into office, testifying to the determination of Horace Mann and his friends to rout their enemies and, in Mann's mind, to root out sin. What difference would they make? History was not encouraging. Complaints about the grammar schools always outnumbered remedies. Since the 1820s, reformers had blasted the double-headed system, overbearing masters, and superficial approaches to judging and comparing schools. But the system seemed impervious to change. Recall that every incumbent master had been reappointed the previous summer. But 1845 became a momentous year in Boston's celebrated system and a watershed for the nation's schools. The inaugural meeting of the School Committee gave no clue to this as it conducted its regular business: the appointment of subcommittees to discuss the selection of textbooks, policies on the primary schools, and other routine matters. By the end of the first meeting, without any fanfare, every one of the nineteen grammar schools also had its own three-member "visiting committee" which promised monthly inspections and quarterly reports. As usual, naming the summer examiners to inspect every school was deferred until May.[1]

Through the coming months, the local visiting committees made their usual rounds and wrote short, hand-written reports to present at the quarterly meetings, after which they were filed and largely forgotten. To read them is to enter a different world from ours, one where impressions about schools sufficed and words rather than numbers ruled. Thus local visitors inspected the Wells School in late January and happily stated that it "continued to enjoy its usual degree of prosperity, & that deserved reputation which a faithful and efficient board of instruction has procured for it." To the masters, staff, and pupils: bravo! Despite periodic laments about the masters, report after report called the schools "satisfactory" or better than before. Their teaching, discipline, and orderly ways were effectively educating Boston's future parents, taxpayers, and leaders. Speaking on behalf of his committee, the Reverend H. A. Graves, a conservative Baptist, typically said a visit to the Lyman School in early February "found very satisfactory evidences of fidelity & competency on the part of the teachers and diligence[,] improvement on the part of the pupils; and nothing more demanding special notice." As committeemen made their rounds, applying the usual subjective standards, everything seemed fine.[2]

Before the summer examiners surprised nearly everyone and tried to turn the system upside down, signs of a gathering storm appeared on the horizon to break the apparent calm. But this was easier to see in hindsight. Much seemed familiar during the winter and spring of 1845. The masters remained preoccupied with their first classes, whose performance usually impressed any visitor. The ushers and female teachers, too, labored as before to teach well and to maintain order and decorum. For pupils, life had its predictable routines, of rising early and walking to school, chatting and jostling with classmates along the crowded and noisy streets, and the inevitable answer to the morning bell. Inside the school was an adult-centered world of textbooks and long hours on hard benches, where boys and girls sat apart in classrooms or buildings and were told to study in silence and prepare for their turn to recite. Those nearest the fireplace on wintry days roasted and those furthest away struggled to stay warm. The year dragged on as temperatures rose and vacation days remained a distant dream. Newspapers stirred fears of an epidemic of fires since the weather seemed unusually hot and dry as spring turned to summer. And, as the heat intensified, the top grammar pupils in late June found themselves subjected to a searching written exam whose results suggested that Boston's schools were in serious trouble.

Between January and June, Mann and a minority of Whig reformers on the School Committee worked out their ingenious scheme to bring the masters to heel. All the while Mann and his friends hardly worried about the weather or what the masters and students, key actors in their unfolding drama, might think about their plans. They met at each other's offices and homes and corresponded regularly, eagerly awaiting news on the smallest detail. In the public arena, newspapers, magazines, and another flurry of pamphlets and reports fed the already overheated passions about the schools, heightening a sense of anticipation among the reformers. Headlines announced new cases of children viciously beaten at school. Abolitionists condemned the shameful treatment of black children at the segregated Smith School. And, said critics, the School Committee overall remained complacent despite these indignities. Reformers saw an opportunity to advance their agenda: to restrict corporal punishment, raise standards, enhance supervision by hiring a superintendent, and eliminate the double-headed system and multi-age classes in the grammar schools. They pinned their hopes on the June exam.

After the summer of 1845, it was impossible to return fully to a time when impressions alone measured a school's worth. To understand the invention and impact of America's first big test requires tracing the steps of the reformers as they planned their next moves.

I

January offered no respite from the bitter feelings between Horace Mann and the grammar masters. Everyone wondered whether the new School Committee would use its power to favor one side or the other. As in the past, the committee included some very prominent, strong-willed, accomplished individuals. Some were alumni of the local schools, high status and successful, certain that Boston's schools were the best in the land. Others arrived in office sewn to Mann at the hip, but they were only a minority on the overwhelmingly Whig board. Whigs believed in the efficacy of well-funded public schools; at the same time, they divided over many contentious issues such as anti-slavery and abolitionism and held different views on the organization of the grammar schools and authority of the masters. One of the veterans on the board, Frederick Emerson, a fellow Whig, despised Mann and his associates. Moreover, Mann's principal ally, Samuel Gridley Howe, was combative and cocksure, with a well-known capacity to annoy even his friends. Adding to the uncertainty of how the stars would align, only eleven of the twenty-four committee members were holdovers. Clashing personalities mixed with divergent political and personal loyalties to make consensus politics unlikely.

Family connections and old school ties bound many elites in antebellum Boston, solidifying allegiances and excluding many outsiders. The School Committee had long been a bastion of well-educated people who expected a certain deference based on their wealth, accomplishments, and, frequently, profession. Two members were elected annually from every ward, and board members presumably exhibited the highest moral quality. Countless educators, citizens, and political leaders agreed that, while schools promoted learning, they should also cultivate pupils' character. Accordingly, a third of the men elected in 1845 were Protestant ministers: three Unitarians, three Baptists, plus one Universalist and one Methodist. But clerics from the same denomination were hardly birds of a feather. For example, some Unitarians and Baptists voted consistently with, and others against, Mann's allies. That Mann had graduated from Baptist Brown and converted from Calvinist Congregationalism to a more liberal Unitarianism enhanced his appeal with certain ministers but deepened the enmity of others. Some orthodox ministers (with friends on the Committee) never forgave him for rejecting their recommendations for the state-approved school library list. (Mann's correspondence is replete with his hyperbolic views on their enduring hatred.) Six physicians, three lawyers, a leading Whig newspaper editor, and a few businessmen helped round out the group.[3]

It was a talented crowd. Many were college graduates and active in benevolent and professional organizations. No less than twenty-one of the twenty-four members in 1845 were Whigs; the others were members of nativist parties or radical abolitionist groups. Some held other political offices during their lifetime. A few of the ministers not only tended to their flock but also edited leading denominational magazines. Public figures, their names were often in the newspaper and, as was said of the Universalist minister, Sebastian Streeter, "about as familiar in our streets, and as well known, as Faneuil Hall, and Boston Common." Who did not know the name Samuel Gridley Howe, whose school for the blind garnered international acclaim and attracted esteemed visitors such as Charles Dickens? Howe's chief nemesis, Frederick Emerson, was an accomplished author of mathematics textbooks and an inventor. Edward Wigglesworth, a political moderate and descendant of a famous minister, was a bank and insurance official and a leading businessman on the India Wharf. Among such over-achieving people, in the tense atmosphere spawned by the *Seventh Report*, school committee meetings might become testy. Indeed, simmering feuds might easily boil over.[4]

In the middle of January, Mann's friends met privately and began a new offensive against the masters. Now that some of their number were in office, they brimmed with optimism. Rumors spread, however, that the masters, miffed by Mann's threats of retaliation if they did not capitulate, planned another rhetorical assault. Some of them seemed overly concerned with defending Boston's reputation and condemning the Secretary, the State Board of Education, and the normal schools. Mann seemed obsessed with discrediting his enemies. And so his allies once more applauded the Secretary's capacious reform program and even pledged $5,000 in matching funds to help establish another state normal school. Recently reelected as mayor, Josiah Quincy, Jr., wrote to Mann on January 13 to inform him of this great vote of confidence. Quincy's name headed this testimonial signed by other Whig luminaries including Howe, Henry Wadsworth Longfellow, and Charles Sumner, the latter recently defeated in his bid for the School Committee. When news of the tribute and matching funds became public, it left little doubt where Quincy's sympathies lay and reinforced the suspicion that Mann was part of a "grand intrigue," as one newspaper alleged. Quincy's group described Mann as a selfless messiah, saving the common schools from unscrupulous foes. "In the warfare with ignorance, there is neither peace, nor neutrality," it warned. "The enemy is always among us, in extensive encampment, wakeful, & ready for the contest. In this warfare you are our leader." Two signatories, Howe and William Brigham, later led the battalion of reformers on the summer examination committees.[5]

The ink was barely dry on Quincy's document when another pamphlet rolled off the press, written by a conservative Congregationalist minister, Leonard Withington. The good reverend lived in the Boston suburbs and was no stranger to public debate. Shunning Unitarian Harvard, he attended Yale, a haven of orthodoxy, and then matriculated to Andover Theological Seminary. While Mann was still working as a lawyer and serving in the Massachusetts legislature, Withington had already staked out some very clear positions on education. Speaking before the august membership of the American Institute of Instruction in 1833, he defended classroom competition, emulation, and the goal of academic excellence. Withington explained that God had made some people smarter, more hard working, and ambitious. "If a boy comes into a school, with twice the abilities of any other, and twice the industry,—why, he has a right to all the fruits of these powers. He has a right to take the standing, which his Maker has given him." Schools could not make everyone equal, but the lazy and slow-witted needed the example of the talented few to rise. Withington preached the conventional Christian view that people were by nature indolent and self-centered. At the very time when Mann labored to shed his Calvinist upbringing, Withington also criticized Unitarian ecclesiology and defended the trinity and that basic tenet of Christianity, original sin.⁶

Insisting he was not in collusion with the grammar masters, Withington nevertheless took their side in an inflammatory pamphlet, *Penitential Tears: Or A Cry from the Dust, or 'The Thirty-One,' Prostrated and Pulverized by the Hand of Horace Mann.* He had sat idly by for too long, he believed, as Mann and the Whigs advanced their dangerous views. Withington left no doubt where he stood. Mann had a "scheming mind," sense of infallibility, and seemed "born to dictate." The "soft and silken reformers" were oblivious to man's sinful nature, leading them to regard corporal punishment a relic of the "dark ages." The masters thus rightly condemned Mann's "moon-shiny speculations" and heretical doctrines. On his six-week tour of Prussia and Saxony, like some modern Don Quixote, the Secretary beheld not an authoritarian state but a fairy tale land of perfectly behaved children and brilliant teachers who miraculously taught without textbooks, the strap, or appeals to emulation. Reality escaped him. Switching metaphors, the reverend assailed Unitarianism as a watered-down version of Christianity, calling Mann "the Münchausen of the moral world." What choice did the masters have but to defend themselves from the slanderous commentaries of impractical dreamers such as Mann and Howe?⁷

Soon after completing *Penitential Tears,* Withington learned that Francis Bowen, the editor of the *North American Review,* had just published an attack on the masters and defense of Mann. In a postscript to *Penitential Tears,* he asked if this learned Whig journal—this "literary synod"—had joined the local "society for mutual admiration." In a long essay, Bowen handled George B. Emerson's October pamphlet and Mann's November

Reply with kid gloves compared with his depiction of the masters, who appeared reactionary if not antediluvian. Bowen believed that all institutions periodically require revitalization. Unwilling to abandon time-worn methods of teaching and discipline, Boston's educational system was clearly in the doldrums. Reorganizing the grammar schools, hiring a superintendent, and initiating other improvements were imperative. Bowen told the masters to *"Mind your own business."* Change was inevitable. To oppose the reform movement led by Mann would only invite more ridicule. "The Boston Teachers might as well attempt to dam up the Mississippi, as to stay its progress."[8]

Bowen's censorious prose only encouraged the opposition, especially Mann's clerical opponents, to ready themselves for another round. Joshua Leavitt, a prominent antislavery and temperance reformer, helped lead the next charge. Editor of the *Emancipator and Weekly Chronicle,* Leavitt and Withington were old friends. Both had graduated from Yale in 1814 and became orthodox Congregationalist clerics. Sharing Withington's disdain for Unitarianism, Leavitt thanked his former classmate for *Penitential Tears,* a "peppery pamphlet, forming a part of the war of words which Horace Mann, the school commissioner, has raised about his ears. Those who delight in earnest and effective sarcasm, will do well to get the pamphlet." Other citizens joined the fray, pummeling the Secretary for his abrasive style and criticisms of traditional classroom discipline. The Baptist *Christian Watchman* published a series of editorials in January and February that praised the masters for holding the line on sound educational and moral principles, which required the measured use of corporal punishment. In mid-February, the *Watchman's* editor defended the masters' right to speak their mind despite the unseemly attempts of Mann and his friends to intimidate. After all, education *was* their business.[9]

By the end of February, as the print wars continued, Mann grew despondent. His enemies would not retreat. Had he not been magnanimous, warning the masters not to respond to his *Reply* to their *Remarks* on his now infamous *Seventh Report?* Mann reached out to George Combe for sympathy and support. The phrenologist had visited Boston a few years earlier and knew how certain people tormented the Secretary. His Scottish friend would understand. "I am sorry to say that my controversy with the Boston school-masters is not ended. They do not accept the propositions of peace which I made. I am told they now have a Rejoinder in press. I think it ought to be out soon, if ever."[10]

As the months rolled by, everyone was prepared to mind everyone else's business.

II

Throughout the early months of 1845, few topics aroused more public debate in Boston than the timeless problem of school discipline. Many people had an opinion on the subject and quite a few willing to share it. How to best control and manage students became intertwined with larger questions of pedagogy and student achievement. Were children motivated more by love or fear? Did they respond best to external motives—grades and prizes—or to the intrinsic love of learning? In their *Remarks*, the masters had accused Mann of promoting pandemonium in the classroom. Like Withington and other Calvinist ministers, they scoffed at his belief that Prussians taught without the use of the rod and said he undermined teacher authority. In contrast, Mann's friends in their testimonial in mid-January praised the Secretary for promoting a more inviting approach to education. "We have learned through you," they wrote, "to appreciate those genial modes of instruction, by which the pupil is won, & not driven into the paths of knowledge; by which he is induced to recognize the sweets of learning & to pursue it for its own sake." Mann and the masters and their respective allies thus continued to speed along on a collision course. When white and black abolitionists intensified their attacks on the disciplinary methods—indeed very existence—of the segregated Smith School, the community became even more polarized as reformers prepared their summer surprise.[11]

The hitting, beating, or humiliation of pupils to temper their youthful spirits had long agitated some parents and committeemen who, like the editors of local magazines and newspapers, embraced distinct political and religious points of view. Indeed, a position on corporal punishment usually rested upon some larger view of human nature often rooted in religious doctrine. Mann had so praised the soft pedagogical methods of the Prussians that he seemed to suggest its elimination, something neither he nor his closest friends including Howe and George Emerson, espoused. Trying to make his position crystal clear, Mann affirmed in

a long essay in 1845 that two factors precluded ending corporal punishment anytime soon: too many children were raised by irresponsible
parents, and too few teachers had studied at the normal schools (which
taught more enlightened approaches to discipline). "But," he added, "a
conclusion in favor of the rightfulness or admissibility of punishment,
in school, does nothing towards sanctioning an indefinite amount of it."
Along with his closest associates, often educators, he hoped that teachers
would largely dispense with the rattan and inspire pupils to study diligently and behave because of its intrinsic moral appeal. The masters and
their supporters, however, interpreted criticisms of physical punishment
as tantamount to favoring its ban, leading them to paint Mann's circle as
irreligious and anti-Christian, reckless and dangerous.[12]

Controversies about physical punishment existed throughout recorded
history, so no one expected any consensus to emerge in Boston, where
the issue attracted heightened attention. Anonymous letters commonly appeared in newspapers, shaping public discussions and debates that
editors, themselves leading figures in political parties, eagerly exploited.
On January 7, a former teacher calling himself "Anti-Busby" published
a long letter to the editor in the Whig *Daily Atlas.* Corporal punishment,
he claimed, was "to an unusual extent, agitating the minds of the community." His *nom de guerre* referred to the Reverend Richard Busby, the
seventeenth-century headmaster at Westminster School in London, one
of the leading floggers of his age who also championed, like so many educators, rote teaching. Flogging and didactic instruction seemed like natural partners, inseparable allies. As Anti-Busby and other reformers knew,
countless educators assumed that only the threat of violence made pupils
dutiful and compliant. To suggest otherwise undermined the whole system of instruction.[13]

Like Westminster, the Boston system's reputation for excellence was
integrally tied to and not discredited by its disciplinary practices. Along
with many contemporaries, Anti-Busby agreed that "the Boston schools
have, from time immemorial, been considered the summit of excellence,
to which all country teachers aspire—and the model of perfection and
beauty, by which all others must be molded. If a reform is to be introduced into the schools in Providence" or the several states, for example,
"the teachers must visit the Boston schools." Accessible by ship, carriage,
or train, the Athens of America was an educational magnet for visitors

domestic and foreign. Local committeemen and other politicians routinely escorted guests on tours of the schools. It was no time for pupils to act up, and they usually behaved. According to our letter writer, the masters usually impressed "strangers with the perfect order" of their schools, where students walked on "tiptoe" if called upon to recite or sat in "perfect silence." Few guests, however, stayed long enough for a worm's eye view. Like spoiled children, the masters, "after having been petted for years," expected deferential treatment, a steady flow of compliments, and a free hand, literally.[14]

There were of course masters known for their kindly manner. Memoirists, however, gave a prominent place to the "raw-hide and the ferrule" in their schoolday memories. The School Committee allowed corporal punishment for cause, with due deference to the master's authority and judgment, though it had long encouraged more gentle measures. In their spirited exchange with Mann, the masters had proudly affirmed their right to hit students; some seemed especially proud of their reputation as disciplinarians. After spending many hours visiting the schools, Anti-Busby found it surprising that "among all the inventions and improvements of the age, no genius has invented a flogging machine for the Boston School Masters!" Such a machine could save time. In one school the master struck eighteen different boys on their hands within a two-hour period. After getting his stripes in the front of the room, one of the "whipped scholars" while returning to his seat grinned at his classmates and "'made faces' behind the teacher's back." Had any good lesson been learned? While numerous observers and primers on teaching noted that cowhide most befriended boys, one girl was hit so hard that "a skillful surgeon could not heal the consequent abscess in less than six weeks." Raising blisters or knocking the heads of two boys together was bad enough, but hitting girls seemed unconscionable.[15]

Complaints about bad-tempered masters waxed and waned for decades but grew louder in the early 1840s. As Mann and the masters squared off, enough discontent existed to force the School Committee to resolve, during the heated campaign season in December 1844, that henceforth teachers had to document every case of corporal punishment. But it also added an important caveat: all records could be destroyed after a quarter. That made it impossible to track trends given the absence of a reliable archive of statistics. Rumors and impressions—the way most aspects of schooling were assessed—trumped hard evidence or facts. Had corporal punishment, as reformers alleged, increased in recent years? No one really knew. But enough people planned to curb its worst abuses and linked this with other reforms, all part of a comprehensive plan for educational improvement. Anti-Busby was confident that "a current of school reform" was sweeping "over this land with irresistible force" that would end all the flogging and treat children with more tenderness.[16]

Enough whipping occurred in the grammar schools to guarantee a steady flow of letters and editorials on corporal punishment in newspapers and magazines throughout the winter term. Undeterred by the altered composition of the School Committee, where known reformers formed a vocal minority, some of the "Thirty-One"—nicknamed "master floggers"—thumbed their nose at the critics, who for decades had often come and gone without consequence. A few of these masters—especially Abner Forbes, Aaron D. Capen, and Barnum Field—were seasoned educators with high name recognition, convinced that they followed sound and time-tested disciplinary methods. The School Committee traditionally deflected complaints about the generous use of the rod, treating it as a minor problem or regrettable reality, given the rebellious spirits of some youth, especially boys. Moreover, enough male students at the annual celebration at Faneuil Hall or old boys at school reunions joked about striped hands and bottoms to suggest that the damage inflicted was inconsequential or justified. Humorists made sport of physical punishment in the newspapers, as seen in the *Boston Courier:* "To what color does a flogging change a boy's complexion? It makes him yell-O."[17]

Schoolgirls and alumnae never seemed to find physical punishment amusing. Neither did Mann's allies, who regarded over-zealous floggers as throwbacks in a progressive age. The Busbys of Boston soon found their reputations sullied and careers threatened, as the reformers made them central figures in the testing controversy that would rock the city.

III

When the Boston School Committee began its quarterly meeting on May 9, it seemed like another ordinary day in the annals of education. It opened with reports from the various visiting committees testifying that "the several schools" were "generally in a flourishing condition." It closed with the seemingly noncontroversial appointment of three committee members each to the summer reading and writing committees. But the main proceedings that Tuesday afternoon were anything but routine. Throughout the winter term, Boston was abuzz with rumors about grammar masters whose tempers ran wild. And in ways few people could have foreseen, scores on the upcoming exams became causally linked in the minds of Mann and fellow reformers with how some masters taught and disciplined their pupils. There was also an important racial component to what was becoming an explosive situation. In recent years reformers and anti-segregationists had assailed the disciplinary methods at the all-black Smith School, and matters came to a head as Mann, the masters, and their allies battled over the *Seventh Report*. Among its many functions, the summer exams became a litmus test on an explosive issue: whether African-American children could receive a high quality education in Boston's racially segregated school system.[18]

For now, the disciplinary practices at a few white schools took center stage. In April, the School Committee appointed a special committee to investigate the behavior of Aaron D. Capen, the writing master of the Mayhew School. Earlier in his career, nearly four hundred people had signed a petition to have him fired because of his penchant for flogging, but they failed to impress the School Committee. Now, according to the *Mercantile Journal*, Capen had hit an eight- or nine-year-old boy "for the heinous offense of whispering." According to the boy, he had a small cut on his hand, which was treated by a physician. Then the master struck him so severely on that very hand that an infection developed and spread. It was relieved only through bleeding, "opening the hand to the bone." In his defense, Capen admitted punishing the boy on March 29 but told a different story. Capen testified that after his whipping, the boy had fallen down while "playing at ball, rubbing off the skin, and drawing blood, by striking his hand against a rough stone." Which version of the events would the investigators believe?[19]

The committee concluded that the boy's tumble, not the flogging, likely caused the infection. The attending physician said the child assured him he had fallen first and been flogged afterwards. It was thus the child's word against the master's, whose staff backed him up. The physician's testimony was weakened when he complained that Boston's teachers relied too heavily on the rattan; he thus appeared predisposed to side with the child, not the master. Master Capen was cleared of all charges. Offering advice heard many times before, Edward Wigglesworth, the committee chair (and member of Mayhew's visiting committee) told the masters and ushers to use "great caution in regard to the infliction of corporal punishment. The rod should be the last resort of the school master," he warned, "and the frequent use of it shows a want of due power to govern pupils or himself."[20]

The Whig *Atlas*, decrying the sensation that the case generated in the press, urged everyone to support Wigglesworth's committee and heed his wise counsel. Teachers should only hit pupils when all else failed. But the editor of a penny press in New York City recognized a good story and ran with it. "Human Butchers for Schoolmasters," read the headlines of the *New York Herald*. Its Boston correspondent, one "Guy Faux," claimed that the Athens of America was in an uproar because of "some recent instances of brutality" by its grammar masters. And now the city had "whitewashed these affairs and excused the Masters!" Citizens familiar with the city schools were hardly surprised that the incident occurred at Mayhew, whose masters were infamous. Decades later, one Bostonian described Capen as a modern-day "Busby" who had an "ungoverned temper and a desire to relieve [his] morbid state of mind by inflicting pain on others." One old boy in the 1890s still remembered the name of a classmate Capen had whipped for a botched recitation.[21]

Other prominent masters viewed the rattan as the main weapon in their armament. At the Franklin School, Barnum Field, whose irritable nature and fondness for the strap, according to many people, terrified the scholars, remained a thorn in the side of the reformers. Sarcastically dubbing him "brother Barnum" in their correspondence, Howe and Mann obsessed over how to depose the incumbent, who seemed entrenched in his position. Field not only headed the list of the "Thirty-One," but he also accused the primary schools in 1845 of having adopted Mann's progressive reading methods, which lowered standards. Teaching words before the alphabet, he said, was a prime example of Mann's mischief. Field was formidable: active in the American Institution of Instruction and a successful textbook author. Even Howe regarded him as an excellent science teacher despite his fearsome reputation.[22]

Born in Taunton, Massachusetts, in 1796, Field became Howe's classmate at Brown University, when Mann was a resident tutor. Perhaps something transpired in Providence to cause Field to dislike both men; perhaps he simply had professional differences and recognized how much the duo threatened his career. Following a brief stint after college in journalism, Field turned to teaching, rising up from his first appointment in Boston in 1826 to become a visible educational presence. Certainly he was no friend to Unitarians: raised as an orthodox Congregationalist, as an adult he converted to conservative Episcopalianism. Mann considered the Episcopalians among his bitterest foes. Everything Howe and Mann believed about pedagogy and school organization offended master Field. Decades after the master's death, a Bostonian recalled that Field scoffed at romantic views of children and that many people thought his discipline "too severe, exacting, violent and over strict." At one professional meeting, Field told educators that when a teacher walked into a room, pupils should immediately know who was in charge. He approvingly quoted Alexander Pope's aphorism, "Order is heaven's first law," else, he added, "anarchy and confusion prevail." The Bible mandated strict obedience to parents and teachers.[23]

Joining Capen and Field in 1844 among the many signatories to the *Remarks on the Seventh Annual Report* was Abner Forbes, the white master of the Smith School. His rise to prominence in the 1830s and precipitous fall a decade later was one of the most dramatic episodes in the epic battle between Mann and the grammar masters. By the early 1840s, Forbes began turning allies into enemies, as both white and black activists demanded the integration of Boston's public schools and the closing of his school. Aligning with his peers against Mann proved unwise, since the Secretary brooked no dissent. Moreover, Forbes's bizarre disciplinary methods and other eccentricities exposed him to more criticism and provoked a full-scale investigation by the School Committee in 1844. As the tensions between Mann and the masters accelerated, his scandalous behavior not only helped generate support for the rule that masters had to document (if only for a quarter) every case of corporal punishment. It also ensured that the summer examiners, especially those sensitive to racial injustice, would likely take special notice of how well Forbes's pupils performed. Like Mann, the key figures on the summer examination committees assumed that teachers largely determined the quality of a school and that antiquated instructional and disciplinary methods inevitably produced low academic achievement.

The fate of Abner Forbes and the disturbing facts about African-American test scores became inextricably linked in Boston's tense political environment.

IV

African-Americans had long struggled to ensure that their children had access to schools and were treated with dignity. In the early 1800s, white philanthropists and black activists funded the earliest schools for Boston's black children, which the School Committee later helped finance and then incorporated into the public system. In 1806, a school for black children opened in the basement of the African Baptist Church on the north slope of Beacon Hill. In 1834, Forbes was appointed to head the school, which was badly underfunded and languishing; the School Committee approved the construction of a new building on the site of the church and named it the Smith School to honor a white benefactor. Many contemporaries viewed the new school and appointment of an experienced master as a sign of educational progress. But there were already some indications of trouble ahead. Since the 1820s, Boston's recently established primary schools were racially segregated, a cause of growing concern as the local abolitionist movement gathered strength.[24]

No one, however, could have predicted the calamitous descent of Abner Forbes, whose star shined brightly upon his appointment as grammar master. A graduate of Williams College, Forbes was classically trained, active in the New England Anti-Slavery Society, and enjoyed the support of William Lloyd Garrison and many black parents. The *Liberator,* Garrison's famous newspaper, applauded his appointment and urged everyone to rally around the new master: *"Let the school be crowded with scholars without delay."* At the dedication of the handsome new Smith School in 1835, a prominent judge praised Forbes for his excellent skills as a teacher and administrator and for his "ardent devotion to the welfare of the colored race." The judge also thanked Frederick Emerson, Mann's and Howe's future antagonist, who had lobbied colleagues on the School Committee for the new facility and became a fixture on the local visiting committee. In many ways Forbes's career depended upon the good favor of Emerson, himself a former teacher who, unlike Mann's network of reformers, empathized with the masters.[25]

Throughout the 1830s, the *Liberator* published numerous articles and editorials that linked education and schooling with the African-American freedom struggle. Essayists stressed the importance of literacy and learning in promoting the common good, echoing mainstream beliefs espoused by many northern citizens: "Knowledge is Power." Judge students by their "merit" and not their inherited condition. A republic depends on a well-educated citizenry. Schools, said one contributor in 1832, were the "almoners of Heaven's bounty." Garrison always praised black striving through education: whether in Sabbath schools, evening schools, manual labor schools, or in Boston's public schools. He and his allies underscored the "natural capacity" of African-Americans to learn, if given a chance, and they fought against the virulent racism of whites who believed that blacks had small brains and could never equal white achievement. The *Liberator* countered these negative images by highlighting school exhibitions where African-American pupils demonstrated their abilities and achievements.[26]

Expectations rose with Forbes's appointment, for he seemed poised to turn the Smith School into a showcase of academic excellence. Working with community activists to expand educational opportunities, he promoted the Adelphic Union, a literary and scientific society that local African-Americans founded for self-improvement in 1837. Meeting at the school in the evenings, it sponsored public lectures that sometimes featured white and black abolitionists. The black chairman of the organization called Forbes "our friend and benefactor." Another contributor to the *Liberator* similarly acknowledged that this "faithful and indefatigable friend of the oppressed" had assembled a fine library for the use of children and adults and frequently performed fascinating scientific experiments, "of which he is a perfect muse." Such accomplishments loom even greater when viewed in context: a very racist world where African-Americans had negligible access to well-paying jobs, decent housing, and the best schools.[27]

While proud of their schools, a growing number of African Americans in the 1830s saw forced segregation as a stigma that marked their children as socially and educationally inferior. Even the "friends" of African-Americans who deemed them educable thought they were far down the scale of civilization, thus dividing them on the question of integration. Boston's African-American community was concentrated near the vicinity of the Smith School. Children who lived in other neighborhoods, however, often traveled long distances to attend segregated primary schools, walking past white schools that refused their admission. Once at school, black children faced various forms of discouragement. One grammar school pupil, a future Garrisonian, was denied a medal despite his superior achievements and could only attend the Faneuil celebration by working as a waiter. That student, William Cooper Nell, never forgot the slight and became one of Boston's leading advocates of equal rights and school integration.[28]

The indignities seemed endless and included the textbooks assigned locally in America's "cradle of liberty." Over the decades, the School Committee adopted several that contained unflattering depictions of Africa and its peoples. Quite a few textbook authors, themselves ordained ministers or pious Protestants, praised missionaries at home and abroad for rescuing Africans and their descendants from idolatry and paganism. Joseph Emerson Worcester's *Elements of Geography,* first published in 1819 and a long-time bestseller, called the enslavement of blacks unchristian and cruel but added that Africa was the "least civilized" of places. "The *Negroes,*" he emphasized, "are chiefly *pagans,* and have the usual habits of barbarous savage life." While lacking great "vigor of mind," Africans were at least, compared to the "swarthy" Moors, "more gentle, faithful, and affectionate." One local standard, Barnum Field's *American School Geography* (1832), presented pupils with the usual racial hierarchies, placing blacks and Indians in the savage or lowest state, and white Americans and Europeans alone on the civilized plane. In time, said most history and geography books, African-Americans would improve their morals and intellect, thanks to the beneficence of white-controlled public schools and Christianity. Few assumed that even well-educated African-Americans would rise very far very fast very soon.[29]

David Walker's famous *Appeal,* published locally in 1830, recounted not just the degraded existence of brothers and sisters in the slave South but the daily insults endured by African-Americans in the free North. Walker complained that racist white teachers allowed black pupils to leave school with superficial knowledge, poor diction and grammar, and an inability to answer basic questions in geography and other subjects. In 1837, a black minister and abolitionist, Hosea Easton, assailed the horrid effects of segregation and Jim Crow policies in housing, schools, and the labor market. Racial prejudice in Boston was strong and intractable. Whites made fun of black physiognomy and capacity to learn. Local teachers reportedly told recalcitrant white pupils they would be assigned to the "nigger-seat, and are sometimes threatened with being made to sit with the niggers, if they do not behave." Easton understandably concluded that Europeans and white Americans, not Africans, were the real barbarians.[30]

By the early 1840s, whatever good will and success Forbes had enjoyed dissipated. Partly this resulted from the rise of a more visible, vocal, and better organized movement of African-Americans as well as white citizens who found racial segregation inimical to democratic principles and Christian ethics. When the Scotsman George Combe visited Boston in 1838, he was appalled to discover that the city's schools were segregated. "This practice," he said, "serves to maintain that odious distinction of colour which is so unbecoming in a country boasting of its Christian spirit." Similar complaints about caste schools intensified in the coming years and helped define political alliances, which hardened after the masters published their *Remarks*. Disagreements over race, discipline, pedagogy, and academic achievement accelerated. By 1844, Forbes had little choice but to join hands with the masters and Frederick Emerson against Mann and his friends. His livelihood depended on it. Mann's allies were often antislavery activists if not always abolitionists, and they viewed the mounting woes of Forbes and the Smith School as another indictment of the grammar schools and their immoral masters. Mann himself privately favored integration but avoided public stands on the explosive subject. He was far more interested in 1845 in shaming the masters collectively.[31]

Beginning in 1840, abolitionists began petitioning for school integration. Sensing that the situation was careening out of control, the School Committee tried to show that Forbes and the Smith School were in fact thriving. In 1841, the local visiting committee organized a well-publicized exhibition. The *Liberator* called it a huge success; the summer event "passed off in a manner highly creditable to the pupils, and greatly to the satisfaction of their parents and friends who were present." Frederick Emerson, who took particular interest in the school's welfare, handed out some "premiums" (not medals) to deserving scholars and reminded parents and guests that Forbes had lifted the institution above its once embarrassing state. If students studied diligently and parents encouraged them to excel, the school would continue to improve. According to Emerson, through "renewed exertions" even the poorest children could rise, and "complexional differences could exert no influence over the mind to restrain its progress."[32]

In 1842, however, abolitionists accused Forbes of poor judgment and an inability to advance the interests of his school. More children of desperately poor fugitive slaves enrolled at Smith, and absenteeism skyrocketed. Moreover, a letter to the editor in the *Liberator* in September noted that only one committeeman attended the recent summer exhibition, and he arrived late. That he favored shipping blacks back to Africa did not help matters. The pupils also seemed unprepared and lethargic, and the School Committee's unwillingness to award medals to the best scholars proof of its callous disregard. Frederick Emerson made sure he attended the exhibition in 1843; some pupils again received premiums and the Smith teachers were finally invited to the Faneuil Hall celebration. But it was too little too late. More petitioners called for Forbes's removal and demanded integrated schools.[33]

That African Americans were themselves divided over whether to close the Smith School further complicated the political scene. Many feared that their children would be ignored, taunted, or mistreated if integration occurred. The issue proved moot, since the primary and grammar school committees voted for the status quo and rejected petitions by the abolitionists. Many white segregationists doubted that blacks were educable and warned that private schools for whites would boom if the School Committee ever forced the issue. Forbes added to his own problems by neglecting his duties, almost inviting a formal investigation of his disciplinary and instructional methods. In response to citizen petitions and complaints, Frederick Emerson and some colleagues investigated the charges against him in the spring of 1844. This was precisely when the "Association of Boston Masters" began considering how to respond to Mann's *Seventh Report,* so Forbes was now fighting for his career and also joining forces against Horace Mann, the nation's most highly regarded school reformer.[34]

Recall that, by this point, Emerson had already locked horns with Mann, opposing the existence of the state board of education, the office of secretary, and tax-supported normal schools. Like most of the masters,

Emerson viewed the Secretary and his associates as dreamers and inter-
lopers. Born in New Hampshire in 1789, Emerson began teaching school
at eighteen after receiving a common school and academy education.
Unlike Mann and his friends, he never attended college but was more an
alumnus of the school of hard knocks. After teaching in nearby towns, he
landed a position teaching math at Boston's Boylston Grammar School
in 1820. A practical-minded, talented man who later invented a popular
system of heating and ventilation for the schools, Emerson left teaching
in 1830, a victim of a short-lived scheme to reduce the authority of the
writing masters. It is unclear if he planned to leave teaching in any case,
since he was an ambitious person. After retiring from the classroom, he
quickly wrote a graduated series of mathematics textbooks. They were
all adopted by the Boston School Committee, on which he served in
the 1830s and 1840s. To help market Emerson's books, old friends who
rose up to become grammar masters, among them Barnum Field, signed
long testimonials on their behalf. In 1836 a local wag complained about
this "great puffing league of schoolmasters" who issued "'tickle me and
I'll tickle you' recommendations" of textbooks. But the endorsements
helped seal political alliances between Emerson and the masters, bonds
strengthened through friendship and shared perspectives on teaching,
discipline, and school organization.[35]

As a teacher, Emerson embodied nearly everything Mann and many
activists detested. George W. Minns, a pupil at the Boylston School in the
late 1820s, reminisced about Emerson and his schooldays a half century
later. Minns graduated from Harvard Law School but then traveled west,
where he taught high school in San Francisco and later headed a state
normal school. Time had not dimmed his memory of Emerson or of the
general atmosphere at Boylston. Its teachers dispensed corporal punishment generously, and Emerson "was the severest disciplinarian among
them. He was very tall, long-visaged, and stern-looking, and we were
all very much afraid of him." He had other personal attributes sure to
offend some Whigs, especially Mann, a teetotaling temperance advocate
who wanted to professionalize teaching. Minns recalled that Emerson
enjoyed a beer—at school—on steamy summer days. Alcohol had also
been served to the medal winners at the Faneuil celebration until pro-
hibitionists intervened. "In hot weather Mr. Emerson would sometimes
send out for a pitcher of strong beer," Minns vividly remembered, and he

and a colleague "would sit at the desk, in plain view of the rising generation, refreshing themselves."[36]

Emerson, like Mann, never seemed to forget a slight. Soon after
becoming chief school officer in Massachusetts in 1837, Mann received
a letter from the former teacher, asking him to endorse his mathematics
textbooks. At the time, the Secretary was the head of the Suffolk County
Temperance Society and counselor to the state organization. To curry
Mann's favor, Emerson pointed out that his mathematics books included
story problems dealing with the evils of intemperance. Years later Mann
described the correspondence in a letter to Loring Norcross, a fellow
Whig and temperance activist. Complicating the situation, Emerson and
Norcross both represented Ward 5, the former on the School Committee,
the latter on the City Council. Mann quoted the math problems verbatim: "If a pint of rum a day will kill a man in a year and a half, how many
men would a cargo of 600 hogsheads kill in the same time?" "If 11 young
men can become fools by drinking 6 bottles of wine, at $3 a bottle, what
would it cost a dinner party of 25, to become fools in the like manner?"
Mann told Emerson that he did not endorse schoolbooks. The Secretary
assured Norcross that, while he didn't want any more trouble with his
adversary, he failed then and now to see how "two or three questions of
that sort, among thousands of others," were especially helpful in teaching
children to love mathematics or better teach them "to cipher."[37]

Like Mann, Sumner, Howe, and most reformers, Emerson was a Whig
but dissented from their notions of educational improvement. And he
was not someone to trifle with. "Tenacious of his opinions" was how one
admirer described him. Moreover, Emerson was deeply rooted in ward
politics, representing the more conservative wing of the party. He often
volunteered as a "vote distributor," on call on election day to ensure a
high turnout. While reformers fumed about the state of the grammar
schools in general and Smith School in particular, local Whigs and the
electorate supported him year after year. As a sign of its appreciation, a
group of citizens in the spring of 1845 presented Emerson with a silver
pitcher with an inscription noting his "zeal, fidelity, and ability" in dis-
charging the "onerous duties" on the School Committee.[38]

If a master accused of excessively flogging pupils wanted a sympathetic
ear on an investigating committee, he could hope for no better choice
than Frederick Emerson. The charges against Forbes were serious. In

May of 1844, a group of citizens accused him of "cruel, unusual, severe, and unjustifiable punishment, neglect of duties of the [Smith] school, loss of the confidence both of parents and pupils, and improper treatment of both." For nearly a week, Emerson's committee met for an average of eight hours daily. Nearly ninety people, divided in their estimate of Forbes, testified before the investigating committee. More petitions circulated, demanding integration. But Forbes was vindicated, his disciplinary methods upheld, and the request to close the Smith School and the segregated primary schools denied. At the annual meeting in August to reappoint masters, Forbes squeaked by, winning twelve of the twenty-three votes cast. Pro-integration activists were furious.[39]

Following the August meeting, a committee of concerned parents and community members attacked the decision to retain Forbes and called for a boycott of the Smith School. Forbes's disciplinary methods again headed the list of complaints. Forbes was unusual among the Boston school masters not for hitting children, but for his range of approaches. Most offensive was the practice of bastinadoing pupils: making them remove their shoes, then caning them on the soles of their feet. In addition, he allegedly made students "stand in a constrained posture on one foot; pulling their hair and ears; pinching; and ferruling a girl on the back of the hand." When some masters, including Barnum Field—well known for his use of the rattan—testified before the investigating committee, they explained that they usually just hit pupils "on the palm of the hand." Forbes also relied on "informers" (teachers as well as pupils) who carried tales of those who misbehaved, poisoning the atmosphere. Some parents and citizens testified that Forbes was patronizing and rude and sometimes threatened to send their children to a reformatory if they misbehaved. One girl, upon being released from the house of juvenile corrections, claimed she would prefer staying there than return to her old school.[40]

Adding to his woes, Forbes was also accused of believing blacks had limited capacities to learn. The *Courier* published an anonymously written article in 1842 that cast doubt on black intelligence, and Forbes was widely believed to be the author. He denied this, but in an attempt to present his views in a better light, claimed that African-Americans could rise in accordance with "*their* natures." The italicized word—which Forbes attributed to a printer's error—stung deeply and his reputation never recovered. Critics also said Forbes was lazy: often found reading the newspaper instead of listening to recitations, and allowing his first class pupils to hear the recitations of the younger children, essentially doing his job. The master never denied these charges but said he had mended his ways.[41]

Forbes believed that Mann's friends, George B. Emerson and Samuel Gridley Howe, were conspiring against him. That is what he told William Fowle in the summer of 1844. Fowle dismissed the idea, telling Mann that abolitionist extremists were his real enemies. To kill the Smith School, integrationists believed, included slaying its master. With his appointment secure and the masters preparing their *Remarks* on Mann's educational philosophy and European trip, Forbes had good reason to be anxious though may have hoped that his worst days were behind him.[42]

The worst was yet to come.

V

The grammar masters, Horace Mann, and their respective allies had thus spent the winter and early spring of 1845 churning in a steady stream of conflicts. Following the acrimony generated by Mann's *Seventh Report* came the partisan hallelujahs that greeted Reverend Withington's pamphlet and the bitterness sustained by reactions to the disciplinary practices at the Mayhew, Franklin, and Smith Schools. In May the local visiting committees nevertheless reported, as usual, that the grammar schools were overall healthy, but such a comforting thought hardly defused the charged political atmosphere. With some high profile, reform-minded Whigs now on the School Committee, Mann's band of reformers dreamed that the grammar schools could be reorganized and the masters collectively shamed and weakened, the most reprehensible ones fired. It did not help their mood to learn that the masters were writing another report, refusing to let Mann's November *Reply* stand as the final word on discipline and pedagogy.

As the masters drafted their report, the Secretary planned his next steps. A seasoned politician and strategist, his skills honed as a lawyer and legislative leader, Mann and his alter ego, Samuel Gridley Howe, hammered out the details of the summer examinations with exquisite forethought and care. Their closest associates, William B. Fowle and

William Brigham (on the writing committee), were perfectly tight-lipped about their revolutionary scheme. The recent, seemingly interminable debates over corporal punishment became a community spectacle. Hearings, meetings, petitions, and resolutions allowed the masters, elected officials, editors, and many citizens to become part of the controversy. Written examinations were different, conceived by a handful of men closeted from the public gaze. Springing the examinations on the pupils and masters without warning would catch everyone off balance.

Apparently most of Mann's contact with the masters throughout the winter and spring came through personal correspondence. There was also the usual gossip about them from Fowle, Mann's local earpiece. Furious that the masters had accused him of being ignorant about local conditions, the Secretary pressed several of them to document his visits to the Boston schools. Recall that in December a few masters, among them some old friends, sought to make peace. Mann thereupon began to pester William J. Adams of the Hancock School, seeking written confirmation of past attendance at exhibitions and graduation ceremonies. Somewhat dumbfounded at his persistence, Mann's several correspondents were not particularly helpful. One took his good-natured time to reply, then claimed that his memory was fuzzy. Adams could only remember Mann visiting once. He tried to help Mann, writing in February to William Shepard of the Brimmer School, prospecting for information but finding none. Shepard was one of the Secretary's main opponents. "Since writing that letter," Adams told Mann in early June, "I have made further inquiries [with other masters], but without obtaining any additional light."[43]

By early May, Mann was nervous about the masters' impending report. But he soon heard that some of the "Thirty-One" were getting cold feet, squabbling among themselves, tiring of the conflict. Fowle relayed other good news, which Mann shared with Howe: a rumor circulated that only four masters planned to write, separately, in the forthcoming report. Perhaps they could be stopped in their tracks and not publish anything, to "save me the trouble and vexation of another reply, and the public the bother and ill will of another newspaper war." "Who are the men," Mann wondered, "that can save me from going into the ring again?" But Howe told Mann on May 8 that "I have tried to stop the forthcoming publication of the masters, but it is unstoppable." Later in the month a report appeared entitled a *Rejoinder to the 'Reply' of Horace Mann. . .* , a two-hundred-page-plus tome that by midsummer provoked a lengthy, visceral response. The masters and the Secretary mostly rehashed their now tiresome debates and produced a yawn among the citizenry. Reacting to another presumed slight, Mann pursued yet another lead. Apparently the minutes of the "Association of Boston Masters" recorded scurrilous attacks on him, so he asked master Shepard to see them. Shepard skillfully dodged Mann's every request, refusing to say whether the records even existed.[44]

All the while Mann was annoying the masters, both friends and foes alike, he was actively working on another front. He was plotting with Howe to embarrass his enemies in a novel way and settle old scores. Howe and Mann colluded every step of the way, predicting that the results of the summer examinations would discredit the masters once and for all. In early May, Mann began feeding Howe some questions for the test and detailed advice about how to proceed. On May 7, he urged Howe to plant some articles in local newspapers about the need for reform. "Why don't something appear in the Boston papers about the organization of the Boston schools?" Another letter underscored the need to keep the opposition completely in the dark about the test. "I do not see in the first place," Mann wrote, "why the regular teacher [i.e. the master] of the school should know anything of the questions put." When the exam is given, make sure the master cannot interfere. "Let him stand aside, or *sit* aside, as they generally do. Let your *regulations* be printed, on the sheet, as well as the questions." Help Brigham prepare the questions in mathematics. Tell him to ask "*practical* questions, that is questions, at least a majority of them, which have relation to the business of life,—as, how much would a pile of wood, 50 ft., 10 in. long, 10 ft. 7 in. high, and 17 ft. 5 in. Wide, come to at $6 a cord? Or what would a piece of land of certain dimensions come etc. at so much an acre. On a note with such payments endorsed on it, as would involve the legal principles on which interest is computed, etc. etc."[45]

On May 8, the day after Mayor Quincy named the members of the reading and writing committees, Howe wrote a revealing letter to Mann about recent events. When the masters heard that Quincy intended to appoint Howe and Brigham, they asked the mayor to reconsider. Perhaps Mann felt a touch of schadenfreude while reading Howe's letter, which exuded an aura of mischievous joy. "They went to the Mayor & endeavored to persuade him not to place either Brigham or myself on either of these *screwing machines* as they call them, because we were openly pledged to support all your measures," Howe explained. "I am told they are in a flutter because the Mayor did put both of us on,—Brigham on the Writing[,] Myself on the Grammar Committee." Seizing the moment, Howe was already strong-arming colleagues about the wholesale reform of the schools, underpinned by modern forms of testing. Howe wanted nothing less than "an entire reformation in our system." That included age-graded classes taught increasingly by female teachers, improved pedagogical methods, the elimination of the double-headed system, and real curbs on corporal punishment. Howe had even tried to persuade Alexander Young, the conservative Unitarian minister of the South Church, that Boston needed to hire a superintendent.[46]

On May 19, William Fowle wrote to Howe regarding news from Abner Forbes, who was increasingly anxious. Forbes learned that one of the masters, William D. Swan, a rattan-wielding master at the Mayhew School and close ally of Frederick Emerson, detected a conspiracy afoot and was organizing to undermine the summer examiners. Swan told Forbes that Barnum Field, the terror of the Franklin School, would thus survive any attempt to depose him. Field had helped lead the charge against Mann in 1844 but now decided to stay on the sidelines as the combatants again donned their battle armor. By early June, Fowle had less news to share. "I hear nothing from the masters. Forbes has been in, but knows nothing." Feeling desperate, Forbes took out a one-year subscription to Mann's journal, "a peace offering. Swan was in just now" but was circumspect when pressed about anything important. The masters obviously regarded Fowle as Mann's toady, telling him only what they wanted the Secretary to hear.[47]

Mann spent the summer with his family in Concord, far enough away that he depended on visitors and the mail for information about the exam. On June 19, barely able to contain himself, he eagerly sought news as Howe and Brigham made final preparations. He pleaded with Howe: "Can you find time to drop me a single line? I saw Brigham when he had gone thro' five schools, & the result was *bad*, for the first class. . . . How is it in your case?" For his part, Howe had decided not only to test the pupils but also to ask the masters and their staff about their teaching philosophy, choice of textbooks, and disciplinary methods. When Howe presented some questions for Mann's approval, the Secretary tut-tut-ted, lecturing his friend to be more direct. How often did the masters strike children? Did they whip them for poor recitations? Hit them on the head? Did the masters spend time with parents? How did they plan to improve the articulation between the primary and grammar schools? Howe revised his questions but the whole effort fizzled; most of the masters and the teachers working under them did not feel obliged to cooper-ate. Examiners and teachers have ever enjoyed such frosty relations.[48]

Throughout June, Fowle and Howe, both resident in Boston, along with the Secretary, spent considerable time preparing the examination. By June 21, Howe was uncharacteristically nervous, telling Mann, "I am told that I am holding a gun which may kick me over—so be it if it kills not a Secretary. I have put in some of your questions and many others of my own." The stress was palpable. Howe feared that "I may break down in the effort, for I have already as much as my weak brain can stagger under. We begin on Monday and go through six schools and I take the odd one, making the nineteen which shall finish in geography on that day. On Tuesday, we take up another subject, and so on through the eight subjects, giving one hour to each subject." That same day, knowing Mann was on the edge of his seat, Fowle confirmed the general details outlined by Howe. "I saw Dr. Howe this morning, & examined some gen-eral questions that he proposes to put to each teacher. They relate chiefly to discipline & attendance."[49]

A few days later, while Howe was busy helping to administer the test, Fowle again contacted the Secretary, providing another bird's eye view of the unfolding events. Fowle could hardly wait to read "Howe's" report (so named already even though he was not the chair of the reading commit-tee). As Howe had indicated, the pupils were examined first in Geogra-phy. Howe and his two colleagues, Theophilus Parsons and the Reverend Rollin H. Neale, divided up responsibility to cover the nineteen grammar schools, scurrying from school to school, arriving at each building at an appointed time with privately printed questions and blank answer sheets. They stood watch as the masters and pupils, who expected a traditional oral exam, coped with the newfangled test. Pupils had one hour to com-plete their answers. Howe told Fowle that some students cheated, either sharing answers with classmates, searching in their textbooks for answers until told to stop, or passing along test items to friends about to run the examination gauntlet at schools nearby.[50]

In the months to come, more serious allegations, of unprofessional behavior by a few masters, would come to light.

VI

Cheating was not invented in 1845 but thus began its unhappy association with written examinations during that fateful week in June. For now, however, pupils and masters tried to make sense of written questions and blank answer sheets, wondering how well they did and how the outcome would affect them. Even before the exams were all graded, Mann had concluded that the results spelled doom for his opponents. Reappointments of the masters occurred every August, and Mann was confident that the final tally would expose the intellectual and moral bankruptcy of the system. Linking test scores to job security thus made its first appearance in the modern world that summer. That some masters would be fired seemed certain. Howe and Mann, in fact, had replacements in mind. During the past year, Mann had urged his good friend, the Reverend Samuel J. May, a fervent abolitionist, to consider becoming master of the Smith School. That Mann had no vote on such an appointment, still held by Abner Forbes, mattered not.[51]

Writing to May on the Fourth of July, Mann felt jubilant. "The 'masters' are in great trouble," he wrote. They had tried but failed to keep Howe and Brigham off the summer examination committees. As for the examiners, "they have adopted a new mode of examination. A list of printed questions is prepared on each subject," which pupils in the first class in the grammar schools had to answer in an allotted period of time, so "all the scholars" can be compared. This would yield a virtual "transcript of the actual condition of the schools; and *rumor* reports that it is anything but flattering." Howe and possibly Brigham had told Mann that many pupils, and by extension the masters, had failed to cover themselves in glory.[52]

At its recent quarterly meeting in May, one member of the School Committee recommended the printing of eight thousand copies of the summer reports. While not approved, it seemed an odd request, but not if one expected something dramatic to emerge from the reading and

writing committees. It signaled the desire of Mann's friends to broad-
cast the results of examinations not yet written, not yet taken, and not
yet graded. Mann told Reverend May that the examiners would publish
numerous statistical "tables" to reveal what children actually knew. The
traditional end-of-the-school-year assessment, based on impressions,
would not do. As one of the Secretary's friends insisted, the "facts" about
the schools would support the "opinions" of those who knew that Boston's schools were in a state of decline.[53]

As he concluded his letter to May, the sometimes somber Horace Mann
almost seemed exultant: "We shall know what condition our boasted
Boston schools are in."[54]

CHAPTER 4

A Pile of Thunder-Bolts

"The seats are narrow, the children crowded, the air close, though the windows are broken, the desks uneasy, the floor ripped up, the plastering falling, the funnel broken, the room smoky, in short, a place for nothing, and everything out of its place." Thus did the Reverend Leonard Withington describe the common schools of New England in 1832, a far cry from any romantic image of America's rural schoolhouses. When the phrenologist George Combe visited Boston a few years later, he was appalled by the noxious odors in the grammar schools. "Many of the school-rooms are deficient in ventilation, and the consequences of which are headache, loss of appetite, and irritability in such of the teachers as do not enjoy exceedingly robust constitutions; and drowsiness in the children, in the latter portion of each meeting, when the air is particularly foul." Since pupils in the various classes in the large halls often recited simultaneously, the rooms were both smelly and noisy. They were often cold and drafty in the winter, hot and a nose-full in the summer. No one disagreed when Horace Mann's friend, the Reverend Emerson Davis, concluded that "the school-house is not generally the most inviting place that ever was to a little child." Especially on examination day.[1]

As enrollments boomed in the 1830s and 1840s, Boston had a difficult time answering the demand for enough buildings and the latest architectural improvements. Despite the fame of the system, its schoolhouses were often dilapidated. One citizen visited a primary school in 1838 that was "nearly as crowded and unventilated as the Black Hole at Calcutta." In the grammar schools, too, pupils sat on uncomfortable backless benches, set up in rows with space between the classes and sections to allow the ushers and female teachers to hear recitations and better maintain discipline. The first class, the elite of the grammar schools, sat nearest the master. Some schools had two furnaces in the basement, each providing warmth for a different floor; but the flues were rarely cleaned and the air drawn into the building wafted over ditches and sewers. Older buildings had fireplaces, spewing heat but also smoke and dust that irritated eyes and lungs, causing teachers to open doors and windows, which invited blasts of cold and clatter from busy city streets. A former pupil vividly remembered "the large rooms, the uncomfortable forms and torturing benches." "The familiar schoolhouse odor," he recalled, "was always perceptible to the visitor as soon as he crossed the threshold." Daily baths were unheard of, adding to the olfactory experience.[2]

As the *Christian Watchman* remarked in 1841, "who can wonder that children under these circumstances become languid and dull?" Those falling asleep might awaken to the snap of the rattan, and singsong drill and rounds of individual recitations could not end the drowsiness. Children during the summer of 1845 faced not the cold but the heat: it was unusually hot and dry. No doubt the appearance of Samuel Gridley Howe and his fellow examiners caused everyone's temperature to rise as they handed out printed questions and answer sheets day after day during the last week of June. A few masters had sharp words with the committeemen, adding to the moment. Some claimed that the examiners, especially Howe, scared the pupils, undermining their performance. Whatever his actual demeanor, tensions grew as the six men scampered from school to school and the news traveled across the city.[3]

After the exams and answer sheets were collected, on the hour for five days, the six committeemen began the arduous task of grading. The public lacked official statements on the nature of the exam until August, when the reading and writing committees traditionally presented their reports at the regular quarterly meeting and the masters faced reappointment. A series of contentious meetings followed, making the earlier conflicts between the masters and Horace Mann over corporal punishment, pedagogy, and the *Seventh Report* seem like child's play. Soon every facet of the summer exams—their invention, purpose, and utility—was analyzed in the city's numerous newspapers and magazines. For now, however, the examiners quietly marked the student papers, tallied the scores, and began preparing their reports.

While Mann had already concluded that the tests would destroy the reputation of the masters and the Boston system, William B. Fowle kept his ears to the ground for the Secretary. On July 7, he relayed some information on recent cases of corporal punishment. Mann must have been disappointed to hear, however, that "I have not seen Dr. Howe, to learn the result of the examination." Other bits of unsettling news began to surface. Soon after the pupils completed their exams, there was a backlash in one East Boston neighborhood. Howe was the target. The previous December, during the run-up to School Committee elections, Howe helped stack a Whig nominating committee with friends to secure Charles Sumner's name on the ballot. But a nativist candidate triumphed, denying Sumner victory. When they heard about the new format for the summer exams, local residents were furious. They surmised that Howe, feeling vindictive because of the election results, was now punishing neighborhood children and the master. Rumors about the exam were beginning to fly.[4]

The rumors, of course, had a basis in reality. Reform-minded Whigs had engineered the election of a minority of activists, including Howe, to the School Committee in 1844 to discipline the masters. Mayor Quincy had placed Howe and some allies on the examining committees, ignoring protests by the head teachers. And the reformers hardly concealed their desire to change the system wholesale by centralizing authority and ending business as usual. That Mann, Howe, and their friends devised their written tests in secret understandably angered some Bostonians and fed more suspicion.

Throughout the spring, the masters had drilled their top students for the summer visits, prepping them for a few oral questions posed to a handful of pupils. No one imagined that the examiners would ask written questions. No one expected them to ask the same questions at all the schools. No one supposed numerical scores would be recorded to compare pupils and schools. Typically, the summer visitors wrote down their observations and impressions; for example, whether reading or history was taught well or needed improvement. But Howe, Brigham, and their colleagues challenged this tried-and-true way of judging a school's quality. Now the children faced, unannounced, a new type of examination that promised to revolutionize the public schools.[5]

America's first big written test not only promoted significant changes in Boston's schools but also sparked a debate about the politics, meaning, and virtues of testing that has never ended.

I

While at least one neighborhood immediately regarded Howe's behavior as intrusive and mean-spirited, no one could have predicted the hailstorm of criticism that soon greeted the summer examiners. The school year was coming to a close and the spring controversies over corporal punishment had apparently faded. By early August, newspaper and magazine editors said very little about the latest report by the masters (now numbering "Twenty-Nine" since William J. Adams and Barnum Field had dropped out) or the recently published reply by the Secretary. It took some stamina on sultry summer days to wade through the *Rejoinder to the 'Reply' of the Hon. Horace Mann, Secretary of the Massachusetts Board of Education, To The 'Remarks' of the Association of Boston Masters, Upon His Seventh Report* and Mann's lengthy *Answer to the 'Rejoinder' of Twenty-Nine Boston Schoolmasters, Part of the 'Thirty-One' Who Published 'Remarks' on the Seventh Annual Report of the Secretary of Massachusetts Board of Education.*[6]

Only the Reverend Joshua Leavitt, the old friend and supporter of Leonard Withington, seemed to think citizens should stay apprised of the latest squabbles between Mann and the masters. Even he thought the feud had reached a stalemate. An editorial in the *Emancipator and Weekly Chronicle* in early August concluded that "as the battle now stands, the parties are at issue upon certain questions in which each maintains itself in the right, and neither seems inclined to yield to the other in the least. The schoolmasters have one advantage; they have kept their temper:—and though severe upon the secretary, have written in a tone and temper becoming gentlemen." In contrast, Mann wrote with "the most bitter sarcasm and lavish abuse, descending sometimes to language so personal and offensive, as to be alike disgraceful to himself and to the position he occupies." Leavitt could not resist reminding readers that Withington's sprightly pamphlet, *Penitential Tears,* "cuts up the honorable secretary without mercy, but in an exceedingly good humored way."[7]

On August 5, the Boston School Committee held its regular quarterly meeting. The subcommittee reports for individual schools were quickly presented and approved. In addition, "the report on the writing schools was read and accepted." But the School Committee then decided that the reading report had to "be laid upon the table." The Whig *Daily Atlas* explained why a few days later. William Brigham had "read a long and very interesting report, giving the results of the very thorough and systematic examination of the writing department" of the grammar schools. But it consumed so much time that consideration of Howe's report was deferred until August 7. At that meeting, something remarkable occurred. Howe, Theophilus Parsons, and the Reverend Rollin H. Neale took turns reading their report aloud—"for over three hours." The length and nature of their presentation precluded absorbing it easily in one sitting. The *Atlas* believed the reports unprecedented in terms of their content and "beautiful" presentation. But some colleagues had heard enough and wanted to bury, not table, them. The examiners had shaken the dog days of summer from their slumber.[8]

Suddenly the accumulated anger, passions, and distrust of recent years exploded as Howe and his colleagues took center stage. On August 9, the *Atlas* published an eyewitness account, since school committeeman Thomas M. Brewer was one of its publishers and editors. Like Howe a Harvard-educated physician, he nearly always voted with fellow reform-minded Whigs. The *Atlas* scooped the story and effusively praised the two committees. "Both reports have not only given a very full and minute account of their examination of the several schools, but both contain suggestions and views in relation to the discipline and improvement in the public schools—much of which will be read, both with pleasure and profit by the public, if they ever are permitted to meet their eye." That was the first hint of trouble. At the meeting, Dr. John Odin, Jr., presented a proposal, first floated in May, to print eight thousand copies of the forthcoming reports (one for every family), which was again voted down.[9]

The reading examiners' oral presentation on August 7 drew upon a working draft. It was easy to grasp its main criticisms and recommendations, since most of them had been around since the 1820s. But the report added something new: numerous statistical tables, impossible to evaluate unless sufficient copies circulated among the board. The *Atlas* thought printing copies for internal discussion beyond dispute. "Yet it was opposed, and bitterly opposed, in the School Committee of the City of Boston." The main obstructionist? Frederick Emerson, who not only "denounced the report" but also "opposed the printing even a single copy, in a spirit and manner that certainly seemed uncalled for, either by the document or the occasion." Staking a position on which he never yielded, Emerson claimed that printing it was akin to "sanctioning all its conclusions, and spreading before the public the most radical and improper views and theories." In the turbulent weeks to come, even his allies agreed that one should read the report before judging it. Only a few men voted with him to block its limited publication. The *Atlas* described Emerson's behavior as "an insult to the gentlemen who compose the annual Committees."[10]

The battle between Mann and the masters had entered a new phase. For the first time ever, test scores had become, literally, front page news and a divisive issue in school politics. Competitive testing was integrally bound to the print revolution that popularized and democratized access to the written word and reflected the fascination of reformers with statistics. As an editor, author, and chief spokesperson for the State Board of Education, Mann was well positioned to publicize innovative ideas. Though he traveled tirelessly by horseback or carriage to countless speaking engagements, Mann knew that the printed word was ever important and vital in securing public support for educational reform, including new forms of school assessment.[11]

Back in May, Mann asked Howe to place some articles in Boston's newspapers on controversial subjects such as the double-headed system to generate more anger against the masters. This would help prime citizens for the impending assault spearheaded by the summer examiners, especially his key allies Howe and Brigham. By mid-August, letters were flowing in abundance. They were often anonymously written, an honored convention, though this only fueled speculation and gossip about the likely authors. No one was above suspicion. Mann's enemies imagined the Secretary and his friends lurking in the shadows. Howe and company saw the masters' devious hands behind any criticism of the exam. Nothing was above politics. Boston's newspapers were owned, edited, and published by party activists such as Thomas Brewer, who perceived no conflict of interest in writing editorials, selling newspapers, and serving on the School Committee. Similarly, Frederick Emerson's math textbooks, adopted by the School Committee in 1832 to the applause of many masters, yielded generous royalties and hardly weakened his popularity with the voters. In Boston, the political was always intensely personal and occasionally profitable.[12]

On August 9, the *Boston Courier*, another Whig paper, published a letter by a "Father," who penned an "eye-witness" account of the factious Committee meeting of three days before. The *Atlas* reprinted it and demanded a mass printing of the reading report. "Father" claimed that the masters, given their arrogance and commitment to outmoded methods of teaching and discipline, had only brought ruin upon themselves. Had they kept up with the times and mended their ways, the first classes might have been spared such a rigorous test, or performed better. The examiners were public benefactors, undeserving of criticism. Who could favor oral over written exams? Every student in June faced the same questions and had the same amount of time to answer. Finally following the official rules to the letter, the examiners devised a way to compare the achievement of different schools. "There can be no perfection in any examination, but this seems to come as near to it as can be expected from poor humanity." What had Howe's committee discovered? Through the ingenious use of statistics, the examiners revealed that the schools were not meeting a "high standard"; they had "exposed a degree of deficiency in every branch [of study], which will astonish our citizens, who have been so long accustomed to consider their schools as superior to all others in Christendom, as they are confessedly more expensive." Was Boston getting its money's worth?[13]

Slivers of information on the contentious August 7 meeting circulated around the city. Who could remember everything heard over a three-hour period? Newspapers tried to fill in the gaps, though they were notorious for confusing fact and fiction, telling bald-faced lies, and promoting their own political causes. Antebellum newspapers routinely reprinted material from other papers, reinforcing partisan politics. But they also helped publicize the issues the committeemen debated and allowed some citizens to voice their opinions. The *Atlas's* article on the controversial meeting appeared verbatim hours later in the *Daily Evening Transcript*. Hoping to stir more interest and sales, other newsmen urged committee members to speak out. The more editors wrote, politicians talked, and copies of the reports multiplied, the more that conflict on the School Committee became likely.[14]

Letters to the editor flooded newsrooms, most taking a stand for or against the examiners. On August 11, the *Daily Journal* presented the views of a "Tax-Paying Citizen," who questioned the motives of both examining committees. Their reports were like a "hurricane" whose creators sought "revolutionary" changes, including the reorganization of the grammar schools and hiring of a superintendent. Was it true, as the documents purported to show, that the schools were "rotten"? Why had examiners traditionally praised them? For decades the masters—widely recognized as "paragons of excellence"—had usually been reappointed without controversy. Cultured and well educated, they added to the luster of the famed school system, despite what the current examiners, possibly moved by "ulterior designs," alleged in their startling report. "Let our citizens be upon their guard, and not allow themselves to be carried into the support of a project which, after all, may not have originated so much in benevolent regard to the public good, as in the motives of a more questionable character."[15]

A day later, the *Journal* reprinted an editorial from the *Atlas*. A "rumor" was circulating that the School Committee planned to block any public distribution of the summer reports. Both papers called for their publication, beyond the copies reprinted for the Committee. The *Journal's* editor evoked the utilitarian spirit of the day: "To enable the public to judge correctly, *facts*, plain FACTS, must be placed before them. We hope that the [reading] report will be published at length, and *that no fact which it contains will be suppressed,* however hard it may seem to bear upon any individual." The oral report had pulled no punches and identified how each school performed, from high to low. Unimpressed, Frederick Emerson continued to oppose further dissemination of the document, which he interpreted as a slur on the system and a personal attack on the masters, whose reappointments were now delayed until the next meeting in mid-August.[16]

Letter writers kept their quills sharpened as the summer exams attracted more public notice. The *Journal* claimed on August 12 that "we are unable to lay before our readers today, the communications on this subject which we have received, for want of room." The next day, three letters appeared on the front page. Two of them endorsed the widespread distribution of the reports, the third defended the "Tax-Paying Citizen" who questioned the motives of the examiners. Those who favored publication said that, whatever one thought of the examiners, everyone knew that reformers had been trying to improve the grammar schools for decades. "That some *reform* is necessary, all admit,—and why should there be any manifestation of *ill temper*, because the Examining Committee have done *their duty*, and have collected a sufficient number of *incontestible facts* to enable *any citizen* to judge respecting the *actual* condition of our schools?" After spending $2,000,000 on the entire Boston school system over the last decade, what did taxpayers have to show for it? Despite complaints about the nature of the test, "the best pupils of all the schools have been required to do their best, and the result is upon paper, in their own handwriting."[17]

Over the next few days, more letters appeared in the city's newspapers. They often called for printing more copies of Howe's report, which infuriated the masters' allies. In a series of weekly editorials, Joshua Leavitt lined up with the head teachers. Like Emerson, he opposed publishing any copies of the reading report and prayed it would "go to its final resting-place in the usual way." He blamed the current controversy on Horace Mann, labeling him the grand conspirator. A former teacher and the author of several schoolbooks, Leavitt was not opposed to educational innovation. Since the 1820s, he supported better classification and grading of students as well as more rigorous school examinations. Like quite a few orthodox ministers, however, he preferred traditional disciplinary methods and opposed centralizing power in the State Board of Education, favoring local control.[18]

Leavitt called Mann thin-skinned and despotic. Offended that the masters stood up for themselves, the Secretary had catapulted cronies to office and to the examining committees. Engaging in "cowardly underhand warfare," Howe in turn was now "blackballing the schools of his own city." If the evidence actually demonstrated that the masters were terrible teachers (which Leavitt doubted), they should be fired. But "public servants" should not "be guillotined in secret for the crime of differing from the secretary of the Board of Education, and without delinquency of some sort proved against them." Regarding the written exams, Mann and his friends had to learn that Boston's public schools "are not playthings for them to try experiments with."[19]

More editorials, letters, and leaks to the press added further heat to the controversy and some light on the issues. It was revealed that Howe's committee had not only given the same exam to the first classes in Boston; it had also administered the test to some schools outside of the city, among them a well-regarded girls' school in Roxbury, to show how well Boston stacked up with competitors. Howe and Brigham were certainly expanding the boundaries of testing, but one letter writer regarded this as another example of the committeemen's bad faith. This author heard that the Roxbury pupils had the questions in advance; they had been drilled in the answers, explaining their high scores. Examiners had traveled there only to make the local grammar schools look bad, another example of Mann's revenge.[20]

Day after day, more news about the exam trickled into the public sphere. On August 14, the enterprising "Father" who earlier gave the "eye-witness" account of the Committee meeting dropped a bombshell. He had taken the liberty to read some of the pupils' answers and was aghast. The condition of the grammar schools was worse than he imagined. Quoting some misfires from the test, he concluded that the top students had learned little at school. "I must say of the *ignorance* of the pupils, as the Queen of Sheba did of the wisdom of Solomon, the half had not been told of me. There is no longer any reason . . . of concealing the facts, and whether the Boston schools are before or behind those of other towns, is less important, than *whether they are what they ought to be*." The system was in tatters. If the first class knew so little, imagine what the pupils below them knew! Boston had better awaken. "She has too long slept on her former well-earned laurels."[21]

That afternoon, the School Committee met again, and it was not pleasant.

II

The meeting on August 14 set the tone for the coming months. William Brigham, head of the writing committee, was among the first to speak. The main item on the agenda was the annual reappointment of the masters. Brigham presented a motion to postpone the vote. At its last meeting, the Committee approved printing copies of the reports for the exclusive benefit of the members, but they were still not ready. According to the by-laws, appointments must occur in August, so Brigham asked for a delay until the end of the month. Immediately there was dissent.[22]

William Hague, a Baptist minister, objected to any delay, having only agreed to it a week earlier because the group ran out of time. Why was it necessary to read the reports before voting? The masters had demanding positions and deserved a holiday to refresh themselves for the fall term; they should not have to worry about whether they had been reappointed. Editor Brewer of the *Atlas* quickly responded. How can anyone vote without reading the summer reports? Asking him to do so was an "outrage on his rights, as a member of the board, to compel him to vote before he knew the merits or claims of the several candidates." Some snickering about "appeals to rights" followed.[23]

Theophilus Parsons was also unhappy. The reading committee consumed many hours, taking time from his law practice, and colleagues worried about the masters' holidays? Reverend Hague could not extend the courtesy of reading the report? Parsons also complained about the persistent rumors, all unfounded, that the summer examiners planned to fire every master. As far as he was concerned, the "worst faults of the schools" resulted from their quirky "organization" and ineffective "supervision." Before joining the committee, he knew few of the head teachers. "For many of the masters themselves," Parsons added, "he had a high respect, especially for some to whom he had been an entire stranger, until he had visited their schools during the year, in the performance of his duties." Parsons planned to vote for "a majority of them." While he was going to vote against one reappointment, he was uncertain about a few others. He wanted to hear from his colleagues before making up his mind—*after* they had read the reports. Asked when they would be available, Parsons said the proofs would soon be corrected.[24]

Once Parsons was quiet, other members chimed in on Brigham's motion. No doubt many colleagues, especially Mann's friends, wondered what to expect from Frederick Emerson, still fuming from the last meeting, the depiction in the *Atlas* unlikely to have improved his mood. It was his turn to speak.

As one contemporary remarked, Emerson had been on the School Committee "almost since time immemorial." Indeed, Mann concluded that "he has been so long on the committee, that he thinks a condemnation" of the masters "is a condemnation of himself." After losing his position as writing master in 1830, he won nomination to office and became a permanent fixture on the board. Emerson explained that he had listened carefully to his colleague's speeches at previous meetings, noting their assaults on the double-headed system, which he had long defended. The examiners, he recalled, had described some schools as "excellent; others as tolerably good, and some as insufferably bad." What could he learn from the written reports? The author of a mathematics trilogy assigned in Boston, he knew how to read "figures and tables," but they would hardly shape how he cast a ballot. A voice rose to interrupt him. Parsons objected to how Emerson described the oral report. No one called any school insufferable. Intolerable? Insufferable? Both men agreed not to split hairs and to drop the subject. But Parsons kept the floor. Still irritated, he returned to the question of summer vacations for the masters. He also heard that some colleagues were caucusing to line up votes for their favorites, which Emerson denied.[25]

After more discussion and a recognition that the votes were against him, Reverend Hague consented to Brigham's motion for a delay. Emerson spoke up again, demanding to know why voting could not proceed as planned. When the votes were counted, however, Brigham's motion passed easily. Dispensing quickly with some routine business, Emerson turned to another matter, not on the agenda.

Emerson questioned Brewer's right to publish editorials and reports on board meetings in the *Atlas*. He found "objectionable" its characterization of the August 7 meeting. Moreover, according to the Democratic *Post*, Emerson accused Brewer of libeling him with "injurious epithets." Brewer interrupted him in the middle of a sentence and called Emerson "to order, for alluding to his having written the article. He asserted that he was out of order thus to allude to a member personally, and to speak of him as the author. . . . Whether he was or was not the author, was no part of the business of the Board." Brewer's friends tried to lower the room's temperature. William J. Dale sought to intercede but Emerson refused to yield the floor. Since the rules forbade personal attacks, Parsons also defended Brewer's right to challenge Emerson. Brigham in turn called for adjournment, but both Emerson and Brewer wanted the floor. Despite support from the chair, Emerson decided he had had enough and the argument ended, thanks to Samuel Gridley Howe, who became a peacemaker.[26]

No friend of Emerson's, Howe defused the accelerating conflict and salvaged the moment by suggesting that henceforth three newspapers should regularly cover board proceedings. He even agreed to serve on a committee to explore the matter. Having played the statesman, Howe then repudiated the rumor that he or his committee leaked anything to the press, which had published "parts" of their report-in-progress in "several of the daily papers." Neither he nor his committee was to blame. Some unknown person had secretly eyed the exams and working copies of their text, innocently left unguarded in the committee chambers. It is unclear how many of Howe's colleagues believed him.[27]

As the School Committee adjourned, Howe must have been relieved that he fared so well. He knew more controversies loomed, beyond the reappointment of the masters, not the least whether the master and pupils at East Boston's Lyman School had cheated in June. Angry neighbors were still meeting and denouncing him. But so far, so good. On August 18, Mann wrote to Howe, knowing there was still time to alter the final draft of the report. Despite his visibility in the local statistical society, Howe struggled with math; any errors in the charts or tables could discredit his committee. Moreover, Mann knew that even well-educated committeemen were not used to reading quantitative material. Few people understood statistics, itself a new and arcane science. For decades, official reports and newspaper articles about schools included some enrollment figures and per capita expenditures. But these did not constitute statistical analyses.

Mann, Howe, and Brigham regarded statistics as a superior means to evaluate schools. The belief that "the teacher made the school" was already a cliché among European and American educational theorists, and these reformers believed that the numbers could prove that low test scores resulted from poor instruction. If the examiners demonstrated that the first class pupils knew very little, this might expose the poverty of conventional teaching and disciplinary methods. The reformers were entering uncharted territory. Lay people on the Committee with little knowledge or interest in statistics had never used quantitative information to assess a teacher's or school's worth. When visiting schools, they looked for signs of order: a tidy room, respectful behavior, a prompt and accurate reply when questions were posed to pupils. That reappointments might hinge on test scores or ranked lists of schools was an alien notion. Emerson and friends thought the idea preposterous, confirming suspicions about the malevolent motives of the reformers. They stood as sentinels in defense of their neighborhoods.

In sharp contrast, Mann and his allies saw themselves as advanced thinkers whose cosmopolitanism lifted them above the din of ward politics, despite their own behind-the-scenes maneuvering. With the benefit of travel abroad, advanced study, and prominence in professional groups that studied phrenology, statistics, and the latest intellectual trends, they intended to use their knowledge and skills to punish their enemies and transform Boston's schools. Having authored major reports on schools that attracted national, even international, attention, Mann in particular was well positioned in 1845 to move schools in a new direction. Long fascinated with how statistics could buttress reform, he tutored Howe on how to talk about and display numbers, to remember, for example, to be precise when commenting on test scores and school quality. He reminded Howe that when comparing schools, he needed to use words such as "relatively" or "comparatively."[28]

Mann knew that Howe was under considerable stress. This was not simply due to the long hours expended on the summer exams and tensions among colleagues. Howe had a stormy relationship with his wife, and he neglected her that summer, when she was pregnant, lonely, and depressed. Mann admitted that he too was worn out and emotionally exhausted by the summer events but exhilarated by what Howe had already accomplished. Still in Concord, Mann planned to pass through Boston in a few days and promised to help his friend in any way. "Call on me, if I can do you any good, for I feel as if my life were nothing in comparison of the value of this enterprise, & if it fails in your hands, we shall have to wait for another great Julian epoch for another opportunity. There is no man but yourself . . . who can carry it thro'." The burdens of office for both men could be offset by thoughts of imminent victory over the masters and their defenders.[29]

As rumors, facts, and opinions about the summer exams multiplied, citizens seized the opportunity to drive home their favorite criticisms of the masters. Hours after the School Committee dispersed on August 14, an anonymous writer in the *Evening Transcript* revived lurid images of disciplinary practices in the grammar schools. One sadistic master was notorious for "pulling hair, pulling ears, taking two boys by the ears and knocking their heads together, taking a boy by the ear and knocking his head upon the desk." "I thank God that *public* attention is aroused to our public schools; if parents will only awake and observe, they will be astonished at their own blindness and apathy." Two days later, the *Boston Daily Times and Bay Street Democrat* printed a detailed police report on a flogging at the infamous Mayhew School. And the next day Brewer published a long article criticizing Emerson's recent behavior and public outburst. He affirmed his right to publish what he pleased about any public official.[30]

There was certainly no shortage of news about the exams or the examiners, as Joshua Leavitt explained on August 20. "The papers of the city," he noted, "abound with communications urging the printing of the report of the committee and its distribution." But neither the public nor the Committeemen should be snookered. Leavitt insisted he had "not the least objection to the most rigid and thorough examination of the schools and a spread of the results broad-cast among the people, *when the examination is made in good faith, and springs only from a desire to make the true condition of the school known.*" But the summer examiners were out for blood, not truth. "The 'three hours' report, and its printing and distribution are in reality the missiles of the secretary, who is fighting behind a masked battery."[31]

Leavitt's tirade continued. He believed the motives of the authors of the reading report—this *"tremendous"* report—had to be considered separately. Parsons, the putative head of the committee, had obviously been brushed aside. "Whether he was not *talented* enough for the dirty work to be done, or whether he was too modest to undertake it, we know not, but by some *hocus pocus* Dr. Howe becomes chairman—Mr. Neale being a kind-hearted man and somewhat unsuspecting, probably did not, we presume, wish to get into any difficulty with the chairman, and thus Dr. Howe has been *the committee* for all practical results." The outcome was predictable. "We firmly believe," wrote Leavitt, "that the schools were examined in a very novel mode, *and on purpose to make them appear badly.*" The former teacher reminded readers that anyone could prepare an exam to embarrass students. "Figures, it is said, cannot lie; but put them together wrongly, and they are the greatest liars in the world." With Mann plotting strategies and Howe leading the charge, the examiners' aim was "to destroy the confidence of the citizens in the masters." The reformers wanted replacements who would be "more obsequious to the secretary of the Board of Education, to have a 'superintendent of schools' with a large salary, and perhaps one or two snug offices for certain men already designated in certain quarters."[32]

Given all the chatter in the local newspapers, rival communities soon delighted in editorials and articles that documented the apparent decline of the Boston school system. Communities living in the shadow of the "Athens of America" must have enjoyed the show. Drawing upon material from the *Boston Courier*, the *Vermont Chronicle*, published in Bellows Falls, published not one but two articles on the summer exams on August 20, before all the committeemen had read the long report. The articles quoted numerous student bloopers, which made the famed grammar masters look foolish. When asked to define "monotony," pupil responses proved imaginative: "the bones of human animals," "thick-headed," "moaning noise," "ceremonious indifference," and a "song by one person." Both articles blamed teachers for the many student "blunders," and one concluded with a lesson from the Bible: "When Ezra and his associates found the book of the Law, and gathered all Israel to hear it, they *'caused the people to understand the reading.'*"[33]

Bellows Falls—Bellows Falls!—was lecturing Boston and lampooning its legendary schools. This would not improve Frederick Emerson's disposition when the School Committee reconvened.

III

With a copy of the examiners' reports finally in everyone's hands, the School Committee once again met on August 28, ostensibly to approve them and vote on the annual appointments. Mayor Quincy barely brought the group to order when John Odin, Jr., upping his previous request, endorsed publishing ten thousand copies of them to guarantee their widest distribution. Very quickly, the sparks began to fly. Sebastian Streeter, a conservative Universalist minister, objected to a section of the writing report on the Eliot School. It erroneously stated, he said, that its pupils were only taught by copying from the textbook. Brigham said the report was accurate and that Streeter was mistaken; but if he wanted the reference removed, fine. Not missing a beat, H. A. Graves, an orthodox Baptist preacher, said other schools were also mischaracterized. His objections carried considerable weight, since he served with Brigham on the writing committee, which examined penmanship and arithmetic. Graves and others who were upset focused on Howe's reading report, which not only covered more subjects but also criticized individual masters and the organization of the system. It was obviously going to be a long meeting.[34]

Everyone on the School Committee seemed agitated. Attorney Sidney Bartlett wondered: were colleagues planning to edit every line? There were many reasons to expect a certain level of conflict: politics, personal animosities, and principled disagreements on any number of school policies. Recall, too, that every grammar school had a three-member visiting committee, including a committeeman from the district; it produced short, handwritten reports every quarter. Even when they suggested improvements, members usually concluded that *their* schools were basically fine. Local representatives often knew the master very well and took pride in their school. So the committeemen, two per ward, would read portions of the annual examiners' report—the sections on their neighborhood—with special care. Since the committee reports ranked all of the schools on the basis of test scores, some inevitably received a black eye, embarrassing the master, pupils, their parents, and the ward representatives, who might dismiss criticisms out of hand. The bearers of bad news, of course, might also be blamed.[35]

Tensions escalated. Alexander Young, a Unitarian minister whom Howe had tried to lobby to his side in May, dismissed Odin's recommendation and opposed any publication of the documents. Other colleagues agreed, saying they were riddled with errors and misrepresentations. The usually moderate Edward Wigglesworth, a businessman who had urged the masters to use the rattan with more discretion after the Mayhew scandal, thought the tables that ranked the various schools very misleading. He wondered how schools would compare if scores were kept on oral exams. He did not address the technical problems or logistics of giving such an exam to hundreds of pupils, but it revealed a preference, shared by others, for traditional means of assessment. The examiners, except for Reverend Graves, must have felt discouraged as the meeting dragged on. Under siege, Howe and Parsons admitted discovering more errors in the tables but promised to fix them.[36]

To gain some footing, Parsons took the floor to explain how the many charts and tables had been assembled. Rumors had spread throughout the summer and he wanted to set the record straight. First he underscored the scale of the tasks facing the examiners. After examining over five hundred students in several subjects, committee work had just begun. After proctoring the test, they had to agree on correct and incorrect responses, grade the answers, compile the statistics, arrange the tables, and interpret the results. Initially, the committee asked some advanced, older pupils (perhaps from the Latin School or English High) to help grade the exams, but that proved unsatisfactory. So the examiners did the grading. Some pupils helped prepare the tables, after which some "skilled mathematicians" rechecked everything. Visibly dismayed by what he was hearing, Reverend Streeter asked if the examiners had gone over everything again. Howe assured his colleagues that they had done so. When one pupil made too many mistakes computing scores, the committee threw her work away and started over. Everything was double- and triple-checked. Contrary to rumors, Howe insisted that "neither boys nor girls had been employed." Even so, some printers' errors inevitably crept into the current draft, since the reading report was running well over a hundred pages.[37]

Reverend Graves of the writing committee then turned to an especially ticklish subject: allegations of cheating at the Lyman School. Graves was a member of Lyman's local visiting committee; the voters had also elected him instead of Howe's friend, Charles Sumner. Graves asked why the Lyman scores were still missing from the report. He was baiting Parsons. The examiners had already explained why. Once again, Parsons said the scores were omitted "because that school had an advantage over the other schools in obtaining a knowledge of some of the words to be defined, before they were examined." This was a story that would not go away and whose facts remained contested in the months to come. Partly the controversy reflected the absence of accepted ground rules for giving or taking written tests. Questionable behavior at exhibitions or visitations was nothing new: sometimes winked at, sometimes ridiculed. Masters often hand-picked pupils for examiners to call upon at oral exams, and examiners occasionally chastised them for prompting students. Since the creators of written exams wanted to raise the stakes for success and failure, to make teachers and pupils more accountable, defining acceptable behavior took on more urgency.[38]

Here is what happened at the Lyman School, according to the examiners. Reverend Neale first showed up to give the test. Soon after, Howe arrived to help his colleague and noticed that pupils were writing down identical answers to a few questions. Suspicious, he asked the master,

Albert Bowker, for an explanation. As it happened, the reading committee could not examine every school on the same day in grammar and definitions. On the evening before that exam, the masters held an emergency meeting, coordinating their defense. They assumed the week-long tests aimed to embarrass them and endangered their careers. That night, the masters shared a few test items. When Howe arrived at the school, he caught Bowker drilling the pupils in the answers but proceeded with the exam, perhaps to avoid a scene. Howe later likened Bowker's behavior to a farmer feeding chickens with the crumbs of knowledge.[39]

Parsons explained that the examiners had set up uniform conditions for taking the test to ensure fairness. "They had examined several schools out of Boston," he continued, "but in none of them, except the Dudley School at Roxbury, were they positively certain that none of the scholars had any previous opportunity of knowing what questions were to be proposed." Reverend Neale had given the Boston exam to pupils in Roxbury, Hartford, New Haven, and New York City. But their scores were all tossed out except for those at the all-female Roxbury School. Since the Lyman pupils had an "unfair advantage in knowing the questions beforehand," the committee had similarly eliminated their scores. Rumors persisted that the Dudley pupils had cheated, but Parsons said no evidence existed to sustain the charge. Since Roxbury's students performed better than any of Boston's grammar schools, critics wanted their scores dropped, but the examiners refused.[40]

Reverend Streeter called the charges against the head teacher outrageous. Master Bowker was a highly moral man who often taught his pupils definitions early in the day. Since the master never told the pupils what would be on the test, he was innocent of wrongdoing. Lawyer Parsons wanted to avoid a debate on ethics with a well-known minister. In response to Streeter's twisted defense, he said he was not interested in judging the master's morals but again insisted that the pupils had an "unfair advantage," which is why their scores were discounted. Parsons believed the two men would never agree and should end the discussion. Apparently sensing he had painted himself into a corner, Streeter lobbed another missile, suggesting that the pupils knew the definitions of difficult words better than the examiners.[41]

Coming to Parsons's aid, Howe recounted a private conversation he had with Bowker. While meeting with the masters in the evening, Bowker told them his pupils had not yet taken their exam on grammar and definitions, so he urged them not to share any questions. They ignored his request, and Bowker admitted drilling the first class in the definitions of four words, right out of the dictionary. Howe did not understand why the master simply didn't tell him, for he could have removed the items from the test. The examiners could not in good conscience count the scores, which were tainted by the master's behavior. Unpersuaded, Graves refused to let the subject die and announced he would not vote to approve the report absent the Lyman scores. Then, unwittingly hurting his own cause, he began reading a nasty remonstrance from his neighborhood against Howe, signed by sixty residents. It was quite personal, leading other committeemen to rush to Howe's defense. Graves stopped reading, but the reverend had violated the letter and spirit of the group's by-laws.[42]

More backbiting and accusations of bad faith ensued as committee members quarreled over whether to approve the report and its wider distribution. Frederick Emerson, still furious, reaffirmed his opposition to printing any part of it. The *Daily Advertiser* paraphrased Emerson's speech, whose message was consistent with his position before and after the meeting. "No committee," he said, "had ever made such a report before. The Boston schools had always been considered as standing as high as any in the country. But now a different impression had got abroad from the report. Parts of it had been published in the newspapers"—even in Albany. This last comment triggered a heated exchange between Howe and Emerson. Howe accused him of playing with the facts, since only a few "written answers" by pupils had been lifted from the committee room. Emerson replied that he did not care what material leaked. The damage was done.[43]

The hour grew late, but Emerson defeated a motion by Howe to make all voting for the masters *viva voce*. Attempts to adjourn were also voted down. Despite protests by Howe and his allies, voting on the reappointment of the masters occurred in secret session. But Brewer won a minor victory: no master could be appointed without a majority in his favor. That could slow down the proceedings, biding some time for the reformers. That evening, however, master Bowker of the Lyman School was reelected, along with a number of other masters. After a few hours in this tense atmosphere, the group adjourned, its work unfinished. It agreed to reconvene in two days.[44]

Before the voting proceeded on the 30th, Howe was allowed to take the floor, since he was the center of the ongoing school controversy. He complained about the abuse he had suffered, both at large and by Reverend Graves and his constituents. When elected to office, he claimed, he never imagined appointment to the summer examiners' committee, a "thankless task." He had not only visited all of the schools in late June but also on other occasions, taking his responsibilities seriously. He was respectful toward the Lyman pupils and their master. In contrast, local residents were in a "state of complete excitement." That not only they but a colleague, a minister no less, had assailed his character and forgotten the Golden Rule, hurt him deeply. When had he ever behaved uncivilly? He never meant to insult the citizens of East Boston by encouraging Charles Sumner, a man with a civic conscience and bright political future, to run for office. To believe he would punish Bowker and his pupils because of the election was especially malicious. Howe asked the board to appoint a special committee to investigate what actually transpired at the Lyman School exam, and whether Bowker had behaved unethically. Graves agreed but replied that he resented Howe's drawing attention to his profession; moreover, he and his constituents were only acting in "self defense." Then he gracefully asked for Howe's forgiveness and that of his colleagues if he had "done wrong." An investigating committee was unanimously approved.[45]

The tenor of the meeting did not otherwise improve. Parsons revived the question of printing the summer reports for general distribution, and Reverend Young rose in opposition. Reappointing the masters was on the agenda, not the reports. Parsons remembered that at their last meeting, Young had attacked the examiners, using "pretty harsh words." While Young might know the schools in his ward, what did he know about the entire system? Parsons had visited all of them, while Young probably knew not their location. Parsons asked how anyone could criticize the use of written exams, which were superior to the usual oral questions and answers in verifying what students knew. And, as Howe said, the examiners visited the schools several times, to get a feel for them. Trotting out numerous tables, Parsons lashed out some more at the Reverends Young and Graves and began chiding them. Was there nothing to learn from the best schools in Roxbury or other communities? The chair of the School Committee called Parsons to order but was ignored. "If attacks like these were to be called out by every inquiry into and exposure of what was wrong in our schools," Parsons concluded, "it was offering little encouragement to fearless examination, and such examination was what was most needed."[46]

Parsons and Howe faced off again at Young and Emerson, and Brigham moved without success to have the reports printed. Brigham said Bostonians had always been left "in the dark" about the actual quality of the schools. Other committee members who had still not read their copy of the documents agreed to discuss them at an upcoming meeting. They were prepared to vote *now* on the masters. Neither tables nor ranked lists of schools would affect their votes. Quite a few masters were then reappointed though several faced considerable opposition. Master Aaron D. Capen, the infamous disciplinarian at the Mayhew School, was voted down with fifteen nays. Others not chosen were among the best-known wielders of the rattan, such as Barnum Field and Abner Forbes. Field, Forbes, and others who failed to win reappointment were among the original "Thirty-One" who attacked Mann's *Seventh Report*. Their fate remained in doubt, subject to more investigation and deliberation. Some masters were obviously in trouble, but Emerson and his allies would not be steamrolled by Mann's allies, a minority on the Committee.[47]

As usual, Mann tried to help Howe navigate the treacherous waters of school politics. On the afternoon of the meeting on the 28th, Mann stopped by Howe's office and waited until 5 P.M. He might have stayed longer but had a fever and wanted to return to Concord before nightfall. The next day, Mann wrote to Howe. Ever alert to the importance of the press, he told Howe to prepare articles immediately "for the papers, containing so much of an analysis of the answers, as will show that the pupils answered common and *memoriter* questions far better than they did questions involving a principle; and it should be set forth most pointedly, that, in the former case, the *merit* belongs to the scholars, in the latter, the *demerit* belongs to the masters." Also link those "abominable blunders" in spelling by the pupils directly to "imperfect teaching." If taught properly, pupils would spell correctly. Once parents saw the printed report, with the actual statistics showing the low test scores, they would demand an explanation. Then came a warning to Howe: "If the odium of such a disclosure is to fall upon the children, the parents will be disposed to punish *you* for it. If on the other hand, it can be fastened where it belongs, they will condemn the teachers." Emphasize "the great difference existing between different schools, on the same subject, showing that the children could learn, if the teachers had taught" effectively. Otherwise the examiners, not the masters, would be vilified, since parents in particular would not blame the children. Mann told Howe to take heart: "You will be hereafter hailed as the regenerator of the Boston schools."[48]

By the end of August, while some masters were in trouble, most had considerable support on the School Committee. Frederick Emerson and his friends had also shown their determination to defend the status quo. The fight over the exams and reappointments continued.

IV

In early September, tensions remained high. Whether the reports would ever be approved, never mind widely disseminated, was unresolved, and some masters still awaited their fate. One adjourned meeting followed another, aggravating already frayed nerves. On September 1, Emerson and Streeter, while disagreeing whether voting should proceed in closed session, agreed that the summer examiners had humiliated Boston's many excellent masters without cause. Following Streeter's suggestion, the voting proceeded behind closed doors, without the presence of spectators and reporters. Theophilus Parsons, who believed that "nine-tenths of the evil done in the world, was done in the dark," only agreed to the motion because of delicate facts surrounding some cases. After they were discussed, the Committee reappointed a few masters and transferred Barnum Field from the all-female Franklin to the all-male Adams School, switching places with Samuel Barrett. Field squeaked by with a bare majority, presumably settling the matter.[49]

On September 3, Howe wrote to Mann regarding recent events. Parsons had broken ranks, voting with the majority to reassign Field, whom Howe described as an "ungentlemanly, coarse, and violent creature." Feeling ill, his wife unwell, Howe dashed out of the meeting but returned in time to vote against the reappointment. Reform was taking its toll: "I have, my dear Mann, been for four or five days in a hell of hot water. They throw it all on me:—some masters have cried, and melted my heart; even F. E. [Frederick Emerson]—says to some, 'If Dr. Howe will go for you, you will be chosen;' but the arch-devil lies, except in one or two cases where he is right. All East Boston is upon me, you see; as for South Boston—they will never send me again. Then the Report! so full of errors—and I so poor an arithmetician." And Parsons, ever talkative, did not really carry his weight. "To hear Parsons speak in the Committee—you would really imagine he had put his blessed eyes on some of the tables! would he might! They will be all right to-morrow." While only a few masters would be fired, scaring the others likely weakened the Association of Masters: "we have scotched that snake if not killed it." But Howe felt weary: "fighting off hornets, I have been exhausted; and going to bed have slept not, but dreamed half awake of ferules, candidates, yeas and nays, ballots, etc. Awake, however, or asleep I am ever yours."[50]

The next day, another meeting. Field's transfer enraged the Adams School parents, spawning a community protest and petition to reverse the decision, their "memorial" read aloud by editor Brewer. It described the master as gruff and hot-tempered, unsuitable for any school. Parents threatened to withdraw their children unless the board came to its senses. Heading the list of petitioners was Edward G. Loring, a prominent Whig, lawyer, and especially close friend of Mann's. Immediately Reverend Streeter defended Field. Emerson, however, urged colleagues to send Field and Barrett back to their old schools. Digging in their heels, the reformers resisted and the conversation grew unpleasant. Quite a few committeemen, said the *Daily Atlas,* "used pretty sharp words." Thanks to lobbying by several members, a committee formed to investigate Field, Howe's old classmate at Brown, to determine his suitability for any teaching position.[51]

More meetings, more breakdowns in civility. The *Evening Transcript* reported on September 5 that "the School Committee, in a more disputatious mood than ever, held another protracted meeting yesterday afternoon, and spent three hours and a quarter in moving one peg backwards." To quell the unrest at Adams, the Committee voted nineteen to four to send Field back to Franklin. Samuel Barrett returned to his old post. That master Field—the original kingpin heading the list of "Thirty-One"—survived while under investigation caused Joshua Leavitt to shout with joy, proclaiming a major defeat for Mann and his co-conspirators. "End of the School War.—The Plotters Defeated," read the headlines on September 8 in the *Emancipator and Weekly Chronicle.* "The famous report of Dr. Howe, which was intended to . . . sweep the masters out of the schools, has been found so full of errors—(to say nothing worse), that it is not yet in a state to print. It has been altered, and altered again." Having never read any draft of the report, he heard that "whole paragraphs have been withdrawn or expunged. At the meeting of the committee last week, even its own concocters could not deny that there were many mistakes." Only a few masters might lose their jobs, and Leavitt predicted that "Dr. Howe will not be elected to the school committee next year." The reverend's obituary for the reform movement proved premature. As Leavitt recognized in August, the recent controversies were one in a series of battles, however pivotal, in a larger war. It was hardly over.[52]

Even though their report was not yet public, the summer examiners had raised public awareness of the schools as never before. Editorials, letters to the editor, and blow-by-blow descriptions of Committee meetings had caused a sensation. The summer examiners had raised serious doubts about the excellence of the Boston schools, causing citizens to wonder who or what to believe; they had aroused and used the press to question whether the School Committee, forced to meet regularly in closed session, screened and supervised their employees very well. For Mann and his friends, despite inevitable setbacks, things were falling into place. Discrediting the masters was a means to larger ends: the destruction of the double-headed system, creation of more age-graded classes, modern forms of assessment, and the appointment of a superintendent. Major organizational and administrative reforms required greater public realization that the system was seriously flawed and broken. A few soldiers might fall, but others could take their place in December.

On the very day that Leavitt pronounced the reformers defeated, the *Daily Advertiser* reported in great detail how Emerson and Parsons had again tangled at the last Committee meeting over reappointments. The *Atlas* reprinted the article on the front page, ensuring wider circulation. That many Committeemen were colorful public figures known for their eloquence—whether preaching to their flock or pleading before a jury—made news reporting all the better. Disagreeing with just about everything he said, Emerson praised Parsons for his rhetorical skills, which made him a formidable rival. Once ensconced in his position, Parsons told his colleagues, a master "is practically regarded as having a vested right. Attempt to remove him, and you are called cruel and unjust, and every impediment is thrown in the way of investigation." Too many masters, he added, gained positions because of personal connections, not merit, becoming "entrenched as in a fortress of strength." But change took time and the firing of the most reviled masters and investigation of Field was "the first blow . . . against this system." Resenting Parsons's tone and suggestion that the board cared little for quality, Emerson accused Parsons of insulting anyone who had ever served on the Committee. Did Parsons really believe that its policies were "an injury and a curse, instead of a blessing" for the schools? Parsons shot back, denying the charge and insisting that the grammar schools should be the best in the nation.[53]

On September 11, the balloting for masters proceeded in yet another adjourned meeting. It did not turn out well for the two masters condemned most vehemently in the press over the last two years: Aaron D. Capen, the writing master of the Mayhew School, and Abner Forbes, the sole master of the segregated Smith School. On the first ballot, with six candidates in contention, Capen received three votes, on the second ballot, none. Six candidates vied for the Smith post; Forbes received seven votes on the first ballot but only one on the second. Called the Boston bastinado by abolitionists and black parents, many of whom were boycotting the school, Forbes was ridiculed as he tried to save his career. He had poor penmanship, apparent when a committeeman, struggling to read his appeal for reappointment, asked in a low voice if Forbes was a writing master, which caused *general laughter around the board.*"[54]

Four masters ultimately lost their jobs but only partly because of their school's scores on the summer exams. Many committeemen ignored the reports or scoffed at the rankings. Some of Mann's allies believed that test scores should seal a master's fate; but Forbes was clearly in deep trouble long before the summer examinations. Howe and Mann discussed possible successors nearly a year before he was fired. Eyewitness reports of board meetings indicated that committeemen were mostly swayed by the usual concerns: complaints by parents, personal impressions of the masters, and other subjective factors.

Forbes and Capen had finally outraged enough parents that petitioners persuaded even reliable defenders of corporal punishment that they were expendable. Low scores certainly weakened the incumbents. The Smith School's rank on Howe's portion of the test was rock bottom. Reverend Neale proctored the examination of the pupils on the morning of July 10, and he transmitted the details that very day in a remarkable letter to

Howe. Neale explained that "the first thought that struck me on looking round upon the school was that which occurred to the Prophet when carried out into the valley, which was fully of bones, he asked despairingly, 'Can these bones live?'" Commenting on their mastery of reading and spelling, the antislavery preacher revealed his low expectations of the pupils. While not expecting them to "comprehend what they read much better than the Ethiopians of old," he was surprised that "on the whole they acquitted themselves in these branches very creditably." But they faltered in grammar. "In geography two or three scholars were able to answer a few questions, but in general there was a marked deficiency in this branch. The same was true in history." Forbes and his female assistant, Neale concluded, "do the best they can in the circumstances of the case. They have evidently a hard set to deal with." Moreover, "the best scholars were absent" on examination day, "in jail for some misdemeanors on the Fourth of July."[55]

Brigham's committee did not have much better news: the Smith pupils lagged so far behind in arithmetic that they were only asked a few questions orally and spared the written test. At the Mayhew School, the cumulative scores in both parts of the exam were mediocre, but master Capen, said one board member, while "a faithful teacher," was seen as "not so successful as those who governed by milder means." Josiah Fairbank, the writing master of the Adams School, which did well in the reading exam but less impressively in mathematics, was also dismissed, but the decision seemed unrelated to the scores. Those voting against him simply said he was a "kind" teacher but lazy and negligent.[56]

On the same day these men were fired, the printing of ten thousand copies of the summer reports, which were merged into a single document, gained approval. This occurred only after Emerson and his allies won a major concession: a disclaimer stating that the report reflected the views of its authors, not that of the Boston School Committee. The *Daily Journal* reported that the reformers conceded after "a somewhat protracted discussion." Recognizing the historical significance of the report, Mann began publishing long excerpts in successive issues of the *Common School Journal* beginning on October 1. He told readers that Boston's schools had never "been subjected to a thorough, scrutinizing examination. . . . Such an examination they have this year received; and their actual condition, as to present proficiency and ability, is now made known to the world."

After conducting a "perfectly fair and impartial" written examination in the grammar schools, committeemen had reduced the results "to a tabular form, so that the common eye can compare them, and determine at a glance [their] relative standing." Mann assured his readers that written examinations, still relatively "novel" in America, were increasingly "common in Europe."[57]

Now a national audience of educational leaders could learn a new way to judge schools and see what Boston's first classes did not know.

V

The reformers were upbeat about what they had accomplished. They were already planning their next assaults on the masters and the double-headed system. William Fowle told Mann that one committeeman thought Emerson could be ousted from office in December. And the key reformers hardly felt defeated by the failure to fire more masters. Mann in particular was in good spirits. Writing to George Combe on September 25, the Secretary viewed the firing of four masters as something "which, twelve months ago, would have been deemed as impossible as to turn four peers out of the British House of Lords." Now all of the masters were in effect put on notice regarding their disciplinary and teaching methods, and their status would presumably sink lower once citizens had access to the reports and saw the horrid test results. The "public mind" had been aroused by the summer examinations and contests over reappointments. Mann was thus optimistic about the upcoming elections, even though politics exacted its price. "I have suffered severely in the conflict, so far as my feelings are concerned," he told his Scottish friend, "and doubtless I have suffered considerably in my reputation."[58]

Mann also realized that the masters had many allies on the School Committee and the allegiance of many ushers and teachers who depended on them. "Between all these there is a natural bond of union. Each has his or her circle of relatives and friends," and the alumni similarly had a vested interest in maintaining the reputations of their old school. But the summer examining committees accelerated the movement toward important changes in the organization and structure of the Boston schools. Despite resistance by Emerson and many others who defended the existing system, the summer exams helped undermine faith in the status quo. Finally, "the old notion of perfection in the Boston grammar and writing schools is destroyed; the prescription by which the masters held their office, and appointed indirectly their successors, is at an end."[59]

Fowle kept Mann informed about any developments. "Nothing new has transpired since yesterday, at least nothing that has reached me," he told the Secretary on October 3. A few days later, Mann told Cyrus Peirce, the principal of the normal school in Lexington, that he was hopeful that the test results would advance the cause of reform. "Have you seen the Report of the Boston School Committee, on the Grammar & Writing Schools? What a pile of thunder-bolts! Jupiter never had more lying by his side, when he had ordered a fresh lot wherewith to punish the wicked." As ever, the Secretary saw the world in black and white, with friends and foes, and in moral terms. Despite the power of the enemy, he seemed confident. "If the masters see fit to assail me again, I think I can answer them in such a way as to make it redound to the glory of God."[60]

While the long-term importance of competitive written tests was unknown in 1845, their significance locally was unquestionable. Some contemporaries sensed that something momentous had happened. After reading a rough draft of Howe's report in early August, a contributor to the *Mercantile Journal* described it as "one of the most extraordinary documents that ever was submitted to any Board, on the subject of public instruction." The pupils' responses—tens of thousands of answers— would literally cover "acres of ground," and the examiners demanded nothing less than a transformation of the local grammar schools, long regarded as without peer.[61]

As copies of the final report began to circulate in the fall, Bostonians could judge what the summer examiners had wrought in the name of reform.

CHAPTER **5**

Thanatopsis and Square Roots

By the fall of 1845, Bostonians were flooded with copies of the sum-mer examiners' reports. They offered readers a blow-by-blow account of what inspired the birth of written examinations, the less than ster-ling performance of the pupils, and recommendations for reform. Once Horace Mann began printing long excerpts in the *Common School Journal,* congratulatory letters began arriving at his office. Writing from Syracuse on October 22, his abolitionist friend the Reverend Samuel J. May told Mann that once they learned the facts the "people of Boston" would never "tolerate" the behavior of the masters. A day later, a job seeker from Colchester, Connecticut, asked how to acquire the actual report. He wanted to learn how to compare his pupils at the Bacon Academy with their counterparts in Boston, but he also quizzed Mann on how to land a position as a grammar master. He was originally from Fitchburg and wanted to move closer to home. He added, no doubt to Mann's dis-pleasure, that he might become a better instructor by observing the head teachers at Boston's legendary schools.[1]

Another correspondent, better informed about Mann's general estima-tion of the masters, found the news about poor teaching in Boston "very remarkable, and startling." The summer examiners confirmed that rote teaching was a failure and demonstrated the necessity of new pedagogical approaches. "Such revelation show how much remains for the reformer to do even in places where the public schools have been uniformly sup-posed to be in the most prosperous condition," said another educator, appalled by the masters' rude treatment of the Secretary. No wonder they tried to avoid "public inspection." But Mann needed to take com-fort when good triumphed over evil and to remember that "the brows of reformers . . . in all ages have been surmounted with the crown of thorns and not a few of them have been destined to expire upon the cross." Here was language the Secretary could appreciate.[2]

Whig journalists in local newspapers and magazines also rallied around the reformers. The editor of the *North American Review* lauded the reading committee. "These gentlemen," he said, "addressed themselves to their duties with a generous spirit of self-sacrifice which deserves all praise." Traditionally the summer exams were oral and "superficial, or, at least, not thorough and searching." But the eminent trio of Samuel G. Howe, Theophilus Parsons, and Rollin H. Neale not only carefully examined the first classes in written tests but also spent months rechecking answers, compiling tables, interpreting the scores, and recommending school improvements. With test results providing the hard evidence on educational decline, the School Committee had to act promptly to eliminate the double-headed system, hire more female teachers, centralize authority in a superintendent, and curb corporal punishment. Even if assailed by "evil tongues," the examiners should recognize "that the abuse which a reformer encounters is exactly in proportion to the need of a reformation."[3]

The fallout from the summer exams nevertheless continued in early November, when the committeemen investigating the Lyman School controversy met with master Albert Bowker and Howe. Hours of meetings produced very little deemed "worthy of investigation or which would injuriously affect Dr. Howe's character," so further "inquiry . . . was impracticable and if practicable would now be inexpedient." Later in the month, William Brigham, chair of the late writing committee, set off fireworks on the School Committee by initiating a discussion about hiring a superintendent. Despite predictable resistance from Frederick Emerson and the Reverends Streeter and Young, colleagues voted thirteen to eight to appoint three colleagues to meet with the city council (which had budgetary authority) to consider the matter. Two of them, Brigham and Parsons, were openly pro-superintendent. Adding electricity to the air, political campaigns were imminent, as the ward caucuses lined up their favorites. "We are now in a state of excitement and anxiety on the subject of the school committee," Mann told Reverend May on December 2. "The 'thirty-one' are exerting every muscle against the reformers. Nothing can exceed their activity, or the baseness of the means that some of them resort to."[4]

Election season always held surprises, not always pleasant. On December 6, the Whig *Atlas* reminded voters in classic understatement that the schools "attracted great attention during the last year." Howe's report had revealed that despite "all our boasting about the state of our Public Schools, errors and defects have crept in, which require a close pruning from skillful hands." Mann's partisans wrote letters attacking Frederick Emerson for profiting on textbooks. Another ally contrasted the low scores on the summer exams with the high expenditures. Happy that four masters were fired and another dozen given a "shaking," he spread the news that Howe and some other reformers lost bids at renomination. Emerson, Streeter, and the forces of darkness were blamed. Another citizen, named "Anti-Bamboozle," assumed that "the masters and their friends are chuckling at their success, and predicting an immediate return to the state of torpidity, when they had little to do but suck their paws."[5]

Even though Howe's stormy tenure on the School Committee neared its end, key allies survived and welcomed a new crowd of reformers. "The Whigs are the 'cocks of the walk' in the city this year," lamented the Democratic *Post*. They seemed invincible. Josiah Quincy, Jr., was reelected mayor and the party retained strong majorities throughout city government. Over the next decade, Parsons, Brigham, Neale, and a succession of like-minded committeemen, inspired by the summer surprise, chipped away at the masters' authority and the double-headed system. Every summer through the mid-1850s, a new set of examiners assessed the first classes. But the ritual survived in a rapidly changing context, as the famine Irish and native poor reconfigured the student body, forcing examiners to reflect upon the strengths and limitations of the new-style examinations. Soon full-time administrators rather than lay people on school committees in Boston and other cities faced these issues directly, for they increasingly wrote the tests and examined the pupils.[6]

The most zealous reformers in Boston believed that written examinations would reveal otherwise hidden truths about the nature of schools. Testing promised to undermine outmoded forms of school organization, identify the best teaching practices, hold teachers and pupils accountable, and provide incontrovertible evidence about what children actually knew: pupil by pupil, school by school, even district by district. In Boston, such heady assumptions clashed with the contemporary limits of quantitative expertise, defensiveness about the quality of neighborhood schools, and traditional forms of assessment. The local examiners on the reading and writing committees, however, were indefatigable as they read acres of answers and provided Bostonians and reformers elsewhere with more detailed analyses of test scores than ever before.

For anyone interested in the birth of the quantitative revolution in the schools, Samuel Gridley Howe, William Brigham, and their colleagues provided a front row seat as they continued to make history in the turbulent world of Boston politics.

I

When the School Committee approved the printing of ten thousand copies of the combined reading and writing reports on September 11, it ensured Howe, Parsons, and Neale a noteworthy place in the annals of education. Together they had administered, graded, and analyzed the meaning of America's first big test. As principal author of the reading report, Howe had revised draft after draft because of his poor mathematical skills and the rancorous response from Frederick Emerson and his allies. Before approving publication, the School Committee resolved that the report only reflected the views of its authors. That said, it was a carefully crafted document, containing fifty pages of prose that recounted the genesis of the exam, explained test procedures, reprinted the test items, documented pupil scores, and recommended several "radical" reforms in the grammar schools. Based on the test scores of 530 pupils, all in the top division of the first classes, it also presented four dozen tables, showing how well each school did on every question, with a cumulative ranking of the schools, outperformed by the girls' school in Roxbury. While commenting on some exam results on electives, the reading report focused on four areas of study taught in all of the schools: history, geography, the definitions of words, and grammar.[7]

In contrast, William Brigham's report on the writing schools was a mere seventeen pages and included only two tables, comparing arithmetic scores school by school. A prominent leader in the local statistical society, Brigham was less abrasive and more adept with numbers than Howe, who regarded him as a "capital fellow," even if too distracted by his legal work to help get "brother Barnum" and another master fired. The writing committee's succinct but equally critical commentaries on student performance and on the mediocre teaching skills of some masters hardly caused a stir. Whether fighting for Greek independence, teaching the blind, opposing slavery, or defending Horace Mann, Howe in contrast always attracted attention. His report not only kept alive the ongoing war between Mann and the masters but also drew upon nearly two decades' worth of complaints about the double-headed system. Without the annoying interruptions of colleagues at public meetings, the committeemen could now fully explain their actions and make their best case against the status quo.[8]

According to the reading committee, the private printing of the exam questions, regarded by critics as malicious, had a benevolent intent. "It was our wish," said the examiners, "to have as fair an examination as possible; to give the same advantages to all; to prevent leading questions; to carry away, not loose notes, or vague remembrances of the examination, but positive information, in black and white; to ascertain with certainty, what the scholars did not know, as well as what they did know; to test their readiness at expressing their ideas upon paper," and to determine whether pupils could spell words correctly and write clear, grammatically sound, properly punctuated sentences. In one long sentence, the examiners had described their break from the past, when colleagues made subjective judgments in their quarterly and annual reports. Howe and his committee knew they were doing something very novel. "The mode of examination by written questions, has been used with great success in many schools and colleges; but we are not aware of any tabularization like this having been attempted."[9]

Based on foreign travel and wide reading, both Mann and Howe realized that written examinations had already posed a limited challenge to the authority of oral examinations and exhibitions. Local usage of written tests also demonstrated their potential, though the examiners never mentioned them. Since 1821, pupils had to pass a short written exam to enter the newly established English High School, a practice widely imitated as other cities created free secondary schools. Before the summer of 1845, however, no one had ever given a common written examination in the United States on such a large scale, systematically analyzed and compared the performance of different classes, or used the statistical results to help change school organization or question teaching practices.[10]

Howe's group had given what later generations would call a "standardized test": an examination bound by common procedures, administered under similar if not identical conditions, and evaluated as much as possible by the same metrics. Every student faced the same questions, had the same amount of time to complete the test, and sat apart to prevent cheating. A few schools were within close proximity, allowing a handful of pupils, only boys it seems, to share some questions with friends at noon time. Despite the brouhaha at the Lyman School, where the master's judgment faltered, the committee believed that pupils were "generally honest" and tried their best. Ominously, most did not need the full hour allotted for each portion of the exam.[11]

The committeemen felt obligated to address the controversial issue of surprising the pupils with a new type of exam. Their justification was that they wanted to prevent the masters from cramming a handful of "show" pupils with answers to impress visitors, the usual practice at oral exams and exhibitions. In contrast, said the reading committee, written tests would demonstrate what the masters' pupils actually knew and document "the real and comparative merits" of the various schools. Accused by Frederick Emerson and other critics of intentionally smearing the pupils—which Howe, Parsons, and Neale again denied—the examiners claimed they even awarded credit for reasonably close answers, overlooking numerous examples of missing punctuation and poor grammar. Since the answer sheets with student names affixed were preserved, anyone doubting their good faith could peruse them themselves. If they had completed every question, pupils would have produced 57,873 answers. In the event, hand grading them was made simpler since nearly half were left blank. But grading 31,159 completed answers and then double- and triple-checking them for consistency was nothing short of Herculean. Despite grading leniently, the examiners still identified 2,801 grammatical and 3,733 spelling errors and 35,947 mistakes in punctuation. The cumulative average score was 30 percent.[12]

Despite such attention to detail, committeemen did not claim omniscience or perfection. Given the scale of the task and time constraints, they acknowledged that some inconsequential errors may have crept into their final report. Howe likely benefitted from Mann's advice on how to turn statistics into readable prose. Occasionally he and his colleagues also assumed a modest pose, perhaps to help defuse criticism.

Admitting human fallibility without losing their authoritative tone, the examiners admitted that they lacked "complete or perfect knowledge of our Schools" and were not judging their "absolute worth." "Far be it from us," the committee insisted, "to consider intellectual activity and intellectual acquirement as alone worthy of consideration." Schools shouldered many important duties, instilling civic and personal responsibility, a "love of knowledge," and "respect for order" in the young. No one doubted that all good teachers embraced such vital goals.[13]

But the summer examiners had their eyes on a different prize: quantitative proof of children's academic achievement. And the results were shocking, sustaining their guiding assumption that reforming the grammar schools was imperative. Even if their carefully gathered statistics were imperfect and did not assess every valuable feature of a school, the written tests had apparently unearthed more reliable evidence on scholastic performance than ever before, in any school system.

Before turning to the test results, the examiners thus felt obligated to explain how they prepared the exam. To determine what the first classes should know, they focused on what pupils were expected to study under the masters' guidance, that is, their textbooks. Test scores, they assumed, gave a clear sense of the quality of instruction, and the new approach to evaluation might lift the conversation about school improvement above personal feelings or partisan politics. Well-designed questions on a common exam, for example, might resolve controversial issues about pedagogy and classroom effectiveness that divided Mann and the masters after the *Seventh Report* appeared in 1844. Did the masters ensure that pupils understood what they studied and memorized? Though their role was not acknowledged by the examiners, Mann and William Fowle helped Howe and Brigham devise a clever way to answer that question and presumably show who taught best. While most of the exam questions were short answer and rote in nature, some sought to show which classes best learned to think, analyze, comprehend, and understand what they memorized. The examiners assumed that scholars taught by textbooks-and-recitation methods might do well enough on rote material but otherwise flounder.[14]

The main instructional tools of the nineteenth century, textbooks contained innumerable questions to answer and problems to solve. So the examiners had abundant grist for the examination mill. J. E. Worcester's venerable *Elements of History* (1843) devoted sixty-four of its four hundred pages to questions, mostly based on recall. Scholars were also assigned textbooks written by master Barnum Field and former master Frederick Emerson, two inveterate enemies of Mann and his circle of friends. Fields's *American School Geography,* adopted in 1832, was in its fourteenth edition at the time of the summer exam; some of its pages had more study questions than text. Similarly, Emerson's *Third Part* of his arithmetic series, first published in 1834 and a local staple, contained hundreds of study problems from the four basic operations through decimals, cube roots, foreign currency conversion, and mensuration. Pupils often remembered the names of the authors of their textbooks, and one scholar decades later at a class reunion remembered his mathematics book well: "There is Emerson staring us full in the face/With his bothering figures and sums."[15]

And so the examiners naturally pulled test items out of the pupils' ubiquitous textbooks. They prepared thirty-one questions in geography ranging from the "very simple" to the "rather difficult." None were beyond the competence of the pupils, said the examiners. But two-thirds of the answers were incorrect. The questions did indeed extend from the simple to difficult and, to modern eyes, from basic to trivial to enigmatic. They mostly asked pupils to remember facts from textbooks, the fountainhead of knowledge. The first question—"Name the principal lakes in North America"—was the easiest: 84 percent answered correctly. Only 65 percent could answer the next question, to name the main rivers. Only 7 percent knew "the rivers, gulfs, oceans, seas and straits, through which a vessel must pass in going from Pittsburgh in Pennsylvania, to Vienna in Austria." Howe and his colleagues were surprised that only 5 percent could explain "the line of perpetual snow" and seemed unaware of the ambiguity of the question, "On which bank of the Ohio is Cincinnati, on the right or left?" Presumably the examiners thought pupils would visualize Cincinnati on a map. Half guessed left, half guessed right. Some must have thought, "It depends on where you are standing."[16]

The tone of the reading report shifted from acknowledging the examiners' imperfect knowledge to affirming what the tests proved. After studying the geography scores, Howe's committee concluded that most masters taught via "verbal or book knowledge" to the neglect of student comprehension or understanding. They harped on how, when asked whether Lake Erie's waters ran into Lake Ontario, or the other way around, only 59 percent of the pupils knew the answer. It seemed outrageous that "our best scholars could not tell which way the waters run, in spite of all the fame of Niagara!" Similarly, while an impressive 77 percent knew the "general course" of rivers in North and South Carolina, only one-third could explain *why* those in some "contiguous states" ran in different directions, one pupil claiming it was "the will of God!" Plucking such answers from the stack persuaded the committee that geography was taught as a dull "catalogue of names."[17]

History enjoyed the same reputation as geography: a potentially engaging subject usually taught dry as dust. Student responses to thirty questions drawn from Worcester's *History* helped pile up more evidence against the masters. The pupils did even worse in history than in geography; only 26 percent of their answers were correct. The examiners had an explanation. As in geography class, "the scholars have, for the most part, learned to recite the words of the text-book . . . without having been accustomed to think about the meaning of what they had learned." On the first, puff question—"What is history?"—82 percent succeeded. On other seemingly easy questions, however, they faltered. Only 20 percent could define "chronology." And, to further expose suspect instruction, the examiners emphasized that 38 percent knew the approximate years of Jefferson's Embargo but only 28 percent could define "embargo." What had been memorized was not understood. "It is worth positively nothing to know the date of an embargo," sneered the committee, "if one does not know what an embargo is."[18]

Reading consumed considerable instructional time, so examiners expected pupils to do reasonably well defining words and using grammar correctly. The scholars were asked to define twenty-eight words (doing about as well as in history) and to answer fourteen questions in grammar (averaging 39 percent). Again, the examiners selected items from assigned schoolbooks. Words to be defined came from the pupils' English reader, and the results were disappointing. "Some of the answers are so supremely absurd and ridiculous," the examiners concluded, that at first they wondered if the students were "attempting to jest with the Committee, were it not that there are marks of honest attempts to trace analogies between words which they did know and words which they did not." Critics lampooned the examiners for asking the scholars to define difficult words such as "Thanatopsis." Fifty-nine percent could define it, the second highest average in that exam. But that failed to satisfy the committee, since pupils had been required to memorize the poem yet many obviously gave little thought to its title. Where teaching apparently excelled, as in the Bowdoin girls' school, 88 percent of the pupils knew the definition while not a single scholar did in three schools and only a quarter or less in six others.[19]

The results of poor teaching had apparently come home to roost. The average scores in geography (34 percent), history (26 percent), definitions (27 percent), and grammar (39 percent) persuaded Howe's committee that pupils in Boston's generously funded system were not receiving a first-rate education. Critics of the grammar schools could now cite the combined reports and say, like the anonymous contributors to newspapers in late summer, that while costs remained high, the achievements were few. The examiners made their criticisms unmistakably clear. Assuming they actually taught the full curriculum and not their favorite subjects, many masters mostly drilled their pupils, strengthening the faculty of memorization at the expense of understanding, analysis, and comprehension. As Horace Mann often said, "hearing recitations from a book, is not teaching."[20]

Aiming at the heart strings, Howe and his colleagues offered a "melancholy" observation. If the best and brightest pupils about to graduate knew so little, what of the masses of children who never reached the first class? Rather than demonize the examiners or complain about their findings, the committee viewed the evidence in their report as incontrovertible. Bostonians had to face the reality that the local grammar schools "have not the excellence and usefulness they should possess." Regrettably, schools elsewhere "are better than most of ours," and "the majority of our Schools are further below the best that we have, than any thing in the peculiar condition of the scholars, or other similar causes can explain." The pupils absolved, the blame rested with the system and the masters.[21]

While hostility among Mann's friends toward the double-headed system and the masters predated the exam, the examiners' conclusions, while buttressed by classroom observations, rested upon statistics. Since the examiners spent so much time examining others, they deserve more scrutiny themselves, especially their understanding of the infant science.

II

Boston helped promote the nation's growing fascination with statistics, and both committee chairs were active in the locally based American Statistical Association. It takes nothing away from the creativity and ingenuity of the examiners to recognize problems, more obvious today than at the time, with some of their procedures and analyses. Some issues about the test that rankled contemporaries, of course, had nothing to do with statistics. Springing new-style tests upon pupils understandably caused discomfort and confusion among some pupils that undoubtedly lowered their scores. It also raised ethical questions about the motives of the examiners, many of whom were openly antagonistic toward the masters and their friends. Critics dismissed their findings by saying that they had looked for problems and found them. As the Reverend Joshua Leavitt remarked, numbers did not lie, but when assembled for malevolent reasons, their ability to deceive was unsurpassed.[22]

To their credit, the examiners were remarkably open about many aspects of their labors. They highlighted the shortcomings of traditional oral exams, which failed to document beyond impressions the "real merits and demerits of our Schools" or assess "their comparative rank." Since examiners were inexperienced, unfamiliar with statistics, and rotated off the committee, the standards of evaluation varied within committees and from year to year. Not only were written tests deemed superior, but the examiners also deliberately asked easy and difficult questions to generate a range of scores. Ingeniously, they asked some questions that required more than a simple recall of facts or rules to determine if pupils understood what they studied. They worried about fairness and tried to standardize test procedures.[23]

At the same time, the six committeemen were neither statisticians nor formally trained mathematicians. They included one physician (Howe), two lawyers (Brigham and Parsons), and three ministers. Howe often pleaded for mercy regarding his math skills. Only Howe and Brigham knew very much about statistics, and there were limits to that knowledge. A product of their time, examiners could know nothing about appropriate procedures for sampling or how to strive for test validity and reliability. While focusing on the masters, they recognized that other factors shaped classroom experiences and how much children learned. But they lacked any knowledge of statistical methods to weigh their relative influence. So, like everyone else, they relied on impressions and observations as well as numbers to reach conclusions. The examiners were part of a generation of pioneers in the forefront of social investigation, gathering statistics, trying to make sense of them, sometimes confusing correlations with causes, sometimes seeing patterns that interested them or confirmed what they assumed while ignoring others.[24]

Howe's committee made passing references to some of the statistics that they had assembled. For example, the examiners mentioned in a footnote that the average age in the "girls' schools" was "about fourteen" (recall that boys had to leave the grammar schools at fourteen, but girls could stay until sixteen). Among the schools they examined, six were all male, five were all female, and the rest had separate male and female departments. One table in Howe's report listed the average ages of the pupils in different schools but did not remind readers whether they were all male, female, or mixed. When the committeemen ranked the schools overall, they did not alert readers to the fact that three of the top four and five of the top ten (out of seventeen included in the final table) were "girls' schools." The examiners seemed not to notice that girls often outperformed the boys.[25]

The Bowdoin female grammar school was ranked best in the city; it was the school whose students shined in defining "Thanatopsis." But, at an average age of fourteen years and eight months, the Bowdoin girls were also the oldest pupils examined in the summer of 1845; they were nearly two years older than the scholars tested at the Adams School, the only boys' school ranked in the top five. The Bowdoin pupils were also two months older than those at Roxbury's Dudley School, the suburban girls' school that beat them out in the final ranking. The examiners buried these bits of information on age and gender in different tables and did not address their possible influence upon performance. Similarly, their claims that Dudley led the pack rested on thin evidence. It beat out Bowdoin by .0008 percent. Either the compilers believed the facts spoke for themselves or did not understand that this was statistically insignificant. Many of the examiners' critics were math innocents and focused on the motives of the examiners, not their procedures or tables. No one hassled the examiners more than Frederick Emerson, whose expertise in mathematics was unrivaled on the School Committee. He brushed off

discussing the tables at committee meetings, and if he thought the statistics or quantitative measures bogus, he seems to have kept his views
to himself.[26]

The reading school examiners also noted that different percentages of
pupils in the first class actually took the exam. Irregular school attendance was the bane of many reformers in the 1840s, and Horace Mann
and other contemporaries complained that many pupils "dodged the
exam" on exhibition day. Public schools lacked any authority to force
pupils to take any test, oral or written. How extensive was the problem in the summer of 1845? The reading committee did not say, but
who showed up or dodged the exams certainly shaped the outcome. In
the writing schools, Brigham's group explained that the pupils in the
first class ranged from eleven to sixteen years of age, averaging "about
twelve or thirteen." The first division averaged about fourteen years of
age and represented 20 to 25 percent of the first class. Brigham's committee affirmed that they tested the "best scholars in each school." But only
three hundred and eight pupils took the arithmetic test compared with
over two hundred more who sat for the reading exam. Brigham's committee started giving the exam in early June, before Howe's, but did not
finish until mid-July, apparently due to scheduling problems. Did that
account for the discrepancy? Or did the percentage of pupils in the "first
division" vary considerably between the reading and writing schools? Did
the examiners consider testing the same pupils, who usually attended
both schools? Or did they assume this was impossible since they had no
leverage over attendance?[27]

The written record is silent on these basic issues. What is fascinating
about the testers of 1845, however, is to watch them work their way
through their novel experiment. Those in the front lines of reform had
guidance from their friends in the American Statistical Association and
were led forward by their own sense of what was feasible. Howe and his
colleagues knew that their "tabularization" was unprecedented, and, like
reformers studying poverty, insanity, or demography, they wanted to use
statistics to understand the world better but also to change and presumably improve it. The examiners underscored the importance of fairness
to every pupil and to report the results "in black and white." But the
exams were inseparable from a political campaign by the key examiners
(especially Howe and Brigham) to discredit the masters, who did not find

"screwing machines" appealing. As lead author on the reading report, Howe felt little restraint in what he said about the individual masters, though Neale and Parsons signed their name to the report and did not endear themselves to the masters and their friends.

Having endured the slings of personal abuse, Howe's committee could not resist retaliating before offering a fulsome list of desired reforms. It was one thing to lash out against the masters behind closed doors among colleagues, another thing entirely to ridicule some of them in a publication distributed to every family in Boston. While they complimented some masters for their pedagogical skills and demeanor, others received rough treatment. They tagged several masters as boring "textbook" teachers who seemed disinterested in their work. A "want of life and energy" pervaded the Eliot School taught by master Sherman and the same was true at Adams. While the examiners favored less flogging and softer forms of discipline, they thought "kindly" master Baker, unable to control the Boylston boys, belonged at a girls' school. Disliking him personally but admiring his talents, Howe thought Barnum Field of the Franklin School favored his *"best"* students. Master Crafts of the Hawes School was uninspiring and should improve his classroom manner. Master Forbes of the Smith School, fired by the time the final report appeared, was a disaster, his school in "deplorable condition."[28]

While they promised not to identify anyone with an "unrestrained and ill-regulated temper," the examiners otherwise hammered away at the masters collectively. History and geography were taught as one fact after another, disconnected from life. Grammar became a formal set of rules, the masters often uninterested in teaching pupils how to write clear and effective prose. Pupils handpicked by the masters to impress guests with their pleasing voices and presence were often clueless if asked to answer basic questions about what they read or recited. The written exams exposed gaps in comprehension even among the strongest students.[29]

William Brigham's writing committee had similar complaints. Pupils memorized rules in arithmetic fairly well but could not explain them or put them into practice. Asked why a particular rule helped solve a certain problem, they grew silent. Separated from the textbook, many were lost. "Elegant school houses and princely appropriations," said Brigham's committee, "do but little without the teacher, who has a sufficient capacity and a proper spirit." Frederick Emerson devoted considerable space in his arithmetic book to fractions and square roots, but only 56 percent of the pupils could solve, "What is the square root of 5/9 of 4/5 of 4/7 of 7/9?" Did he grimace upon learning that the pupils only scored 35 percent overall? Emerson seemed implicated in their failures since he defended the masters and they assigned his textbook.[30]

Both committees believed that the test results proved that some teachers taught more effectively than others. Some masters were fine teachers and taught more than the facts while many were doing a terrible job. Howe's committee did not think their expectations were unreasonable. "If it is thought that we insist too strongly that the children should *understand* what they study, and if it is said that this cannot be perfectly accomplished, we answer, that we do not demand the impossible." Testing promised to help identify the best instructional methods, which could be imitated in underperforming schools. Brigham's committee also noticed differences in teacher quality. Even if many factors influenced learning, "the zeal, capacity, or efforts of the teachers themselves" were often decisive. "Upon the teachers must, in a great degree, depend whether the pupils shall confine their acquisitions to the letter and rules of the text book, or whether they shall understand the principles of the studies they pursue." Observing the masters and checking pupil scores revealed "a striking difference in our schools. In some the pupils seem to understand what they have studied; and to know how to apply it to the cases which may arise." But too many masters seemed content to have pupils recite rules and definitions, tackle some problems on slates and blackboards, and call it a day.[31]

The two committees also endorsed a series of reforms, all of them embraced since the 1830s by reform-minded Whigs. The newly elected reformers who joined the School Committee in 1844 had meant business, as the summer examinations demonstrated, but their work had only begun. Both committees emphasized the interlocking nature of intended reforms and used the test results to try to undermine the status quo. To move the system forward, Boston had to join other cities and appoint a superintendent. A full-time administrator could set the "same standard" for children in similar classes and expand the testing regimen to reveal the "exact condition" of every school, top to bottom. Currently the masters only taught the first class, a huge expense, hardly justified by the embarrassing test scores. Currently no one had the authority to set standards and benchmarks to measure progress. The turnover of lay people on the School Committee, until now wedded to outmoded ways of assessing teachers and children, made the "systematic and continuous observation" of teachers and pupils impossible.[32]

Next, the double-headed system had to be eliminated. It was a "strange" and costly arrangement apparently found only in nearby Charlestown. At the time of the summer exam, Boston employed thirty-five masters, double what was needed. Seventeen male ushers taught the boys just below the first classes, while the lowly paid female teachers, seventy of them, taught the youngest girls and boys. Why spend so much money on the masters and ushers? Reducing their number dramatically would enable the School Committee to hire more female teachers, who earned considerably less and were regarded as superior instructors. While not endorsing a ban on corporal punishment, the reading committee also emphasized that recent reforms, including required recordkeeping on the practice and the firing of a few masters notorious for their disciplinary methods, proved that change was possible; if more women were hired, more rattans would gather dust.[33]

Having spent months embroiled in controversy, the summer examiners did not naïvely think that the masters and their allies would suddenly warm to their side. Bitter feelings prevailed. Howe and his colleagues asked the masters to complete a survey on their attitude toward corporal punishment and thoughts on assigned textbooks. Both were delicate subjects. Since they rejected romantic views on discipline, were angry about the surprise exam, opposed hiring a superintendent, and had little reason to insult Barnum Field or Frederick Emerson, most of the masters refused to cooperate. And they probably resented the recommendation, near the conclusion of Howe's report, that they embrace new approaches to teaching. Instead of motivating children to excel through fear or emulation, they should inspire pupils through nobler ideals such as the love of learning. Once this occurred, and a superintendent and more female teachers were hired, "every School in Boston will be as one or two are now, a place to which children delight to resort."[34]

One or two schools, out of nineteen? The words seemed to slip out, suggesting that the schools were generally nightmarish and belying the concluding words of the reading committee. Contrary to what their critics believed, Howe and his colleagues had not forgotten, despite their "desire to find out and reform . . . errors and deficiencies," that Boston's schools had many "excellences." "That many of our Schools are far better than they once were, we well know, and gladly acknowledge. But the knowledge that there are such improvements, has only made us look to the possibility of farther progress, and resolve to do all in our power to leave for our children Schools as much better than the present, as the present are better than those of olden time." Brigham's group similarly affirmed that the system was "capable of great improvement" in the coming years.[35]

Whig reformers were euphoric. Horace Mann broadcast excerpts from the examinations nationwide in successive issues of the *Common School Journal* and in his widely read state reports. In early November, he predicted "that the mode of examination, *by printed questions and written answers*, will constitute a new era in the history of our schools." Written tests were "impartial," ensured that everyone, not just the show pupils, were tested, and measured how well teachers taught and pupils learned. Once experts set commonly agreed upon and measurable standards, school improvements were inevitable. And test results were real and authentic, providing a "transcript, a sort of Daguerreotype likeness, as it were, of the state and condition of the pupils' minds," available to all interested parties "for general inspection." There was little doubt, Mann proclaimed, of "the superiority of the written over the oral method of examination," and no school committee "will ever venture to relapse into the former inadequate and uncertain practice."[36]

The events of the summer and fall of 1845 were a sensation. New York's *District School Journal* found the test results "astonishing." They proved that Boston's schools did "not come up to that standard, which has ever been claimed for them throughout the Union." But what difference would written, competitive tests make in practice? How would the local committeemen respond to the recommendations of the summer examiners?[37]

III

Delivered during the first week of January in 1846, Mayor Quincy's annual address applauded the summer examiners. After all, he had appointed the six committeemen, the key figures personal friends. Quincy endorsed the appointment of a superintendent, who could set a "high standard" for the schools, examine their "comparative merits," and (in a dig at the masters) "check the tendency" of those "in an honorable and lucrative station to relax the efforts by which it was obtained." A superintendent would ensure both fiscal responsibility, accountability, and the adoption of "all the modern improvements." The conflict between Mann and the masters had entered yet another phase.[38]

A week later, with Quincy in his familiar post as chair, the new School Committee held its first meeting. Following tradition, Quincy made the usual committee assignments. Then the mood of the meeting changed. Master Albert Bowker resigned, adding another notch in the belt of the reformers. Frederick Emerson asked the Lyman School's subcommittee to report whether it approved of the escalating effort to abolish the double-headed system. Seizing the moment, his ally the Reverend Sebastian Streeter moved that every master and usher receive a copy of the examiners' reports, which had endorsed hiring a superintendent and replacing many of the ushers with female teachers. Then George S. Hillard, the Whig head of the Common Council, took the floor. A friend of the Secretary and a fellow lawyer, Hillard explained that Boston violated state law by failing to advertise teaching positions or interview finalists. Theophilus Parsons predictably urged compliance. Samuel Gridley Howe may have been bounced off the School Committee, but over the next decade a revolving roster of friends and allies, inspired by the summer experiment, showed persistence and resolve.[39]

In late January, Charles Brooks, one of the newly elected allies of Horace Mann, recommended requiring prospective teachers to take written examinations to test their knowledge of subject matter and the latest pedagogical methods. Like Hillard, Parsons, and so many reformers, Brooks, a Unitarian minister, was a Harvard graduate. In the 1830s he traveled extensively in Europe, fascinated by the latest educational reforms. Upon returning home he campaigned with other Whigs to establish state normal schools and, with Hillard, Howe, and others, signed Quincy's long petition in defense of Mann. Repeating the well-known European refrain—*"As is the Teacher, so is the School"*—Brooks had long embraced the belief, reinforced by the summer examiners, that teachers made the crucial difference in student achievement. "Take the poorest school in this State, and put into it an intelligent, skillful, and conscientious master, and he will raise it to his own level; for all streams flow level with their fountains. Put into that school a stupid, selfish, and vicious master," warned Brooks, "and he will drag it down to his own degradation."[40]

Fitfully implemented, Brooks' proposal was nevertheless another example of the determination of reformers to end business as usual in the schools. Indeed, everywhere the masters, Frederick Emerson, and their friends turned, Mann's allies seemed to appear. In a detailed speech before the Common Council later in the month, Hillard threw his lot with the pro-superintendent lobby. Last year's examiners' reports, he said, "produced a great sensation in our community, and gave rise to much discussion. I am not going to plunge into the troubled waters of that strife." But plunge he did. Admitting that he was Mann's friend, not his "mouthpiece," Hillard chastised the masters for their hostile treatment of the Secretary and reactionary pose. Boston's schools were "the best jewels in her crown" but, changing metaphors, he accused the masters of "dry-rot of the mind." All institutions tended to ossify. "The search-ing and penetrating inspection of a superintendent," however, would "correct this injurious tendency." William Wordsworth had rightly said that "the child is father of the man," and Boston had to regain its first rank in public education. Through regular "examination and inspection," a superintendent would "learn in minute detail the condition of each school." This would "encourage the faithful" and "quicken the sluggish," teachers as well as pupils.[41]

Hillard called the typical quarterly and summer exam "superficial and unsatisfactory." An examiner, he said, should have "knowledge, skill, and time." "How many sub-committees combine all these elements? I assure you few, very few." Most quarterly exams were "mere ceremonies." The examiners enter the room, the master gives the signal, the pupils leap to attention. The master gives a textbook to the examiner who, feeling awkward and unfamiliar with the subject matter, returns it. The master knows "the strength and the weakness of his school, where the ice is thick, and where it is thin." With eyes trained on the students who will perform best, the charade continues, the pupil answers the agreed-upon questions, and newspapers duly report that the schools are flourishing. To expect the master to expose any weakness, as Howe's written test had done, would require "superhuman magnanimity and self-sacrifice."[42]

Throughout the spring, Hillard lobbied colleagues to petition the leg-islature for permission to hire a superintendent. Quincy endorsed the proposal in a long report, saying only a full-time expert could uncover the "actual condition of the schools," compare how well teachers taught, and identify what worked best. At the Common Council and School Committee, debates on employing a superintendent were fierce; as expected, Democrats and conservative Whigs, including friends and allies of Frederick Emerson, openly attacked the proposal. Not-so-veiled slurs against the former master surfaced, one critic claiming that "three little books—Arithmetics—were the cause of all the opposition." Several councilmen denounced the summer examiners, accusing them of libeling the schools and promoting centralized power over republicanism. Amid these debates, a local newspaper, the *Traveller*, partly owned by former master Bowker, sent sparks flying by alleging that Reverend Neale had admitted that the examiners had always planned to embarrass the masters, which Neale promptly denied. The reformers had more clout on the School Committee than on the Council, which decisively voted down the motion to petition the legislature.[43]

Assaulting the integrity of the examiners was exquisitely timed and generated a lengthy response from Howe and other committee members. Defending their motives and their European-inspired experiment in competitive written exams, they continued to lobby for numerous reforms, whether on or off the School Committee. Mann opened the pages of the *Common School Journal* to Howe and other allies and kept interested readers informed about the fate of testing and the local effort to transform Boston's schools. The struggle to hire a superintendent triumphed in 1851, when the Council finally secured the authority and approved funding for the position. A master campaigned for the post but lost, one in a string of defeats in defense of the double-headed system. Nathan Bishop, superintendent of the Providence, Rhode Island, schools since 1839, became Boston's first chief school officer. He was well known for advancing mainstream reforms such as the improved classification of pupils and the replacement of ushers with women. Mann had earlier tried to lure the fellow Brown alumnus to head one of the state normal schools. He arrived at his new post as local reformers whittled away at the double-headed system.[44]

Since the 1820s, school reformers had endorsed better forms of grouping and classifying students as the most efficient and effective way to organize classrooms. In his controversial *Seventh Report* in 1844, Mann reaffirmed his support for the hiring of more female teachers, preferably trained in normal schools, and the construction of buildings with separate classrooms, with one instructor per class. One-room or poorly graded schools that included a range of children were standard in the countryside as well as in many cities. Boston's primary schools, governed by a separate committee, were typically one-room, often rented, found all across the city. The grammar schools, typically divided into two floors with long halls on each, segmented internally by classes and divisions, were obviously in the line of fire. The masters could not help but see the import of the new architectural ideals, which favored replacing benches with single seats and desks. In 1847, the School Committee, despite heated opposition, approved the construction of some new grammar schools, all single-headed.[45]

The Quincy School, named for the current mayor's father, epitomized the trend and was the most celebrated. It was a four-story building with a large assembly hall and twelve separate classrooms, the third built on the new plan. Together they cost the princely sum of $200,000. Quincy's lone master, chosen from dozens of applicants, was John D. Philbrick, a former usher at the English High School and current writing master at Mayhew. The dedication ceremonies in 1848 featured several of Frederick Emerson's adversaries. Reverend Neale offered the dedicatory prayer. Dr. Thomas M. Brewer, head of the local subcommittee and proprietor of the *Atlas,* joined him on the program; he had defended the examiners from the start. Josiah Quincy, Jr., the trusted ally of Howe and Mann, must have beamed with delight. Mann had recently attended other school dedications in the city, and, begging forgiveness, sent a long and flattering letter to be read in his absence. After the younger Quincy left office in December and was criticized by his successor for extravagant school construction, he wrote a stinging reply, saying that the single-headed plan was superior and saved money. Besides Philbrick, who earned the standard $1,500 salary, the Quincy School employed two male teachers (earning $1000 and $800) but fifteen females (who only earned $300). Each master, then, earned as much as five women. By the spring, the education committee of the Council, responsible for construction and remodeling projects, adopted the Quincy School as its model. The days of the double-headed plan seemed numbered.[46]

The reformers on the committee after 1846 won the battle against the double-headed system but allowed the old masters to bide their time, as old age, disability, or death swept them away. Even the reformers admitted that some of them were excellent teachers, though the system had to go. So the School Committee phased in the single-headed plan as new schools were built and existing ones remodeled after the old masters left the scene. Frederick Emerson and a few colleagues voted consistently to preserve the double-headed plan, but no one made an effective case that two masters were better than one. Ominously, masters were increasingly called "principals," head teachers still but with a less dignified title.[47]

Year after year, reformers attacked everything the masters held dear. Reminders of the embarrassing test scores and importance of written examinations were regularly thrown in their face and used to champion the appointment of a superintendent and female teachers trained at normal schools. In 1847, George B. Emerson, the long-time champion of these reforms, suggested that the masters teach the fourth as well as the first class. While vociferously opposed by Frederick Emerson and not approved, the proposal showed the ease with which masters' perquisites faced regular challenge. Some colleagues liked one of Reverend Neale's pet ideas, to require the masters to live in the city and dismiss anyone who commuted from the suburbs. There seemed to be no end to the threats on customary privileges. Resolutions by Charles Brooks and other Whig activists to make every grammar school single-headed as soon as possible must have grated on the old-timers still in service, as articles praising self-contained classrooms, female teachers, and related reforms filled local newspapers and magazines. Reformers even introduced a resolution in 1850 that mandated examinations of every class, not just the top students, much easier to pass than actually implement.[48]

Frederick Emerson increasingly played the role of obstructionist, voting with the minority opposed to the superintendency and other means of weakening the old regime. Seeing the inevitability of defeat, he channeled his prodigious talents elsewhere, serving regularly on the "building committee," perfecting ventilation systems for schools as well as ships. Snide remarks about collusion between the masters and "bookmakers" appeared often enough in the press that its intended target was obvious; it did not help Emerson's reputation when the dignified, gray-haired gentleman escorted the infamous courtesan Lola Montez on a tour of the city schools. Unlike Lola, apparently, whatever Emerson wanted, he did not get, at least in terms of turning the clock back on the schools. Successive summer examination committees in the post-Howe era endorsed the

single-headed system, and an organizational revolution seemed imminent. In 1852, the *Evening Transcript,* applauding a recent examiners'
report, warned that some of the old masters resisted every change and,
"their craft being in danger . . . will cry out against those who will no
longer afford them patronage."[49]

One by one, many of the original "Thirty-One" who had signed the
Remarks in response to Mann's *Seventh Report* slipped into history. Barnum Field died in 1851 at the age of fifty-five. By the early 1850s, retire-
ments and resignations and rumors of masters pushed out of the system
were commonplace. Once superintendent Nathan Bishop arrived in the
city, several received severance pay to soften the blow. John Harris of
the Hawes School, remembered for placing disobedient girls under his
desk or his hung-up long coat, retired in 1852 along with other veterans.
Finally, in 1855, the *Evening Transcript* reported that Cornelius Walker,
reading master of the all-female Wells School, on whose subcommittee
Frederick Emerson had long served, submitted his resignation. After several years at the Eliot School, Walker had taught at Wells since it opened
in 1833. Resolutions duly recorded his decades of service and announced
the final shift to the single-headed plan.[50]

Between the summer of 1845 and Walker's retirement, the city had
undergone enormous demographic and social changes. The Whig activists aimed to transform the schools, using examination results to promote a variety of reforms, some organizational, some pedagogical. Grand
plans circulated to create age-graded classrooms from the lowest classes
through high school. By the early 1850s, Boston had even opened a
normal school, bringing the Prussian-inspired reform in full view of the
masters. It would ultimately train hundreds of female teachers. Due to
charter reform, the Primary School Committee was abolished in 1855,
expanding the superintendent's supervisory authority.[51]

That same year, the Massachusetts legislature abolished racially segregated schools, ending the legal basis to Jim Crow. A decade earlier,
abolitionists such as Samuel Gridley Howe had publicized the embarrassing test scores at the Smith School, but their opponents warned that
African-American pupils would struggle academically if they attended
integrated schools. Members of the Grammar Committee pointedly asked
whether a "poor colored boy" could succeed in any competition with
"some rich man's son,—of like age and capacity, but in the enjoyment

of immeasurably superior facilities for progress, from books, and leisure, and study . . . amid the seclusion and comforts of a quiet and genial home?" Many white Bostonians continued to doubt the mental capacity and potential of African-Americans, reinforcing entrenched racial views and casting doubt on whether integration would improve achievement among the most disadvantaged, impoverished pupils.[52]

Without question, however, the reformers who had rallied around Horace Mann and his allies had reason to cheer. Looking back at the era, William T. Harris, America's most prominent school administrator in the post-bellum era, believed that in less than a generation Boston had discarded "the old shell" of its largely ungraded system and "adopted a new organization better fitted for a city school system." Written examinations had been central in its transformation, but their place in Boston's schools and in the nation at large remained a work in progress.[53]

IV

Advocates of graded classrooms, soft pedagogy, the hiring of female teachers, and the appointment of a superintendent often pointed to the 1845 examination results as evidence that only wholesale reforms would end the costly and ineffective tradition-bound practices of the grammar schools. George Hillard believed that despite their unpleasant reception, the examiners' reports gave "an impulse to the public schools of Boston, as any thing which has happened for the last ten years. It was the blowing of a sharp and strong wind through them." Whether serving as mayor or councilman or on the School Committee, reformers claimed that the only way to judge the "comparative merits" of different schools, teachers, and pupils was to better classify the scholars and centralize power in the hands of a superintendent. Otherwise, as Charles Brooks and his allies repeatedly argued, no one actually knew how well the schools performed.[54]

The unsettling war of words over written examinations had nevertheless cast a pall over them. It was common knowledge that committeemen usually had neither the time nor the interest in grading tens of thousands of answers. Most committeemen were busy people who, unless they had inherited wealth, had (except for some clerics) little leisure time. Having seen Howe's head in the lion's jaw, few followed his lead.

Even friends of Howe like Hillard, who had higher political ambitions, worried about angering parents by ranking their schools low and rating their children below average. As enrollments expanded, grading the tests became daunting indeed. Superintendent Bishop helped all he could, but his responsibilities grew dramatically once the primary schools became part of his bailiwick.[55]

Few people had the stamina or desire to repeat Howe's and Brigham's experiment. The opposition had treated them so scornfully that Mann's old law school classmate and former business associate Edward G. Loring conducted the reading examination by himself in 1846. Loring had enormous faith in the power and authority of written exams, so he was a perfect volunteer. Like Howe, he favored written examinations because they revealed "facts, authentic facts, instead of uncertain, varying opinions," and the accumulation of facts, when gathered "from year to year, become reliable statistics, by which the condition, improvement, or deterioration of our schools can be ascertained and shown." Sharing Mann's faith that test scores were veritable "transcripts of the children's minds," Loring said they assured each master "his deserts of praise or censure." Loring's exam resembled Howe's and also tried to discern if pupils understood what they memorized. "The boy who knows by heart every word" of a textbook "and knows no more," Loring believed, "knows little which of itself is worth knowing." As in 1845, the pupils performed better on the rote questions. Reprinting and comparing scores from 1845, Loring claimed that the previous year's exams stimulated the masters to teach better and discipline more gently. The average cumulative score jumped to 51, an improvement of 21 percent! Such was the examiner's faith in the power of shaming teachers and in the absolute trustworthiness of statistics.[56]

Like Howe's committee, Loring provided detailed analyses of pupil responses, tables on each school's score on every question, and comparative rankings. He also remarked upon the growing diversity of pupils in different schools and wondered how to assess its influence upon achievement. Before the 1840s, poor children typically attended school for only a few years, often sporadically; some never attended at all. Those in attendance concentrated in the primary schools, while the nineteen grammar schools often had children from a higher social class. With the arrival of thousands of impoverished Irish immigrants, the situation changed. Loring said the famine Irish were a topic of "daily" conversation by the time he examined the schools. That very year, Theophilus Parsons wrote a major report on truancy and with other reformers secured legislation in 1850 that made nonattendance of idle children a crime. Though the law was largely ineffective, examiners increasingly wondered whether schools could be both excellent and more socially inclusive. The Irish were transforming neighborhoods and some grammar schools overnight, especially in east and south Boston. Editorials and articles in newspapers and magazines routinely complained about the flood of immigrants and the attendant problems of vagrancy, truancy, and crime. Feeling outnumbered, Boston's native elite condemned the children who panhandled and loafed "on wharves and in stables, spending their time in idleness, profanity, and all the modes of juvenile vice."[57]

Loring and a succession of examiners through the mid-1850s could hardly avoid noticing the new demographic patterns, and they worried about how the rising numbers of poor children would shape pedagogy and discipline. Some reformers joined sides with anti-Catholic nativists, who were growing in political power, and reminisced about their childhood days, when Boston was more homogeneous. Like everyone else, Loring recognized that class and ethnicity influenced student achievement. "The child of intelligent parents, growing up in a well ordered and instructed household, in which grammar and language are correctly used, and the subjects of daily conversation are akin to his school studies, is far better fitted for, and furthered in, those studies, than the child, whose home is darkened by the ignorance, and the mental and moral degradation of his parents; and the results of the same degree and quality of instruction at school, would be in the two children entirely different." If that was true, how could one hold teachers accountable? Loring felt stymied, lacking a statistical means to weigh out-of-school factors, which currently "cannot be stated in figures in the tables, nor accurately ascertained by the annual visit of the annual committees."[58]

Even the most outspoken advocates of written tests and teacher accountability soon realized that ranking and comparing schools was foolhardy and unfair to many masters. The wounds of 1845 had not healed, and the examiners, unable to compel anyone to take a test, allowed the masters to hand-pick pupils for some exams. In schools where the number of Irish pupils multiplied, native-born parents increasingly insisted on transfers for their children and, if refused, often pulled them from the system. In this atmosphere, examiners were more cautious in berating the worst schools and applauding the best on the basis of test scores alone. Like its recent predecessors, the 1847 reading school committee, headed by Mann's old ally, George B. Emerson, gave a comprehensive written test; but instead of ranking the schools, its report listed them in alphabetical order (with the scores provided in the tables) to help disguise the winners and losers. The committee then wrote long descriptions of each school, some very critical of the masters but also cognizant of the pupils they worked with. "In those parts of the city occupied by permanent, native residents, the materials are the best possible; in those parts occupied chiefly by foreigners, or their immediate descendants, the materials are very poor; and between these extremes, there are many varieties." Setting a "common standard" for the entire system of schools would have been whimsical. Emerson's committee also noted that the girls who were tested were older and often better students, so it made little sense to compare boys to their betters.[59]

While immigration from Ireland exploded, examining committees after 1845 continued to blast the double-headed system, endorse the hiring of a superintendent, and say more often in words than statistics that teachers, despite the varying "materials" in their classrooms, decisively shaped student achievement. At the same time, written examinations were downplayed in the summer ritual and soon were dropped completely. John Codman, a Unitarian minister, chaired the reading committee in 1848 and 1849 and did most of the work alone. Reverting to the pre-Howe and Brigham era, he did not use written exams but relied upon oral recitations. At the Smith School, he mostly discovered "noise and confusion." As one pupil tried to recite, wrote a flustered Codman, another imitated "the sound of a harmonicon or some other musical instrument" and had to be reprimanded. In his report, Codman provided his own impressions of every school visited and criticized rote teaching and uninspiring masters. Endorsing the hiring of a superintendent, he had few good words for existing methods of examining pupils, whether written or oral. The annual turnover of examiners meant each group began "without practice, without experience, without any fair standard of comparison fixed in their minds." He was nevertheless struck by the "marked inequality in the condition of the schools." Unwilling to let the masters off the hook, Codman concluded that "the varying degrees of attainment" in different schools "are hardly to be accounted for by alleging the differences of materials and situation."[60]

Following Codman's lead, a succession of examiners also relied almost exclusively on oral examinations and impressions to assess the schools. Some years the size of the examining committee ballooned, the labor divided up into teams who visited schools, heard recitations, and jotted down their observations, which a committee chair drew upon for the final report. Common written examinations disappeared, along with tables and ranked lists. In 1850, the examiners thought that the use of printed questions was "a happy and valuable process when first introduced, as a basis for calculating the percentage of correct answers." But the Committee found the method was "injudicious" since the numbers failed to explain why any school did well or poorly "with the unerring accuracy such an array of figures would apparently demonstrate." Testing every pupil, as the new rules required, was tantamount to "counting the leaves of the forest, and equally profitless."[61]

Still, no one had trouble confirming what Howe and his colleagues described statistically, that the schools and pupil achievement varied enormously. And nothing prevented them from speculating about what they saw. "Comparison of schools cannot be just," said the reading committee in 1850, "while the subjects of instruction are so differently situated as to fire-side influence, and subjected to the draw-backs inseparable from place of birth, of age, of residence, and many other adverse circumstances, all of which should be carefully weighed, in deciding upon the condition of any one school." Some pupils were still in double-headed schools; some were in shabby facilities on busy streets, others in model buildings such as the Quincy School.[62]

But committeemen, while recognizing the complexity of the issue, still put the onus on teachers. The examiners in 1851 said that "the best teachers usually succeeded in securing the most uniform *attendance* of their pupils," which led to better scores. The following year, their colleagues said that even though pupils varied considerably, if teachers "are well qualified for their office, we have invariably found, under all circumstances, the state of discipline and instruction to be good." As the examiners concluded in 1854, "it is the ability, industry, and fidelity of the teachers, which, more than all other causes combined, determine the character of a school." And the master was responsible for setting the tone and "direction" for the entire building.[63]

V

Written questions disappeared from the summer exams but not from schools, whether in Boston or in other districts. After all, written examinations already existed to some degree in towns and cities that had better groupings of pupils than ungraded schools. As urban high schools proliferated, so did the numbers of pupils taking written entrance exams, and citizens sometimes judged, rightly or wrongly, the quality of the schools below by the number of successful applicants to secondary school. As editors sent free copies of their newspapers to colleagues across the nation, more people read about Boston's experiment. Leading educators corresponded with each other and attended professional meetings that spread the gospel of testing. Nearby communities quickly found the novelty of written examinations appealing and joined the future. The *Daily Atlas* reported in the spring of 1846 that New Bedford had already adopted the "Boston" method of school examinations. Charlestown, Salem, Worcester, and other communities began testing, ranking, and comparing pupils, teachers, and schools. Some even used items from Howe's examination, concluding that their schools were superior to Boston's.[64]

At midcentury, in America's "Athens" as in other towns and cities, scores on written examinations appeared alongside oral reports and exhibitions to educate the public on how well schools fared. Written examinations became more common throughout the school year, as pupils competed in weekly, monthly, end-of-year, or promotion exams. Statistical information often clashed with impressions. Boston's subcommittees, for example, continued to issue quarterly reports that claimed that the local schools were "flourishing" even when they documented low standards, uninspired teaching, and high truancy rates. Making critical comments about one's own neighborhood school remained unpopular, and exhibitions and the annual summer festival for medal winners also retained their cachet. These time-tested activities coexisted with the new world that reformers popularized: a world of tables, ranked lists, and quantitative analyses of pupil achievement. The first major written examinations in Boston did not transform local schools overnight, but they represented a new way of thinking about education that would never disappear, even when challenged and overshadowed by traditional forms of assessment in different times and places.[65]

Reforms rarely have a straightforward effect, and those that survive usually have unintended consequences. Some reforms miss the mark or linger for a time and then disappear; others, like competitive testing, have a long, unpredictable gestation, taking decades to mature to a fuller bloom.

The adoption of various Whig-inspired innovations, for example, hardly eliminated hidebound school practices in Boston. No less a figure than John D. Philbrick, who succeeded Nathan Bishop as superintendent in 1856, was renowned for whipping pupils and even lost a celebrated court case for hitting a student. Decades later, a former student at the Quincy School recalled that Philbrick used the rattan on "frequent occasions." Neither did hiring female teachers guarantee kinder and gentler classrooms. Examiners in 1854 expressed shock that corporal punishment, apparently in decline a few years before, prevailed in some schools. The perpetrators were not gruff old bastinadoes but young women disciplining the unruly children of Erin. Rote instruction seemed common enough, too. William B. Fowle, who played no small role in the summer intrigue, concluded that "the removal of many old teachers . . . and the appointment of new ones, has not materially altered the method of instruction" or "improved the quality." A visitor to the Hancock School, a model facility with self-contained classrooms, heard pupils on command rattle off the names of English kings and queens from Egbert to Victoria, hardly an example of enlightened pedagogy but not an unusual spectacle anywhere. It remained to be seen whether an expanding world of written tests would weaken traditional pedagogy and disciplinary practices.[66]

Written examinations never supplanted other forms of assessment in antebellum cities. Yet they spread in ways no one could have imagined when Howe's and Brigham's committees launched their summer surprise. In 1849, the editor of the *Massachusetts Teacher*, well aware of the recent commotions in Boston, recognized that assessing schools by "statistical" measures had grown very popular. Skeptical that teaching and learning could be evaluated with mathematical precision, he recognized that many teachers and pupils now inhabited a new educational universe. "Any one who has perused the annual reports of our town committees," he wrote, surely noticed that evaluating committees, whose definitions of merit and standards seemed arbitrary, used old as well as new methods to assess schools. Yet "the supposed excellences, or short-comings of teachers, tried by these several standards, are paraded before the public," as school officials subjected them to "their official approval or animadversion." Teachers humiliated at seeing their names and schools rated low in reports and in local newspapers had little recourse if they felt "the lash of their official superiors," having "no means of resistance or redress." To complain about rankings sounded like an apology for poor performance.[67]

Soon other innovators discovered new uses for statistics and written tests, which proliferated after the Civil War. Up-to-date schools were unimaginable without them. Whenever awakened by their creators, the genies of testing promised all manner of school improvement.

CHAPTER 6

Chewing Pencil Tops

Professional educators in the post-Civil War era never forgot what had occurred in Boston in 1845. While Horace Mann, Samuel Gridley Howe, and their friends and enemies passed from the scene, the idea of testing children in written, competitive examinations to measure student achievement and teacher quality gained more champions and grew ever powerful. In 1800, exhibitions, recitations, and visual displays of learning were the central means to assess a school. A century later, these seemingly timeless practices had hardly disappeared, but they had lost much of their legitimacy. Except in the most backwoods districts, no one confused an exhibition with an actual examination. Parents everywhere still enjoyed seeing their loved ones on stage in a play, delivering a speech, or answering arcane questions about the lengths of rivers and the wives of Henry VIII. But Boston had catapulted written tests forward. Once adopted by school systems, they assumed many shapes and forms and would never disappear.[1]

"Since writing has entered so extensively into school exercises, examinations have largely taken the written form," was the matter-of-fact way that H. S. Jones, superintendent of the Erie, Pennsylvania, public schools, described recent trends. Tests had become so common that Jones chaired a blue-ribbon committee for the National Education Association in 1886 to study their proliferation. He and his colleagues concluded that too many urban administrators had an uncritical faith in standardized exams, which had produced a backlash. Howls of protest sounded in many cities where test scores strongly determined who was promoted, entered high school, or graduated. Marks and grades, ranked lists of scholars and teachers, and more elaborate record keeping signified a new pedagogical order that challenged centuries of tradition.[2]

Superintendent Jones and his peers recognized that the rising popularity of written tests occurred in an age of vast social changes: the transition from a world of craftsmen to factories, population movement from the countryside to the city, Civil War and a still-divided nation that schools might help unify. A rising national faith in mathematical precision undergirded everything from standard gauge railroad tracks to properly graded bushels of wheat to factory-made consumer goods. This found expression in the charts, graphs, and tables that filled ever-swelling school reports. How to draw upon the accumulating reams of statistics to improve instruction and raise standards remained controversial, but leading educators embraced the utilitarian belief that uncovering the facts of student achievement would yield the greatest good to the greatest number. There was no turning back to a world where impressions about schools sufficed.[3]

True to its origins, competitive testing remained controversial, precisely because it eroded familiar practices. Moreover, Jones's contemporaries knew that rancorous debates over testing were nothing new. As the superintendent from small-town Erie realized, the utopian faith of Boston's reformers in 1845 in the merits of testing had ignited a firestorm of criticism, anger, and dissent. "When the written examination cyclone struck Boston, over forty years ago, and the numbers of wounded and killed were presented in complicated per cent tables for the inspection of the public," Jones noted, school reformers, oddly enough, seemed overjoyed. "Horace Mann, in discussing the mortifying results, grew eloquent in praise of what he termed the 'novel mode,' and 'the new method.' To him it seemed to meet every want, real and imaginary. In fact it seemed to him 'a new education.'"[4]

That statistics continued to mesmerize many reformers and educators hardly made them universally popular. Samuel Gridley Howe was not the last elected official enamored with testing to suffer the wrath of angry parents, and school committeemen and urban administrators in post-bellum America proceeded carefully or faced the consequences. Testing would not have dramatically expanded unless enough school board members and administrators, faced with burgeoning numbers of students, recognized the benefits of the innovative ideas promoted by Mann and other antebellum reformers. The concept of the division of labor made famous by Adam Smith assumed a greater hold on the schools after midcentury. Administrators assigned pupils to classes and grades, grouping them in an ascending hierarchy from the primary level through high school. Increasingly taught by women in the lower grades, students in villages, towns, and cities encountered a cascade of written exams which, as superintendent Jones noted, depended upon greater attention to the art of writing. Access to common textbooks and mastery of the pencil and pen also ensured a wider market for competitive testing.[5]

Even though they never met everyone's grandiose expectations, the spread of written examinations was impressive. In 1888, William B. Harlow, a high school teacher in Syracuse, New York, described an increasingly familiar image. "Who of us has not been amused by the ludicrous scene which an examination room presents?" he asked in *Education*, a prominent northern journal. "Youthful faces are screwed into all sorts of hard knots; hair is made to stand on end, presumably for a free passage of ideas; heads are held together as if to prevent them from bursting." Some pupils appeared calm, others terrified, a few resigned to their fate. "Others are looking furtively around as if to discover whether the coast is clear for examining certain formulae inscribed in microscopic characters on cuffs, fingernails, and pinafores. Some are eating pencil-tops," Harlow added, "and others seem to be writing with their noses." Pupils joked that someone might invent a "marking machine." Then the examination papers could be "cast into a hopper, and passing through a series of chambers containing balances, tape-measures, yardsticks, pecks, quarts, and gills" would ultimately emerge marked, graded, and ranked. "What a savings of eyes, midnight oil, and of that patience which every teacher is supposed to possess in unlimited quantities!"[6]

By the mid-nineteenth century, teachers who had often succeeded as pupils through public displays of learning found themselves coaching their classes to do well in competitive exams, as nervous students faced a new round of tests.

I

From Boston to San Francisco and countless places in between, testing assumed significance far beyond what Horace Mann's generation of reformers could have anticipated. Since state and federal authority in education was relatively weak, America's public schools, organized and governed locally, adopted innovations through experimentation and imitation and at their own pace. In 1883, Thomas Tash, a school superintendent in Portland, Maine, believed that as far as cities were concerned "whatever is found to be good in one place is soon appropriated by others, and whatever is found harmful is gradually discarded by all." As testing spread to more districts, it became widely discussed in specialized school journals, teacher training manuals, and the proceedings of professional organizations. That hardly secured consensus on all aspects of written tests or eliminated oral examinations anywhere, especially in ungraded rural schools, which still enrolled the majority of children in 1900. Even in the countryside, however, the outstretched arms of testing extended whenever schools were large enough for broad groupings of pupils and enterprising teachers assigned more written assignments. But cities pioneered new forms of school assessment.[7]

To begin to unlock the history of testing after midcentury, consider its impact upon one person, a teacher who became a prominent educational figure, before exploring nationwide trends. In the span of a single lifetime, schools changed in some fundamental ways. Recall the fictional character invented in 1833 by the Reverend Warren Burton in New Hampshire. Mr. Spoutsound served as the prototype of a rural schoolmaster. Committeemen examined a few of his pupils through oral questions in class before the more important evening event, the public exhibition that showcased pupils whose speeches and skits entertained family and friends. For actual teachers, especially in more urbanized districts, Spoutsound's world increasingly faded from history. Exhibitions lost status while competitive examinations became common and influential.

In a reminiscence published in 1911, the educator John Swett recalled that by the 1870s "all the city schools of the United States were running wild on the subject of written examinations." Indeed, the contrast between his student days and subsequent career illuminates this transformation. Like many contemporary school leaders, Swett and his family had deep rural roots. Born in 1830 on a farm near Pittsfield, New Hampshire, Swett attended a one-room school on the outskirts "of the village, near the mill pond and cotton factory." There, he remembered, writing was the weakest part of his education. His teachers, typically male college students, expected pupils to memorize material from their textbooks, work alone solving arithmetic problems on their slates, recite when called upon, then return to silent study. "We had no nature study, no drawing, no singing, no composition writing." To learn grammar, he memorized rules and parsed sentences, "but we had no exercises in writing our mother tongue. The teachers kept no record of checks [for daily recitations] or credits. We had no written examinations."[8]

Swett's parents ran a boarding house for mill workers. In 1844 he entered Pittsfield Academy, which taught the higher branches and employed traditional pedagogy. He was assigned compositions "every other week" at the academy but lacked any guidance. Teachers assumed that if pupils mastered basic grammatical rules from a textbook, the art of writing would follow. While attending another academy, Swett taught for a few terms, ultimately teaching in West Randolph, Massachusetts, not far from Boston. Following tradition, committeemen quizzed some of his students orally at the end of the term. Aspiring to improve his pedagogical skills, Swett resigned his position and enrolled at a normal school.[9]

Like Spoutsound, this real-life son of the Granite State headed west, sailing out of Boston harbor in 1852 and landing four-and-a-half months later in California. After a less-than-profitable fling with gold mining, he passed the requisite oral examination to certify his fitness to teach in San Francisco's fledgling school system. Within a year he was a principal, with instructional as well as administrative responsibilities. By his own account, because he was "not handicapped by written examinations," he followed the customary practice of classifying pupils in groups "according to their ability or their own individual needs" and not on their age or test scores. Like most educators, he prepped pupils for oral examinations at an annual exhibition and organized traditional May Day celebrations and other festivals. And, like teachers everywhere who lacked tenure or multiyear contracts, he had to pass an oral exam annually for reappointment, which was never guaranteed since school board members doled out the positions to cronies and relatives. Thus far, Swett's experiences as a teacher and principal were hardly unusual, since both he and his pupils had to run the familiar gauntlet of oral tests. Customary means of assessment, however, were about to lose their authority.[10]

San Francisco's school board included many men who also hailed from New England. They advocated the usual innovations endorsed by northern reformers: better age-graded classrooms, uniform textbooks, women teachers for the lowest grades, and the establishment of a high school (founded as the Union Grammar School in 1856). Granted a leave of absence to visit his family and city school systems on the East Coast, Swett returned to find the schools reorganized; they were divided into primary and grammar divisions and the new high school, each level sub-dividing into grades. Imitating Boston, Philadelphia, and other cities, the school board also approved a written entrance test for high school pupils. To Swett's horror, teachers and principals now had to pass a "long and tedious written examination" to reapply for their positions. Swett thought the Board treated its employees disrespectfully, but he was a striver with a family to support, so he complied. Then his career took an unexpected turn. From 1862 to 1867 he served as the state of California school super-intendent. Returning to San Francisco, he was rehired as a principal and became deputy superintendent in 1870, second-in-command.[11]

Swett could not escape from written exams. His main responsibility during his three-year term as deputy superintendent was to prepare pro-motion tests, which students had to pass to advance from grade to grade. Like the hierarchical organization of grades, textbooks were increasingly published in graduated series, whether in reading or arithmetic, and they were the source of test items. Swett spent April and May preparing the tests while teachers drilled pupils for the ordeal. Unlike teachers prep-ping pupils for an old-time exhibition where some spouters shined, every student in San Francisco faced a promotion test. Exams were graded by hand, and Swett had the unenviable task of monitoring whether teach-ers marked them accurately, fairly, and uniformly. Little wonder that he later described his administrative labors as mind-numbing and bemoaned the baleful effects of written examinations. "The position of deputy had not proved a bed of roses. The endless preparation of sets of questions for written examinations, in which I had little faith," was "distasteful."[12]

There was simply no way, however, to advance as a teacher or admin-istrator without recognizing that written examinations now ruled the roost. While Swett's autobiography highlighted the downside of exams, he prospered in a budding profession increasingly shaped by the world of print. His mastery of prose and skills as a public speaker and administra-tor helped secure his national reputation as a thoughtful, well-published professional. His name graced the pages of prominent educational jour-nals, which advertised his books and quoted him. Swett was a living ste-reotype of a fastidious, hard-working, ambitious Yankee, who seemed to save every scrap of paper or news clipping that traced his movements and applauded his achievements. Eager to lift the status of teaching and administration, he authored numerous reports, articles, and books on the latest pedagogical trends, the long list of publications strategically placed in the opening pages of his memoir. Curiously, he left out one important contribution, published in 1872. It was among the first of its kind, its omission perhaps no mere oversight but a revealing clue about the man and his times.[13]

Questions for Written Examinations: An Aid to Candidates for Teachers' Certificates, and A Hand-Book for Examiners and Teachers was the missing title. It was more than two hundred pages long and included 2,200 questions on the basic school subjects. It also contained detailed rules on how to conduct and take written exams. As deputy superintendent, Swett was the point man for written questions with an ample supply on which to draw. Identifying his own contributions with an "S," he also reprinted hundreds of questions written by colleagues in Chicago, Cincinnati, and other eastern cities. What was happening in San Francisco obviously reflected broader trends, which his book both documented and publicized. Whatever Swett's misgivings then or later regarding competitive exams, his book placed him in the forefront of the testing movement. The volume helped fuel an emerging cottage industry of articles, reports, and books on testing, a subject that stirred endless debate. *Questions for Written Examinations,* which remained in print for decades, promised to lighten the labors of examiners and teachers and testified to the popularity of the new form of school assessment.[14]

Stepping down from his high-level post when a Democrat became superintendent, Swett, a Republican, returned to the trenches as a principal before beginning a thirteen-year tenure as head of the Girls' High School in 1876. Once again, written exams remained central to his career despite his periodic grumbling. In 1880, he complained in a book on teaching methods that "in most city schools, written examinations are carried to great extremes." Admission to the Girls' High School required passing an entrance test, and Swett protested loudly when, later in the decade, the school board admitted dozens of students who had flunked the exam. If, as he and other critics said, written tests improperly reduced learning to a numerical score, they also presumably rewarded merit, screened students, and enhanced the quality and prestige of his school. In 1893, now writing as city superintendent, Swett again railed against the tests, singling out Boston for setting a bad example for everyone.[15]

Given his extraordinary success, John Swett was hardly a typical teacher-turned-administrator. But the transit of his career, like the lives of millions of pupils and countless teachers, became inextricably bound with testing. "The old-fashioned, public, oral examination is fast going by, or rather is being separated into its component parts," an advocate of written exams announced in the *New England Journal of Education* in 1875. "The part intended to entertain the public is taken out and improved, and called an exhibition; but the part intended as a test of scholarship, is private, and written, and called an examination. 'To everything there is a season, and a time to every purpose under heaven,' saith the preacher," and while exhibitions were popular, written examinations were the only accurate way "to test what each pupil" learned.[16]

Like evangelicals predicting Christ's imminent return, some educational leaders thought the triumph of written tests was at hand.

II

Waiting for educational improvements, never mind the millennium, required patience. What distinguished an exhibition from an examination remained especially fuzzy in rural areas and villages, where some pupils were "examined" at the annual show. Oral traditions persisted despite the intrusive world of print. After midcentury, children everywhere still recited one by one or in groups, searching their memories for the names of state capitals or the answer to 12 x 12, as they once did in charity schools or still did in a multitude of one-room schools. Textbooks might rule, competitive exams multiply, but certain rituals survived. In Washington, DC, pupils marched behind their school's banner in the scorching July heat despite the adoption of written tests and promotion exams. In San Francisco as elsewhere, May Day celebrations, spelling bees, and exhibitions remained popular. Boston held its seemingly timeless summer festival, sans alcohol for the medal winners, since the teetotaling reformers of 1845, offended by the sight of inebriated youth, had corked the wine jugs.[17]

Even the most sober advocates of written tests conceded that exhibitions and festivals generated welcome publicity and financial support. In the 1860s, as testing gained ground, children in Des Moines, Iowa, as in so many places, performed on stage to raise money for the schools. According to the *Dakota Republican,* the good folks in Vermillion also opened their wallets, contributing $30 for a new building. In Prescott, Arizona and other newly settled western communities, white settlers sought the familiar in unfamiliar surroundings. The *Weekly Arizona Miner* typically noted in 1869 that parents had recently enjoyed "one of those old-fashioned pleasantries," a school exhibition. The rituals, however, lingered in a new educational landscape, where numerical scores mattered more.[18]

Traditional ways of judging schools increasingly surrendered to modern methods, especially in towns and cities. As John Swett had learned after a short trip home, change did sometimes occur almost overnight. As the San Francisco *Daily Evening Bulletin* explained in 1863, the school board "very sensibly decided that a fairer test of the progress of scholars in the various branches of education can be had by private examinations and by examinations in writing, than by one conducted in a public manner." Tests remained bound to other reforms: better-grouped classes, high schools, and more centralized, expert supervision. Every major change seemed to advance competitive testing. As northern cities converted charity schools into more inclusive public schools, open to children of all social classes (if not always to all races), written tests proliferated. Better grading meant a more uniform curriculum and reading materials and more high schools meant more entrance and diploma exams, soon followed by grade-to-grade promotion tests for many pupils. The public often judged the quality of grammar schools by their average scores on high school admission. To augment scores, principals and teachers assigned more written work and administered additional tests, which school boards often required weekly, monthly, and end-of-term. Their reputations on the line, teachers often tested more than officially allowed.[19]

Communities adopted written exams at varying rates, but enough did so that discussions about them became commonplace. Newspapers disseminated the latest knowledge about testing practices and often reported on local scores. Not long after the 1845 experiment, teachers' associations began debating the pluses and minuses of "printed questions." Teachers trying to keep up with the latest ideas attended institutes taught by superintendents or professors from the new normal schools. As early as

1848, teachers in a village in Vermont discussed "Written Answers for Printed Questions." By 1876, a contributor to the *New-England Journal of Education* listed twenty-six topics of vital interest to teachers and placed written tests on the top. Educational periodicals throughout the country reprinted questions from recent exams for pupils and teachers, who in many places had to pass written tests to earn a teaching certificate. No forward-thinking educator or citizen wanted to remain behind the times, though where all this testing would lead was anyone's guess.[20]

By the early 1870s, as deputy superintendent Swett kept his nose to the grindstone, complaints about exams accelerated, a sign of their growing influence. Superintendent William T. Harris of St. Louis concluded in 1873 that the testing craze would inevitably generate a reaction against them. Had "examination fever" infected the schools, asked some citizens? Were teachers trying to produce "walking encyclopedias"? One critic in 1874 said too many pupils equated the final exam with the "Day of Judgment" and confused high marks with being educated. "Examinations and reports are positive manias in our schools at the present time—especially written examinations," said another observer. By the 1880s, Bostonians complained about the "incessant examining" and citizens elsewhere said schools were stuck in the "rut of everlasting examinations." One flamboyant writer accused the "examination octopus" of squeezing every ounce of creativity out of teachers and pupils, who should focus on the joys of learning, not impressive report cards. By 1898, a contributor to the *Ohio Practical Farmer* believed that "examinations have about reached the chronic stage of monomania."[21]

The hyperbole notwithstanding, schools were undergoing real change, and the transition to new forms of assessment was bumpy and often unpleasant. To transform schools from ungraded to better classified institutions, urban reformers found written examinations invaluable. As in every city, children attending Cincinnati's public schools in the 1840s concentrated in the elementary grades, where pupils attended poorly graded classes taught by young, inexperienced female teachers. Late in the decade, however, reformers on the school board, usually Whigs, pressed for various interrelated improvements, including a tougher entrance test to the "central" secondary school. The school board appointed a "Committee on Printed Questions," which gave written tests to the grammar school pupils. It was the only way, said committeemen, to know what children had learned and ensure placing them in the proper grade. Emphasizing that teachers were the key to raising standards, they acknowledged that "local causes" (a euphemism for the character of neighborhood families and children) prevented schools from producing equal results. As in Boston, teachers and principals in the lowest-performing schools soon felt aggrieved as their failures were paraded before the public in tabular form, offering unflattering school-by-school comparisons.[22]

The Committee on Printed Questions did historians an unusual favor by recording the reactions of many teachers and principals. Explaining failure was on everyone's mind. Principal H. H. Edwards in the First District hated to whine, but his school suffered from high pupil turnover and truancy. One boy—James Dick—showed up for the exam after missing half of the school year. None of the First District's teachers felt qualified to teach history, and the departure of Mr. Butler, strong in math, caused pupils to flub "Simple Subtraction." Though the circumstances were beyond his control, Edwards admitted that many pupils were tested on subjects they never studied. Echoing longstanding problems, another principal said too many students dodged the exam; another felt he was being punished for promoting his best pupils to the "central" school, which depressed his overall score; still another conceded that his pupils never made it to the chapters on Asia and Africa in their geography book and, with obvious frustration, added that they did worst in English grammar even though he had drilled them "the most thoroughly. I know not how to account for this."[23]

Principal Marilla Clarke in turn complained that her best female students dropped out of school. Blaming teachers for embarrassing scores, she added that she could not "find ten girls who had studied American History; and of those who were examined, not one had been through the book we use." Another principal offered a different explanation for failure. The exam coincided with a religious holiday for German immigrants in his district, so he had trouble locating pupils. Only four took the exam on "definitions." While he collared fifteen who had studied arithmetic, "only four" had studied the whole book, "three had been to Interest, and the remainder as far as to Decimal Fractions." Clearly, reformers seeking higher, uniform standards had their work cut out for them. Each school seemed autonomous, a world unto itself.[24]

In the early 1850s, in a pattern repeated countless times in countless places, Cincinnati's administrators labored to increase academic quality through regular personal visits, the purchase of uniform textbooks and apparatus including globes and blackboards, and the adoption of more written tests, including in the primary grades. Superintendent Nathan Guilford made principals require more written assignments. He and his successors spent hundreds of hours visiting classrooms and testing pupils, and the opening of two high schools in 1852 deepened the spirit of emulation encouraged by reformers. H. H. Barney, the principal of Hughes High School, linked rigorous entrance tests with rising quality in the grades below. "We hazard nothing," he wrote in 1853, "when we say that a child learns now, especially in the two highest departments [of the grammar grades], more than twice as much as he would learn if the hope of promotion to the High Schools did not exist to stimulate him and his Teachers to the utmost exertions." High school advocates everywhere made similar claims. While critics rightly complained that only a few ambitious (usually middle-class) pupils aspired to high school, defenders rightly retorted that rigorous entrance tests raised the standards for everyone in grammar school.[25]

In 1854, Andrew J. Rickoff, who rose up through the system, was promoted to the superintendency and built upon the work of his predecessors. While sharing Mann's hope that the desire to excel was intrinsic, he accepted reality, recognizing that "few, very few, of the pupils of our public or private schools study for the love of it." Like their elders, pupils sought tangible rewards for doing well: high grades, prizes, and diplomas. Working closely with allies on the board of education, Rickoff instituted better record keeping and more tests. In 1856, board president Rufus King noted that "printed examinations have been much more in use of late as a means of obtaining an accurate test of scholarship of the different schools." Criticized by teachers and the parents of failing students, he challenged them to prove that oral assessments were superior to written exams. In an environment promoting improvement, Rickoff sought to make the grades more distinctive and by 1857 had implemented promotion exams for all of them.[26]

Like chief administrators elsewhere, Rickoff wrote the annual promotion questions. Like his peers, he tried to make schools more uniform by devising timetables and standard procedures for taking and evaluating written exams. He read Mann's essays and reports and the news coming out of Boston and other cities. Rickoff similarly applauded the utility of written tests, which promoted a more coherent curriculum, and he dreamed of devising exams that pinpointed the most effective teaching methods, which would yield the highest scores. Cincinnati's schools were soon awash in written tests. In addition to annual promotion tests, the board of education mandated quarterly exams and some principals and teachers required many more.[27]

Implementing dramatic changes very quickly, superintendent Rickoff, long remembered for his iron will, wore out his welcome in Cincinnati after only a few years, especially among teachers and principals, who were held accountable for what pupils learned, spelled out in black-and-white for everyone to see.[28]

III

What happened in John Swett's San Francisco and in Andrew Rickoff's Cincinnati mirrored changes occurring across America's cities. In 1855, the nation's capital adopted the new-style exams. As the *Daily National Intelligencer* reported, pupils spent an entire day answering questions "in writing to printed questions, unaided by books, teachers, or communication with each other. This mode of examination . . . much in use elsewhere . . . furnishes a rather severe though nearly correct test of the extent and accuracy of the pupils' acquaintance with their school studies, their ability to express their ideas with a proper regard to construction of sentences, the use of capitals and marks of punctuation." This was the first time local pupils competed in such an exam, and there were more to come. Whenever systems grouped enough pupils, competitive testing, like seeds finding suitable ground, took hold. Using another metaphor, one educator noted in the Spring of 1881 that "the annual torture of the final 'examination' for promotion, graduation, and general standing" now existed "all the way across the continent," suffered by "myriads of children, in all sorts of schools."[29]

Always the trendsetters, the larger cities, facing the most rapid changes soonest, set the pace, though they were never perfectly imitated since reforms always had to adapt to local circumstances. Not surprisingly, Boston often remained in the national spotlight, its relationship with written tests ever colored by the bruising battles of 1845. Recall that common written examinations for the first class of grammar school pupils disappeared there by the late 1840s. Written admission tests for the various secondary schools, however, continued, controlled not by a central office but by the individual institutions. Applicants to the Girls' High and Normal School in 1852 faced ninety printed questions. The *Daily Atlas* informed its readers that the examinees answered "in writing, and each candidate was separately examined in reading." While Mann's allies had successfully abolished the double-headed system, built more age-graded grammar schools, and hired a superintendent, two more decades passed before Bostonians entertained reviving centrally administered common tests. Old wounds healed slowly.[30]

Compared to some peers elsewhere, the authority of Boston's superintendent was fairly weak. The School Committee hired and fired employees, nepotism was rampant, and the grammar masters remained powerful. The masters still controlled admission to their schools and eligibility for the next level of entrance tests. Critics still accused them of retaining older students to enhance their school's reputation and ensure the highest scores possible on admission exams. The superintendent visited and "inspected" the schools but did not examine them. The absence of centralized control did not mean a ban on written tests, which were growing in importance. In 1860, the School Committee noticed that "examinations have more frequently than heretofore been conducted by means of written or printed questions." Cautioning against interpreting scores as an "exact measurement" of what children learned, the committeemen, like their counterparts in many cities, nevertheless endorsed written exams in no uncertain terms.[31]

Boston's primary schools, mostly one-room and long governed by a separate board, came under the control of the School Committee in 1855. Appointed superintendent a year later, John D. Philbrick, the former master of the well-graded Quincy grammar school, initiated several changes that promoted more tests. By 1862, Philbrick had converted all but thirty-two of the two hundred and fifty primaries into "graded" facilities. Every class enrolled children of different ages, but the average increased as one ascended the graded ladder. Imitating the reforms instituted in the grammar schools, Philbrick ensured that primary classrooms had one teacher (usually a woman) per room and single desks. In addition, Philbrick persuaded the School Committee to provide young children with slates to upgrade their writing skills. He was proud of these achievements. By the time they faced the grammar school entrance exam, he argued, children "were taught to write on their slates a fair, bold hand, a better hand" than ever before.[32]

Given the anger generated in 1845, Philbrick was surprised to see how popular written tests had become. Certainly the decision to end centrally administered tests contributed to a more harmonious atmosphere in the 1850s and 1860s. As superintendent, Philbrick noticed that a "high pressure" system of testing nevertheless flourished, especially above the primary schools. This resulted less from edicts from his office than a gradual appreciation among principals and teachers for the value of timed, competitive exams. It was becoming impossible to imagine modern urban schools without them. Moreover, grammar masters still loved to brag about how many of their pupils passed high school entrance tests, and grading the primary schools and improving writing instruction opened the door to more competitive behavior.[33]

Philbrick regarded written exams as valuable but did not see them as a panacea. And on some issues, especially testing, it was best to tread lightly. Philbrick knew first hand that some grammar masters were prickly characters, so he often made suggestions, not demands, given his limited authority. In 1867, he suggested spending less time recording marks for daily recitations. Endorsing a practice already underway in some schools, initiated by the masters themselves, he favored "a series of *examinations* at regular and not very distant intervals" including monthly and end-of-term. A decade later, as committeemen debated ticklish problems associated with testing, Philbrick explained that "it is difficult to conceive how to manage a system of schools, without any regard to rank and distinction, based on intellectual attainments; for there must be examinations, at least for the purposes of classification and promotion; and the examination determines the rank, the rank necessitates discrimination, and distinction, in some form, follows inevitably."[34]

No one, including Philbrick, wanted to resurrect the hard feelings of the 1840s, but the spread of testing and passage of time enabled the School Committee to explore making assessment more effective and systematic. In 1876, it established a Board of Supervisors—full-time examiners—which led to a dramatic increase in testing. Offended by a further erosion of his power, Philbrick clashed with the group. But the supervisors strengthened the testing culture. They tested prospective teachers and gave grammar and secondary pupils exams for diplomas. In 1883, they established the first common entrance exam for the grammar schools.[35]

Most cities did not create a formal Board of Supervisors. Boards of education typically placed the superintendent in charge of testing programs. In large cities, the superintendent often delegated the work to subordinates such as the deputy superintendents in San Francisco, which in a short-lived experiment appointed two full-time inspectors in the 1880s. Whatever the local arrangement, the division of labor reflected in graded classrooms thus found expression in school administration. Testing teachers and pupils became more onerous as student populations soared along with demands for accountability in a society where nepotism honeycombed all levels of government, all the way to the Potomac. No one looked to the federal government for ethical guidance, and the U.S. Bureau of Education was ineffective and weak. So testing spread from city to city, starting on the East Coast, then traveling near and far.[36]

In the 1850s and 1860s, for example, Chicago joined the larger national effort to build modern public schools. During the tenure of superintendent William Harvey Wells (1856–1864), Chicago became well known in national educational circles. Like many reformers, Wells was of New England stock, born on a Connecticut farm in 1812. Reminiscent of John Swett, he was educated at a variety of institutions: district school, academy, and teachers' seminary. Wells became a normal school principal in Massachusetts before heading west, where he grew prominent as a system builder. A friend remembered that soon after arriving in Chicago, Wells "set in motion, in a prompt and intelligent way, machinery containing all the essential elements of a perfect school-system. The schools were graded. The high school, as an inspirer and a goal for pupils in all the grades below, was firmly and permanently established. The normal school began to turn out a picked class of teachers." Another admirer concluded that "as Augustus found Rome brick and left it marble, so Mr. Wells found Chicago in chaos and left it in order, school-wise."[37]

The author of well-regarded textbooks on English grammar, Wells gained renown for *The Graded School*, published in 1862. Lengthy and widely distributed, it served as a how-to guide on what and how to teach in each grade, and how to test, too. Drawing upon "the best elements of the different systems adopted in Boston, New York, Philadelphia, Cincinnati, St. Louis, and other cities," Wells emphasized the importance of written examinations, "among the most successful means that can be employed for securing thoroughness and accuracy of scholarship. They afford a reliable test of the pupil's knowledge of a subject, cultivate habits of freedom and accuracy in the use of language, and afford a valuable discipline to the mind, by throwing the pupil entirely upon his own resources." To succeed, even the youngest pupils had to hone their writing skills through regular practice on slates and blackboards. Quoting Andrew J. Rickoff, he called for better record keeping and statistics and, following the example of other cities, implemented annual promotion exams and more written assignments. Like many superintendents, he was fascinated with numbers and wished someone would invent superior tools to measure intellectual development.[38]

Wells regretted that "we have no means of measuring and recording from day to day the successive steps of mental growth. Heat and cold, the lapse of time, the speed of lightning, are made tangible, and measured with ease and exactness." But schools lacked anything as sophisticated as a thermometer to measure learning. Judging school effectiveness was still so much guesswork, leaving written tests as the best and most impartial means of assessment. As superintendent, Wells used graded classrooms and tests to centralize authority and impose more uniform practices upon Chicago's schools. Still, attaining the precision in measurement of contemporaries associated with industry seemed unlikely anytime soon. Wells resigned his post and became an insurance executive, where statistics also documented vital trends.[39]

Numerous towns and cities in the old Northwest Territory and high plains adopted written tests with alacrity. Boosters in the larger towns and cities in Ohio, Indiana, and Wisconsin did not want their communities to become backwaters. Late in the spring of 1866, the *Daily Cleveland Herald* reported that the local superintendent was preparing "thirty-four different sets of printed questions" for the annual written examinations, including thirteen for the high school. That same year, superintendent Abram C. Shortridge, working with Republicans on the Indianapolis school board, implemented a range of written examinations to shore up standards and strengthen the high school. The board favored written over oral tests and approved annual promotion exams. "Questions based upon the studies pursued in each grade were prepared by the Superintendent," wrote the Committee of School Visitors in 1866, "and printed copies furnished the teachers." Pupils were separated to prevent cheating, and no questions were allowed "until written answers were returned. Their answers were examined by the teacher and School Visitors, and their correctness and incorrectness determined the relative rank of each scholar."[40]

In west central Illinois, the *Quincy Whig* took pride in the evolution of the local school system. In the middle of June in 1874 it announced that "all the boys and girls who aspire to a seat in the Grammar school will have a chance to show what they know by being on hand at 9 o'clock in their respective district schools. The written examination will commence at that hour and all who are on hand and make the required percentage will have the pleasure of handling the certificate that will admit them to the coveted seat." Small-town boosters and city superintendents alike regarded the new mode of testing as a sign of progress. As rural children poured into villages and cities, they left behind small, ungraded schools for something new.[41]

In Omaha, Nebraska, superintendent A. F. Nightingale's pressing task in the 1870s was to better classify the students. So he gave oral examinations to the younger pupils, who had little experience holding a pencil, and written examinations to the older pupils, to determine grade placement. The transition to graded schools was complicated. "The examinations," he wrote in 1873, "did not meet my expectations." Many of the children showed "manifest nervousness and fright," which hurt their performance, while most of the principals, teachers, and pupils in the new system were "unacquainted with each other. Children, on the first day of the term, flocked to school by fifties and hundreds; many from private schools, where they were ungraded; many from public schools; and many still who had not been to school for years." In a lament heard elsewhere, Nightingale met resistance from parents who thought better of their children's achievements than test scores indicated. "The time may never come when parents will believe that other people's children are almost as bright as theirs," but he firmly believed that "one set of examination papers" provided "more reliable information concerning the real condition of a school, and the real character of instruction given, than could be gained by personal visitation for an entire month." Teachers denied this, parents and students balked, but Nightingale pressed ahead—before seeking better professional opportunities in Chicago. Promotion exams and related reforms survived his swift departure.[42]

Sixteen hundred and fifty miles away, school leaders in Portland, Oregon, also used tests to smooth the always-difficult transition from ungraded to graded schools. The very first annual report of the city schools, issued by superintendent S. W. King in 1874, explained the importance of systematic recordkeeping and highlighted the percentage of pupils promoted in the primary, intermediate, and grammar departments. While still perfecting his examination system, he emphasized that "the importance" of written tests "is too well established to need any comment in favor of their continuation." Pupils who failed the promotion examination "had not performed the work required" and should try again. As a fellow reformer remarked, before the adoption of these tests, each school functioned "like so many separate units or 'feudal baronies,'" and the grades "were in a decidedly nebulous state." Superintendent King thought a healthy competition among teachers and pupils produced academic excellence. "System, order, dispatch, and promptness have characterized the examinations," he wrote in 1877. "Next to a New England climate, these examinations necessitate industry, foster promptness, and encourage pupils to do the right thing *at the right time*."[43]

Public schools were often associated with Yankee culture, but tests penetrated every region. Cities in the border states and Deep South also adopted written examinations after the Civil War. In Memphis, superintendent W. Z. Mitchell praised teachers aspiring to higher professional status; in the late 1860s, he noticed several of them were reading Wells's *Graded School,* an improvement on the behavior of those caught reading novels or "knitting or sewing" as children recited their lessons. Mitchell endorsed graded schools and written promotion exams, which were soon required of the more than two thousand children in the system. As the president of the school board, J. T. Leath, explained in 1869, pupils faced a mix of oral and written exams, the latter "less superficial and more searching than public examinations. They often bring tears to the eyes of the sensitive pupil." Progress obviously came at a price. No doubt tears also flowed in Louisville, Baltimore, and other places as competitive examinations gained credibility. One observer noted that Nashville shared in the era's "mania" for tests, required "in writing from the time the children learn how to write."[44]

During Reconstruction, Little Rock implemented written exams for pupils and prospective teachers. As the *Morning Republican* explained in 1871, written examinations were now used in "the best schools in the country." Within a year, the *Arkansas Gazette* reported that pupils faced all-day tests once a month in every class above the fifth grade. The low scorers might be held back, while the highest achievers had their names published in local newspapers. New Orleans, with a strong concentration of transplanted Yankees, worked diligently to bring northern reforms to their new home, adding the usual written tests to supplement the ubiquitous daily recitations. The rise of Jim Crow ensured that every aspect of education was racially determined. Monthly written examinations were adopted in the white schools in Columbus, Georgia, and other small cities throughout the region. Underfunded schools for African-Americans became the norm, despite heroic efforts by ex-slaves to expand educational opportunities.[45]

Atlanta also advanced a well-developed, albeit racially segregated, system for testing pupils and teachers. As in other cities, the school board set the minimum score for admission to the white high school. In 1874 it was set at 75 percent both in English grammar and arithmetic. The following year, superintendent Bernard Mallon reported that oral and written examinations were common throughout the system and included monthly competitions. Reflecting a broader trend toward better record-keeping and accountability, Atlanta issued report cards to keep parents informed of their children's progress. By the summer of 1881, competitive testing was so routine that the *Atlanta Constitution* simply mentioned that "the usual written" examinations were underway.[46]

As exhibitions and displays lost their salience, school officials and administrators developed detailed rules and regulations on testing, which teachers and pupils were expected to embrace and, most importantly, honor.

IV

When Samuel Gridley Howe, William Brigham, and their colleagues examined the reading and writing schools in 1845, they worked behind the scenes to reach some agreement on how to proceed while setting norms and procedures. The pupils faced the same questions and time restrictions and were told to work alone, without books; the examiners identified correct answers and tried to mark them consistently. Howe and his colleagues issued lengthy reports on the process, after the fact; they did not say so, but they likely drew upon the basic, similar rules governing high school entrance tests, first written in Boston in the 1820s and developed by one of their allies, George B. Emerson. By the 1840s, Howe and Mann, like colleague William Brigham active in the local statistical society, also had the benefit of wide reading on examinations and relevant knowledge from Europe.[47]

As written tests became more common, school boards everywhere typically approved the rules and regulations and printed them, and examiners were enjoined to follow them. Administrators who read reports from Boston and other cities afterwards drew upon a growing body of knowledge about how to write, conduct, and interpret written tests. The customary practices at exhibitions were insufficient; written tests involved everyone—not a few hand-picked students—and some tests such as promotion exams, which were common by the 1870s, had high stakes. Failing them could mean repeating a grade. Professional literature and the annual reports of urban districts increasingly underscored the differences between exhibitions and examinations and explained why the latter were a superior and "impartial" way to assess achievement. As the editor of *The Teacher, and Western Educational Magazine* in St. Louis claimed in 1853, "the time has gone by, when an exhibition will be taken for an examination, or what was specially prepared for the occasion, as an evidence of intellectual attainments." As towns and cities abandoned one-room schools modeled on the countryside and buildings with long halls used by charity schools, their replacement with more age-graded facilities, with one teacher per room, allowed more school-to-school and grade-to-grade comparisons.[48]

Urban school boards usually created standing committees on student classification and promotion whose responsibilities included hearing appeals from disgruntled parents or teachers. Once superintendents were hired, committeemen approved passing grades for promotion but preferred leaving the daily operations of tests and grading to the central office, which regularly complained that it was understaffed. Teachers set their own grading standards for the accelerating number of regular tests in their classrooms, many mandated by their superiors, others added as examination day drew near.

In 1858, superintendent Rickoff outlined the testing policies emanating from his office in Cincinnati. He prepared the annual promotion tests for every grade and had them printed, placed in "sealed envelopes," and sent to the various principals, who were instructed to begin and end on time. A few wrinkles had to be ironed out. "In some schools," Rickoff discovered, rules were not honored "as faithfully as it was desirable they should have been, on account perhaps of the novelty of the plan." To compensate, he prepared "quarterly examinations" to confirm the overall results on the annual test. "The classes were in this way thoroughly sifted, and . . . the standard established by the Board . . . quite stringently applied to every class within the city." The principals agreed upon a "specific standard" and graded the answers accordingly. Rickoff emphasized that the process allowed "little or no margin for differences in the marking." In other words, the exam consisted of short, rote-oriented questions.[49]

Glimpses of how tests worked in theory and practice appeared periodically in official reports. In 1869, Chicago superintendent J. L. Pickard described the rules in detail; it is impossible to know if they were followed to the letter. Pickard prepared the exams and wanted them to be fair. Here are the basic rules for one test. Pupils should begin at 9:25 sharp and end two hours later. On the top of the answer sheet, they should write down the grade and their name and their teacher's. Each pupil should receive "two sheets of paper" plus the printed questions, with "nothing else allowed upon the desk, or about the desk, except a slate, slate-pencil, and pen." Pupils should work out answers on their slates, then copy them neatly on the answer sheets. "No books nor helps of any kind allowed on the desks, and none to be used during the examination. All communication to be avoided. Pupils to receive no information from teachers, or others, respecting any of the questions." Students should also show the "steps" in solving math problems, thus minimizing cheating and guessing.[50]

Knowing that exams made pupils and teachers anxious, schoolmen sometimes offered tips on how to succeed and to lower stress. A normal school professor in Indiana urged prospective teachers to make a good appearance; examiners would notice if they were unkempt, dressed "foppishly," or had too much "'real estate' . . . under the finger nails." Avoid "twirling your hair with your fingers, drumming on the table," and other irritating behaviors. More advice: do not arrive late, do not cram, but do write clearly, use time effectively, and "keep cool. If you get excited you cannot tell half you know." Such advice flowed generously to teachers and pupils alike. John Swett's how-to book on written examinations also told test-takers that, when stumped by a question, skip it and return to it later. Other educators reminded pupils not to write outside the lines on ruled paper. In 1872, superintendent Pickard sent the following note to pupils facing a high school entrance test: "Let your answers be models of accuracy and neatness, remembering how much pleasure a well written page may give your examiner, and that good penmanship makes bad spelling appear more unsightly." He signed it "Very Truly Your Friend."[51]

Did any of these efforts calm racing hearts, eliminate sweaty palms, or improve one's score?

There is always slippage between rules and behavior, and testing was no different. Ignoring the rules, students would raise their hands and examiners would try to clarify an ambiguous question. Despite injunctions against cheating, teachers reminded scholars that to err was human but unacceptable. Pupils sometimes cheated, especially in high-pressure exercises, even if teachers separated pupils as required and the basic rules on honesty became common knowledge. In 1879, the *Cincinnati Daily Gazette* printed a student's poem:

> The rules of examination are,
> That no student can bring with him or her
> Any book, and that none through word or sign
> Shall with any neighbor at all confer. . . .[52]

While pupils had to face the music, John Swett was not the only adult to recoil from the tedium of testing. One of his successors as deputy superintendent in San Francisco, Joseph O'Connor, concluded in 1883 that he had had enough. "Any person possessing even a slight appreciation of the wear and tear of mental strain," he said, "must see that the labor of conducting the usual annual written examinations is something fearful." Students "sit scarcely a foot apart, each one eagerly hoping to obtain the required percentage. The teacher, by a cat-like vigilance, is required to enforce honesty upon fifty or sixty persons whose undeveloped judgement often recognizes the advantage in the opposite course. Then commences the work of poring over quire upon quire of nervously written answers which, when deciphered, reflect lines of thought just as different from those of the examiner, as the reasoning and motives of the child are from those of the adult." O'Connor seemed happy to resign.[53]

The work involved in writing, distributing, monitoring, grading, and interpreting written scores was staggering. In one eight-month stretch in New York City in the early 1860s, assistant superintendent Henry Kiddle visited over one hundred grammar schools, listening to thousands of pupils recite their lessons. And then there was all the grading. The annual exams and ranking of schools angered so many teachers and principals in 1868 that the central office held several day-long meetings to allow dissidents to let off steam. Kiddle and the other chief administrators defended the system, but the spiraling increase of students made supervision and examinations difficult. In Milwaukee, a much smaller city, the superintendent already had two hundred classes to examine by 1872. The rules on promotion, written years earlier, required the superintendent to administer and grade all of the annual exams. Joshua Stark, the chair of the Committee on Rules and Regulations, noted in 1874 that the city had twenty schools and enrolled around eight thousand pupils. "A moment's reflection must convince anyone," he thought, "that this system [of examinations] has become impracticable. It may have been possible, when there were but six or seven public schools in the city, and the whole number of pupils in attendance did not exceed two or three thousand, for one person to perform this labor." That now seemed impossible. Unless the principals started evaluating them, the number of tests would have to shrink, undermining the graded system.[54]

That Stark believed that a busy administrator could drop everything and grade two to three thousand exams—even short-answers—shows that the testing tiger already had very sharp claws. In city after city, superintendents, their assistants, principals, and teachers confronted an escalating number of exams. High school entrance tests alone produced many sore eyes and backs, and they were only one of the many competitions. Secondary schools often gave monthly, end-of-term, and diploma exams. At the all-day exit test at Louisville's Male High School in 1863, each pupil generated between eleven and thirty pages of foolscap, keeping teachers busy and students anxious for weeks before and after the event. "If a pupil gets a low grade he knows it is not guess work, it means something," said one observer, and "if he gets a high grade, he knows that . . . he really has merit." Tests, said many educators, helped guarantee strong standards. To raise academic quality at San Francisco's high schools in the early 1870s, deputy superintendent Swett prepared a three-day exam for the top grammar grades. The high school teachers did the grading: a mere ten thousand answer sheets, which Swett double-checked.[55]

Elsewhere on the West Coast, the Portland *Oregonian* gave a clear account of the labor consumed in testing. In 1875, superintendent S. W. King worked long hours on the annual exam. "The questions, consisting of 31 different sets and covering 100 pages of closely written foolscap, and 25 pages of letter paper, were carefully prepared by the superintendent a month before the examination." King and the principals agreed on the usual protocols, and teachers evaluated the answers. As in most cities, teachers were not allowed to grade their own pupils' high-stakes tests, and the superintendent and his staff reviewed their work. Exams aimed to hold every teacher accountable and verify that every pupil stood "on his own merits." In 1877, on the other side of the nation, Portsmouth High School in New Hampshire received kudos from the *New England Journal of Education* for its academic quality. At Portsmouth High "none but good scholars can stand high. Few are aware how much work . . . written examinations make for the teachers, but they are faithfully carried through, month after month, and with the best results." A handful of supervisors in Boston anticipated marking twelve to fifteen thousand examinations in the summer of 1882. A year later, the local superintendent visited every primary school three times, and the supervisors again had their hands full preparing and marking a variety of entrance and exit exams. No wonder that complaints about "incessant" and "perpetual" testing were heard locally as well as nationwide.[56]

One school periodical concluded in 1883 that "the marking of examination papers is the teachers' treadmill. It is drudgery. It is slavery." Marking exams was the least of it. Since the first recording of high school admission scores in the 1820s, teachers endured public humiliation, since the results often appeared in local newspapers. As in 1845, leading educators believed that tests measured teacher quality as well as pupil performance. Given the absence of appropriate statistical tools, no one could pinpoint the exact influence of teachers upon achievement. That mattered not. Superintendents often ranked schools by average entrance scores, and newspapers sometimes printed every pupil's name and scores on major tests down to the first decimal point. The *Chicago Tribune* regularly published this information. Chicago also had a unique custom: the principal whose school scored highest bought peers a crate of oranges, the lowest, "a convenient measure of peanuts."[57]

In 1873, Cincinnati's Committee on Examinations ranked the schools and teachers alike. Miss Julia Kellogg, top-ranked and at a highly ranked school, must have beamed when her pupils averaged 83 percent. But, in the lowest-performing school, Miss Melissa Sprague's pupils sat on the bottom, scoring 35 percent. She was repeatedly named the worst teacher. "It is certain," the committee added, "that where the average in a room is down to thirty-five, the pupils are receiving no good. Is it not certain that they are receiving positive harm?" Reminiscent of Samuel Gridley Howe's nasty comments on particular masters decades earlier, the no-holds-barred practices were mitigated whenever citizens condemned such cruelties, and printing names and scores became less common by the 1880s. As children learned after receiving a score or report card, the numbers seemed etched in stone, never wished away. In 1869, John S. Hart, who gained national attention for creating well-regarded admission tests as principal of Philadelphia's Central High School, noted that the most eloquent spoken words disappeared unless preserved for posterity. "But the written word remains."[58]

While school officials and administrators worked out the rules, teachers prepped their students, who soon decided whether to dodge the test, evade the rules, or prepare for the ordeal.

V

There was no shortage of spoken or printed words in America's public schools. Oral recitations—whether one by one or in sing-song fashion—still helped classroom teachers assess pupil progress, and textbooks remained everyone's constant companion. But the expansion of testing rested upon a revolution in the teaching of writing, which was closely tied to the better grouping of pupils. Previously taught as a separate subject, writing was now taught across the curriculum.

"There has been no change in school training in the past thirty years more marked or general than the use of written exercises," Cincinnati's superintendent, Emerson E. White, observed in 1886. "This change has occurred not only in the higher grades, but even more notably in elementary schools. Pupils are now very generally taught to write from the beginning of the school course, several years earlier than was formerly permitted; and the skill in writing, thus early acquired, is utilized in many ways." Educators regularly chided students for sloppy penmanship, but writing had become "an important means in nearly all school work." Slates and pencils were basic to every grade, "and their use is required not only in the work and study of pupils in their seats, but also in class exercises." Graded-school teachers routinely had pupils write out lessons on slates and, whenever possible, on paper. The "amount of written work" grew dramatically.[59]

John Swett also marveled at this pedagogical transformation. Before the Civil War, writing was closely linked with preparation for the learned professions or commerce, mostly dominated by men. When writing entered the school curriculum, it was usually taught as a separate subject and by means of copy books that presented models for pupils to imitate. As Swett explained, copy books declined after midcentury as writing lessons expanded in every subject. Like most people of his generation, Swett had learned to spell the old-fashioned way: by memorizing lists of words. While some rural schools still used copy books late in the century, even there spelling was often taught in a new way. Pupils increasingly learned to spell by writing words on blackboards, slates, and paper and using them in written assignments. Teachers made pupils write compositions and letters on familiar topics such as a trip to the seaside. Swett was impressed by the spread of "written exercises and written examinations, the written work in elementary science, in history, in geography, and in letter-writing," and the overall attention paid to the written word.[60]

In the 1850s and 1860s, superintendents often pressured committeemen to furnish schools with more blackboards, slates, pencils, and paper. Pens became more common later in the century. Superintendent Rickoff said Cincinnati's teachers initially resisted the adoption of slates; but soon children were composing short sentences as well as solving math problems on them. By 1858, with annual tests in full force, slate exercises became popular among the staff. Teachers dictated spelling words and asked questions in other subjects that required written answers. In Cincinnati, New York, and other cities, manuals of instruction mandated slate work in every grade. In 1875, one of Rickoff's successors, John Hancock, gave a test that assessed "slate writing." He averaged the scores for every school and ranked them from "moderate" (5 percent) to "excellent" (2 percent). The spread resembled what statisticians later called a bell curve.[61]

Urban districts everywhere increased and dramatically altered writing instruction. The change moved an amateur poet to write:

> Learned sages may reason, the fluent may talk,
> But they ne'er can compute what we owe to the chalk. . . .
> Go, enter the school-room of primary grade,
> And see how conspicuous the blackboard is made.
> The teacher makes letters and calls them by name,
> And says to the children, 'Now you do the same,'
> Mere infants, you see, scarcely able to walk,
> But none are too feeble to handle the chalk.[62]

A woman visiting Boston's schools in 1881 was amazed at the change. "When I was a girl," she remembered, "we had writing-books, pen, and ink given to us, with instructions to 'write,' and we imitated the copy laboriously. Sometimes the teacher would look over our shoulders and say, in a rather neutral manner, that our pen-holding wasn't quite right, but she neither offered to correct it nor seemed to attach much importance to the subject, and so we toiled on as best we might." Many commentators noticed that young children and rural transfers struggled most learning to hold a pencil, pen, or chalk properly and to write at the proper slant. Slates and blackboards existed in schools before midcentury but now came into general use, as classroom photographs demonstrate. Boston, without any graded primary schools in 1855, had slates in many of them by 1864. Twenty years later, superintendent Edwin P. Seaver told the *Boston Morning Journal* that children in the lower grades routinely wrote compositions, an impressive change.[63]

Visitors to schools in many cities often commented on the spread of writing assignments. Whether responding to printed questions or those on a blackboard, children seemed to be continually writing down answers. A former teacher in New York City's charity schools, where slates were not uncommon, was astounded to see their more extensive use in primary schools by 1860. Faced with an annual examination, the older pupils especially were now "required to write words correctly," which meant more written spelling lessons. By 1875, Atlanta implemented "written examinations, copying, dictation exercises, and compositions, so that every scholar has had at least one written exercise each day besides the daily drill in penmanship." In 1883, a Chicagoan said children spent considerable time "filling [a] slate with words only to erase them and fill it again—that modern combination of pillory and thumb screw."[64]

Throughout history, most schools had emphasized recitations—oral responses by pupils to questions posed by teachers or examiners—but the enhanced importance of writing made a familiar word lose its traditional meaning. By the 1880s, guides on teaching and testing described a new phenomenon: "written recitations," a neologism indicating a notable change. Increasingly, teachers who asked pupils questions expected written, not oral responses, in effect turning "so-called recitations" into yet another competitive test. By 1899, James M. Greenwood, the superintendent in Kansas City, Missouri, estimated that half of the recitations and question-and-answer periods at school generated written work, yielding more paper to mark and grades to record. Greenwood believed "the written work affords better opportunity for the teacher to reach and criticize the work of every one."[65]

Greater awareness of the mutual dependence of writing, graded classes, and testing seeped into student doggerel and poems that were often widely reprinted. In 1883 the *Idaho Avalanche*, published in Silver City, described the stress a pupil experienced at a spelling exam as a graded-school teacher dictated the words.

> How the victim's bosom swells
> With a desperate desire
> To be higher—one grade higher—
> And with resolute endeavor
> To be perfect now and ever
> He spells, spells, spells
> With his pen or pencil spells.
> Disaster could strike
> If he spells the word believe
> As he would the word receive
> Or if he puts too many l's
> In the simple word propels
> It may mean another year
> In the grade he hopes to clear.[66]

Testing was part of a larger transformation of the school, which included a changing sensory and perceptual experience for teachers and pupils.

The noise and dust associated with slates abated as schools purchased more pencils, paper, and pens. Annoying scratching sounds on slates gave way to spilled ink bottles and the sound of pencils, engraved with teeth marks and chewed up tops, perpetually dropping on the floor or needing a sharpened point. Moreover, the shift from oral to written examinations involved a novel way of thinking and understanding on the part of students. "To read a printed question so as to understand it and think out the answer, is a very different thing from receiving the same question from the teacher's lips," superintendent Seaver of Boston sensitively explained in 1884. In an oral exam, if a student was confused, a teacher could use "emphasis, inflection, and repetition" to help the child, but printed words and figures sat silently on a page. A pupil able to solve a particular arithmetic problem in class might freeze on the same item in a timed, competitive test. Tests were "impartial" but adapting to them was not always easy. And teachers, always identified by superiors as the key to academic success, told their pupils that learning was intrinsically good though everyone's eyes, including their own, were inevitably drawn to marks and percentiles.[67]

In 1892, an amateur poet tried to portray the everyday world of "The Modern School Teacher." The teacher "sat alone" on a Saturday night, in Boston, appropriately enough, grading papers. "She averaged this and she averaged that/Of all her class was doing." She computed percentages and fell asleep, dreaming she had died. A gravedigger named Pat exhumed her skull and found it "lined with figures." A postmortem confirmed the obvious. "'Just as I thought,'" said a "young M.D."

> "How easy it is to tell 'em!"
> Statistics ossified, every fold
> "Of cerebrum and cerebellum."
> "It's a great curiosity, sure," said Pat.
> "By the bones you can tell the creature!"
> "Oh, nothing strange," said the doctor,
> "That was a nineteenth-century teacher."[68]

By the 1870s and 1880s, competitive testing proliferated in America's urban school systems, changing them in fundamental ways, but then as now its power was neither absolute nor unchallenged.

CHAPTER 7

The Culture of Testing

As competitive testing spread after the Civil War, Americans accommodated themselves to the changing world of schools in a variety of ways. The most smitten advocates of competitive tests believed they had found a tool that measured both teacher competence and pupil performance, to identify who deserved promotion from grade to grade, academic honors, or a diploma. Critics complained that the statistics were not very reliable and worried about the harmful effects of testing upon pupils, teachers, pedagogy, and the curriculum. Some romantic, progressive educators took a more radical position, calling for the elimination of competitive testing and letting children learn as much as ambition and talent allowed. Parents and pupils in turn sometimes contested the test scores and appealed to teachers, principals, or those higher in the chain of command to nullify the results. Amid these often heated debates came yet another response: nostalgia for the educational values and practices of the past. Both the purveyors of cultural longing and the most outspoken critics of statistical measures reacted differently to the sometimes sudden transformation of urban schools. Neither halted the growth of testing.

While educators in the late nineteenth century still used displays to publicize innovations such as model kindergartens or student projects in the manual arts, exhibitions became less important in urban schools. In San Francisco, the *Daily Evening Bulletin* reported in 1858 that the Committee on Examinations retained exhibitions "merely for the gratification of the parents and friends of the scholars." A few years later, assistant superintendent Henry Kiddle in New York City reduced the number of exhibitions, restricted to one per school per year when he became superintendent in the 1870s. Rules were not always followed,

188

and age-old customs proved resilient. "Nearly all the schools closed with exhibitions more or less extensive," wrote J. L. Pickard, Chicago's superintendent, in 1868. "The exercises were varied and pleasant, but, as I conceive, far from profitable on the whole. The displays that accompany these exhibitions are without doubt pleasing to fond parents, and gratifying to youthful vanity, but the time taken for preparation is so much time taken from the more profitable work of the schools. In them parents see not the real work of the schoolroom" but a "few precocious ones" on stage. The "real work" expressed itself in numerical scores on the end-of-year written exams.[1]

The number and significance of "public examinations" in city schools declined, and spoofs of exhibitions remained common in urban newspapers, which increasingly called them "old-fashioned." In 1870, the *Hartford Daily Courant* in Connecticut poked fun at rural clodhoppers and their dialects. "Hark, I hear an angel sing!" said a student at an exhibition in Indiana, to which a farmer allegedly yelled, "'No, 'taint, it's only my mule that's hitched outside.'" "Three Killed and Fifteen Wounded," read the more sober headlines in rural North Carolina, after one teacher, for reasons unknown, went berserk after a school's closing exercises. Whenever comical or deadly disturbances involving fisticuffs or gunplay occurred at rural events, the telegraph and faster mail service sped the news far and wide. After the Civil War, newspapers reported that one school (in Jerusalem, Illinois, no less) reenacted Lincoln's fatal night at Ford's Theater. An old gun with a live round discharged, the student playing Lincoln catching the bullet in a molar. No doubt the tale grew taller in the telling, but it hardly made rural schools seem like a model for the nation. Student costumes caught on fire, schoolhouse floors collapsed, and exhibitions and displays, in rural areas especially, became fodder for urban writers, many of whom originally hailed from village or countryside.[2]

As early as 1867, theatergoers in Cincinnati laughed uproariously at the silly questions and answers of examiners and pupils at a minstrel show entitled "High School Examination." As farm families and youth seeking work flooded into cities, playwrights both American and English, knowing their market, slipped funny exhibition scenes into sentimental stories for comic relief. Everyone laughed as examiners and spouters mixed up their facts. In the early 1890s, amateurs published poems that spoke of "simpler" times, and the very newspapers that announced upcoming exams and publicized test scores frequently reprinted them. The most popular one appeared in 1893:

> O, the old school exhibitions! Will they ever come again.
> With the good, old-fashioned speaking from the girls and boys so
>   plain. . . .
> The girls don't speak in calico, the boys in cotton jeans:
> They've changed the old time dresses, 'long with the old time
>   scenes. . . .
> O, the old school exhibition! It is gone forever more!
> The old schoolhouse is deserted, and the grass has choked the door.[3]

As far as schools were concerned, city folk seemed to have little to learn from rustics. A reminiscence about "The Old Red School House" in *McClure's Magazine* in 1905 affirmed that "the city schools are now the pattern of the country schools." One could take solace and reminisce, however, by singing along to "School Days/School Days" (1907), a product of New York's Tin Pan Alley and cowritten by a native Philadelphian.[4]

Many decades before most rural schools were consolidated, urban-based writers not only satirized rural life but also nurtured gentler memories for urban residents of a world gone by, before schools were better graded and test scores were posted.

I

America was still very rural in 1900, with tens of thousands of one-room schools. But the more centralized bureaucratic structure and changing classroom practices in towns and cities tapped a popular longing for a familiar world that would never return. The creators of nostalgia not only reminded contemporaries that deep-seated changes were transforming American culture. While their invention of idealized pasts helped cushion the blow, nostalgia about schools also testified to the enhanced authority of tests. And, as was so often true in the story of testing, important roads often connected Boston to the wider society, exemplified by the cultural influence of the sculptor John Rogers, who became the most commercially successful artist in America, and Charles H. Hoyt, one of its most successful playwrights.

Boston's secondary schools played a part in the growth of educational nostalgia. Established in 1635, the famous Latin School prepared boys for college. Recall, too, that in 1821 Boston created the English Classical School, soon more accurately named English High, which provided an "English" or "modern" education; it taught boys practical subjects such as English, mathematics, and nonclassical languages, useful in a commercial city. John Rogers's path to English High had been circuitous. Born in nearby Salem in 1829, John soon moved with his family to Cincinnati when his father became co-owner of a sawmill, which failed within a few years. Ultimately the family returned to Massachusetts, settling in Roxbury, where John graduated from its Latin grammar school. Too poor to attend college, he took the entrance test to English High, where he excelled in mathematics. In 1846, Rogers dropped out of English High after two years and became a clerk.[5]

After working as a machinist in Manchester, New Hampshire, where he pursued clay modeling in his free time, Rogers labored at an iron works and then as a master mechanic in a railroad shop. Committing himself to art, he studied in Europe, eschewing strictly classical forms in favor of subjects drawn from "everyday life." The practical orientation of studies at English High served him well, though he did not miss the "torture" of its rigorous examinations. Rogers's specialty was miniature plaster sculptures, which were mass produced from bronze molds, widely advertised, and soon found in many middle-class parlors. Just as identical copies of "printed questions" promoted uniform testing, mass production enabled Rogers to sell identical products to consumers. By 1900, Rogers had sold an estimated eighty to one hundred thousand copies of his miniatures, the themes ranging from the Civil War to sentimental images of Americana: old men playing checkers, the village blacksmith, the local school master. In 1869, Boston's *Daily Advertiser* dubbed him the "Burns of sculpture," his democratic sensibilities capturing "the quaint enjoyments of lowly life." The *Daily Miners' Journal* in Pottsville, Pennsylvania, believed that Rogers's "far-spreading fame" among ordinary citizens was easy to explain: "his subjects touch their hearts, enlist their sympathies, stir memories, [and] recall the past."[6]

Inspired by Oliver Goldsmith's poem "The Deserted Village," Rogers created sculpted imaginings of a world slipping away. One of his well-known miniatures, "The School Examination," appeared in 1867, precisely when competitive written tests in graded systems were becoming common. Three individuals are in this miniature, which stood twenty inches tall. A whiskered examiner is seated, gently correcting a girl standing next to him, his spectacles resting upon her slate. Behind both individuals is a young female teacher (Rogers had married one), who is holding a book but seems reassured that the "examination" will turn out fine. Available as a stereograph, sold in jewelry shops, and raffled off at county fairs, "The School Examination" became a perfect retirement gift for teachers. The more pupils were tested, schools were graded, and cities set the standard, the more marketable Rogers's sentimental objects depicting children, families, and schools.[7]

The nostalgia that sold so well for Rogers assumed other cultural forms, inspired in part by the transformations occurring in schools. Acclaimed as the most popular play of the 1890s, Charles H. Hoyt's comedy, *A Midnight Bell*, premiered in New York City in 1889 and was pure sentimentality, with an obligatory bow to the old-time school. Hoyt was born in Concord, New Hampshire, in 1859. His father managed a hotel, then moved in-state to Charlestown, becoming a railway clerk. Young Hoyt later attended the Boston Latin School, studied law, worked out West, and then became a journalist, covering music, drama, and sports at the Boston *Post*. Between the early 1880s and the turn of the century, he wrote nearly twenty plays, *A Midnight Bell* his most memorable achievement.[8]

The play is a combination melodrama-farcical comedy, set in a New England village. The story line is simple, the characters stock figures from the past. A banker has been wrongly accused of stealing money, the culprit is exposed, and a set of stereotypical characters—an old maid, an Irish schoolmarm, her suitor—populate the play. The second act deals with a school exhibition, something any urban resident could recognize. The property list for opening night in New York City included a "school bell on the teacher's desk. Pens, pencils, ink, and paper on teacher's desk. Schoolbooks on teacher's desk. Chalk at blackboard." It's snowing outside the one-room school as Deacon Lemuel Tidd, assisted by a local attorney, Napier Keene, arrives to inspect the school.[9]

As Tidd approaches, pupils bombard him with snowballs. More laughs follow as the Deacon slips on the icy doorstep, regains his composure, and takes the lead in the exam. First he berates the teacher for imparting such impractical knowledge as the definition of "equator," which, he snarled, was an imaginary line no one would ever see. Lawyer Keene then poses a typical rote question. "What's the largest city in the world?" A pupil replies: "Chicago!" Uncertain if that's correct, the Deacon asks another question: "Largest city in New England?" The students shout: "Boston." A disagreement ensues over whether Boston is better known for baseball or boxing.

Deacon: "What two rivers join to make the Ohio?"
A female student: "The Allegheny and the Monongahela."
Deacon: "Not at all, Why an Allegheny is one o' them critters they hev
   down South that bit Fin Never's leg off when he was in the army, and
   now he's gittin' a pension 'cause he said he had it shot off. Monongahela is whiskey—you can't fool me on Monongahela."[10]

Asked to locate the North Pole, a pupil responds: since many explorers could not find it, why ask me? In other versions of the play, a pupil simply points skyward.[11]

A Midnight Bell attracted a multitude of fans. Within a few months of opening night, the *New York Times* applauded its sentimentality; it had already played one hundred times at the Bijou. As the show hit the road, its reception in cities large and small remained impressive. In the fall of 1889, the Chicago *Tribune* called it an excellent "farce," its popularity assured since "everyone who has lived in a village or has read about one, recognizes the characters." Theater critics often praised the timely delivery of lines at the school exhibition, and laughing at the rustics sold tens of thousands of tickets coast to coast and from Duluth to New Orleans.[12]

Working in different mediums and famous in their day, John Rogers and Charles Hoyt touched the sensibilities of many adults whose family members confronted difficult challenges: where they lived, how they worked, how they bonded with neighbors, how the young were judged at school. For as long as anyone remembered, school exhibitions were a familiar and time-honored part of community life. Memories of the mundane not only reminded people of America's rural roots but also of how different America had become.

Those who admired a Rogers's miniature or laughed during Hoyt's play helped celebrate and remember the past, but the reaction of many citizens to the birth of modern schools, in which testing became common, was less than sentimental.

II

Between the 1860s and 1890s, John Rogers and Charles Hoyt responded to dramatic social change through their artistry. Contemporaries who labored in schools or observed the changes underway had their own vantage points. They too tried to understand how the new culture of testing altered the inner dynamics of schools and their relationship to the community. Written, in-class exams had noticeable effects upon the lives of teachers, children, and local schools. Once timed, written exams became more central to classroom routine, the private nature of testing became apparent and the public, when invited, rarely showed up to watch pupils compete. In 1861 a Midwesterner dryly commented that "a school examination is not exactly as entertaining as a school exhibition." "Stillness reigns, broken only by the scratching of pens upon the paper, or by the clicking of pencils upon the slates," said another citizen. Even elected officials had to be nudged to attend. In 1865, superintendent Anson Smyth contacted every member of Cleveland's school board regarding the date and time for final exams. "Written examinations are not particularly entertaining to visitors," Smyth admitted. "Still, I earnestly request all Visiting Committees to be in attendance at their respective schools." Duty called but visiting committees were becoming largely honorific. "Printed questions" had replaced them.[13]

As William T. Harris of St. Louis predicted in 1873, written exams generated a loud, angry response. Numerous educators and lay people marshaled impressive arguments against them and catalogued their baneful effects on schools. So-called progressive educators in particular believed that tests destroyed creative teaching and undermined freedom for the child. Less radical critics also worried that tests caused teachers to tailor instruction to likely exam questions, which lowered standards and narrowed the curriculum. Objections to tests, especially their exaggerated use, were extensive. Angry Bostonians had not been shy about voicing their opposition to the summer surprise of 1845. But complaints accelerated once testing became more widespread as schools became larger, better graded, professionally administered, and seemed obsessed with measurable results. Cities had the concentration of pupils and wealth necessary to adopt innovations and advance professional careers, especially for male administrators; the attack on tests was one way to express unhappiness about how much change so many people absorbed as they left farming and the countryside. Since they directly affected some of the weakest members of society, the young, some critics hyperbolically compared the new-style tests to the ball and chain on prisoners, the machines controlling factory operatives, the shackles on southern slaves, and "the despotism of Turkey and China."[14]

Complaints about tests in general and promotion exams in particular generated anger reminiscent of the first round of battles in the testing wars. By the early 1870s, newspapers frequently published editorials and letters to the editor that condemned the "testing mania," a product of the "percent" or "marking system" and "examination mill." They blamed the exams for rote teaching, dependence upon textbooks, and impaired health among teachers and pupils. In the 1840s, although Boston's reformers had championed written tests to expose overreliance on rote teaching and textbooks, the new exam system only aggravated the problem. Contributors to teachers' magazines as well as to the *Atlantic Monthly, Harper's,* and *The Forum* vilified the schools for inhumane, soul-destroying pedagogy. Articles with titles such as the "Murder of the Innocents" heaped scorn on tests. Joined by John Swett and some other prominent administrators, John B. Peaslee, Cincinnati's school superintendent in the early 1880s, cheered on the critics. Over-zealous testing, Peaslee wrote, had understandably created enemies. After all, examinations "were held in every subject in which it was possible to hold them. The per cents were posted up in the offices of superintendents, exhibited and commented upon in the different schools, carried around in triumph by the principals, paraded in the daily newspapers, and published in school reports."[15]

That competitive written tests, which had dramatically increased across the curriculum, had undesirable effects upon pupils and teachers seemed self-evident to many people. Innumerable articles in newspapers and educational and medical journals boldly claimed that test preparation and "over-study" undermined physical health and mental wellbeing. Themselves victims of the new system of assessment, teachers forced students to memorize a surfeit of facts, definitions, and rules, sometimes ostensibly leading to insanity, debilitation, even death. The faculty of memory, as Howe and Mann had claimed in the 1830s and 1840s, was becoming over-developed at the expense of understanding, perception, and observation, a view sustained by many phrenologists and physicians who worried about health risks if children's brains were over-stimulated. As high school enrollments expanded, the pernicious effects of academic success on girls' health became a raging issue. By midcentury, educators often remarked that girls were better students in every grade, and their visible presence as the majority of high school pupils brought them more scrutiny. If the largely white middle- and upper-middle class girls who dominated in secondary schools later in life could not bear children, some citizens feared a weakened society already wracked by labor unrest, immigration, and crime.[16]

While no one expected pupils to perform equally well, girls stood out as a group. Girls were more studious and responsible and were retained less often in-grade, thus graduating at higher rates from high school. Periodic attempts to ban homework for girls in Boston, New York, and other cities were routinely ignored by the students, especially those aiming for high school and aspiring to teach. Boys were generally more disruptive and filled the small but growing number of "ungraded," special classes that cities established to segregate pupils with troublesome behaviors and learning problems. Though examiners lacked statistical techniques to isolate precisely how gender, age, social class, or other factors influenced grades or scores, girls on average outperformed boys. The presence of so many higher-achieving girls in high school (and now in college) at a time when evolutionary theories posited survival of the most fit unsettled many adult men. In 1871, the *Cincinnati Times and Chronicle* editorialized that white males might lose their dominant position in society. Test score disparities caused the editor to ask "whether our boys have ceased to be the intellectual equals of the girls" and were "overwhelmed by . . . all that pertains to intellectual culture and power."[17]

Thanks to a simple equation of cause and effect in the minds of critics, any pupil who studied diligently and became ill was proof positive that "over-study" was to blame. In Boston, Cleveland, and other cities, physicians, who often served on school committees, frequently denounced tests, which led to eye-catching headlines in local newspapers anxious to outsell their competitors. By the 1850s, magazines and newspapers began to claim that the ranking system, fears of failure, and the mad dash for prizes, honors, or promotion to the next grade or school added stress to the already difficult lives of urban families. Canadian and American "insane asylums" now included adolescent girls thanks to the testing culture. One article on "over-study" in Cleveland's *Plain Dealer* in 1859 told the sad story of a local "lunatic" who was traveling west to begin life anew among strangers, who would not know his condition. Suicides by over-wrought scholars in foreign lands also made the news.[18]

The writings of Samuel Gridley Howe, trained as a physician, added to the cavalcade of complaint, the loquacious reformer silent on who helped get the testing ball rolling. Howe and his allies had denounced emulation, which the exam system exacerbated. Boston's *Daily Advertiser,* which had applauded the reformers in 1845, claimed in 1867 that "the medical books are full of instances of the injurious results of over-study in the schools." Nearly all of the primary school teachers were women, and many physicians in Boston feared they were collapsing from the strain "largely due to the needless and ever increasing complexity of the school machinery," said one local observer in 1882. This included "the minute 'marking' of recitations, the recording and averaging of the 'marks,' the many written examinations, with the correcting and marking of the same, to say nothing of other written exercises, compositions, etc." which have "been enormously increased in recent years." Despite their dwindling numbers, phrenologists also spoke out, reaffirming that memorizing too much academic material ruined mind and body.[19]

Newspapers from New England to Hawaii speculated that John Jacob Astor's son's mental distress resulted either from "a blow on the head or over-study" at the University of Geneva in Switzerland. Ordinary people also suffered if they studied too much. In the 1870s, a girl in Jersey City reportedly ran away out of fear of academic failure, one of a legion of examples in the popular press. In 1881, another excessively studious girl in New Jersey sank into a coma, and a physician said that electrical shocks failed to produce one nervous twitch. In the Chicago courts, a so-called Insane Day was scheduled once a week, when over-zealous students joined the ranks of those committed. A girl in Baltimore allegedly committed suicide because of the stress of exams. Before taking her life, she became delirious and "incessantly repeated her studies, figuring out large sums and spelling one word after another" for nearly thirty hours. An M.D. identified the cause of death as "congestion of the brain."[20]

Throughout the post-bellum decades, test preparation or test results ostensibly produced a steady stream of tragedy: students in Cincinnati jumping into the Ohio River, fatal drug taking, and mysterious disappearances. In Maine, the *Bangor Daily Whig and Courier* said a body found along the railroad tracks in 1884 was a worn-out, recent high school graduate. Lurid details abounded about the latest victim claimed by the testing Moloch. Suicide notes and those penned by runaways recounted how embarrassing test scores, lousy report cards, and academic failure made life unbearable. Such simplistic, single-cause explanations for personal tragedy were frequently at odds with reality but a boon to newsies hawking papers, which advertised stomach bitters that promised to undo the ill effects of test preparation and "brain exhaustion." One "Celery Compound" promised to fix whatever ailed students, and a quack remedy in Colorado promised to cure almost any illness, including over-study, for $5. In 1881, one clever writer poked fun at the proliferating tales of ill-health, tests, and tragedy. The Philadelphia *North American* recounted the story of a delinquent hauled before the courts in New York. When the judge asked the miscreant why he preferred a life of crime over school, where he might improve himself, the boy replied that he feared "dying from over-study."[21]

The urban stories, like Rogers's miniatures or Hoyt's old-fashioned scenes, rested upon a larger truth: tests were transforming schools. "Over-study" deserved its send-up, but for many people exams were no laughing matter. Excessive testing and its attendant evils—too much memorization and homework, the ranking of teachers and pupils, and health-destroying competition—not only helped sell newspapers. The subject also attracted experts from all walks of life: teachers, phrenologists, physicians, social scientists, traveling lecturers, and the first generation of psychologists. Some denounced the tests and called for their elimination, while most urged restraint and the elimination of the high-stakes promotion exams.

Critics and advocates of testing often agreed that testing had not only raised academic standards but also produced real if not life-threatening anxieties among teachers and children while making boring classrooms even more so.

III

The new testing culture did not create but reinforced didactic practices in America's schools. Most pupils clustered in the lower grades, and only a small percentage of the relevant age-cohort entered high school.

Elementary teachers were usually young and inexperienced; they usually did not attend any normal school; their turnover was high (at least
10 percent annually in many cities); they earned far less than secondary teachers despite having the largest classes; and administrators often
ranked, judged, and evaluated them on the basis of pupil scores. Advocates of vigorous testing programs admitted that they had made teachers'
lives more stressful. The *Journal of Education* more darkly concluded in
1884 that written examinations were the "greatest evil" in the schools
and created perpetual "warfare between the teacher and examiner."
John Swett added that school inspectors were about as welcome among
teachers as informers in Ireland.[22]

Elementary teachers after midcentury had typically received a gram-
mar-level or few years of high school education. Some secondary schools
established normal training classes, but plentiful teaching positions in
the countryside, villages, and towns led many female students to depart
before earning a degree. In New York City, many primary teachers in
the 1860s had only graduated from grammar school. The meager education of many teachers ensured their dependence upon textbooks, the
source of nearly all test items. Memorizing and reciting were the norm
in schools everywhere. Numerous observers noticed that tests, aided by
the spread of written assignments, strengthened traditional pedagogy, in
which teacher and text prevailed. The leading progressive educator of the
last half of the nineteenth century, Francis W. Parker, advocated more
inductive, child-centered methods and repeatedly claimed that written
exams were the "greatest obstacle" to "real teaching," destroying creativity and individual expression.[23]

Born in New Hampshire in 1837, Parker began teaching when he was
sixteen years old and became a principal in his early twenties. A Union
veteran, he returned to teaching and administration after the Civil War,
traveled to Germany to imbibe the latest child-centered ideals, and had a
short but celebrated tenure as superintendent of the Quincy, Massachusetts, schools between 1875 and 1880, leaving Boston after a stint as a
supervisor to head the Cook County Normal School in Chicago. Parker's
fame rested on his years in Quincy. There Parker replaced rote-oriented
teachers, dispensed with spelling books, and introduced story-telling and
innovative number work into the primary grades. Charismatic and outspoken, Parker loved to lecture others while occupying the moral high
ground. In a meeting of superintendents in 1877, he attacked competitive

exams, endorsed freedom for the teacher, and called the typical school examiner "ignorant." A year later, a countywide test in Norfolk County revealed that most pupils had not mastered the Three R's, averaging 57 percent. Quincy's schools, however, scored highest, ostensibly proving the superiority of progressive pedagogy, which Parker and his followers boasted about for decades afterwards.[24]

In a speech to Chicago's teachers in 1883 that gained national attention, Parker explained that he was not opposed to tests per se, since if constructed differently they might reveal how well teachers taught and how much pupils learned. In their current form, however, competitive exams typically asked pupils to recall "disconnected facts" and were thus "the greatest curse" upon the schools. Always taking the side of teachers—especially if they were progressive, avoiding the evils of textbooks and rote exams—Parker believed that "if the teacher really teaches, and faithfully watches the mental growth of her pupils . . . she alone is the best judge of their fitness to do the work of the next grade." Most mainstream leaders, however, believed that the profession varied in terms of talent; not everyone was a skilled practitioner or an objective judge of student achievement. Thus, written tests, despite their imperfections, remained invaluable in holding teachers and students accountable. "We entertain no Utopian ideas on the subject of perfect teachers," Baltimore's chief administrator wrote in 1875. "There are, in proportion to the number employed, as many imperfect teachers as there are imperfect lawyers, doctors, preachers, editors, etc." To think otherwise was to deny the obvious.[25]

Progressives and traditionalists alike agreed that rote teaching, textbooks, and written exams were inextricably bound. Agreeing on a solution to mechanical forms of instruction was another matter, since educators had long complained that many pupils memorized subject matter they did not understand. The situation did not improve once printed questions and written examinations became fashionable. The lowest primary grades had the largest class sizes—sometimes fifty, sixty, or many more pupils squeezed into a room—yet the novices placed in charge were frequently berated by superiors for not treating each pupil as an individual or not adopting more child-friendly pedagogy. "It is only when the reason and understanding are enlisted with the memory," the president of Baltimore's school committee insisted in 1860, "that the school can be attractive and study a pleasure." If true, many pupils were doomed to many unhappy schooldays.[26]

Nearly every visitor to city schools after midcentury bore witness that rote instruction was not only alive and well but aligned beautifully with the new culture of competitive testing. As pupils scratched away on their slates or answered questions orally or on paper, trying to remember what the textbook said, their minds seemed like "an encyclopedia of facts." Listen to superintendent John Philbrick after he made his rounds in Boston's primary schools in 1857. "It was very uncommon to hear . . . a single question or remark by the teacher which had any reference to the understanding of the children. In many cases, the reading was but little more than the mechanical pronunciation of an unknown tongue. There is a text-book in daily use . . . entitled *Spelling and Thinking Combined*" but "I never saw the slightest evidence of any attempt at the combination indicated in the title." Forty years later, a Bostonian noted that "the deadening influence of routine in teaching is well known and . . . too familiar to need description."[27]

With many individual recitations impossible in classrooms squirming with children, teachers frequently used "concert" or "simultaneous" recitations to keep pupils focused and busy. Citizens walking along the streets of Baltimore heard what sounded like "chanting choristers" as they approached a school, where the noise inside was deafening. In 1865, one local official lamented that "the recitation of the multiplication table is frequently conducted in a manner as equally reprehensible with that of the spelling lesson. It is shouted forth vociferously as if intended as an exhibition of the lung-power of the school room." When not filling in their slates and erasing them, pupils in unison in school after school blasted out the names of capitals, lists of presidential successions, times tables, and rules, definitions, and facts galore. A visitor to Chicago's elementary schools in 1884 was happy to see pupils writing more with crayons and pencils, but many classes were mired in an "unmeaning, benumbing routine." "Of all the relics of the past that have been embalmed and sent down to us," he concluded, nothing matched grammar instruction, with "the routine parsing, 'common noun, third person, singular number, neuter gender, objective case,' year in and year out." But this might be on the test.[28]

"Teacher and textbook may be full of knowledge," as John M. Gregory, the former president of the University of Illinois, remarked in 1886 in a primer on teaching. Unless a pupil actually understood the subject matter and absorbed its wider meaning, however, what was learned seemed quickly forgotten. Too often, teachers regarded the mind as a receptacle, "a bag to be filled with other people's ideas, a piece of paper on which another may write, a cake of wax under a seal." However, Gregory recognized that the reputations of teachers rested on test scores, so they often deposited information nonstop into children's heads. As a result, they "drone on through dull hours and dreary routine, reading commonplace questions from books," boring students to death. As one Bostonian concluded, "not one in a hundred examined retains any wish to know more of the subject under examination." Pupils experienced tests "as a bad dream from which they have waked, never, they hope, to dream it again."[29]

Critics employed many different metaphors to describe America's classrooms, few of them complimentary to teachers. Pupils, they said, resembled an over-wound alarm clock, spouting answers recklessly and prematurely. Others said teachers stuffed students like a Christmas goose. Still others said that pupils were stretched or chopped to conform to the graded system, a modern version of a Procrustean bed. Some called teachers gradgrinds, invoking the name of the fact-obsessed pedant in *Hard Times* (1854), Charles Dickens's protest against utilitarian education. *Puck*, the English satirical magazine, also skewered the human "cramming machines" in a widely-reprinted poem.

> Ram it in, cram it in,—
>   Children's heads are hollow!
> Slam it in, jam it in,—
>   Still there's more to follow:
> Hygiene and history,
> Astronomic mystery,
> Algebra, Histology,
> Latin, Etymology,
> Botany, Geology,
> Greek and Trigonometry—
> Ram it in, cram it in,
>   Children's heads are hollow![30]

Obviously, not all teachers were pedantic, unable to tap pupil interest, or the living embodiment of Thomas Gradgrind, who told teachers to impart "nothing but Facts." Reports of uninspired teaching nevertheless littered the educational landscape.[31]

After observing many classrooms in Cincinnati in the 1850s, Andrew J. Rickoff concluded that "teachers to a greater or less degree, teach as they themselves were taught; at least, the forms are handed down from generation to generation, alas, too often without the spirit." As Horace Mann had said years before, "hearing recitations," not teaching per se, filled their day. In 1855, Rickoff described a typical scene. "With such teachers, it is not an unfrequent custom to hold the text-book of Geography in one hand, and the map in the other, glancing from question to map as questions are asked and answered, and I have seen classes delayed at every step, to give the teacher time to find the answers. So in History, have I seen the questions at the back of the book used while time was taken in hunting up the answer in the text." Similar criticisms surfaced everywhere. School was "a dull, uninteresting, tiresome place," Nebraska's chief school officer concluded in 1873, since so many teachers "simply stand before their classes, book in hand, asking the printed questions, and requiring answers in the exact language of the book!"[32]

While progressive educators in particular condemned these practices, they were teachers' bread and butter, and most school officials and administrators shared a wider Enlightenment faith that mass-produced books, readers, encyclopedias, and even the dullest of textbooks advanced the cause of popular education. Unscrupulous drummers might bribe a school board member to adopt inferior textbooks. Teachers might drone on and never go beyond the knowledge found between the covers of a textbook, causing supervisors to shudder. For many educators, however, textbooks were the "storehouse" of knowledge, a democratizing force that enabled pupils with even the worst teachers to stand a chance at learning. And, with every passing decade, schoolbooks were better aligned with the graded system, with promotion as the carrot and tests as the stick. Defenders as well as critics of stale pedagogy recognized that teachers both leaned on textbooks excessively but also keyed their instruction to probable test questions. Teaching and testing were inseparable, each powerfully shaping the other.[33]

Seasoned administrators, who had usually climbed up the ranks, found it unsurprising that teachers taught to the test. In 1857, John Philbrick noted in the *Massachusetts Teacher* that they "are ever strongly tempted, even against their better judgment, to conform their teaching to the kind of examination expected. They cannot be blamed for adopting such a course." Philbrick was a survivor of the testing wars in the 1840s, becoming master of the model Quincy School, fully graded and a blow against the double-headed system. He thought it would have been odd if teachers did not align their teaching with tests. In Boston, primary teachers prepped pupils for admission to grammar schools, whose teachers in turn prepped students aspiring to the next level. The bragging rights always went to the schools with the top scores. In Boston no one dared to publish the results, but the word always got out. Testing had other unintended consequences. Even though cities had manuals of instruction and time-tables for each subject, Philbrick and colleagues elsewhere knew that teachers "will more or less neglect those branches on which their pupils are not examined" or not used to judge "the merit and standing of their schools." Tests therefore not only narrowed teaching but also the curriculum.[34]

A contributor to the *California Teacher* put it succinctly: "teaching can never rise higher than the examination." Emerson E. White, a much respected administrator and longtime editor of school periodicals, told colleagues at the National Education Association (NEA) meetings in 1874 that tests had been instrumental in classifying and promoting pupils but had a deleterious effect on instruction. Like Philbrick, he said that teachers constantly worried about test results since their careers depended on them. "I have seen blackboards covered with 'probable' questions, and classes, meeting before and after school to be crammed with set answers to them, as a preparation for a test examination. I have known classes to memorize the names of all the bones in the human body, hundreds of dates in American history, and scores of the mechanical processes of mensuration, because these things were known hobbies of the question maker."[35]

Principals, White said, told critics they were preparing their *"wares for the market,"* so teachers had to drill pupils constantly. Publishing "tables of examination per cents," White added, "often put a premium on special cramming and false teaching, and sometimes on downright dishonesty." Rules against cheating did not ensure honesty any more than harping about cramming ended it. Joseph O'Connor, a deputy superintendent in San Francisco, explained in 1883 that since pupils

faced highly stressful promotion tests, "the great majority of teachers
. . . spend nearly all of their time in *drilling and preparing the pupils for
the annual examinations.*" Teachers felt they had to genuflect before the
authority of "the question maker."[36]

From the Atlantic to the Pacific, another contemporary affirmed,
schools were obsessed with "Questions and Questioners."[37]

IV

The "grooving" of instruction to match test requirements created a market for quiz books and assorted volumes to help teachers and pupils beat
the system. Recall that John Swett, who sometimes protested too much,
very early profited from the trade. Like many educational practices, quiz
and review books were modeled on traditional religious instruction. Protestants published numerous question-and-answer books on the Bible in
the nineteenth century utilized by teachers at Sunday schools, which
many school leaders had attended and later taught. After midcentury,
many public school textbooks remained broadly Christian and Protestant
but usually softened their sectarian tone; pedagogy, however, retained
its didacticism. Questions often appeared at the bottom of the page or at
the back of the book. To help teachers, publishers also printed separate
"keys" to textbooks: special volumes of questions and answers. A citizen
complained in 1852 that the "keys" were available "for every lazy student
who has wit enough to know the road to the bookstore." Another said
the keys should be declared "contraband," since they undermined "self-
reliance" and fostered "indolence" among pupils.[38]

"The word 'coach'," the *Brooklyn Daily Eagle* explained in 1878, "in
these days is a painfully familiar one." Coaching and cramming were the
natural offspring of the testing movement. Once written scores assumed
greater prominence, quiz books and guides on testing and the tricks of
the trade proliferated. By the 1870s and 1880s, they were advertised
nationwide in newspapers and especially in teachers' magazines. Pitched
to pupils studying for entrance or promotion tests, and to teachers inse-
cure about their knowledge and prepping for class or certification exams,
the study books contributed to the "testing mania" of the era. Many of
the authors were former teachers who became school administrators.
The quiz books tried to help teachers and pupils gain some command

over the explosion of knowledge occurring in every domain of learning. In an age of written tests and heightened accountability, educators rushed in offering assistance, for a price.[39]

Books such as *The Teachers' Pocket Manual* (1876), *Treasury of Facts* (1884), and *Hughes' Common School Branches in a Nutshell* (1893) promised to alleviate the stress and strain of test preparation. The author of the *Pocket Manual,* an experienced teacher, said his "only excuse" for publishing it was to help teachers elevate youth "from its primeval state of ignorance" and to "assist the pupils in their arduous task of storing the mind with useful knowledge." And "there is a demand for it." Published in West Virginia, *Common Branches in a Nutshell* told pupils to "REVIEW! REVIEW!! REVIEW!!! REVIEW!!!!" A blurb on its back cover said the book "Makes Examinations Easy, and Removes Many Difficulties Encountered by the Teacher." All for fifty cents, postpaid.[40]

As school enrollments exploded after the Civil War, authors upped the ante and tried to best their competitors, just like pupils squaring off in the nation's classrooms. It would take a very large nutshell indeed to hold all the knowledge available in schoolbooks. In 1872, Asa H. Craig, who lived in Caldwell's Prairie, Wisconsin, started out modestly with *The Question Book: A General Review of Common School Studies, For the Use of Teachers, and Those Intending to Teach.* It covered the basic subjects and only had 1,047 questions and answers, though many of the selections had multiple parts. *The Question Book* sold extremely well, merited several editions, and was the basis for *The New Common School Question Book,* which was keyed more closely to textbooks. The 1887 edition bulked up to 3,700 questions, without counting the questions within questions. One on Canadian geography, for example, asked for the names of the various provinces, the location of twenty-one cities, eight capes, twelve gulfs and bays, and the descriptions of nine lakes (including Abbitibbe, Mistissinnie, and Nipissing) and thirteen rivers. One platform speaker concluded that study guides such as Craig's covered everything since "pre-historic man sat chattering in his cave, gnawing the bones of his slain adversary."[41]

From the 1870s onward, authors competed for their share of an expanding market. Not to be outdone by Asa Craig, the author of *The Practical Question Book* (1887) had "Six Thousand Questions and Answers." The editor of *The Normal Teacher* in Indiana, J. E. Sherrill, showed restraint (only three thousand questions) in the *Normal Question Book* (1882). Like his competitors, however, Sherrill peddled his volume broadly to pupils and teachers in "Common Schools, High Schools, and Institutes, for Daily, Weekly, and Monthly Reviews." A few authors specialized, providing numerous facts about literature or history. In 1888, J. Dorman Steele, a prominent author of American history and science books, published his own *Manual of Science for Teachers, Containing Answers to the Practical Questions and Problems in the Author's Scientific Textbooks.*[42]

By 1880, some of the standard-bearers approached five hundred pages, but not everyone wanted comprehensive guides to the whole of schoolbook knowledge. A few enterprising individuals spotted a market for shorter, less expensive publications. Thus appeared a series of "Dime Question Books"—each one on a separate subject—to help students and teachers bone up on their weakest subjects. B. A. Hathaway of Lebanon, Ohio, ran a cottage industry that produced a string of slightly larger quiz books, offering "1001 Questions and Answers" on individual subjects for fifty cents apiece. Whether a dime or half-dollar, these volumes helped students and teachers prep for the next test. Despite these cheaper alternatives, critics said the quiz books encouraged cramming and put students without expendable income at a competitive disadvantage.[43]

As attacks on testing and its excesses accelerated in the 1880s, some compilers of study guides pushed back against the critics. They brushed aside the dreamers who wished the world was different. A. C. Mason, the author of *1000 Ways of a Thousand Teachers,* said his guides dealt with schools *"as they are."* Albert Henry Thompson, the author of *The Examiners' Companion* (1887), offered readers a mere 1,060 questions and answers and with a sweep of the hand simply dismissed "would-be critics" opposed to "the use of Question Books by Teachers and Students." Some authors even reduced Francis Parker's writings on pedagogy, including his criticisms of tests, to the question-and-answer format, since rote questions on child-centered pedagogy, ironically enough, could appear on teachers' exams. Gradgrind conquered all.[44]

Criticisms of excessive testing appeared in a wide range of newspapers, books, and periodicals after the Civil War. Since teachers' magazines usually operated on a shoestring, even those that regularly assailed testing regularly advertised quiz books. In the spring of 1866, the *Central School Journal* in Keokuk, Iowa, assailed the "examination fetish" and called for "more teaching and less cramming for useless examinations. For years the horrible Juggernaut of examination has done its best to crush the progressiveness of teachers and the mental growth of pupils." The editor thus prayed that America's "odious examination system" received its "death-blow." But the journal advertised B. A. Hathaway's popular series of question-and-answer books, which focused on the basics. As one reviewer explained, even in his slender volumes Hathaway tried "to ask and answer any conceivable interrogatory likely to come before the student."[45]

The keys, quiz books, and review guides available in bookshops and through the mail testified to the new culture of testing enveloping the schools. Some of these volumes contained enough facts to make Thomas Gradgrind's head spin. They rarely asked questions beyond recall, in line with expectations on examination day. The first edition of Craig's *Question Book* had 232 history questions; only one began with the word "why." The rest asked about names, dates, places, and events, with little attention to causation or analysis. In Sherrill's *Normal Question Book,* only 2 percent of the questions in grammar (out of 278) began with "why," 1.7 percent (out of 339) in history. These books emphasized what textbooks and exams stressed including rules and procedures in arithmetic, definitions of words and parts of speech, correct punctuation, and countless facts in history, geography, and other subjects.[46]

For many school children in graded systems, the tests never seemed to end, but they also never quite worked in the ways some critics and advocates claimed or implied.

V

By the 1880s, criticisms of tests seemed to reach fever pitch. "The reaction against the examination mania has fully set in," said a contributor to the *Ohio Educational Monthly* in 1884. Thomas W. Bicknell, editor of the *Journal of Education* in New England, warned readers that "examinations are necessary, both for teachers and pupils, and must always be. . . . The tendency has been and is to misuse and overdo a good principle, and we have today the reaction, which would overthrow all test-examinations and leave teachers and pupils to move into and out of grades by a sort of moral gravitation, each seeking his own true level. Now the angels in light may have a celestial gradation on that heavenly principle," he added, but here on earth the elimination of tests would encourage teachers and pupils to slough off and undermine academic quality. Later in the year, S. A. Ellis, the chief school administrator in Rochester, New York, sensed "a general revolt throughout the country from the excessive number and quantity of the written examinations" but warned that no other method better determined "the real scholarship of a pupil."[47]

The pendulum seemed to be swinging away from written tests, and rhetoric for and against them heated up. In 1891, a U.S. Bureau of Education survey of seventy cities discovered that a growing number of districts had recently abolished high-stakes promotion tests. For decades, mainstream educators as well as high-profile progressives such as Francis Parker attacked these exams for encouraging cramming, "over-study," needless anxiety, and excessive labor for teachers and supervisors. Now promotion decisions, especially below high school, increasingly rested upon teachers' or principals' recommendations based on scores on weekly, monthly, end-of-term, and year-end exams as well as daily recitation marks, oral and written. High-pressure tests were clearly giving way to a broader range of assessments, the formula for promotion varying from district to district. High schools had first adopted written admission tests in the 1820s and were the most resistant to change. Nearly 50 percent of the cities surveyed still relied upon them almost exclusively, but they were also trending in the same direction. Hold-outs such as New Orleans that ruled in 1886 that the "yearly record" did not count for high school admission were soon in an ever-shrinking minority.[48]

As the attacks on promotion exams accelerated in the 1870s and 1880s, defenders of written examinations responded forcefully to the over-heated rhetoric about the evils of promotion tests by accusing critics of plotting to end competitive testing altogether. Nostalgia about old-time schools, complaints about cramming, and taxpayer concerns about the costs associated with the appointment of examiners and supervisors added to the tensions surrounding testing. It soon became evident, however, that once written tests entered the schools, they were never going to leave. A vote against promotion tests was not usually a vote against testing but a mandate to evaluate pupils more frequently, to obviate the need for one annual exam.

Defenders of tests formed the mainstream within administrative circles and drowned out the most strident opponents of testing. While complaints about rote teaching, mindless memorization, and too much testing resounded through the end of the century, most criticisms focused on high-stakes exams. Testing advocates agreed that promotion tests were undesirable but stopped short of assailing written exams in general, ensuring their survival and growth. Like graded classrooms or textbooks, tests had their enemies within the educational community, who routinely criticized them for promoting uniformity, excessive competition, and lifeless pedagogy. Very few school board members or administrators, however, suggested eliminating them. As an educator from little Steubenville, which like many towns had joined the testing movement, told listeners at the Ohio Teachers' Association meetings in 1881, no subject attracted more "conflicting opinions . . . than examinations. Many teachers are ready to condemn the whole system, yet all were making use of one method or another. The very nature of school work compels their use. No satisfactory substitute has been found, nor is any likely to be offered." Written tests had become as common as chalk and blackboards and didactic instruction.[49]

Quite a few educators, independent-minded physicians, and an assortment of writers pooh-poohed the notion that "over-study" ruined the health of young people. Instead, they pointed to late nights at the skating rink, dime novels, and laziness as more serious concerns. "Hard Study Kills Nobody," read one headline in the San Francisco *Evening Bulletin* in 1870. The *Milwaukee Sentinel* also rejected the "Over-Study Humbug" while the *Providence Journal* in Rhode Island told scholars to work harder and get more sleep. In 1878 the *Teetotaler,* a temperance journal in Wisconsin, sarcastically concluded that "in the school, as in the world, far more rust out than wear out." Teachers and principals often disliked excessive or exclusive reliance upon entrance, promotion, or exit exams but had little interest in ending competitive exams per se, which they believed forced pupils to study. In 1881, teachers in San Francisco met to discuss written tests and voted strongly against abandoning them or replacing them with oral exams. Even strong opponents of promotion tests such as Chicago superintendent George Howland recognized that written scores and reports generated hard proof about pupil achievement, which protected teachers from parents who demanded without merit that little Johnny deserved promotion. Hearings on "over-study" in Portland, Maine, as elsewhere, allowed critics to let off steam, but they had to listen to their opponents say that pupils were pampered, unlike young farm hands or factory operatives.[50]

Even though Francis Parker claimed that in theory tests could be valuable, his much-quoted attacks on their harmful effects exposed progressive educators to the charge that they cared little for academic standards. An anonymous contributor to the *Massachusetts Teacher* in 1874 said the world will always be "a hard place for shirks," and tests got the students' attention. Various superintendents dismissed the "flippant," ad hominem attacks by child-centered educators and others on tests and textbooks. How, they asked, could schools function without them? In 1883 superintendent John Dowd of Toledo, Ohio, said Parker's ideas—fewer textbooks and tests and more child-centered approaches—would lead to classroom bedlam. Dowd's counterpart in Columbus, Ohio, said only utopians opposed tests. He told listeners at the NEA in 1885 that written exams were "indispensable—they are the goad for the lazy, the reward for the industrious, and the crown of glory for the gifted and ambitious." If the "new education" proposed by progressives meant "no examinations, no . . . work for the teacher and none for the child, I am not prepared to give up the old and adopt the new." Other administrators claimed that getting high marks was like earning a dividend from a successful business. They often paraphrased what Howe, Mann, and others had said in the 1840s: written tests were the best way to measure achievement, lift standards, and hold everyone accountable.[51]

Lost in all the hubbub over the evils of cramming, "over-study," and school competition was the reality that test scores were never as omnipotent as their champions hoped and critics feared.

VI

Beginning with Samuel Gridley Howe's committee in 1845, a new way of thinking arose about how to assess schools that linked better-grouped classes, the hiring of women teachers on the elementary level, centralized authority in terms of uniform texts and administrative control, and written exams and statistics. As competitive tests became ubiquitous in graded systems, their successors after midcentury confidently asserted that test scores demonstrated pupils' "actual proficiency" and "true rank" and the "real workings" of classrooms. As one administrator in

Memphis insisted in 1869, the new quantitative approach better captured reality and was "less superficial" than old-fashioned methods and impressions. In 1882, however, *The Century Magazine* offered the usual retort that the "teachers of grades" now existed "to fetch a pupil through a certain stage of his education, and then pass him along to the driver of the next." The health and efficiency of the system, not the welfare of the individuals within it, guided decisions, and "the high regard paid to the quantitative analysis of learning in examinations, has pretty much done away with the school-master. The individual genius and personal quality of the teacher has been crowded to the wall by the overloaded course of study and the exactitude of system." The teacher was now "a hearer of lessons, a marker of registers, a worker for examination week."[52]

While written examinations certainly shaped pedagogy and the curriculum, urban schools were never that efficient or meritocratic despite concerted attempts by reformers to make them so. Prospective teachers usually had to pass competitive tests to be considered for appointment, but board members often favored candidates with personal or political connections. The much-vaunted "quantitative analysis" on which dreams rode and fears arose was also less than met the eye. That truth resided in numbers clashed with the reality that despite rising mountains of statistics, few administrators were sophisticated in interpreting them. At best most had college-level proficiency in mathematics and very little in statistics, even if scores, enrollment figures, and promotion rates were dutifully gathered and printed. The hard facts about schools had illusory qualities. As early as 1849, an observer in the *Massachusetts Teacher* concluded that local school reports, filled with tables on academic performance, "are often even more deceptive than those of our Railroad Corporations."[53]

Like railroad reports, school records were often poorly assembled. Educators were not angels but apparently never kept separate ledgers as some railway executives did to hide the truth from stockholders and Congressional investigators. In many instances, administrators sometimes were simply unaware of how certain fact-gathering procedures invalidated claims about instruction or academic performance. As early as the 1860s, NEA committees tried to establish uniform methods to accurately measure academic achievement within and across school districts, as Howe's committee attempted in 1845. But they failed to reach any consensus. Implementing a standard policy, of course, would have been impossible given the decentralized nature of the nation's school systems.[54]

Many administrators recognized that statistics were often untrustworthy and merited a skeptical eye. Comparisons of schools on centrally administered exams frequently rested upon incomplete data or unreliable numbers that invalidated claims etched in "black and white." Incipient bureaucracies were incapable of collecting information in a uniform, systematic way. In New York City, assistant superintendent Henry Kiddle remarked in 1858 that families were "constantly moving" and students might be truant, rebellious, or inattentive, some enrolling in one school in September while finishing in a different one in the spring. Which teacher, then, should be credited or blamed when the grades were posted? In 1861, Baltimore's chief school officer wanted to make decisions based on "facts" but complained that principals and teachers sometimes kept poor records. Principals were key to implementing policies and, like every group in society, varied in their competence and reliability. In San Francisco, breakdowns in the chain of command caused the central office to send memos repeatedly to principals asking for their missing reports. Moreover, judging teachers on high-stakes tests encouraged some to tell weak students to dodge the exam or transfer. In 1878 superintendent T. H. Crawford in Portland, Oregon, criticized teachers who "openly advised" pupils likely to drag down scores "to withdraw from the school. Parents have been requested, *in writing*, to find some other employment for their children." Crawford warned the public not to take the table comparing schools seriously.[55]

Whenever too many people conducted and evaluated an exam, gathering valid statistics became extremely difficult. George A. Walton, an agent of the Massachusetts state board of education, prepared a common test for the school districts in Norfolk County in 1878. It tried to compare the achievement of pupils who had attended school for four and eight years, respectively, in basic subjects. When Walton's lengthy report was released, it received national publicity, the first time any one test had received so much attention since 1845. Once again, the dismal scores convinced some citizens that public education was a failure. The technical problems involved in testing nearly 5,000 students in 276 classes spread across many districts were huge. Walton relied on numerous people as examiners, and problems quickly emerged, including deciding who to test. It soon became apparent that asking rural children untutored in using pencils to compete in a written test was farcical, so some examiners provided them with extra help.[56]

For a variety of reasons, only 58 percent of the primary and 79 percent of the grammar pupils' answers were included in compiling the final report. How different examiners kept or tossed out exams likely varied, making the results as slippery as an eel. Contemporaries who knew enough about standard testing procedures scoffed at Francis Parker's boasts that the results proved the superiority of child-centered pedagogy. But Parker was hardly alone in condemning tests in one breath while citing scores that made him look good in another. Fans and opponents of public schools and testing interpreted the numbers as personal preferences and situations demanded. Articles in national magazines and numerous newspapers including the *New York Times* discussed the Norfolk study, many editors and contributors concluding that the county's pupils overall had performed miserably. In response, J. W. Dickinson, secretary of the state board in Massachusetts, glibly replied that the students did fine even though the average score was an F, which already had enough meaning to the general public that it hardly inspired universal confidence in public schools. The schools, Dickinson believed, "deserve credit for their best products" but were only "somewhat responsible for their poorest," adding that children elsewhere would probably perform similarly before concluding that Massachusetts's schools had "no superiors." Every claim rested on his word alone.[57]

Administrators often admitted that they could not ensure that subordinates followed standard procedures in district-wide exams and, while pupils were often assigned numbers to conceal their identities, hand-marked tests led to errors despite due diligence and honesty. Since some examiners were tougher than others, uniform assessments were unlikely unless a supervisor reexamined everything. In San Francisco, superintendent John C. Pelton by 1867 remarked that "the fewer examiners, the better—the more just and reliable the results obtained." But rising numbers of pupils and tests to grade multiplied the number of examiners and brought "into play scores of minds with their differing judgments and varying standards of calculations." Even rote questions gave graders wiggle room on ambiguous items. When they had more say in promotion decisions after high-stakes tests disappeared, some teachers and principals took the path of least resistance and advanced everyone, making life difficult for colleagues with higher standards.[58]

By the 1870s, with testing in full throttle in many graded systems, educators realized that explaining precisely which factors shaped achievement remained a mystery despite a growing archive of statistics. To account for low scores, administrators frequently blamed the teachers, the safest strategy. But some agreed that student traits such as native intelligence, ambition, and family characteristics such as poverty, ethnicity, and race were also influential; absent sophisticated statistical tools to weigh their relative influence, however, explanations necessarily rested upon impressions. No one knew how long an "average" child, itself impossible to define precisely, should take to master a subject. An essayist in the *Maine Journal of Education* wrote that once experts could "definitely tell what the human mind can do in a given time, then education will be a science, and not until then. We will never know this until accurate statistics have been kept." Superintendent H. S. Jones in Erie, Pennsylvania concluded in 1879 that despite reams of statistics, educators still judged schools "upon a basis of opinions, impressions, and theories." A superintendent in New York or Chicago might boast that since this year's average scores rose (though on a different set of tests), schools were definitely improving, an exuberant claim resting on dubious evidence.[59]

Personal testimony notwithstanding, no one could prove on the basis of statistics that any schools were improving or declining or which teaching methods worked best. Test scores, charts, and ranked lists supplied administrators with abundant information on academic performance, leading to comparisons of average scores in different classes and many bulky reports. In 1889, the county superintendent in Pottsville, Pennsylvania, nevertheless reached the conclusion that "in all our printed statistics we have comparatively nothing by which we can compare anything." Statistical analysis was too unsophisticated to fulfill the dreams of its many devotees, and factors other than test scores shaped promotion decisions.[60]

At times rules on promotion were meant to be broken.

VII

Over-crowded classrooms often played a significant role in determining grade-to-grade promotions. The vast majority of pupils concentrated in the first four grades, and throughout the century big cities in particular could not build schools fast enough to accommodate everyone. In New York City, whose system could never admit every applicant, assistant superintendent Joseph McKeen pointed out in 1856 that "instances are not infrequent when it is necessary to relieve an over-crowded primary department, and increase a small grammar department . . . to give each teacher a due share of employment, and to regulate the equilibrium of the whole house." As in Boston, grammar school principals, McKeen thought, refused to accept enough pupils, which exacerbated over-crowding in the grades below. He warned that "persons who do not go behind the scenes . . . are likely to be deceived, or to remain ignorant with regard to the condition and wants of a school." Ward-based board members in New York and other cities sometimes decided to promote pupils because of over-crowding, ignoring issues of academic readiness. Accommodating everyone lowered standards but seemed preferable to more children prowling the streets. In many places, the city council decided whether, when, and where to build a new school, a situation ripe for corruption and scandal.[61]

Keeping up with demand was challenging enough before the nation sank into economic depression in 1873; soon after, an estimated nine thousand children in Chicago only attended half-day sessions. Two decades later, in the midst of the century's worst depression, thousands were still relegated to rented spaces including cellars and spare rooms in saloons. In many cities, severe over-crowding in the first and second grades often forced "premature promotions," a popular euphemism. As population surged in Chicago and New York as well as in smaller places such as Milwaukee, pressure on the lower grades intensified. Administrators could never predict how many children would apply to attend particular schools, so districts allowed families, which moved frequently in search of jobs or better housing, to enroll children wherever space existed. In 1890, Milwaukee's superintendent remarked that once "word is passed from house to house that So and So's children" were "refused admission," parents stopped applying. He compared the typical sixteen-room school with a "train of so many passenger coaches,—the vacant seats of one room filled by the overflow from other classes," irrespective of academic preparation. When promotion tests were in vogue before the 1890s, low scores could mean repeating a grade, the fate of a reported 10 to 20 percent or more of first graders in many cities. But if pressure to open up seats for others became too great or parents insisted on promotion, teachers, principals, and school officials might capitulate.[62]

Repeating a grade was not uncommon after midcentury, with the highest failure rates usually in the first and second grades and usually due to poor reading and arithmetic skills. Emerson E. White, superintendent of Cincinnati's schools in the late 1880s, believed that in a "well-graded system," 80 to 90 percent of pupils should pass, and that "the higher the grade the greater should be the per cent of pupils promoted." But promotion rates for the same grade within school districts could still vary widely. After children sat in the same class for two years and became frustrated, bored, and disruptive, administrators often moved them forward, making them the next teacher's responsibility while opening up seats for others. A sizeable minority of pupils entered first grade late or attended irregularly, contributing to the high retention rates, which usually dropped by third and fourth grade. Those who missed the fall term frequently needed two years to master first grade; immigrant children still learning English also might need additional time. When parents believed children merited promotion, however, they were unafraid to lodge complaints. An inspector in San Francisco who graded promotion exams sighed: "When the papers are marked and returned to the class examined, the objections of pupils, parents, and teachers to the crediting come thick and fast." When teachers did the grading, they bore the brunt of any criticisms.[63]

From coast to coast, school officials noticed that Americans were always in a rush. In 1891, the superintendent in Council Bluffs, Iowa, not exactly a metropolis, faced a familiar issue. "Some pupils are always in a great hurry to complete the course of study." Their parents regularly told him to promote "their children against the judgment of himself and teacher. Men and women who are liberal in dealing with the ordinary phases of human experience are absolutely irrational when confronted by the question of their children's educational welfare." Considerations besides test scores, then, shaped decisions. If a grammar or high school was full and demand increased, admission bars were raised or, as a superintendent euphemistically said in New Orleans, "the standard . . . changed." Sometimes pupils were promoted if they had a strong overall record but flunked an admission test. And if parents yelled enough, someone might listen.[64]

Tension between maintaining standards and keeping schools accessible, for white pupils especially, lay at the heart of many testing battles after the Civil War. School board members were usually elected by ward, and voters expected their representatives to defend neighborhood interests. Jobs for teachers were a lucrative source of graft and power, and setting academic standards too high eroded public support. During economic downturns especially, critics openly condemned high schools, which were expensive and enrolled relatively few students, unlike the lowest grades, usually jammed with pupils. But without respectable high schools, the "better class" of families might abandon the system, leaving it stigmatized as suitable only for paupers. So educational leaders tried to be flexible about promotion standards, especially below the secondary level, when space allowed or seemed politically wise. San Francisco's Committee on Classification, which handled complaints, made the reasonable point in 1868 that "we must take humanity as it is in the real live boys and girls which we meet in the street" and "consider the circumstances, thoughts, and feelings of parents and friends, and put their influence into the scale . . . otherwise we can scarcely expect to have our schools continue to reflect the interests and wants of the public."[65]

Maintaining standards while serving diverse student populations was never easy. Samuel Gridley Howe's committee confirmed in 1845 what everyone knew without any comparative scores: not everyone performed equally well at school. His successors also recognized that achievement within social groups varied, and in their minds the numbers demonstrated that girls generally outperformed boys and that African-Americans in the segregated Smith School fared worst. Over the rest of the century, similar claims about the influence of gender and race echoed in numerous reports, but it remained unclear how more evidence about achievement would alter the situation and improve the scores of children from groups that were left behind.

Despite the establishment of better age-graded classes, where the average age of pupils usually rose with each grade, "premature promotions" and other factors ensured that city systems could never create enough classes with pupils roughly equal in achievement. Children from a wide range of ages and achievement levels were enrolled in most classes, especially below high school. "In spite of all that has been said and done," said an official in Baltimore in 1882, "in many classes pupils are found who are not equal to the work of the grade, and whose presence in the class is an injury to themselves, and continual drag upon the class and the teacher." As the president of the local school board said the following year, teachers differ in talent, and "pupils of the several schools vary in character, the result of different home surroundings and influence, making "the labor of some teachers" more difficult "than others." One San Francisco administrator wondered whether teachers in schools on the "Barbary Coast" deserved more pay than those working on Nob Hill.[66]

Widespread discrimination, segregation, or exclusion from public schools ensured that African-Americans generally suffered egregiously in America's cities, depressing their academic achievement. Statistics regarding their test scores are scanty, but in cities that published them, the story was grim. In the Deep South, the freed people sought every opportunity to become educated after the Civil War, though underfunded Jim Crow schools, violence against them by white vigilantes, poverty, and other obstacles blocked many paths to improvement; self-help and churches supplemented the existing schools, impressively lifting black literacy rates, but this was achieved despite everything white society did to prevent it. Access to public high schools was negligible or nonexistent in many communities of the border and former slave states. In Baltimore, which like other urban districts in the border states had segregated schools, a smaller percentage of African-Americans than whites was promoted; dire poverty ensured that the boys frequently had to choose work over school, which depressed their attendance and achievement. As with whites, girls generally attended more regularly and advanced more rapidly.[67]

Racial segregation was rampant in the North. Many northern and southern educators, reflecting the values of the larger society, often doubted the mental capacity of African-Americans, depicted in textbooks as far down the evolutionary scale. Occasionally an educational leader would speak out, if not forcefully challenge racial injustice. For example, before and after the Civil War, African-Americans in New York City attended segregated schools that were built in very inconvenient locations. Henry Kiddle noted that African-American children often walked many miles and were often "greatly annoyed, and often abused and seriously injured, by the persecution of ruffian boys, who . . . waylay and assail the children on their way to and from school." Segregation was common in other cities, whether by law, custom, or gerrymandering. Chinese students, when not excluded entirely, attended separate schools in San Francisco, where hostility against them was severe, even though white administrators said some of the students excelled in science and mathematics. Statistics on achievement were unreliable for white students and were often simply not gathered for African-American and Chinese students.[68]

By the 1890s, however, neither nostalgia for the past, complaints about cramming and teaching to the test, "over-study," the diverse talents of teachers and pupils, nor the limitations of statistical knowledge and "premature promotions" stopped competitive tests from spreading across America. The solution to the problems associated with testing was always the same: more testing.

Epilogue

By the 1890s, promotion exams increasingly disappeared and daily, weekly, monthly, end-of-term, and end-of-year tests proliferated in graded school systems. In Chicago, superintendent Albert G. Lane applauded the elimination of promotion exams and growing variety of written alternatives, which when combined with traditional oral questions and answers gave teachers better insights into how well children learned. Beginning in the lowest primary grades, he said, "written tests are constantly given to determine the spelling, punctuation, exactness of thought, and power of expression. They show the teacher the defects of individual pupils as well as those which are common to a class, thus enabling her to give specific instruction to correct them. They constitute a standard for determining the relative power and advancement of pupils." Critics of high-stakes tests at the meetings of the National Education Association in 1895 typically started out assailing student competition and ended up calling for more exams year round. Written tests were so common that popular writers now listed them among the various reasons young people had nightmares.[1]

While sensitive to recurrent complaints about the evils of "over-study," advocates and defenders of written tests abounded. Once competitive exams became routine, no one offered more credible ways to raise and maintain standards. The chief administrator in Knoxville, Tennessee, eager to upgrade its schools, proudly announced in 1893 that he was preparing written questions for the district's four thousand students. Urban superintendents, the most ardent champions of testing and the professionalization of the schools, noticed that hyperbolic criticisms of written exams had generated a counter-defense on their behalf. "However much we may deprecate the evil of cramming and other mis-directions of energy, and deplore its waste," said an educator from Jersey City, New Jersey, in 1895, "it must be admitted" that rigorous, mandatory examinations "mean the thorough awakening of the schools."[2]

In New York state, where passing a Regent's exam was the ticket to academic certificates and diplomas, the expansion of school enrollments at all levels led to a surfeit of high-pressure competitions. The Regents' tests covered a variety of subjects from high school through post-secondary education. Citing a Regents' report for 1896, the *Journal of Education* gave a clear indication of what mass testing, still in its infancy, already entailed: "Two million seven hundred twenty-eight thousand five hundred question papers were printed. Four hundred thousand answer papers were written, and nearly 300,000 were received . . . and rated by university examiners." Some educators complained that the pressure to pass the high school diploma exam had led to cramming and, occasionally, "crooked work," a euphemism for cheating. While districts in many states increasingly abandoned high school entrance and exit examinations and promotion tests, New York illuminated the various ways testing had already expanded. The utility of competitive written exams, first championed enthusiastically by the antebellum Whigs, seemed to have won the day.[3]

Throughout the 1890s, leading educators repeated a familiar mantra, calling for more consolidated schools, graded classrooms, uniform curricula, and greater attention to written classroom exercises, key elements in the spread of testing. Indeed, they reminded their colleagues and the public that criticisms of entrance, exit, or promotion exams were hardly a condemnation of tests in general. William T. Harris, the U.S. Commissioner of Education, stressed the superiority of age-graded instruction, standardized curricula and uniform textbooks, and written assessments. So did his well-known contemporary, Emerson E. White. As superintendent in Cincinnati in the 1880s, White had helped eliminate promotion tests in the local schools. Like most leading educators, he was also familiar with educational developments in England, where special teachers—crammers—prepped pupils for exams at Oxford and Cambridge. He thus worried about making the regular teacher here a "hireling coacher and crammer," reducing teaching "to the trade of preparing pupils for examinations." "When the teacher and crammer are united in one person," he feared," the degradation of the teacher's office is complete." In the twilight of a long career, White nevertheless called competitive exams "the eye of teaching," a window onto reality. "As a rule," he concluded, "teachers overestimate their pupils' attainments, and pupils as a class know much less than they think they know. The searching test is an eye opener. It undeceives teacher and pupils; may, indeed, take the conceit out of them," improving both "teaching and learning."[4]

Absent any viable alternative, save a return to relying upon old-fashioned recitations, written examinations became ubiquitous by the end of the century. Progressive educators such as Francis Parker still lectured on the evils of tests and classroom competition. Parker still loved to tell audiences that grades, prizes, and other academic honors were a form of "bribery" and that pupils should study for its intrinsic value. But even he faced critics who said students at his normal school in Chicago performed two years below grade average. Turning the tables on Parker, given his boasts about his success in Quincy, did not stop him from attacking report cards, statistical data, and competitive testing. But the rising tide of quantification, which would become a tsunami in the twentieth century, was already rolling over the progressives. In 1900, superintendent William B. Powell of Washington, DC, an outspoken champion of child-centered education and vehement critic of competitive exams, was hauled before a Congressional committee, berated for allegedly lowering standards, publicly humiliated, and sacked.[5]

By then, urban officials everywhere affirmed the centrality and importance of written exams in modern school systems. In Cincinnati, Emerson E. White's successor praised the new-style tests for lifting educational standards during "the last half century." "Examinations," he said, "are excellent preparatory exercises for the ever-recurring tests in the sterner matters of life. They toughen the mental fiber, and prepare mind and heart for that which is beyond the school room." The allusion to the 1840s, of course, conjured up the world of Horace Mann, Samuel Gridley Howe, and William Brigham, whose yeomen labors were long remembered in America's Athens. "Shall written examinations be abolished, or restricted, or let alone?" asked Edwin P. Seaver, Boston's superintendent, in 1893. "Far be it from me to join in any hue and cry against written examinations," since they stimulated teachers and pupils to excel. "To relapse into the barbarism of oral examinations or into the laxity of no examinations at all—the conditions of things in this city about a half century ago—is not to be thought of for a moment."[6]

Seaver recognized that every reform could be overdone and condemned testing zealotry. While he could not have predicted the future, no one who suggested returning to the past was taken very seriously by mainstream educators and administrators in the coming years. Parker's generation would be replaced by another wave of progressives, who also criticized various aspects of testing. Once competitive testing entered the schools, however, the issue became not whether there would be written exams, but whether, as the authors of quiz books believed, educators could teach pupils subject matter more effectively and enhance their test-taking skills. As one commentator wryly commented in 1897, "passing examinations is an art, almost a 'trick,' to which one must be trained, and the hot-house training keeps a youth at this 'trick' every week or two for years, until he is as skillful with the question as is a baseball expert with the twirled sphere." The sports metaphor was well chosen, and critics ever since have complained about how some pupils game the system.[7]

Not surprisingly, a succession of key administrators in Boston beginning with John D. Philbrick never forgot about its pivotal role in the early testing wars. Over time, the passions and bitterness engendered by the events of 1845 slowly dissipated. As the principal participants in the summer surprise passed from the scene, however, few people remembered or knew very much about the broader context and complicated origins of testing. What happened behind the scenes—in private meetings and correspondence between Horace Mann and his friends, and the grammar masters and their allies—was hidden from view and never made public. But an opportunity for public reflection arose on May 4, 1896, the centenary of Horace Mann's birth. Boston made a special effort to honor the famous reformer, whose statue along with Daniel Webster's stood on the grounds of the state house. In school after school, pupils listened to short lectures on the outsized role that Mann played in promoting educational reform. Speakers mostly emphasized his endorsement of better teacher training, the hiring of female teachers, and the establishment of a uniform curriculum and age-graded classrooms. At the Bowdoin Grammar School, among the nineteen tested in 1845, pupils learned a few facts about Mann's legendary battles with the masters. At the Quincy School, whose name was once synonymous with the demise of the double-headed system, "the exercises were of a very simple nature" since the master was busy with other responsibilities. None of the masters or speakers elsewhere emphasized Mann's advocacy of written examinations, which might have generated catcalls from some students.[8]

Newspapers and magazines across the nation remembered Mann on his birthday. Phrenology journals reprinted his image, praising his "magnificent forehead." The *Troy Times* rightly pointed out that before becoming the chief school officer in Massachusetts, Mann had had a successful political career, which "gave him the opportunity of securing the ends for which he fought." Others simply called attention to Mann's patriotism, humanitarianism, and support for a range of reforms, especially normal schools. In Portland, the *Morning Oregonian* nostalgically recalled a golden age of political leadership, noting that Mann had succeeded John Quincy Adams in Congress and that he helped place the nation's schools "on a sound and scientific basis." In Houston, Texas, superintendent William S. Sutton held an institute at the high school and required the teachers to provide written responses to a series of questions, including one that dealt with Mann, the grammar masters, and the *Seventh Report*. Regarding the battles between the Secretary and his enemies, they were asked: "who was right?" A day later, the *Galveston Daily News* reprinted one response, which said Mann's trip abroad had convinced him that Europe's schools were superior, raising the ire of the masters. Rather than take sides, the teacher concluded that "mistakes were made by both parties to the controversy," uncertain if Mann understood Boston's schools well.[9]

Educators elsewhere also tried to assess Mann's legacy. S. Y. Gillan, editor of the *Western Teacher*, published in Milwaukee, addressed the alumni of the Illinois Normal School. "Teachers," said Gillan, "are often told by orators who talk for effect that the destiny of a Republic is in their keeping." But everyone knew that "the home, the press, the pulpit," government, and "the money power" especially molded the character of the nation. The schools reflected these broader factors in society and moved "with its current far more than they help to direct its current." So Mann should be understood in the context of his times, an era of widespread change. Among Mann's lasting contributions, Gillan thought, was his championing of "the graded school system with its machinery of examinations and promotions." Neither Gillan nor other speakers across the land, however, said very much about the rise of statistics, the nature of the double-headed system, or the role that numerous Whigs such as Samuel Gridley Howe and their allies played in the events of 1845. Their great adversary and loyal friend of the masters—Frederick Emerson— was also forgotten.[10]

Gillan had nevertheless remembered that competitive testing was one of Mann's most significant legacies. Through his speeches, publications, and active involvement in the first big test in Boston, Mann had seized an opportunity to shame the masters in the light of superior European child-centered practices and to imagine a new way to evaluate pupils and teachers. Echoing Gillan's sense of the importance of historical context, William T. Harris told an appreciative audience at the National Education Association meeting in Buffalo that Mann was a system builder who rose to leadership, "just at the beginning" of the era of railroads and paralleling "the growth of cities." Between 1840 and 1890, the number of communities with at least eight thousand residents—enough to build age-graded facilities and a high school—jumped from 44 to 443. Harris explained that as trunk rails connected cities to villages and suburbs, America was becoming an urban nation, which hastened the process of educational change as communities consolidated their schools and adopted the usual city-based reforms, including testing.[11]

The nineteenth century, as Gillan and Harris recognized, has to be understood on its own terms, and it does seem far removed from contemporary debates on testing and academic standards. But more than a glimpse of the future had appeared in 1845. The testing experiment was predicated on the belief that America's schools were lagging behind the best international standards—then, presumably, found in Europe. At least one master and some students cheated to raise scores, and no one accused the reform-minded Whigs who initiated testing of modesty or unwillingness to argue beyond their evidence. For the first but hardly the last time, citizens read about the shocking test results in newspapers and magazines and debated whether they signified a school system in decline. The major political parties and their intensely partisan newspapers—the leading "media" of the day—were forced to take a stand. Their flawed statistics notwithstanding, reformers then and later compared cities unfavorably with suburbs or smaller communities, whether Roxbury or Quincy, based on test scores. In response to their numerous critics, examiners also claimed on the front page of the *Boston Daily Atlas* in 1846 that the local schools were inferior to "the public schools of Scotland and Holland, to say nothing of Prussia," anticipating the modern movement to rank schools across national boundaries.[12]

The bearers of bad news, the examiners had thus set numerous precedents whose import outlasted the specific battles over school reorganization and administration that preoccupied them in antebellum Boston. Thanks in part to the final rankings, reformers, especially abolitionists, tried to buttress their case that segregation, dreadful pedagogy, and draconian methods of punishment inevitably led to dismal academic achievement at the Smith School, in the heart of America's "cradle of liberty." Following Boston's lead, urban administrators elsewhere soon ranked schools by average scores, applauding the best teachers and pupils while embarrassing the worst. Defenders of tests, who said the written scores generated incontrovertible knowledge about achievement, championed their use as a tool of educational reform, sometimes using them to discredit teachers, accused among other things of teaching to the test and truncating the curriculum. Horace Mann proved prescient in his prediction: after the 1840s, there was no retreating to a time when competitive written tests did not exist or oral exams sufficed.

The nineteenth century acclimated many teachers, pupils, taxpayers, and administrators to a world where schools were expected to produce measurable results: hard facts, not impressions, about educational achievement. Statistics transformed how many people understood reality, and true believers ever since have reduced the purpose of public schools to whatever appears in a table, chart, or graph. Recall that as Mann anxiously awaited the final tallies in Boston, he told a friend that written scores, unlike traditional assessments, provided a virtual "transcript" of their "actual condition." Even the pioneer examiners of 1845, including Mann, nevertheless warned that statistics could never measure a school's "absolute worth" or full meaning. In addition to promoting "intellectual activity and intellectual acquirement," schools had a responsibility to teach students right from wrong and "respect for order" and to help them internalize that which was ineffable and unmeasurable: "a love of knowledge."[13]

That hardly exhausted the many expectations beyond cognitive training that reformers had for the public schools, whether preserving the republic and social order or promoting social mobility for the most talented pupils. Boston's reformers believed that competitive testing would expose the failures of rote instruction, for whites and African-Americans alike, but they never considered whether judging teachers by test results might reinforce hidebound teaching methods. As pupils in graded systems everywhere faced an increasing number of competitive tests, they were no doubt prodded to study more and not rest on their laurels. For reformers in Boston and other communities, written examinations were the indisputable way to raise standards and lift academic achievement. Later generations of educators, however, would rediscover what had genuinely distressed reformers such as Samuel Gridley Howe: that children often left school with minds filled with undigested knowledge, unable to think critically or analytically, and paralyzed if asked to explain or apply what they memorized and regurgitated on tests.

The explosion of knowledge—its sheer expansion in every academic subject—made teaching ever more complicated and demanding by the late nineteenth century. Ungraded or partially graded classrooms were still the rule where most people lived, especially outside of towns and cities; pupils there still memorized subject matter, recited what they knew when called upon by teachers or examiners, and were not tested in common exams. But the innovations that Mann, Howe, and their colleagues forged in the city became the template for schools in modern America. Report cards and the routine gathering of scores on an increasing abundance of exams provided everyone with facts, not as entertaining as an exhibition, parade, or play, but reality pure and simple. Schools, Mann and fellow activists believed, now had the ability to capture, document, and preserve that reality, much like the well-known daguerreotype of the Secretary, so grave and dignified, his hair parted in the middle and brushed to the side to highlight his impressive brow.

Testing was an integral part of the broader movement for free public schools, as Whigs labored to centralize authority and make schools modern and efficient. Over the course of the nineteenth century, reformers and critics of the schools agreed that written examinations would bring discipline, order, and uniformity to the system. The more pupils attended age-graded classes, the more they could be tested and compared. The proliferation of promotion exams and written tests more generally had helped transform urban schools, the models for the nation as districts consolidated and quantitative techniques matured in the early twentieth century. Newly invented intelligence tests and an array of achievement tests would identify children's innate capacity and pinpoint what they learned at school. By World War I, multiple choice exams and machine-readable formats afterwards added to the appeal of standardized testing. Thanks to a swelling tide of foreign immigration, more children poured into the schools, where they faced textbooks that brimmed with facts and subject matter whose boundaries ever expanded. And, like educators throughout the nineteenth century, teachers and administrators struggled to accommodate themselves to the continual spread of knowledge and information in a global economy, a still-familiar challenge. Standardized testing and the tools of measurement became more sophisticated, ever-present features of modern education.[14]

As more schools consolidated in the twentieth century, competitive written examinations seemed like a natural part of the educational system, even though they were in historical terms of recent lineage. With every passing decade, fewer children could escape the ever-lengthening arms of the testing movement, strengthened by modern demands for accountability and a national network of professionals, publishing houses, and corporations.

What educational reformers wrought in the pre-Civil War North thus resonates loudly in the early twenty-first century. Pioneers in using statistical knowledge to advance various social reforms, Mann and his friends knew that many factors shaped school achievement. But they were also politically astute, unafraid to wield power and demonize their opponents. They recognized that when low scores were posted, the safest response was not to emphasize pupils, families, poverty, cultural issues, or other out-of-school influences, but to blame teachers. In 1845 Samuel Gridley Howe identified which teachers deserved public censure or praise, based in part on test scores, a practice abandoned in the late postbellum period but recently revived in some cities. Shaming is cruel and foolhardy but reflects a faith in the inviolability of statistics and quantitative measures and the twined assumption present at the birth of the testing movement: that teachers are primarily responsible for children's academic performance.[15]

Over the last generation the chasm between rich and poor widened, ethnic and racial divisions persisted, and schools failed to achieve the impossible: to make everyone meet the standards associated with the white middle classes. In a world of accountability, past or present, someone must bear the blame. Judged ever relentlessly by standardized measures, teachers and principals have sometimes cheated in Atlanta, Philadelphia, Washington, DC, and other cities, changing student responses on test-bubbles if necessary to preserve their reputations and jobs. In Atlanta, the superintendent humiliated and fired many teachers for not lifting scores. According to Michael Winerip, a columnist for the *New York Times*, investigators discovered in 2011 that "178 principals and teachers at nearly half the district's schools—desperate to raise test scores—had cheated." In various states, students, too, have found new, clever ways to excel, using cell phones hidden in their jeans to text answers to friends during state-mandated exams. Test security companies have arisen to profit from such malfeasance. Politicians who are more comfortable regulating the lives of teachers and children than holding the titans of commerce and finance accountable take credit if test scores rise and blame others if they fall. In the case of New York City, recent claims about rising scores due to mayoral control of schools rested on quicksand, since independent evaluators discovered that pupils had taken easier tests.[16]

The *Testing Wars in the Public Schools* helps explain why school reformers implemented competitive testing in the first place and demonstrates that standardized exams have long been a central part of the American school system, longer than most people realize. Competitive testing arose in an age of reform marked by deep social, racial, and political conflicts, and the debates and controversies of the nineteenth century and of our own times bear an uncanny resemblance. But we live in a different age, and the past and present are not interchangeable. History helps document a wide range of human behaviors and actions, its ability to identify the main roads to the present its basic claim to relevance. Can it guide citizens who seek to respond thoughtfully to enduring problems associated with testing? In a nation obsessed with student competition and measurable outcomes?

History provides perspective and can illuminate the origins of testing and its challenges, benefits, and shortcomings. It cannot offer prescriptions to cure current educational ills. Consider, for example, the successful assault on high-stakes tests in the late nineteenth century. While those tests declined, other forms of testing nevertheless expanded and proliferated, growing more intrusive and consequential in the twentieth and early twenty-first century as school-going expanded and educational credentials became better linked with middle-class jobs and access to the professions. High-stakes exams also reappeared due to federal policies such as *No Child Left Behind* (2002), which currently faces extensive criticism, allowing states to opt out of its testing requirements. As in previous eras disenchanted with unpopular aspects of testing, new and advanced forms of assessment such as "value-added" metrics have arisen to measure how individual teachers influence pupil scores, the latest battleground for friends and foes of standardized testing. Given constant demands for educational accountability from policy makers and elected officials, now moving upward to include colleges and universities, high-stakes tests in many expressions will remain the raison d'etre of schools unless citizens create alternatives that receive political endorsement and the imprimatur of science. Obviously, history cannot tell us whether modern critics of standardized testing will do so.[17]

As experts invent new ways to measure the contents of children's minds, it is crucial to emphasize the importance of historical context, which gives meaning to testing. When competitive testing originated in the nineteenth century, the vast majority of children typically attended schools for a few years. Failure at school had its price, from the shame of repeating grades to the failure to progress very well or very far academically. But most children by the age of twelve or so often entered the workforce to help families survive. Attending school was a small part of most working-class lives. As late as the mid-twentieth century, many poorly educated citizens, whites in particular, had access to factory jobs with some benefits and perhaps union protections, and decent middle-class jobs did not always require college attendance or completion. Compared to the nineteenth century, however, when ungraded classrooms were common and state and federal influence on educational policy was relatively weak, tests today are now more tightly woven into the fabric of school and society.

That remains true even though academic credentials in the early twenty-first century cannot guarantee economic opportunities once more easily enjoyed by degree holders. By the time students complete high school, now a mass institution, they have run through an impressive gauntlet of exams: endless quizzes, aptitude, achievement, and I.Q. tests as well as untold short-answer, essay, and multiple-choice exams prepared by their classroom teachers, test prep tutors, state-level experts, or national testing services. Like the quiz books of an earlier day, Kaplan, Princeton Review, and the authors of a widening array of test prep books beckon consumers to win the race to the top. Tutoring companies flourish as pupils from affluent families scramble for admission to the right school, whether to kindergartens in Manhattan or the most selective colleges and professional schools across the nation. For many politicians, taxpayers, parents, and pupils, high test scores and effective schools have become one and the same.[18]

Since tests in their innumerable expressions help determine grade-to-grade promotion, classroom success, and access to college and professional schools, their grip on teachers and students and their families seems secure. Tests are part of big business and corporate culture. As the Educational Testing Service, the largest "non-profit" organization in the business, explains, its reach is global, for it "develops, administers and scores more than 50 million tests annually in more than 180 countries, at 9,000+ locations worldwide." High school students aspiring to higher education face standardized exams administered by ACT, Inc., and the College Board, rival organizations, ensuring that tests are among the most common features of everyday life. Countless individuals—the authors of guides to testing, psychometricians, economists, guidance counselors, and statisticians and technical staff, among others—have professional identities and livelihoods anchored in a world of testing. And, for teachers and students, tests seem ever present, another one just around the corner.[19]

The fate of the schools rests in the hands of the living, not the dead, but history is an important educator. It helps shape an informed citizenry, which the Founders of the nation saw as a central goal of literacy and learning. The history of testing reveals the high hopes of antebellum reformers, who so enthusiastically advanced policies that judged teachers, pupils, and schools in novel ways, pointing public schools in a new direction from which they have never veered. History also offers many cautionary tales about the effects of high-stakes testing, which contrary to expectations strengthened rote pedagogy and narrowed the curriculum. Knowledge about the fascinating and long-forgotten history of testing seems indispensable to anyone who seeks humane, informed, and sensible policies to improve the lives of students and teachers. If history is any guide, no one should expect consensus as citizens pursue those indefinable though worthy ends, since conflict cast a long shadow over the dramatic events of 1845 and the growing number of communities that imitated the Athens of America.

Anyone who hopes to separate politics from testing, which were intertwined from the start, will have to look to something other than history for guidance. Anyone who imagines that recurrent attacks on high-stakes exams will lead to a diminution in the number and authority of tests is surely mistaken. Anyone who believes that more and better exams will resolve problems endemic to standardized testing, however, can find kinship with numerous Americans who dreamed such dreams before.

Notes

Introduction

1. "Preceptor and Pupil," *Daily Inter-Ocean* (Chicago), January 11, 1878.
2. John Scales, ed., *Biographical Sketches of the Class of 1863: Dartmouth College, With Historical Memorabilia of the College, 1859–1863* (Published by the Class, 1903), 447–448. On urban leadership in school innovation, see Carl F. Kaestle, *Pillars of the Republic: Common Schools and American Society, 1780–1860* (New York: Hill and Wang, 1983), Chapters 3 and 6; William J. Reese, *America's Public Schools: From the Common School to "No Child Left Behind"* (Baltimore, MD: The Johns Hopkins University Press, 2011), 56–68.
3. George S. Counts, *The American Road to Culture* (New York: The John Day Company, 1930), 147; David B. Tyack, *The One Best System: A History of American Urban Education* (Cambridge, MA: Harvard University Press, 1974), 198–216; Michael M. Sokal, ed., *Psychological Testing and American Society, 1890–1920* (New Brunswick, NJ: Rutgers University Press, 1987); Henry L. Minton, *Lewis Terman: Pioneer in Psychological Testing* (New York: New York University Press, 1988); Nicholas Lemann, *The Big Test: The Secret History of the American Meritocracy* (New York: Farrar, Strauss, and Giroux, 1999); and Diane Ravitch, *The Death and Life of the Great American School System: How Testing and Choice Are Undermining Education* (New York: Basic Books, 2010). Ellen Condliffe Lagemann juxtaposes child-centered and efficiency-minded educators in *An Elusive Science: The Troubling History of Education Research* (Chicago: The University of Chicago Press, 2000).
4. Reese, *America's Public Schools*, 322–328.
5. Garrison Keillor, *Lake Wobegon Days* (New York: Viking, 1985); R. J. Montgomery, *Examinations: An Account of their Evolution as Administrative Devices in England* (Pittsburgh, PA: University of Pittsburgh Press, 1965), Introduction and Chapter 1; Christopher Stray, "The Shift from Oral to Written Examination: Cambridge and Oxford 1700–1900," *Assessment in Education* 8 no. 1 (2001): 33–50; and William Clark, *Academic Charisma and the Origins*

of the Research University (Chicago: The University of Chicago Press, 2006), 109–117, 130–137.

6. David M. Henkin, *The Postal Age: The Emergence of Modern Communications in Nineteenth-Century America* (Chicago: The University of Chicago Press, 2006); Daniel Walker Howe, *What Hath God Wrought: The Transformation of America, 1815–1848* (New York: Oxford University Press, 2007), Chapters 6 and 14; and especially Brian Balogh, *A Government Out of Sight: The Mystery of National Authority in Nineteenth-Century America* (New York: Cambridge University Press, 2009).

7. For a summary of federal involvement in education, see Donald R. Warren, "United States Department of Education," in *Historical Dictionary of American Education,* ed. Richard J. Altenbaugh (Westport, CT: Greenwood Press, 1999), 370–372.

8. William Shakespeare, *Measure for Measure,* in *The Complete Works of William Shakespeare* (New York: Avenel Books, 1975), 107.

1. Festivals of Learning

1. Warren Burton, *The District School As It Was, Scenery-Showing, and Other Writings* (Boston: Press of T. R. Marvin, 1852), 75–76, 84. The 1833 edition of Burton's book was entitled *The Distric School As It Was: By One Who Went to It.*

2. "Warren Burton," *American Journal of Education* Issue 44 (Spring 1866): 430; and Burton, *District School,* 76, 80. See the positive reviews of the book: "Article V," *Christian Examiner and General Review* 14 (July 1833): 324–327; "Common Schools," *Family Lyceum* 1 (August 1833): 203; and the gushing review in *The Pearl and Literary Gazette* 3 (November 10, 1833): 48. Burton was an antislavery activist, and his work was reprinted in numerous magazines and newspapers, including William Lloyd Garrison's *Liberator,* March 8, 1834; and Horace Mann's *Common School Journal* 1 (April 15, 1839): 124–126.

3. Burton, *District School,* 78, 79, 80–81, 84.

4. Burton, *District School,* 80. Complaints about the parsimony of hiring committees abounded in newspapers and magazines. See the caricature on teacher salaries in J. Orville Taylor, *Satirical Hits on the People's Education* (New York: Published by the "American Common School Union," 1839), 38.

5. Untitled editorial, *Boston Commercial Gazette,* August 29, 1825. On school exhibitions, see Carolyn Eastman, *A Nation of Speechifiers: Making an American Public after the Revolution* (Chicago: The University of Chicago Press, 2010), which came to my attention after completing this chapter.

6. Nathan Schachner, *The Medieval Universities* (New York: A. S. Barnes & Company, c. 1938), Chapter 33; Alan Cobban, *English University Life in the Middle Ages* (Columbus: Ohio State University Press, 1999), Chapter 5; Christopher J. Lucas, *American Higher Education: A History* (New York: St. Martin's Griffen, 1994), Chapters 1–2; Nicholas Orme, *Medieval Children* (New Haven, CT: Yale

University Press, 2001), 188–189, 232; Steven Ozment, *Ancestors: The Loving Family in Old Europe* (Cambridge, MA: Harvard University Press, 2001), 72–73; and Simon P. Newman, *Parades and the Politics of the Streets: Festive Culture in the Early American Republic* (Philadelphia: University of Pennsylvania Press, 1997), Chapter 1.

 7. On the celebratory traditions in Great Britain, the American colonies, and the new nation, see Gary Nash, *The Urban Crucible: Social Change, Political Consciousness, and the Origins of the American Revolution* (Cambridge, MA: Harvard University Press, 1979), 260–262; David Cressy, *Bonfires and Bells: National Memory and the Protestant Calendar in Elizabethan and Stuart England* (Berkeley: University of California Press, 1989), 197–199, 205–206; David Waldstreicher, *In the Midst of Perpetual Fetes: The Making of American Nationalism: 1776–1820* (Chapel Hill: The University of North Carolina Press, 1997), 18–24, 145; Newman, *Parades*, 20–21; Steven Mintz, *Huck's Raft: A History of American Childhood* (Cambridge, MA: Belknap Press of Harvard University Press, 2004), 28–29; and Brendan McConville, *The King's Three Faces: The Rise & Fall of Royal America, 1688–1776* (Chapel Hill: The University of North Carolina Press, 2006), 56–63.

 8. On the rise of charity schools and fund-raising at Lenten sermons, read *An Account of Charity Schools in Great Britain and Ireland: With the Benefactions Thereto; And of the Methods Whereby They Were Set Up, And Are Governed* (London: Joseph Downing, 1712), 9.

 9. Lucas, *American Higher Education*, 105; Robert Middlekauff, *Ancients and Axioms: Secondary Education in Eighteenth-Century New England* (New York: Arno Press & The New York Times, c. 1971), Chapter 3; Carl F. Kaestle, *Pillars of the Republic: Common Schools and American Society, 1780–1860* (New York: Hill and Wang, 1983), Chapter 3; and Margaret Nash, *Women's Education in the United States 1780–1840* (New York: Palgrave Macmillan, 2005), 5–7.

10. Kaestle, *Pillars*, Chapter 1. The spread of print culture is the subject of many historical works; see the excellent essays by Richard D. Brown, "Early American Origins of the Information Age," and Richard R. John, "Recasting the Information Infrastructure for the Industrial Age," in *A Nation Transformed by Information: How Information Has Shaped the United States from Colonial Times to the Present*, eds. Alfred D. Chandler, Jr., and James W. Cortada (New York: Oxford University Press, 2000), 39–53, 54–105.

11. "The Vogue," *Norwich Packet*, April 1, 1791.

12. Limping Lingo, "Advertisement Extraordinary," *The New-York Journal, & Patriotic Register*, August 4, 1792.

13. William B. Fowle, "Memoir of Caleb Bingham," *The American Journal of Education* 5 (September 1858): 325–349. On the charity school, see James Axtell, *The European and the Indian: Essays in the Ethnohistory of Colonial North America* (New York: Oxford University Press, 1981), Chapter 4. On emulation and the charity school, read David M'Clure and Elijah Parish, *Memoirs of the Rev.*

Eleazar Wheelock, D. D., Founder and President of Dartmouth College and Moor's Charity School (Newburyport, NH: Published by Edward Little & Co., 1811), 19.

14. "Miscellanies," *Massachusetts Spy: Or, Worcester Gazette,* October 6, 1785.

15. "Miscellanies."

16. In addition to Nash, *Women's Education,* see Theodore R. Sizer, ed., *The Age of the Academies* (New York: Teachers College, Columbia University, 1964).

17. Untitled article, *Baltimore Gazette and Daily Advertiser,* August 28, 1827; untitled article, *Providence Patriot & Columbian Phenix,* September 2, 1826; and Z., "For the Federal Gazette," *Federal Gazette, and Philadelphia Evening Post,* November 20, 1788. The standard histories of charity schools include three volumes by Carl F. Kaestle: *The Evolution of an Urban School System: New York City, 1750–1850* (Cambridge, MA: Harvard University Press, 1973); *Joseph Lancaster and the Monitorial School Movement: A Documentary History* (New York: Teachers College Press, 1973); and *Pillars of the Republic,* Chapter 3.

18. "Celebration of the Fourth of July, By the Tammany Society, or Columbian Order," *New-York Daily Gazette,* July 2, 1791; untitled article on the Masons, *The Argus, or Greenleaf's New Daily Advertiser,* June 25, 1795; "Tammany Festival," *The Argus, or Greenleaf's New Daily Advertiser,* May 12, 1796; A Spectator, "New-York Free School," *The Columbian,* December 11, 1809; and "City Intelligence," *The New York Herald,* July 30, 1847.

19. "The New-York Free School," *New-York Commercial Advertiser,* May 10, 1810; and "New-York Free School," *National Advocate,* reprinted in *New-York Herald,* May 10, 1815.

20. See the following articles in *The Sun:* "Primary Schools," July 23, 1842; "Public Schools—Admission to the High School," August 4, 1842; "Local Matters," December 23, 1842; "Popular Education in Baltimore—The High School," January 13, 1843; "May Festival of Female Public School No. 3," May 29, 1843; "Local Matters," July 27, 1843; and "May Festival of the Public High Schools," May 31, 1845.

21. "The Schools and the President," *The Farmer's Cabinet* (Amherst, New Hampshire), August 23, 1849; and *Annual Report of the Trustees of Public Schools of the City of Washington, August 1850* (Washington, DC, n.d.), 33.

22. "New-York African Free School," *New-York Statesman,* reprinted in *New-Hampshire Repository,* April 28, 1823. Also read "African Free School," *New York Daily Advertiser,* reprinted in *National Gazette and Literary Register,* May 11, 1824; "Juvenile Department," *The Liberator,* May 28, 1831; "Examination of the Albany School for Colored Children," *Albany Evening Journal,* November 15, 1837; and Charles C. Andrews, *The History of the New-York African Free-Schools, From their Establishment in 1787, to the Present Time* (New York: Mahlon Day, 1830), 34–35. On racism and public celebrations generally, read Waldstreicher, *In the Midst of Perpetual Fetes,* Chapters 4–6; on the horrid condition of schools, Davison M. Douglas, *Jim Crow Moves North: The Battle Over Northern School Segregation, 1865–1954* (New York: Cambridge University Press, 2005), 44–45.

23. Frederick Douglass, *Narrative of the Life of Frederick Douglass: An American Slave* (New York: Penguin Books, 1982. Originally published in 1845), 83–84; J. B. Anderson, "Communications," *The North Star,* January 5, 1849; and "Exhibition of the Colored School," *The North Star,* April 27, 1849.

24. "Miscellany," *Columbian Centenil,* December 14, 1791; and "How It Strikes a Spectator," *Christian Reflector* 5 (August 31, 1842): 2. On the importance of oratory and nation-building, see Eastman, *A Nation of Speechifiers* as well as Kenneth Cmiel, *Democratic Eloquence: The Fight over Popular Speech in Nineteenth-Century America* (New York: William Morrow and Company, 1990).

25. "Portland," *Cumberland Gazette* (Portland, Maine), June 15, 1787. Caroline Winterer explores the importance of Cicero in *The Culture of Classicism: Ancient Greece and Rome in American Intellectual Life, 1780–1910* (Baltimore, MD: The Johns Hopkins University Press, 2002), 10–11, 13, 25–26. On Bingham and social justice, read Granville Ganter, "The Active Virtue of *The Columbian Orator,*" *The New England Quarterly* 70 (September 1997): 463–476; and Eastman, *A Nation of Speechifiers,* 89, 93.

26. See the untitled articles in the *Boston Gazette,* November 15, 1802; *Carolina Gazette* (Charleston), April 19, 1823; and *The Baltimore Gazette and Daily Advertiser,* March 27, 1826. On tickets and police, see "Annual Exhibition of Ward School No. 5," *New York Herald,* July 30, 1847; and "Examination of Public Schools," *The Sun,* April 3, 1849.

27. "School Exhibition," *The Maryland Herald and Hager's-Town Weekly Advertiser,* March 28, 1804; and "Lancasterian School," *Connecticut Herald,* February 13, 1827.

28. *The Hawes School Memorial, Containing an Account of Five Re-Unions of the Old Hawes School Boys' Association, One Re-Union of the Hawes School Girls' Association, and a Series of Biographical Sketches of the Old Masters* (Boston: David Clapp & Sons, 1889), 100.

29. "Fable," *The Norwich Packet or, The Chronicle of Freedom,* February 24, 1785; Publicus, "Messrs. Printers," *The Daily Advertiser,* January 17, 1791; A Correspondent, "School Oratory," *Salem Gazette,* July 31, 1792; "Juvenile Elocution Society," *Connecticut Herald,* February 19, 1828; and Eastman, *A Nation of Speechifiers,* 33–34.

30. Quoted in John Franklin Reigart, *The Lancasterian System of Instruction in the Schools of New York City* (New York: Teachers College, Columbia University, 1916), 90; and A Visitor, "Perry Academy," *The Georgia Telegraph,* December 19, 1848.

31. "Third Lecture: On the Faults of Teachers," *Southern Literary Register* 2 (July 1836): 478; and "American Education: Its Principles and Elements," *Southern Quarterly Review* 11 (April 1855): 463.

32. "The Following Address," *Salem Gazette,* April 13, 1798. On the nature of the adult political culture caricatured in the student's address, see Joanne B. Freeman, *Affairs of Honor: National Politics in the New Republic* (New Haven, CT: Yale University Press, 2001).

33. Untitled letter to the editor, *New-York Daily Advertiser,* August 5, 1818; "Adversaria," *Hallowell Gazette,* June 20, 1827; and Burton, *District School,* Chapter 12. Complaints about parents who thought their son was a genius were common; see, for example, the spoof "Common Sense, In Dishabille," *Farmer's Weekly Museum,* reprinted in *The Philadelphia Minerva,* October 7, 1797.

34. "On the Evil Consequences of Public Exhibitions and Acting Plays in Elementary Schools," *The Juvenile Mirror; Or, Educational Magazine* 1 (March 1, 1812): 265; and "Town Schools," *Salem Gazette,* April 19, 1825.

35. "Local Matters," *The Sun* (Baltimore), March 31, 1849. Examples are legion; see, for example, the untitled article in the *Semi-Weekly Eagle* (Brattleboro, Vermont), November 20, 1848; and "Punctuation," *Wabash Courier* (Terre Haute, Indiana), March 17, 1849.

36. "The High School," *The Vermont Phoenix,* May 24, 1839.

37. *A Dissertation on Employing Emulation to Encourage Literary Excellence* (Cambridge, MA: Brown, Shattuck, and Company, 1832), 39. J. M. Opal highlights how academies fostered classroom competition and emulation in *Beyond the Farm: National Ambitions in Rural New England* (Philadelphia: University of Pennsylvania Press, 2008), Chapter 4, especially 117–124; in the broader public school context, including high schools, see William J. Reese, *The Origins of the American High School* (New Haven, CT: Yale University Press, 1995), 46, 132–133, 179, 191, 196.

38. "Tirocinium: Or, A Review of Schools," in *The Poetical Works of William Cowper,* ed. H. S. Milford (London: Oxford University Press, 1959), 252–253.

39. "On the Principle of Emulation," *Christian Observer* 13 (March 1814): 151–159; T. S., "Cursory Remarks on the Subject of Emulation," *Christian Observer* 13 (September 1814): 570; and Alpheus Crosby, *A Lecture on the Use and Abuse of Emulation as a Motive to Study: Delivered Before the Essex County Association of Teachers, At Newburyport* (Lynn, MA: Butterfield & Kellogg, Printers, 1852), 11.

40. "Emulation," *Episcopal Recorder* 9 (August 6, 1831): 73; Samuel R. Hall, *Lectures on School-Keeping* (Boston: Richardson, Lord, and Holbrook, 1829), 72–115; S. R. Hall, *Lectures to Female Teachers on School-Keeping* (Boston: Richardson, Lord, & Holbrook, 1832), 161–162; S. R. Hall, "Emulation," *American Annals of Education* 2 (April 1832): 206, where he claimed that pupils who mastered their lessons quickest became idlers; Reese, *Origins,* 132; and Opal, *Beyond the Farm,* 75–76. George B. Emerson, former principal of the English High School in Boston, regretted awarding prizes; see *Reminiscences of an Old Teacher* (Boston: Alfred Mudge & Son, Printers, 1878), 25–26, 54, 61–63. Catherine Beecher, the most famous champion of women's education, also had regrets but mended her ways. See Beecher's essays, "Moral Education," *American Annals of Education* 2 (April 1832): 218; and "The Best Motives in Education," *Vermont Chronicle* (Bellows Falls), January 11, 1833.

41. Caleb Bingham, *The American Preceptor; Being a New Selection of Lessons for Reading and Speaking* (Boston: Manning and Loring, c. 1811), 9. On

Quintilian, see "Communication," *The Repertory* (Boston), August 19, 1806; and "On Exciting Emulation in Children," *Charleston Courier* (South Carolina), May 17, 1810; on Francis Bacon, see his *Essays* (London: Penguin, 1985, third edition originally published 1625), 180; and on Smith, "Common Schools," *Brattleboro Messenger* (Vermont), June 20, 1828.

42. "Extracts, Moral and Prudential," *Weekly Wanderer,* July 17, 1802, and "Modern Education," *Boston Courier,* August 29, 1831. On markets and school culture, see David Hogan, "'To Better Our Condition': Educational Credentialing and 'The Silent Compulsion of Economic Relations' in the United States, 1830 to the Present," *History of Education Quarterly* 36 (Autumn 1996): 243–270.

43. "Article VIII," *The North American Review* 43 (October 1836): 499, 500–501, 513; "The Abbot Festival," *Portsmouth Journal of Literature and Politics,* September 1, 1838; "Emulation," *The Massachusetts Teacher* 1 (May 1, 1848): 131; and Opal, *Beyond the Farm,* 75–77.

44. "Pittsfield," *Spirit of the Times* (New York), reprinted in *The Madisonian* (Washington, DC), March 10, 1842.

45. "Communicated for the *Spy,*" *Massachusetts Spy, or Worcester Gazette,* August 15, 1810.

46. "Trenton," *The New Jersey Gazette,* July 3, 1786; and "Young Ladies' School," *Philadelphia Repository, and Weekly Register,* March 14, 1801.

47. In addition to the classic works by Kaestle, cited earlier, also see two articles by David Hogan, "Modes of Discipline: Affective Individualism and Pedagogical Reform in New England, 1820–1850," *American Journal of Education* 99 (November 1990): 1–56; and "The Market Revolution and Disciplinary Power: Joseph Lancaster and the Psychology of the Early Classroom System," *History of Education Quarterly* 29 (Autumn 1989): 381–417.

48. Joseph Lancaster, *Improvements in Education, As It Respects the Industrious Classes of the Community* (New York: Collins and Perkins, 1807), 74–85. On the tickets and signs, see *The British System of Education: Being a Complete Epitome of the Improvements and Inventions Practiced by Joseph Lancaster: To Which is Added, A Report of the Trustees of the Lancaster School at Georgetown* (Georgetown, DC: Joseph Milligan, 1812), 74; J. L. Rhees, *A Pocket Manual of the Lancasterian System, In Its Most Improved State* (Philadelphia: n.p., 1827), 26–29; and Reigart, *The Lancasterian System,* 52.

49. Anonymous letter to the editor, *The Albany Gazette,* March 22, 1813; "Extenuation of Lancasterian Schools Through the Whole State," *Northern Sentinel* (Burlington, Vermont), April 19, 1816; "Lancaster School," *Ulster Plebian* (Kingston, New York), August 5, 1816; and Publicola, "The Lancastrian Schools," *The Portsmouth Oracle,* April 7, 1821.

50. "Lancasterian Schools," *Kentucky Gazette,* reprinted in *The Western Monitor* (Lexington, Kentucky), August 2, 1817; "Primary Schools," *The Sun,* July 23, 1842; and "Oahu Charity School," *The Friend* (Honolulu), January 1, 1845.

On the teaching methods employed in Baltimore and other charity schools, see William R. Johnson, "'Chanting Choristers': Simultaneous Recitation in Baltimore's Nineteenth-Century Primary Schools," *History of Education Quarterly* 34 (Spring 1994): 1–23.

51. "Summary," *Salem Gazette,* July 11, 1797; "New Orleans Schools," *New Orleans Commercial Times,* reprinted in the *Boston Daily Atlas,* February 10, 1846; and "Ward School No. 3," *New York Herald,* February 12, 1848.

52. "Newark Academy," *The Daily Advertiser* (New York City), April 20, 1799; W., "Communication," *New-York Spectator,* May 13, 1820; and "Report of the School Committee for the Town of Concord, 1822–23," *New-Hampshire Patriot & State Gazette,* March 24, 1823.

53. "Communication," *Providence Patriot and Columbian Phenix,* January 31, 1818; "Examination," *American Repertory,* April 9, 1822; and untitled editorial, *Barre Gazette* (Vermont), November 27, 1835.

54. Untitled article, *State Gazette of South-Carolina,* December 15, 1792; "Our Public Schools," *Salem Gazette,* August 26, 1823; "Academy at Germantown," *National Gazette and Literary Register* (Philadelphia), August 21, 1823; "Hartford Central School," *The Connecticut Mirror,* March 31, 1832; and "School Examination," *Albany Evening Journal,* July 29, 1848.

55. "Portsmouth High Schools," *The Portsmouth Journal,* March 13, 1847. Morpheus was the god of sleep.

56. "School Examinations and Exhibitions," *The Connecticut Common School Journal and Annals of Education* 4 (May 1857): 152. Also see Charles Northend, *The Teacher and the Parent: A Treatise Upon Common School Education* (Boston: Jenks, Hinkling & Swan, 1853), 180.

57. See "Massachusetts," *Newburyport Herald,* September 2, 1803; "An Inhabitant," *Salem Gazette,* September 2, 1803; untitled article in the *Salem Register,* September 5, 1803; and Reese, *Origins,* 179.

58. E., "Lancasterian School," *Connecticut Herald,* December 27, 1825; "Augusta High School," *The Age,* October 17, 1840; "High School," *The Constitution* (Middletown, Connecticut), April 12, 1843; A Spectator, "Mr. Editor," *Morning News* (New London, Connecticut), April 8, 1846; "Female School, No. 5," *The Sun* (Baltimore), March 27, 1847; and "Local Matters," *The Sun,* April 1, 1847. Also see *The Common School Journal,* edited by Horace Mann: "Examination of Schools," 1 (February 15, 1839): 53–56; "First Examination of Schools," 1 (December 2, 1839): 358–361; "Extracts from the Report of the School Committee of the Town of Athol," 4 (June 15, 1842): 177–181; and "Salem Schools," 6 (December 16, 1844): 377–380.

59. Reese, *Origins,* 142–161; and William J. Reese, *America's Public Schools: From the Common School to "No Child Left Behind"* (Baltimore, MD: The Johns Hopkins University Press, 2011), 62–63.

60. "Examination at the Central High School," *Public Ledger,* July 10, 1840; "Twenty-Second Annual Report of the Controllers of the Public Schools,"

Public Ledger, October 22, 1840; untitled article, *The North American and Daily Advertiser,* July 14, 1841; "High School Examination," *The North American,* February 11, 1846; Reese, *Origins,* 146–148, 160, 204, 221; Reese, *America's Public Schools,* 62; and the classic analysis of merit and academics at Central High by David F. Labaree, *The Making of an American High School: The Credentials Market and the Central High School of Philadelphia, 1838–1939* (New Haven, CT: Yale University Press, 1988).

61. *Abstract of the Massachusetts School Returns, for 1839–40* (Boston: Dutton and Wentworth, 1840), 352. Examples of pupils "dodging" exhibitions to avoid examinations were legion in the state abstracts throughout the 1840s.

2. A-Putting Down Sin

1. Henry Barnard, "Report on a System of Common Schools, For Cities and Large Villages," *New-York District School Journal* 3 (August 1, 1842): 19. The standard history of the Boston schools is by Stanley K. Schultz, *The Culture Factory: Boston Public Schools, 1789–1860* (New York: Oxford University Press, 1973). On the annual celebration, see "Schools Visitation," *The Columbian Phenix, or, Boston Review* 1 (July 1800): 449; and "Annual Visitation of the Boston Free Schools," *American Federalist Columbian Sentinel,* August 24, 1822. On school expenses, see Leonard P. Curry, *The Corporate City: The American City as a Political Entity, 1800–1850* (Westport, CT: Greenwood Press, 1997), 72, 78; and Rachel Regina Remmel, "The Origins of the American School Building: Boston Public School Architecture, 1800–1860," (Ph.D. diss., University of Chicago, 2006), 9–10, 38. On the significance of Boston, read William J. Reese, *The Origins of the American High School* (New Haven, CT: Yale University Press, 2005), Chapter 1.

2. "Public Schools," *Evening Gazette,* reprinted in *Boston Courier,* March 3, 1828; and letter to the editor by J. R. Friendlander, "Boston Public Schools," *Boston Courier,* November 22, 1832.

3. "School Establishments of Boston," *The Repertory,* August 19, 1806; "The Schools," *Boston Weekly Messenger,* September 9, 1824; "Boston Public Schools," *Daily Advertiser,* reprinted in "Boston Schools," *Boston Recorder* 24 (August 30, 1839): 140; and "Public Schools of Boston," *Christian Register* 23 (August 24, 1844): 134. Also read Stephen Farley, "On the Improvement Which May Be Made in the Condition of Common Schools," in *The Introductory Discourse and the Lectures Delivered Before the American Institute of Instruction, in Boston, August 1834, Including the Journal of Proceedings, and A List of the Officers* (Boston: Carter, Hendee and Co., 1835), 70.

4. "Miscellany," *The Massachusetts Centinel,* July 15, 1789; "Boston, May 24," *Salem Gazette,* May 25, 1790; *Regulations of the School Committee of the City of Boston* (Boston: Printed by Joseph W. Ingraham, 1823), 14 (Boston Public Library; hereafter BPL); and United States Literary Gazette, reprinted in

"Public Schools in Boston," *Daily National Intelligencer* (Washington, DC), September 7, 1824.

5. *Minutes of the Boston School Committee* (May 6, 1845), 225. (Boston School Committee Archives, Rare Books and Manuscripts, BPL).

6. B. A. Hinsdale, *Horace Mann and the Common School Revival in the United States* (New York: Charles Scribner's Sons, 1900), 183; Isaac F. Shepard, "The Public Schools of Boston," in *Sketches of Boston, Past and Present, and of Some Few Places in Its Vicinity* (Boston: Phillips, Sampson, and Company, 1851), 207; and, for specific examples on the college training of the masters, Leah L. Nichols-Wellington, *History of the Bowdoin School 1821–1907* (Manchester, NH: The Ruemely Press, 1912), 118–124; and the numerous examples sprinkled throughout Arthur Wellington Brayley, *Schools and Schoolboys of Old Boston: An Historical Chronicle of the Public Schools of Boston from 1636 to 1844, To Which Is Added A Series of Biographical Sketches, With Portraits of Some of the Old Schoolboys of Boston* (Boston: Louis P. Hager, 1894). On profit-making on school texts and supplies, see Scrutator, "Our Public Schools," *Boston Courier,* July 16, 1838, which notes that the masters ignored the School Committee's ban on the practice. On the extra two years allowed to girls, see *Regulations of the School Committee of the City of Boston* (Boston: Press of John H. Eastburn, 1830), 13 (BPL). The prohibition on teaching their own private schools is described in "Public Schools," *New-England Galaxy & Masonic Magazine* 2 (April 30, 1819): 115.

7. Schultz, *Culture Factory,* 107; Lemuel Shattuck, *Report to the Committee of the City Council Appointed to Obtain the Census of Boston for the Year 1845, Embracing Collateral Facts and Statistical Researches* (Boston: John H. Eastburn, City Printer, 1846), 67; *Bowen's Picture of Boston, or the Citizen[']s or Strangers' Guide to the Metropolis of Massachusetts, And Its Environs* (Boston: Otis, Broaders and Company, 1838), 28–31; and Nichols-Wellington, *Bowdoin School,* 16.

8. Shattuck, *Report to the Committee,* Appendix R, 28, and Appendix T, 32; and *Regulations of the School Committee* (1823), 10.

9. "Publick Schools," *Boston Gazette, and the Country Journal,* January 24, 1791; "Public Schools," *Columbian Centinel,* August 23, 1817; "Boston Town Schools," *Columbian Centinel,* August 26, 1820; "Visitation of the Public Schools," *Boston Gazette,* reprinted in *Christian Register* 5 (August 26, 1826): 136; and "Public Schools of Boston," *Christian Register,* 135. The *Boston Weekly Messenger* continually praised the summer events; see, for example, "Town Schools," August 31, 1820; "Visitation of the Schools," August 30, 1821; and "Town Schools," reprinted from the *Gazette,* September 2, 1824.

10. *Regulations of the School Committee* (1823), 5.

11. B., "Visitation of the Schools," *Boston Commercial Gazette,* September 1, 1825. A reporter in 1826 added that the exhibition allowed the masters "to show the Committee, parents and others, what improvements the youth have made under their care." Also see "Visitation of Public Schools," *Boston Commercial Gazette,* July 21, 1826.

12. *Regulations of the School Committee* (1823), 6.

13. Nichols-Wellington, *Bowdoin School*, 42; "The Schools," *Boston Weekly Messenger*, September 9, 1824; and "Communication," *Boston Patriot and Daily Chronicle*, August 28, 1818.

14. Letter to the editor, Jerry, "Primary Schools," *Boston Courier*, March 17, 1828; "The Public Schools," *Boston Courier*, May 27, 1830; Editorial, "The Public Schools," *Boston Courier*, November 18, 1830; and S. A. Wells, *The Committee Appointed, 'To Consider the Expediency of Adopting a Uniform Mode of Classification of the Schools, Of Prescribing and Assigning the Studies to Each Class, and the Term of Time To Be Applied to Them, Respectfully'* (Boston, 1830), 2 (Rare Book and Special Collections, Library of Congress; hereafter referred to as LC). On Wells and the high school, see Reese, *Origins*, Chapter 1.

15. Wells, *The Committee Appointed*, 9–10; and Reese, *Origins*, 56, 152.

16. The various reforms can be traced in the following articles in the *Boston Courier:* "The Public Schools," May 27, 1830; "Public Schools," August 19, 1830; "The Public Schools," December 9, 1830; Justice, "Our Public Schools and the School Committee," December 13, 1832; Justice, "Boston Public Schools," December 20, 1832; "Our Schools," *Transcript*, reprinted on September 5, 1836; P., "To the Editor of the Courier," March 3, 1836; and *Report of a Sub-Committee, Recommending the Introduction of a New Organization for the Public Grammar Schools of the City of Boston. 1836* (Boston: John H. Eastburn, 1836), 12–14 (LC).

17. Nichols-Wellington, *Bowdoin School*, n.p.

18. Nichols-Wellington, *Bowdoin School*, 17–18, 62; and *The Hawes School Memorial, Containing An Account of Five Re-Unions of the Old Hawes School Boys' Association, One Re-Union of the Hawes School Girls' Association, and a Series of Biographical Sketches of the Old Masters* (Boston: David Clapp & Sons, 1889), 97, 192.

19. Untitled article, *Montgomery Phoenix*, reprinted in the *Daily Evening Transcript*, April 22, 1843. Also see "Recommendations to the School-Masters, By the Committee Appointed to Carry the Preceding System Into Execution," *Massachusetts Centinel*, January 9, 1790; and A. B., "For the Centinel," *Columbian Centinel*, July 16, 1791.

20. George M. Minns, "Some Reminiscences of Boston Schools Forty-Five Years Ago," *The Massachusetts Teacher* 26 (November 1873): 411; "Visitation of the Public Schools," *Boston Gazette*, reprinted in *Christian Register* 5 (August 26, 1826): 136–137; and a broadside, *Written for the Anniversary Dinner of the Public Schools of the City of Boston* (Boston: J. H. Eastburn, City Printer, 1833), n.p. (BPL).

21. Brayley, *Schools and Schoolboys*, 59, 61; and "A Boston Public School Twenty Years Ago," *The Knickerbocker; or New York Monthly Magazine* 51 (April 1858): 397–400. The rise of soft pedagogy and romanticism is explored in William J. Reese, *America's Public Schools: From the Common School to "No Child Left Behind"* (Baltimore, MD: The Johns Hopkins University Press, 2005), Chapter 3.

22. H., "The Public Schools," *Boston Courier,* January 4, 1838.

23. *Abstract of the Massachusetts School Returns, for 1841–42* (Boston: Dutton and Wentworth, 1842), 1–3.

24. "Josiah Quincy, Jr.," *Boston Daily Advertiser,* July 27, 1893. On Quincy's legislative activities relative to education and friendship with Mann, see Jonathan Messerli, *Horace Mann: A Biography* (New York: Alfred A. Knopf, 1972), 240, 277, 300–301, 349, 364–365, and 425.

25. Among the six summer examining committees (three each for the reading and writing committee), two of them, Samuel Gridley Howe and William Brigham, signed a January 1845 testimonial in defense of Mann. See the list of signatories in the Raymond B. Culver, *Horace Mann and Religion in the Massachusetts Public Schools* (New Haven, CT: Yale University Press, 1929), Appendix C, 289. For a short biography of Brigham, see Frederick Clifton Pierce, *History of Grafton, Worcester County, Massachusetts: From Its Early Settlement by the Indians in 1647 to the Present Time* (Worcester, MA: Press of Chas. Hamilton, 1879), 465–466. The lone non-Whig on the writing committee was H. A. Graves, a Baptist minister and member of the Native American Party, which was virulently anti-immigrant and anti-Catholic; see Schultz, *Culture Factory,* 139–140. Graves received the Whig party nomination for School Committee from Ward Four in 1845. According to William B. Fowle, *The Scholiast Schooled: An Examination of the Review of the Reports of the Annual Visiting Committees of the Public Schools of the City of Boston, for 1845* (Cambridge, MA: Metcalf and Company, 1846), 55, Brigham was a close friend of Quincy's and prominent in the Native American party. He was a longtime Whig and ran on the Whig ticket in December 1844.

26. On the elder Parsons, see Ronald P. Formisano, *The Transformation of Political Culture: Massachusetts Parties, 1790s–1840s* (New York: Oxford University Press, 1983), 132. On the younger Parsons, see Augustus A. Gould, "Notice of the Origin, Progress, and Present Condition of the Boston Society of Natural History," *The American Quarterly Register* 14 (February 1842): 236; "Great Whig Meeting," *Boston Daily Atlas,* June 7, 1844; Messerli, *Horace Mann,* 168; and untitled article on Parsons's death, *Boston Daily Advertiser,* January 27, 1882.

27. "Installation," *Christian Watchman* 14 (September 20, 1833): 150; "Christianity Against War," *Christian Watchman* 16 (November 27, 1835): 1; "Address to the Baptist Churches in the Northern Part of the United States," *Christian Secretary* 3 (May 22, 1840): 1; Rev. Luther Farnham, "Boston Pulpit," *Gleason's Pictorial Drawing* 5 (November 26, 1853): 348; "Death of the Rev. Dr. Neale," *Boston Daily Advertiser,* September 18, 1879; and "The Late Dr. Rollin H. Neale," *Boston Daily Advertiser,* September 23, 1879.

28. On the Latin school incident, Julia Ward Howe, *Memoir of Dr. Samuel Gridley Howe* (Boston: Printed by Albert J. Wright, 1876), 3. The definitive biography, while dated, is by Harold Schwartz, *Samuel Gridley Howe: Social Reformer, 1801–1876* (Cambridge, MA: Harvard University Press, 1956).

29. On the deep friendship between Mann and Howe, see the correspondence between them cited in George Allen Hubbell, *Horace Mann: Educator, Patriot and Reformer: A Study in Leadership* (Philadelphia: Wm. F. Fell Company, 1910), 242–246. In addition to Schwartz, *Samuel Gridley Howe*, also read Mary D. Vaughan, *Historical Catalogue of Brown University 1764–1904* (Providence, RI: Published by the University, 1905), 38, 126, 131.

30. Mark Rennella, *The Boston Cosmopolitans: International Travel and American Arts and Letters* (New York: Palgrave Macmillan, 2008), 6–7; and Thomas H. O'Connor, *The Athens of America: Boston, 1825–1845* (Amherst: The University of Massachusetts Press, 2006), a concise, general history.

31. *Seventh Annual Report of the Board of Education; Together With the Seventh Annual Report of the Secretary of the Board* (Boston: Dutton & Wentworth, State Printers, 1844), 24–25; Deborah Pickman Clifford, *Mine Eyes Have Seen the Glory: A Biography of Julia Ward Howe* (Boston: Little, Brown and Company, 1979), 57; and Samuel G. Howe to Horace Mann, undated, ca. 1845, in Laura E. Richards, ed., *Letters and Journals of Samuel Gridley Howe* (Boston: Dana Estes & Company, 1909), 2: 178. On Calvinism and metaphysics, read Messerli, *Horace Mann*, 22–23, 350–351. Also see John D. Davies, *Phrenology: Fad and Science A 19th-Century American Crusade* (Hamden, CT: Archon Books, c. 1971), 85–88. On Howe and religion, Schwartz, *Samuel Gridley Howe*, 4. Both Mann and Howe (who helped fund John Brown's raid on Harper's Ferry) left the Whig Party, which collapsed over the issue of antislavery, in the late 1840s.

32. Messerli, *Horace Mann*, 224, 318–319, 350–353, 465; Schwartz, *Samuel Gridley Howe*, 93, 116, 144; Harold Schwartz, "Samuel Gridley Howe as Phrenologist," *American Historical Review* 57 (April 1952): 648–649, 651; and Hubbard Winslow, "On the Dangerous Tendency To Innovations and Extremes in Education," in *The Introductory Discourse*, 176. On the appeal of phrenology among elite Bostonians, see James H. Cassedy, *American Medicine and Statistical Thinking, 1800–1860* (Cambridge, MA: Harvard University Press, 1984), Chapter 7. On Howe and Spurzheim, also read Steven A. Gelb, "'Not Simply Bad and Incorrigible': Science, Morality, and Intellectual Deficiency," *History of Education Quarterly* 29 (Autumn 1989): 363.

33. S. G. Howe, *A Discourse on the Social Relations of Man; Delivered Before the Boston Phrenological Society, At the Close of Their Course of Lectures* (Boston: March, Capen & Lyon, 1837), 25.

34. Several excellent histories of quantification help place the rise of written tests in a broad Western European context. Read Ronald Edward Zupko, *Revolution in Measurement: Western European Weights and Measures Since the Age of Science* (Philadelphia: The American Philosophical Society, 1990); Alfred W. Crosby, *The Measure of Reality: Quantification and Western Society, 1250–1600* (Cambridge: Cambridge University Press, 1997); Oz Frankel, *States of Inquiry: Social Investigations and Print Culture in Nineteenth-Century Britain and the United States* (Baltimore, MD: The Johns Hopkins University Press, 2006); and two

books by Theodore M. Porter, *The Rise of Statistical Thinking, 1820–1900* (Princeton, NJ: Princeton University Press, 1986) and *Trust in Numbers: The Pursuit of Objectivity in Science and Public Life* (Princeton, NJ: Princeton University Press, 1995). Also see Reese, *America's Public Schools,* 112. On the harvest of souls, R. H. Neale, "Revival in the First Baptist Church," *Christian Reflector* 5 (April 13, 1842): 2.

35. The central role of Boston and Massachusetts in popularizing statistical analysis, and Howe's importance in that effort, is underscored in Cassedy, *American Medicine,* 164, 193, 201, and by Frankel, *States of Inquiry,* in many sections of his excellent book. Also see *First Annual Report of the Board of Education, Together With the First Annual Report of the Secretary of the Board* (Boston: Dutton and Wentworth, State Printers, 1838), 36, 69; Messerli, *Horace Mann,* 124–128, 247; Howe, *A Discourse,* 36–37; and "The Common School Journal," *Christian Register and Boston Observer* 20 (July 31, 1841): 122.

36. George M. Towle, "Theophilus Parsons," *Appletons' Journal of Literature, Science, and Art* 7 (March 2, 1872): 237; R. H. Neale, "Letter from Rev. R. H. Neale," *Christian Watchman* 24 (June 23, 1843): 98; and R. H. Neale, "Letter from Rev. R. H. Neale," *Christian Watchman* 24 (August 18, 1843): 131.

37. Quoted in Robert L. McCaul, "Educational News and Comment," *The Elementary School Journal* 58 (October 1957): 6.

38. Schwartz, "Samuel Gridley Howe as Phrenologist," 647; and Messerli, *Horace Mann,* on Mann's temperament, which is explored throughout his probing biography.

39. On the Whig educational platform, see Reese, *America's Public Schools,* 20–27, 32, 43, and 183.

40. The definitive analysis of the battle over the creation of (and attempt to eliminate) the State Board of Education is by Carl F. Kaestle and Maris A. Vinovskis, *Education and Social Change in Nineteenth-Century Massachusetts* (Cambridge: Cambridge University Press, 1980), Chapter 8; Messerli, *Horace Mann,* Chapter 14; and Horace Mann to Samuel Gridley Howe, March 17, 1842 (Reel 6, Horace Mann Collection, 1669–1926, Massachusetts Historical Society, microfilm edition; hereafter cited as HMC); this letter was reprinted with a note on the reference to the masters in Laura E. Richards, "Horace Mann to Samuel G. Howe," *New England Quarterly* 12 (December 1939): 732.

41. M. J. Cullen, *The Statistical Movement in Early Victorian Britain: The Foundations of Empirical Social Research* (New York: Barnes & Noble Books, 1975), and Frankel, *States of Inquiry,* document the English fascination with statistics, Benthamite politics, and other innovative ideas concerning measurement in the early nineteenth century. On the exam systems developing at Cambridge and Oxford Universities, see R. J. Montgomery, *Examinations: An Account of their Evolution as Administrative Devices in England* (Pittsburgh, PA: University of Pittsburgh Press, 1965), Introduction and Chapter 1; Sheldon Rothblatt, *The Modern University and Its Discontents: The Fate of Newman's Legacies in*

Britain and America (Cambridge: Cambridge University Press, 1997),148–160; Christopher Stray, "The Shift from Oral to Written Examination: Cambridge and Oxford 1700–1900," *Assessment in Education* 8 no. 1 (2001): 33–50; and William Clark, *Academic Charisma and the Origins of the Research University* (Chicago: The University of Chicago Press, 2006), 109–117, 130–137. On Mann's trip abroad, read Messerli, *Horace Mann,* 385–408. Mann approvingly described written tests in "Examination of Candidates for Admission to a Superior Grade," *Common School Journal* 3 (July 15, 1841): 217; and in "School Examinations," *Common School Journal* 5 (March 1, 1843): 70. Also see Reese, *Origins,* 142–161.

42. *Seventh Annual Report* (1844), 133; and Messerli, *Horace Mann,* 407.

43. C. S., "Mr. Mann's Report on Education Abroad," *Niles' National Register* 16 (April 6, 1844): 85; "Report of the Secretary of the Board of Education," *The Monthly Religious Magazine* 1 (April 1844): 143; "Seventh Annual Report of the Board of Education," *North American Review* 58 (April 1844): 518; and *Boston Post,* reprinted in "Seventh Annual Report," *Boston Cultivator* 6 (March 30, 1844): 104.

44. Comments from the *Athenaeum,* reprinted in "Seventh Annual Report of the Massachusetts Board of Education," *Littell's Living Age* 7 (June 29, 1844): 428; and Horace Mann to George Combe, April [?] 1844, in Mary Peabody Mann, *Life of Horace Mann* (Washington, DC: National Education Association of the United States, c. 1937), 225–226.

45. Reese, *Origins,* 127, 142–143; George B. Emerson, S. R. Hall, and E. A. Andrews, *Memorial of the American Institute of Instruction Praying for the Appointment of a Superintendent of the Common Schools* (Boston: House Document No. 27, Legislature of the Commonwealth of Massachusetts, 1836), 10–12; and GBE, "Common Schools," *Christian Examiner and Religious Miscellany* 36 (May 1844): 414, 419–420.

46. "Schools in Prussia," *Common School Journal* 1 (May 15, 1839): 154–158; Samuel G. Howe, "Letter from Dr. Samuel G. Howe," *Common School Journal* 2 (August 1, 1840): 238; and "Remarks on the Seventh Annual Report of the Honorable Horace Mann," *The North American Review* 60 (January 1845): 228–229; Reese, *America's Public Schools,* 86; and, though from a later period, Mann's "Ninth Report of the Secretary of the Board of Education," *Common School Journal* 8 (July 1, 1846): 199. On Howe's admiration for Pestalozzi, see Samuel Gridley Howe to Horace Mann, July 19, 1838 (Howe Family Papers, MS Am2119. Houghton Library, Harvard University; hereafter cited as HFP).

47. On Fowle, see "Phrenology Applied to Character," *Ladies' Magazine and Literary Gazette* 6 (June 1, 1833): 277–278; "William Bentley Fowle," *The American Journal of Education* 10 (June 1861): 290–305; Rev. Elias Nason, "William Bentley Fowle," *The New-England Historical and Genealogical Register and Antiquarian Journal* 23 (April 1869): 109–117; Robert T. Brown, "William Bentley Fowle," *American National Biography Online* (New York: Oxford

University Press, American Council of Learned Societies, c. 2000); and William B. Fowle to Horace Mann, July 11, 1844 (Reel 7, HMC).

48. George B. Emerson to Horace Mann, July 16, 1844 (Reel 7, HMC); and Theodore Parker to Horace Mann, September 17, 1844 (Reel 7, HMC).

49. Horace Mann to Samuel Gridley Howe, August 19, 1844 (Reel 7, HMC).

50. Association of Masters, *Remarks on the Seventh Annual Report of the Hon. Horace Mann, Secretary of the Massachusetts Board of Education* (Boston: Charles C. Little and James Brown, 1844), 8, 26, 35, 38 for the quotations, and 13–15, 19, for commentary on Howe. Messerli, *Horace Mann,* 413, sees a touch of paranoia in the masters.

51. Edward L. Pierce, *Memoir and Letters of Charles Sumner* (Boston: Roberts Brothers, 1877), 1: 162; and Charles Sumner to Samuel Gridley Howe, September 11, 1844, quoted in Pierce, *Memoir and Letters of Charles Sumner,* 2: 319. Sumner was defeated in his bid for election to the School Committee in December 1844, losing to a nativist Baptist minister.

52. See the following letters from Horace Mann to Samuel Gridley Howe, September 25, 1844 (Reel 7, HMC); October 8, 1844 (Reel 7, HMC); October 11, 1844 (Reel 7, HMC); and November 1, 1844 (Reel 7, HMC). Also see Samuel Gridley Howe to Horace Mann, October 9, 1844 (HFP).

53. Orestes Brownson, "Remarks on the Seventh Annual Report of the Hon. Horace Mann," *Brownson's Quarterly Review* 1 (October 1, 1844): 547; and Horace Mann to Samuel Gridley Howe, October 8, 1844 (Reel 7, HMC).

54. Horace Mann to Samuel Gridley Howe, October 8, 1844 (Reel 7, HMC); Horace Mann to Rev. S. J. May, October 16, 1844, in *Life of Horace Mann,* 227; George B. Emerson to Horace Mann, October 19, 1844 (Reel 7, HMC); George B. Emerson, *Observations on a Pamphlet, Entitled "Remarks on the Seventh Annual Report of the Hon. Horace Mann, Secretary of the Massachusetts Board of Education"* (n.p., 1845), 1–2; and Horace Mann, *Reply to the "Remarks" of Thirty-One Boston Schoolmasters on the Seventh Annual Report of the Secretary of the Massachusetts Board of Education* (Boston: Wm. B. Fowle and Nahum Capen, 1844), 143–164.

55. Dr. Fischer to Horace Mann, November 7, 1844, regarding Odin's displeasure with the masters (Reel 7, HMC).

56. "Seventh Annual Report of the Boards of Education," *Boston Daily Atlas* (November 26, 1844); and "Remarks on the Seventh Annual Report," *The North American Review,* 231.

57. Samuel Gridley Howe to Horace Mann, October 9, 1844 (HFP); and Samuel Gridley Howe to Horace Mann, November 26, 1844 (HFP).

58. Horace Mann to George Combe, December 1, 1844, in *Life of Horace Mann,* 230–232.

59. S. G. H., (i.e. Howe), "Mr. Mann and the Boston Teachers," *Boston Daily Atlas,* December 7, 1844; "The Thirty-One Boston School-Masters," *Boston Evening Transcript,* November 23, 1844; Joshua Bates, Jr., to Horace Mann, December

8, 1844 (Reel 7, HMC); W. J. Adams to Horace Mann, December 8, 1844 (Reel 7, HMC); and Horace Mann to George Combe, December 1, 1844, in *Life of Horace Mann*, 232.

60. "School Committee—Complete," *Boston Daily Atlas*, December 13, 1844; "Mr. Mann and the Boston Schoolmasters," *Christian Watchman* 25 (December 27, 1844): 207; and J. T., "Matters and Things in Boston," *New York Observer* 22 (December 21, 1844): 202.

3. Screwing Machines

1. "School Committee," *Boston Daily Atlas*, January 18, 1845.

2. February 1845 quarterly school reports, (File Folders for 1845, Boston School Committee Archives, BPL).

3. This collective portrait is based on numerous sources: especially local city directories, biographical sketches in Boston's various newspapers and magazines, and obituaries.

4. On Streeter, see the Rev. Luther Farnham, "Boston Pulpit," *Gleason's Pictorial Drawing-Room Companion* 5 (October 15, 1853): 252; on Emerson, G. H. T., "The Late Frederick Emerson, Esq.," *The Rhode Island Schoolmaster* 3 (June 1857): 113; and on Wigglesworth, "Edward Wigglesworth," *American Academy of Arts and Sciences* 12 (May 1876–May 1877): 303–307.

5. The testimonial is reprinted in Raymond B. Culver, *Horace Mann and Religion in the Massachusetts Public Schools* (New Haven, CT: Yale University Press, 1929), 287–289; and Josiah Quincy, Jr., et al., to Horace Mann, January 13, 1845 (Reel 8, HMC). On the "grand intrigue," see "The School Committee Report," *Emancipator and Weekly Chronicle*, August 20, 1845. Sumner had led the committee that raised the money to help fund a normal school; see Jonathan Messerli, *Horace Mann: A Biography* (New York: Alfred A. Knopf, 1972), 421.

6. Franklin Bowditch Dexter, *Biographical Sketches of the Graduates of Yale College With Annals of the College History* (New Haven, CT: Yale University Press, 1912), 6: 722–727; and "The Rev. Leonard Withington," *The New York Times*, April 23, 1885. On debates over self-discipline and emulation, see Michael B. Katz, *The Irony of Early School Reform: Educational Innovation in Mid-Nineteenth Century Massachusetts* (Boston: Beacon Press, 1968), 131–153; on romanticism and education, William J. Reese, *America's Public Schools: From the Common School to "No Child Left Behind"* (Baltimore, MD: The Johns Hopkins University Press, 2005), Chapter 3. One of Withington's contemporaries proudly noted that emulation was a positive good, producing habits of study and leading to prizes and honors in the local grammar schools. See Caleb H. Snow, *A History of Boston, The Metropolis of Massachusetts, From Its Origin to the Present Period; With Some Account of the Environs* (Boston: Published by Abel Bowen, 1828), 354; Rev. Leonard Withington, "Emulation in Schools," in

The Introductory Discourse and the Lectures Delivered Before the American Institute of Instruction, in Boston, August 1833, Including a List of Officers and Members (Boston: Carter, Hendee and Co., 1834), 141, 149, 150; and Leonard Withington, "Review of Channing's Works," *Literary and Theological Review* 1 (June 1834): 304–335.

7. Leonard Withington, *Penitential Tears; Or A Cry from the Dust, By "The Thirty-one," Prostrated and Pulverized by the Hand of Horace Mann, Secretary, &c.* (Boston: C. Stimpson, 1845), 3, 5, 8, 10, 17, 18, 22, 32, 35, 38–39.

8. Withington, *Penitential Tears,* 58–59; and Francis Bowen, "Article IX," *North American Review* 60 (January 1845): 231, 246.

9. Dexter, *Biographical Sketches,* 6: 673–75; Hugh Davis, *Joshua Leavitt: Evangelical Abolitionist* (Baton Rouge: Louisiana State University Press, 1990), 20, 29; "Penitential Tears," *Emancipator and Weekly Chronicle,* January 29, 1845; and "Mr. Mann and the Boston Schoolmasters," *Christian Watchman* 26 (February 11, 1845): 30.

10. Horace Mann to George Combe, February 28, 1845, in Mary Peabody Mann, *Life of Horace Mann* (Washington, DC: National Education Association of the United States, c. 1937), 237.

11. The testimonial is reprinted in Culver, *Horace Mann and Religion,* 287–289.

12. Horace Mann, *Lectures on Education* (Boston: Wm. B. Fowle and N. Capen, 1845), 311; and E. W., "Massachusetts Board of Education," *Christian Examiner and Religious Miscellany* 38 (March 1845): 229–231. George B. Emerson had used corporal punishment extensively as a young teacher and regretted that it was still necessary in some cases. See "On Corporal Punishment and Emulation, in Schools," *Common School Journal* 4 (August 15, 1842): 246. Samuel Gridley Howe, in his otherwise sprightly defense of Mann and criticisms of the Boston masters, pointed out that he did not fully agree with the Secretary on corporal punishment. This hardly led Howe to condone the flogging meted out by Boston's teachers. See S. G. H., "Mr. Mann and the Boston Masters," *Boston Daily Atlas,* December 7, 1844.

13. Anti-Busby, "School Discipline," *Boston Daily Atlas,* January 7, 1845.

14. Anti-Busby, "School Discipline."

15. Anti-Busby, "School Discipline." One of Mann's allies, an educator and minister, wrote that "It is very common for teachers to address boys in ruder, rougher, and coarser language, than they do girls; boys too are often punished for offenses which are overlooked in girls; or they receive five blows when a female would receive but two." See Emerson Davis, *The Teacher Taught; or, The Principles and Modes of Teaching* (Boston: Marsh, Capen, Lyon, and Webb, 1840), 21.

16. Anti-Busby, "School Discipline."

17. "News," *Boston Courier,* May 18, 1843.

18. "School Committee," *Boston Daily Atlas,* May 9, 1845.

19. *An Appeal to the Public: In a Case of Cruelty, Inflicted on a Child of Mr. Jacquith, At the Mayhew School in Hawkins Street. . . .* (Boston: Published for the Benefit of

the Public, 1832), 13–14, 19–20 (LC); "Corporeal Punishment," *Mercantile Journal*, reprinted in *Boston Daily Atlas*, April 25, 1845; and "School Committee," *Boston Daily Atlas*, May 9, 1845. Another master had allegedly knocked a little girl down and kicked her, though her parents had yet to file a grievance.

20. Wigglesworth's report is reprinted in "School Committee," *Boston Daily Atlas*, May 9, 1845. The physician, H. B. C. Greene, presented his side of the story in a letter reprinted in the *Boston Daily Atlas*, May 12, 1845.

21. "Boston," *New York Herald*, May 24, 1845; and Arthur Wellington Brayley, *Schools and Schoolboys of Old Boston: An Historical Chronicle of the Public Schools of Boston from 1636 to 1844, To Which Is Added A Series of Biographical Sketches, With Portraits of Some of the Old Schoolboys of Boston* (Boston: Louis P. Hager, 1894), 60, 252.

22. On the squabbles over teaching methods, see *Report of a Committee of the Association of Masters of the Boston Public Schools, On a Letter from Dr. John Odin, Jr., and in Relation to a Report of the Special Committee of the Primary School Board* (Boston: William A. Hall & Co., 1845) (LC); and William B. Fowle to Horace Mann, June 26, 1845 (Reel 8, HMC), regarding the strong performance of Field's pupils in science in the summer examination. On the reference to "brother Barnum," one of many letters dealing with the irascible master, see Samuel Gridley Howe to Horace Mann, May 8, 1845 (HFP).

23. For some memories (and a defense of Field), see *The Hawes' School Memorial, Containing An Account of Five Re-Unions of the Old Hawes School Boys' Association, One Re-Union of the Hawes School Girls' Association, and a Series of Biographical Sketches of the Old Masters* (Boston: David Clapp & Son, Printers, 1889), 128–130. Also read W. H. W., "Mass. State Teachers' Association," *The Massachusetts Teacher* 1 (December 15, 1848): 373. On Mann and the Episcopalians, see Horace Mann to George Combe, April [?] 1844, in *Life of Horace Mann*, 225–226. On the Brown connection, see Mary D. Vaughan, *Historical Catalogue of Brown University 1764–1904* (Providence, RI: Published by the University, 1905), 38, 130, 131.

24. There is a huge literature on the subject of African-American education in antebellum Boston. Read especially Carleton Mabee, "A Negro Boycott to Integrate Boston Schools," *The New England Quarterly* 41 (September 1968): 341–361; Donald M. Jacobs, "The Nineteenth Century Struggle Over Segregated Education in the Boston Schools," *The Journal of Negro Education* 39 (Winter 1970): 76–85; Stanley K. Schultz, *The Culture Factory: Boston Public Schools, 1789–1860* (New York: Oxford University Press, 1973), Chapters 7–8; and Stephen Kendrick and Paul Kendrick, *Sarah's Long Walk: The Free Blacks of Boston and How Their Struggle for Equality Changed America* (Boston: Beacon Press, 2004), 71–73.

25. Biographical information on Forbes is found in "Obituary," *Boston Evening Journal*, October 26, 1877. Also see "Grammar School in Belknap-Street," *The Liberator*, April 5, 1834; "Grammar School—Belknap Street," *The Liberator*, August 23, 1834; *Mr. Minot's Address: Delivered at the Dedication of the Smith*

School House in Belknap Street, March 3, 1835 (Boston: Webster and South-ard, Printers, 1835), 2; and J. Morgan Kousser, "'The Supremacy of Equal Rights,': The Struggle Against Racial Discrimination in Antebellum Massa-chusetts and the Foundations of the Fourteenth Amendment," *Northwestern University Law Review* 82 (Summer 1988): 952–953.

26. See the following articles in *The Liberator:* "Education," *National Intelligencer,* reprinted January 1, 1831; "The Infant School Exhibition in Philadelphia," June 4, 1831; R. T., "Incentives to Get Knowledge," March 10, 1832; J., "School for Colored Children," *Catskill Recorder,* reprinted June 2, 1832; "School for Colored Youth," September 29, 1832; "African Free Schools," June 22, 1833; "Capacity of the African Race," October 19, 1833; and "Edu-cation," December 14, 1833.

27. In *The Liberator,* read "Formation of a Literary and Scientific Society," Janu-ary 2, 1837; "Scientific Lectures," January 14, 1837; and "Adelphic Union," May 11, 1838.

28. Leonard W. Levy and Douglas L. Jones, *Jim Crow in Boston: The Origin of the Separate but Equal Doctrine* (New York: Da Capo Press, 1974), ix–x; and Mabee, "A Negro Boycott," 341. Also read *William Cooper Nell: Selected Writ-ings 1832–1874,* eds. Dorothy Porter Wesley and Constance Porter Uzelac (Baltimore, MD: Black Classics Press, 2002).

29. J. E. Worcester, *Elements of Geography, Modern and Ancient With a Modern and Ancient Atlas* (Boston: Published by Lewis and Sampson, 1844), 195, 197; and Barnum Field, *The American School Geography, Embracing A General View of Mathematical, Physical, and Civil Geography, Adapted to the Capacities of Children* (Boston: Otis, Broaders, and Company, 1844), 136. Racism was endemic in schoolbooks; see Ruth Miller Elson, *Guardians of Tradition: American School-books of the Nineteenth Century* (Lincoln: The University of Nebraska Press, 1964), Chapter 4; and Reese, *America's Public Schools,* 32.

30. David Walker, *Walker's Appeal, In Four Articles, Together With a Preamble to the Coloured Citizens of the World, But in Particular, and Very Expressly, to Those of the United States of America* (Boston: Revised and Published by David Walker, 1830), 35–39; and Reverend H. Easton, *A Treatise on the Intellectual Charac-ter, and Civil and Political Condition of the Colored People of the U. States; and the Prejudice Exercised Towards Them: With a Sermon on the Duty of the Church to Them* (Boston: Printed and Published by Isaac Knapp, 1837), 6–7, 19–20, and 40–41; and, for appraisals of both men, see Schultz, *The Culture Factory,* 172–175, 179.

31. George Combe, *Notes on the United States of North America during A Phrenologi-cal Visit in 1828–9–40* (Edinburgh: Maclachan, Stewart, and Company, 1841), 1: 159. Hillary J. Moss analyzes Mann's private views and public posture on integration in *Schooling Citizens: The Struggle for African American Educa-tion in Antebellum America* (Chicago: The University of Chicago Press, 2009), 149–157.

32. Kendrick and Kendrick, *Sarah's Long Walk,* 40–41, 79–80; and "Smith School," *The Liberator,* August 27, 1841.

33. Kendrick and Kendrick, *Sarah's Long Walk,* 81–84. The declining fortunes of Forbes can be traced in *The Liberator:* Justice, "Smith School, Belknap-Street," September 2, 1842; One of the School Board, "The Smith School," October 7, 1842; and Telemaque, "Smith School, Belknap-Street," August 25, 1843. Also see two letters by Wilberforce in the *Boston Courier:* "The White Race in Boston," July 18, 1842 and "The Colored Race in Boston," August 8, 1842.

34. Kendrick and Kendrick, *Sarah's Long Walk,* 80–84.

35. Basic biographical information appears in G. H. T., "The Late Frederick Emerson," 113. On Emerson's removal from the Boylston School, read Isaac F. Shepard, "The Public Schools of Boston," in *Sketches of Boston, Past and Present, and of Some Few Places in Its Vicinity* (Boston: Phillips, Sampson, and Company, 1851), 216. Also see Henry Barnard, *School Architecture; Or, Contributions to the Improvement of School-Houses in the United States* (New York: A. S. Barnes & Co., 1850), 144; and "School Books," *The Boston Pearl: A Gazette Devoted to Polite Literature* 5 (February 13, 1836): 174.

36. George W. Minns, "Some Reminiscences of Boston Schools Forty-Five Years Ago," *The Massachusetts Teacher* 26 (October 1873): 375; and George W. Minns, "Some Reminiscences of Boston Schools Forty-Five Years Ago," *The Massachusetts Teacher* 26 (November 1873): 411. Drinking alcohol was commonplace, at all sorts of private and public events, in the antebellum period. See William J. Rorabaugh, *The Alcoholic Republic, An American Tradition* (New York: Oxford University Press, 1979); and Ronald P. Formisano, *The Transformation of Political Culture: Massachusetts Parties, 1790–1840s* (New York: Oxford University Press, 1983), 181, 297–298.

37. Mann recounted the story of Emerson's textbooks and his refusal to endorse them in letters to Loring Norcross, March 10, 1846 and March 11, 1846, in Robert L. Straker, compiler, "Notes on the Life of Horace Mann," 1571–1572. (Robert L. Straker Collection, Antiochiana, Antioch College). On Norcross and temperance, read "Great Temperance Meeting in Faneuil Hall," *Boston Daily Atlas,* February 24, 1842.

38. G. H. T., "The Late Frederick Emerson," 113; "At a Meeting of the Whigs of Ward 5," *Boston Courier,* November 13, 1843; and "Tribute of Respect to Frederick Emerson, Esq.," *Boston Daily Atlas,* March 14, 1845.

39. See three articles in the *Boston Daily Atlas:* "The Investigation," May 21, 1844; "Report of a Committee of Parents," July 25, 1844; and "The Handsome Vote," August 20, 1844. In a committee report dated June 12, 1844, Emerson admitted that Forbes was "indiscrete" in meting out discipline and dealing with parents. ("School Committee Papers," BPL).

40. "Report of a Committee of Parents," *The Liberator,* August 2, 1844.

41. "Report of a Committee of Parents."

42. William B. Fowle to Horace Mann, July 11, 1844 (Reel 7, HMC).

43. W. J. Adams to Horace Mann, February 19, 1845; Samuel A. Eliot to Horace Mann, June 2, 1845; William J. Adams to Horace Mann, June 9, 1845; and S. Mason to Horace Mann, June 16, 1845 (all on Reel 8, HMC).

44. William B. Fowle to Horace Mann, May 3, 1845; Horace Mann to Samuel Gridley Howe, May 5, 1845; Horace Mann to William Shepard, May 30, 1845; William Shepard to Horace Mann, June 10, 1845; Horace Mann to William Shepard, June 12, 1845; and William A. Shepard to Horace Mann, June 13, 1845 (all on Reel 8, HMC). On Howe's inability to stop publication of the *Rejoinder,* see Samuel Gridley Howe to Horace Mann, May 8, 1845 (HFP). Also see *Rejoinder to "Reply" of The Hon. Horace Mann, Secretary of the Massachusetts Board of Education, to the "Remarks" of the Association of Boston Masters, Upon His Seventh Annual Report* (Boston: Charles C. Little and James Brown, 1845); and Horace Mann, *Answer to the "Rejoinder" of the Twenty-Nine Masters, Part of the "Thirty-One" Who Published "Remarks" on the Seventh Annual Report of the Secretary of the Massachusetts Board of Education* (Boston: Wm. B. Fowle and Nahum Capen, 1845). On the redundant arguments in both reports, also read Messerli, *Horace Mann,* 417–418.

45. Horace Mann to Samuel Gridley Howe, May 7, 1845 (Reel 8, HMC); and Horace Mann to Samuel Gridley Howe, May [?] 1845 (Reel 8, HMC).

46. Samuel G. Howe to Horace Mann, May 8, 1845 (HFP).

47. William B. Fowle to Horace Mann, May 19, 1845 (Reel 8, HMC); and William B. Fowle to Horace Mann, June [?] 1845 (Reel 8, HMC).

48. Horace Mann to Samuel Gridley Howe, June 19, 1845 (Reel 8, HMC); Horace Mann to Samuel Gridley Howe, June 20 1845 (Reel 8, HMC); and Harold Schwartz, *Samuel Gridley Howe: Social Reformer, 1801–1876* (Cambridge, MA: Harvard University Press, 1956), 130.

49. Samuel G. Howe to Horace Mann, June 21, 1845, in Robert L. Straker, "Samuel G. Howe to Horace Mann," *New England Quarterly* 16 (September 1943): 477–478; and William B. Fowle to Horace Mann, June 21, 1845 (Reel 8, HMC).

50. William B. Fowle to Horace Mann, June 26, 1845 (Reel 8, HMC).

51. Horace Mann to Samuel Gridley Howe, October 8, 1844 (Reel 7, HMC).

52. Horace Mann to Rev. S. J. May, July 4, 1845, in *Life of Horace Mann,* 238.

53. "School Committee," *Boston Daily Atlas,* May 9, 1845; and William B. Fowle to Horace Mann, June 26, 1845 (Reel 8, HMC).

54. Horace Mann to the Rev. S. J. May, July 4, 1845, in *Life of Horace Mann,* 239.

4. A Pile of Thunder-Bolts

1. "Rev. L. Withington—On Common Schools," *Newburyport Herald,* reprinted in *The New England Farmer* 11 (October 24, 1832): 120; George Combe, *Notes on the United States of North America During a Phrenological Visit in 1838–9–40* (Edinburgh: Maclachlan, Stewart, & Company, 1841), 1: 160–161; and

Emerson Davis, *The Teacher Taught; or, The Principles and Modes of Teaching* (Boston: Marsh, Capen, Lyon, and Webb, 1840), 25.

2. One of the School Committee, "Boston Primary School Rooms," *American Annals of Education* 8 (December 1838): 547; "Order of Lessons and General Arrangement in the Hancock School, Boston," *Common School Journal* 5 (May 1, 1843): 134; and Arthur Wellington Brayley, *Schools and Schoolboys of Old Boston: An Historical Chronicle of the Public Schools of Boston from 1636 to 1844, To Which Is Added A Series of Biographical Sketches, With Portraits of Some of the Old Schoolboys of Boston* (Boston: Louis P. Hager, 1894), 111.

3. "Ventilation of School Rooms," *School Journal*, reprinted in *Christian Watchman* 22 (February 26, 1841): 36.

4. William B. Fowle to Horace Mann, July 7, 1845 (Reel 8, HMC); Stanley K. Schultz, *The Culture Factory: Boston Public Schools, 1789–1860* (New York: Oxford University Press, 1973), 139–140; and Harold Schwartz, *Samuel Gridley Howe: Social Reformer, 1801–1876* (Cambridge, MA: Harvard University Press, 1956), 128–131.

5. Schwartz, *Samuel Gridley Howe*, 130; and Jonathan Messerli, *Horace Mann: A Biography* (New York: Alfred A. Knopf, 1972), Chapter 17.

6. *Rejoinder to the "Reply" of The Hon. Horace Mann, Secretary of the Massachusetts Board of Education, To The "Remarks" of the Association of Boston Masters, Upon His Seventh Annual Report* (Boston: Charles C. Little and James Brown, 1845); and *Answer to the "Rejoinder" of Twenty-Nine Boston Schoolmasters, Part of the "Thirty-One" Who Published "Remarks" on the Seventh Annual Report of the Secretary of the Massachusetts Board of Education* (Boston: William B. Fowle and Nahum Capen, 1845).

7. "Mr. Mann's Answer," *Emancipator and Weekly Chronicle*, August 6, 1845.

8. *Minutes of the Boston School Committee* (August 5, 1845), 227 (BPL); and "School Committee," *Boston Daily Atlas*, August 9, 1845.

9. "School Committee," *Boston Daily Atlas*, August 9, 1845. Emerson and his allies recognized that Brewer had long been allied with Mann, Howe, and the reform-minded Whigs. Brewer had introduced the motion to force the masters to record all incidences of corporal punishment at the final meeting of the School Committee in 1844. See "School Committee," *Boston Daily Atlas*, reprinted in *Daily Evening Transcript*, December 28, 1844.

10. "School Committee," *Boston Daily Atlas*, August 9, 1845.

11. On Mann's amazing ability to tap every available means of communication and transportation to spread his educational message, see Messerli, *Horace Mann*.

12. On the growing connections between political parties and newspapers in the late 1820s, see Paul Starr, *The Creation of the Media: Political Origins of Modern Communication* (New York: Basic Books, 2004), 85.

13. A Father, "The Report on the Boston Schools," *Boston Courier*, reprinted in *Boston Daily Atlas*, August 11, 1845.

14. "School Committee," *Boston Daily Atlas,* reprinted in *Daily Evening Transcript,* August 9, 1845. On the politics of newspapers, see Ronald P. Formisano, *The Transformation of Political Culture: Massachusetts Political Parties, 1790s–1840s* (New York: Oxford University Press, 1983), 324–325.
15. "A Tax-Paying Citizen," *Boston Daily Journal,* August 11, 1845.
16. "School Committee," *Boston Daily Journal,* August 12, 1845.
17. "School Committee," *Boston Daily Journal,* August 12, 1845; and three letters on August 13, 1845: Another Citizen, "The Grammar Schools"; Citizens of Boston, "Our Schools"; and Shawmut, "Our Schools."
18. "The Public Schools," *Emancipator and Weekly Chronicle,* August 13, 1845; and Hugh Davis, *Joshua Leavitt: Evangelical Abolitionist* (Baton Rouge: Louisiana State University Press, 1990), 34–40.
19. "The Public Schools," *Emancipator and Weekly Chronicle,* August 11, 1845.
20. Shawmut, "Our Schools."
21. Father, "The Report on the Boston Schools, No. 2," *Boston Courier Semi-Weekly,* August 14, 1845.
22. "School Committee," *Boston Daily Atlas,* August 15, 1845.
23. "School Committee," *Boston Daily Atlas,* August 15, 1845.
24. "Boston School Committee," *Boston Daily Advertiser,* August 16, 1845.
25. Horace Mann to Rev. Samuel J. May, July 4, 1845, in Mary Peabody Mann, *Life of Horace Mann* (Washington, DC: National Education Association of the United States, c. 1937), 238; "Boston School Committee," *Boston Daily Advertiser,* August 16, 1845; and "The School Committee and the Atlas," *Boston Daily Atlas,* August 19, 1845.
26. "Election of School Teachers Postponed," *Boston Post,* August 15, 1845; and "School Committee," *Boston Daily Atlas,* August 15, 1845.
27. "Boston School Committee," *Boston Daily Advertiser,* August 16, 1845.
28. Horace Mann to Samuel Gridley Howe, August 18, 1845 (Reel 8, HMC).
29. Deborah Pickman Clifford, *Mine Eyes Have Seen the Glory: A Biography of Julia Ward Howe* (Boston: Little, Brown and Company, 1979), 84–85; Mary H. Grant, *Private Woman, Public Person: An Account of the Life of Julia Ward Howe from 1819 to 1868* (Brooklyn, NY: Carlson Publishing Inc., 1994), 64–65; and Horace Mann to Samuel Gridley Howe, August 18, 1845 (Reel 8, HMC).
30. A, "For the Transcript," *Daily Evening Transcript,* August 14, 1845; "The Flogging Case in the Mayhew School," *Boston Daily Times and Bay State Democrat,* August 16, 1845; and "The School Committee and the Atlas," *Boston Daily Atlas,* August 19, 1845.
31. "The School Committee Report," *Emancipator and Weekly Chronicle,* August 20, 1845.
32. "The School Committee Report," *Emancipator and Weekly Chronicle,* August 20, 1845.
33. "Who Can Do Better, Children?" and "Teaching Geography," *Vermont Chronicle,* August 20, 1845.

34. "The School Committee," *Boston Daily Atlas*, August 29, 1845; and "Boston School Committee," *Boston Daily Advertiser*, August 30, 1845. On Graves, see Schultz, *Culture Factory*, 139–140.

35. "The School Committee," *Boston Daily Atlas*, August 29, 1845; and "Boston School Committee," *Boston Daily Advertiser*, August 30, 1845.

36. "Boston School Committee," *Boston Daily Advertiser*, August 30, 1845.

37. "Boston School Committee," *Boston Daily Advertiser*, August 30, 1845.

38. "Boston School Committee," *Boston Daily Advertiser*, August 30, 1845. On Sumner's defeat, see Schwartz, *Samuel Gridley Howe*, 128.

39. Letter to the editor, "Another of the School Committee," *Boston Daily Times and Bay State Democrat*, August 15, 1845; "Boston School Committee," *Boston Daily Advertiser*, August 30, 1845; and Samuel Gridley Howe to Horace Mann, September [?], 1845, in Laura E. Richards, *Letters and Journals of Samuel Gridley Howe* (Boston: Dane Estes & Company, 1909), 2: 182–183.

40. "Boston School Committee," *Boston Daily Advertiser*, August 30, 1845. On Neale's travels to other cities, see Messerli, *Horace Mann*, 419; and Mark Antony De Wolfe Howe, *Review of the Reports of the Annual Visiting Committees of the Public Schools of the City of Boston, For 1845* (Boston: Charles Stimpson, 1846), 20, 38.

41. "Boston School Committee," *Boston Daily Advertiser*, August 30, 1845.

42. "The School Committee," *Boston Daily Atlas*, August 29, 1845; "Boston School Committee," *Boston Daily Advertiser*, August 30, 1845; and "Election of Schoolmasters Further Proceeded In," *Boston Post*, September 1, 1845.

43. "Boston School Committee," *Boston Daily Advertiser*, August 30, 1845. Howe and Emerson were no strangers to public debate. At the 1841 meetings of the American Institute of Instruction, Emerson attacked Mann and his friend, George Combe, which provoked a heated reply from Howe. See "Normal Schools," *Salem Gazette*, reprinted in *Common School Journal* 3 (November 1, 1841): 328–333.

44. "The School Committee," *Boston Daily Atlas*, August 29, 1845.

45. "Boston School Committee," *Boston Daily Advertiser*, September 1, 1845; "School Committee," *Boston Daily Atlas*, September 1, 1845; and *Minutes of the Boston School Committee* (August 30, 1845), 241 (BPL).

46. "Boston School Committee," *Boston Daily Advertiser*, September 1, 1845.

47. "Boston School Committee," *Boston Daily Advertiser*, September 1, 1845.

48. Horace Mann to Samuel Gridley Howe, August 29, 1845 (Reel 8, HMC).

49. "School Committee," *Boston Daily Atlas*, September 1, 1845; and "School Committee," *Boston Post*, September 2, 1845.

50. Samuel Gridley Howe to Horace Mann, September 3, 1845, in Richards, *Letters and Journals*, 2: 180–181.

51. "The School Committee," *Boston Daily Atlas*, September 5, 1845.

52. "The School Committee," *Daily Evening Transcript*, September 5, 1845; "School Committee," *Boston Daily Times and Bay State Democrat*, September 5,

1845; and "End of the School War.—The Plotters Defeated," *Emancipator and Weekly Chronicle,* September 10, 1845. (The editorial was dated September 8 but published two days later.) Schwartz, *Samuel Gridley Howe,* 136, describes the long-term victories by the reform group.

53. *Boston Daily Advertiser,* "The Proceedings of the School Committee," reprinted in *Boston Daily Atlas,* September 8, 1845.

54. "School Committee," *Boston Daily Atlas,* September 12, 1845.

55. R. H. Neale to Samuel Gridley Howe, July 10, 1845 (HFP).

56. *Reports of the Annual Visiting Committees of the Public Schools of the City of Boston, 1845* (Boston: J. H. Eastburn, City Printer, 1845), 149, 159, 161–163; and "School Committee," *Boston Daily Atlas,* September 12, 1845.

57. "School Committee," *Boston Daily Atlas,* September 12, 1845; "School Committee," *Boston Daily Journal,* September 12, 1845; "Another Meeting of the School Committee," *Boston Post,* September 12, 1845; "Boston Grammar and Writing Schools," *Common School Journal* 7 (October 1, 1845): 289; and "Boston Grammar and Writing Schools," *Common School Journal* 7 (November 1, 1845): 330.

58. William B. Fowle to Horace Mann, September 23, 1845 (Reel 8, HMC); and Horace Mann to George Combe, September 25, 1845, in Mann, *Life of Horace Mann,* 240–241.

59. Horace Mann to George Combe, September 25, 1845, in Mann, *Life of Horace Mann,* 241.

60. William B. Fowle to Horace Mann, October 3, 1845 (Reel 8, HMC); and Horace Mann to Cyrus Peirce, October 7, 1845 (Reel 8, HMC). My characterization of Mann's personality, shaped by reading his personal correspondence and published writings, was also guided by Messerli's psychological portrait in *Horace Mann.*

61. "The School Committee's Report," *Mercantile Journal,* reprinted in the *Boston Daily Atlas,* August 11, 1845.

5. Thanatopsis and Square Roots

1. *Reports of the Annual Visiting Committees of the Public Schools of the City of Boston, 1845* (Boston: J. H. Eastburn, City Printer, 1845); Samuel J. May to Horace Mann, October 22, 1845 (Reel 8, HMC); and James Eaton to Horace Mann, October 23, 1845 (Reel 8, HMC).

2. William Hamilton to Horace Mann, October 27, 1845 (Reel 8, HMC); and James Henry to Horace Mann, December 29, 1845 (Reel 8, HMC).

3. "Report of the Committee Appointed to Make the Annual Examination of the Grammar Schools in the City of Boston," *North American Review* 61 (October 1845): 524, 527. The *Boston Daily Atlas* typically endorsed most of the reforms advanced by Mann and his friends.

4. *Minutes of the Boston School Committee* (November 4, 1845), 273; and (November 25, 1845), 276–277 (BPL). Also see "School Committee," *Boston Daily*

Atlas, November 27, 1845; and Horace Mann to Samuel J. May, December 2, 1845, in Mary Peabody Mann, *Life of Horace Mann* (Washington, DC: National Education Association of the United States, c. 1937), 245. Like Howe, Brigham failed to win nomination to the school board, but the latter was elected in the spring, filling a vacancy. See "Election in Ward Eleven," *Boston Daily Atlas,* May 26, 1846. The editor viewed the outcome as support for the reformers and endorsement for hiring a superintendent, which Brigham championed.

5. Read the following articles in the *Boston Daily Atlas:* L., "The School Committee," December 2, 1845; "The Municipal Election," December 6, 1845; Free Schools, "The Public Schools," December 8, 1845; Anti-Bamboozle, "Bamboozling," December 8, 1845; and Horace Mann to Samuel J. May, December 2, 1845, in Mann, *Life of Horace Mann,* 245.

6. "All Sorts of Paragraphs," *Boston Post,* December 9, 1845; and "Our City Election," *Boston Daily Atlas,* December 9, 1845. On the changing social context, Stanley K. Schultz, *The Culture Factory: Boston Public Schools, 1789–1860* (New York: Oxford University Press, 1973); and Oscar Handlin, *Boston's Immigrants: A Study in Acculturation* (New York: Atheneum, c. 1977).

7. *Minutes of the Boston School Committee* (September 11, 1845), 254; and *Annual Visiting Committees* (1845), 2, 9, 39.

8. Samuel Gridley Howe to Horace Mann, September [?] 1845 (HFP); and *Annual Visiting Committees* (1845), 154, 161. Active in the American Statistical Association since its formation in 1839, Brigham became an officer in the organization. See "American Statistical Society," *Boston Daily Atlas,* January 19, 1846; and "The American Statistical Association," *Daily Evening Transcript,* February 5, 1852.

9. *Annual Visiting Committees* (1845), 6–7, 54.

10. On the English High School and entrance tests, see William J. Reese, *The Origins of the American High School* (New Haven, CT: Yale University Press, 1995), 1–15, 142–161.

11. *Annual Visiting Committees* (1845), 7, 8. I'm indebted to Daniel Koretz, *Measuring Up: What Educational Testing Really Tells Us* (Cambridge, MA: Harvard University Press, 2008), a very accessible volume on the nature, benefits, and pitfalls of testing.

12. *Annual Visiting Committees* (1845), 6, 9–10. William B. Fowle published a defense of the examiners pseudonymously, *The Scholiast Schooled. An Examination of the Review of the Reports of the Annual Visiting Committees of the Public Schools of the City of Boston, For 1845, by "Scholiast"* (Cambridge, MA: Metcalf and Company, 1846), 33, and noted the "Herculean" effort.

13. *Annual Visiting Committees* (1845), 18–19.

14. *Annual Visiting Committees* (1845), 10–11; and Horace Mann to Samuel Gridley Howe, May [?] 1845 (Reel 8, HMC); and William B. Fowle to Horace Mann, June 21, 1845 (Reel 8, HMC).

15. See J. E. Worcester, *Elements of History, Ancient and Modern: With a Chart and Tables of History, Included Within the Volume* (Boston: W. J. Reynolds, 1843),

316–400; Barnum Field, *The American School Geography, Embracing a General View of Mathematical, Physical, and Civil Geography* (Boston: Otis, Broaders, and Company, 1844); and Frederick Emerson, *The North American Arithmetic. Part Third, For Advanced Scholars* (Boston: Russell, Odiorne, & Metcalf, 1834). Textbooks *were* the curriculum in most schools; see William J. Reese, *America's Public Schools: From the Common School to "No Child Left Behind"* (Baltimore, MD: The Johns Hopkins University Press, 2005), 28–38. Also see *The Hawes' School Memorial, Containing An Account of Five Re-Unions of the Old Hawes School Boys' Association, One Re-Union of the Hawes School Girls' Association, and a Series of Biographical Sketches of the Old Masters* (Boston: David Clapp & Sons, 1889), 26.

16. *Annual Visiting Committees* (1845), 10–11, 66–75. See the criticism of the question in Mark Antony De Wolfe Howe, *Review of the Reports of the Annual Visiting Committees of the Public Schools of the City of Boston, For 1845* (Boston: Charles Stimpson, 1846), 26–27.

17. *Annual Visiting Committees* (1845), 10–11, 66–75.

18. *Annual Visiting Committees* (1845), 12–13, 56–65. On the reputation of geography and history, see Reese, *Origins*, 137–138; and Reese, *America's Public Schools*, 32, 37–38.

19. *Annual Visiting Committees* (1845), 13, 14, 76–85. Perhaps the masters in the low-achieving schools, of course, had not even required their pupils to study or memorize "Thanatopsis." The examiners assumed that what was assigned should have been read and studied.

20. See three articles in the *Common School Journal:* "Examination of Schools," 1 (February 15, 1839): 53–56; A Parent, "The First Examination of Schools," 1 (December 2, 1839): 358–361; and "Boston Grammar and Writing Schools," 7 (November 1, 1845): 332.

21. *Annual Visiting Committees* (1845), 18, 30.

22. "The School Committee Report," *Emancipator and Weekly Chronicle,* August 20, 1845.

23. *Annual Visiting Committees* (1845), 6, 9.

24. On the importance of statistics and social investigations, see Oz Frankel, *States of Inquiry: Social Investigations and Print Culture in Nineteenth-Century Britain and the United States* (Baltimore, MD: The Johns Hopkins University Press, 2006); and Theodore M. Porter, *The Rise of Statistical Thinking, 1820–1900* (Princeton, NJ: Princeton University Press, 1986) and *Trust in Numbers: The Pursuit of Objectivity in Science and Public Life* (Princeton, NJ: Princeton University Press, 1995).

25. *Annual Visiting Committees* (1845), 9, 148–149.

26. *Annual Visiting Committees* (1845), 148–149.

27. *Annual Visiting Committees* (1845), 153, 154, 161. Commentary on Brigham's exam, and on the delays administering it, appeared in Horace Mann to Samuel Gridley Howe, June 19, 1845 (Reel 8, HMC); and William B. Fowle to Horace Mann, June 26, 1845 (Reel 8, HMC).

28. *Annual Visiting Committees* (1845), 19–23.

29. *Annual Visiting Committees* (1845), 23, 29.
30. *Annual Visiting Committees* (1845), 160–161, 164; and Emerson, *The North American Arithmetic. Third Part,* Chapters 10 and 19.
31. *Annual Visiting Committees* (1845), 30, 31, 152, 164.
32. *Annual Visiting Committees* (1845), 30–33.
33. *Annual Visiting Committees* (1845), 34–40, 46. On the teaching staff, see Lemuel Shattuck, *Report to the Committee of the City Council Appointed to Obtain the Census of Boston for the Year 1845, Embracing Collateral Facts and Statistical Researches* (Boston: John H. Eastburn, City Printer, 1846), Appendix R, 28 and Appendix T, 31.
34. *Annual Visiting Committees* (1845), 46–49.
35. *Annual Visiting Committees* (1845), 51, 168.
36. "Boston Grammar and Writing Schools," 330, 334, 335; and *Abstract of the Massachusetts School Returns, for 1845–46* (Boston: Dutton and Wentworth, 1846), 2–10.
37. "Boston School Examination," *The District School Journal of the State of New York* 6 (December 1845): 172.
38. "Mayor Quincy's Address," *Daily Evening Transcript,* January 6, 1846.
39. "School Committee," *Boston Daily Atlas,* January 14, 1846.
40. "Remarks of Rev. C. Brooks, in School Committee–On Examining School-masters, According to the Law," *Boston Daily Atlas,* January 22, 1846. For examples of test questions for prospective teachers, see untitled article, *Common School Journal* 9 (December 15, 1847): 378–381. On Brooks and school reform, see Jonathan Messerli, *Horace Mann: A Biography* (New York: Alfred A. Knopf, 1972), 241, 261–262, 298, 316; and Jurgen Herbst, *And Sadly Teach: Teacher Education and Professionalization in American Culture* (Madison: The University of Wisconsin Press, 1989), Chapter 2. See the list of signatories to the petition in Raymond B. Culver, *Horace Mann and Religion in the Massachusetts Public Schools* (New Haven, CT: Yale University Press, 1929), Appendix C, 289. By early February of 1846, Mark Antony De Wolfe Howe, an orthodox Episcopalian minister, had issued a lengthy pamphlet attacking the examiners, accusing them of vilifying the grammar masters on behalf of the Secretary. Howe had taught in the local schools before entering the ministry, and he ridiculed the idea that pupil responses to a handful of "written questions" proved that the system, whose alumni included numerous distinguished citizens, was in tatters. See Mark Antony De Wolfe Howe, *Review of the Reports,* 18, 22, 38; and the condemnation of his report in "Multiple News Items," *Boston Daily Atlas,* February 7, 1846.
41. "Superintendent of the Schools," including "Remarks of Mr. Hillard," *Boston Daily Atlas,* February 25, 1846.
42. "Remarks of Mr. Hillard."
43. Follow the political narrative in the *Boston Daily Atlas:* "Superintendent of the Public Schools," February 26, 1848; "Common Council," *Boston Courier,*

reprinted on March 7, 1846; "Remarks of Otis Clapp, Esq.," March 19, 1846; "Mr. Neale's Stated," April 8, 1846; "It Affords Us Pleasure," April 9, 1846; and "Superintendent of Schools," April 18, 1846.

44. S. G. Howe, William Brigham, and J. I. T. Coolidge, "Boston Public Schools, and Appointment of a Superintendent," *Boston Daily Atlas*, April 23, 1846. Adjoining this long article were letters by Rollin H. Neale and Theophilus Parsons. Mann often published articles by or about his friends, including Samuel Gridley Howe, George B. Emerson, and Charles Brooks. See for example "Progress of Reform in the Boston Schools," *Common School Journal* 8 (March 2, 1846): 65–69; and Howe, "Superintendents of Public Schools," *Common School Journal* 10 (August 1, 1848): 240. On Mann's interest in Bishop, see the reply from Nathan Bishop to Horace Mann, April 24, 1843 (Reel 7, HMC). Mann also published flattering comments on him; read H. B., "Rhode Island," *Common School Journal* 5 (November 15, 1843): 339–340. On the campaign to appoint a master to fill the superintendent's position, see "Superintendent of the Public Schools," *Boston Evening Transcript*, May 20, 1851.

45. *Seventh Annual Report of the Board of Education; Together With the Seventh Annual Report of the Secretary of the Board* (Boston: Dutton & Wentworth, State Printers, 1844), 84–85; and Reese, *America's Public Schools*, 33. On the importance of single seats and desks to ensure more uniformity and pupil responsibility, see "Affairs In and Around the City," *Boston Daily Atlas*, June 27, 1851; and Reese, *Origins*, 195.

46. "School Committee," *Boston Daily Atlas*, August 31, 1847; "Quincy School," *Boston Daily Atlas*, June 27, 1848; "Popular Education," *Boston Daily Atlas*, June 28, 1848; "The Quincy School," *Boston Post*, reprinted in *Daily Evening Transcript*, June 27, 1848; "Address of Hon. Josiah Quincy, Jr.," *Boston Daily Atlas*, January 6, 1849; "The New School House at South Boston," *Daily Evening Transcript*, March 29, 1849; "Learning," *Boston* Almanac, reprinted in *The Youth's Companion* 24 (September 26, 1850): 87; and Howard P. Chudacoff, *How Old Are You? Age Consciousness in American Culture* (Princeton, NJ: Princeton University Press, 1989), 35–36.

47. The casual use of the word "principal" can be seen in "Superintendent of Public Schools," *Boston Evening Transcript*, May 19, 1851; and "Affairs In and About the City," *Boston Daily Atlas*, August 4, 1852. Typical behavior by Emerson is recorded in "Grammar School Committee," *Boston Daily Courier*, October 11, 1849.

48. On the linkage of written tests and a proposed position for a superintendent, see *Superintendent of Public Schools* (Boston: City Document No. 14, March 10, 1847), 6–8. Also see "School Committee," *Boston Daily Atlas*, September 7, 1847; and "In School Committee," *Boston Daily Atlas*, September 13, 1847. George B. Emerson also presented a detailed report to the School Committee in August of that year and served on a committee to advance the "reorganization" of the grammar schools. See "School Committee," *Boston*

Daily Atlas, August 31, 1847. On the residency question, see Howe's report in *Annual Visiting Committees* (1845), 50; "List of Non-Resident Instructors in Public Schools and the Salaries Paid to Each, November 1849," ("School Committee Papers," Folder 24, Boston School Committee Archives, BPL); and "School Committee," *Boston Daily Advertiser*, reprinted in *Daily Evening Transcript*, May 8, 1850. On Brooks and his enthusiasm for the single-headed system and hiring of female teachers, see "Our Public Schools," *Daily Evening Transcript*, February 28, 1850; and, on the resolution on examining every class, see "Local Intelligence," *Boston Daily Atlas*, January 31, 1850. Once hiring a superintendent was imminent, more resolutions on behalf of the single-headed system emerged; see "Affairs In and About the City," *Boston Daily Atlas*, December 17, 1851.

49. Poz., "The Superintendent of Schools," *Boston Courier*, March 5, 1846; and M., "The Public Schools of Boston," *Daily Evening Transcript*, October 22, 1852. The Montez scandal churned for months before the School Committee issued a statement saying that Emerson had not acted on its behalf, but as a private citizen; see "Affairs In and About the City," *Boston Daily Atlas*, November 10, 1852. On support for the single-headed plan, see *Reports of the Annual Visiting Committees of the Public Schools of the City of Boston* (Boston: J. H. Eastburn, City Printer, 1846), 39; *Reports of the Annual Visiting Committees of the Public Schools* (Boston: J. H. Eastburn, 1847), 45–52; and *The Report of the Annual Examination of the Public Schools of the City of Boston* (Boston: J. H. Eastburn, 1849), 5–6, which noted the trends toward the single-headed system but said the old plan worked fine if both masters cooperated.

50. "Grammar School Committee," *Boston Post*, reprinted in *Daily Evening Transcript*, May 14, 1851; "The Following Important Report," *Boston Daily Atlas*, March 5, 1852; "Affairs In and About the City," *Boston Daily Atlas*, September 4, 1852; and "School Committee," *Boston Post*, reprinted in *Boston Evening Transcript*, November 7, 1855, and Walker's letter of resignation to the Boston School Committee, September 24, 1855 ("School Committee Papers," BPL).

51. Uniting the primary schools, grammar schools, and secondary schools into a more cohesive, uniform system became more popular. See the proposal to establish four grades for each of the three divisions, similar to modern schools, in "Meeting of the Grammar School Committee," *Boston Courier*, January 18, 1849. Also read *Normal School* (Boston: City Document No. 40, 1852), which explains its rationale. On the administrative needs following charter reform, see "The School Committee," *Boston Daily Advertiser*, January 9, 1855.

52. *Report of a Special Committee of the Grammar School Board, Presented August 29, 1849, on the Petition of Sundry Colored Persons, Praying for the Abolition of the Smith School: With an Appendix* (Boston: J. H. Eastburn, City Printer, 1849), 54.

53. William T. Harris, "Public Services," in *A Memorial of the Life and Services of John D. Philbrick*, ed. Larkin Dunton (Boston: New England Publishing Company, 1887), 62.

54. "Remarks of Mr. Hillard"; "Rev. Mr. Brooks' Letter to the Mayor," *Daily Evening Transcript*, February 20, 1850; and "Our Public Schools," *Daily Evening Transcript*, February 28, 1850.

55. *The Report of the Annual Examination of the Public Schools of the City of Boston* (Boston: J. H. Eastburn, City Printer, 1852), 3–4; and, on Bishop's expanding duties, "Affairs In and About the City," *Boston Daily Atlas*, January 25, 1854.

56. *Annual Visiting Committees* (1846), 11, 14, 16, 21, 28; Messerli, *Horace Mann*, 86; and Reese, *Origins*, 156. The *Boston Daily Atlas* provided editorial support for Loring and written exams; see "School Committee," October 9, 1846.

57. *Reports of the Annual Visiting Committees* (1846), 34; and *Reports of the Annual Visiting Committees* (1847), 55. See "School Committee," *Boston Daily Atlas*, November 2, 1846, for the full report written by Parsons. Newspapers were filled with commentaries, too numerous to cite, on the rising tide of Irish immigration.

58. *Reports of the Annual Visiting Committees* (1846), 23. William B. Fowle waxed nostalgic in "Boston Free Schools," *Common School Journal* 13 (February 1, 1851): 33–34; also see "The Police Report of Boston," *Common School Journal* 13 (February 15, 1851): 55–57. The summer examiners frequently commented on how the Irish were changing the schools; for example, read *Reports of the Annual Visiting Committees* (1847), 53–56; and *The Report of the Annual Examination of the Public Schools of the City of* Boston (Boston: John H. Eastburn, 1850), 27, 32, 36–37. Often, instead of naming the Irish by name, examiners referred to the poor "materials" in the various schools; see also Schultz, *Culture Factory*, Chapters 9–11.

59. *Reports of the Annual Visiting Committees* (1847), 4, 5, 12, 35, 53, 106–110, 113. The writing report is in the second half of this publication; see p. 4 on the policy of allowing masters to select pupils from the first class for its examination. On transfers, read *The Report of the Annual Examination* (1849), 28.

60. *The Report of the Annual Examination of the Public Schools of the City of Boston* (Boston: J. H. Eastburn, 1848), 7, 11–12, 13, 42; and *Report of the Annual Examination* (1849), 42–43. An editorial in the *Atlas*, which endorsed written examinations, nevertheless warned that "equal attainments" were impossible given the diversity of pupils; it thus warned against making too much of rankings and comparisons based on test scores. See "Report of the Examining Committees of the Public Schools," *Boston Daily Atlas*, January 18, 1848.

61. *The Report of the Annual Examination* (1850), 13, 14, 19. On the impossibility of examining everyone, also see *The Report of the Annual Examination* (1852), 3–4; and *The Report of the Annual Examination of the Public Schools of the City of Boston* (Boston: J. H. Eastburn, 1854), 7–8.

62. *The Report of the Annual Examination* (1850), 14; *The Report of the Annual Examination of the Public Schools of the City of Boston* (Boston: J. H. Eastburn, 1853), 27; and *The Report of the Annual Examination of the Public Schools of the City of Boston* (Boston: J. H. Eastburn, 1854), 11.

63. *The Report of the Annual Examination of the Public Schools of the City of Boston* (Boston: J. H. Eastburn, City Printer, 1851), 14; *The Report of the Annual Examination* (1852), 9; and *The Report of the Annual Examination* (1854), 11.

64. "New Bedford Schools," *Boston Daily Whig*, reprinted in Boston *Daily Atlas*, April 29, 1846. Also see *Annual Report of the School Committee of the City of Charlestown* (Charlestown MA: William H. Wheildon, Printer, 1849); 5–13; *Annual Report of the School Committee of the City of Salem* (Salem, MA: Printed at the Gazette Office, 1850), 21–37; *Report of the School Committee of the City of Worcester, For the Year Ending December 31, 1854* (Worcester, MA: Printed by Henry J. Howland, 1854), 71–72, which notes that written examinations were increasingly given in Lowell, Hartford, and other towns and cities. On rating grammar schools by how well pupils did on entrance exams to high school, see Reese, *Origins*, 154–157.

65. For decades, local examining committees typically described their own neighborhood schools as "flourishing." Newspapers usually dutifully repeated the claims. Occasionally a reporter said the quarterly reports were "couched in the usual favorable terms." See "Grammar School Committee," *Boston Daily* Atlas, reprinted in *Boston Evening Transcript*, August 2, 1854.

66. "Address of Granville B. Putnam," in *Memorial of the Life and Services of John D. Philbrick*, 209; *The Report of the Annual Examination* (1854), 20–21; William B. Fowle, "The Boston Schools," *Common School Journal and Educational Reformer* 14 (August 15, 1852): 242; and W. A. E., "A Visit to Boston Schools," *Connecticut Common School Journal and Annals of Education* 3 (January 1856): 520–521. Female teachers were cheaper than men, but they typically left teaching after about three years; see "Affairs In and About the City," *Boston Daily Atlas*, November 19, 1851.

67. "School Examinations and Reports," *The Massachusetts Teacher* 2 (November 1849): 321, 323.

6. Chewing Pencil Tops

1. By the 1850s, mainstream teachers' magazines in the northern states especially underscored the distinctions between examinations and exhibitions. See "Resident Editor's Department," *The Connecticut Common School Journal and Annals of Education* 4 (May 1857): 152–154; A. C. "School Examinations," *The Massachusetts Teacher* 13 (June 1860): 225–234; and X.Y.Z., "Some Views in Regard to Exhibitions and Examinations," *The Massachusetts Teacher* 17 (January 1864): 3–8.

2. H. S. Jones, "Report of the Committee on City School Systems. Pupils,— Classification, Examination, and Promotion," *The Journal of Proceedings and Addresses of the National Educational Association* (Salem, MA: Observer Book and Job Print, 1887), 280.

3. Many educational leaders believed that only written exams, which generated numerical scores, were the appropriate basis for comparing student

achievement precisely. See A. C., "School Examinations," 229. On social change in the late nineteenth century, see especially Robert H. Wiebe, *The Search for Order 1877–1920* (New York: Hill and Wang, 1967); Allan Trachtenberg, *The Incorporation of America: Culture and Society in the Gilded Age* (New York: Hill and Wang, 1982); Richard Franklin Bensel, *Yankee Leviathan: The Origins of Central State Authority in America, 1859–1877* (New York: Cambridge University Press, 1990); and William Cronon, *Nature's Metropolis: Chicago and the Great West* (New York: W. W. Norton & Company, 1991), 116–117.

4. Jones, "Report of the Committee," 280.

5. On grading and its adoption in villages and towns, see Joel Perlmann and Robert A. Margo, *Women's Work: American Schoolteachers, 1650–1920* (Chicago: The University of Chicago Press, 2001), 94–96; as well as David B. Tyack, *The One Best System: A History of American Urban Education* (Cambridge, MA: Harvard University Press, 1974), 44–46; and William A. Fischel, *Making the Grade: The Economic Evolution of American School Districts* (Chicago: The University of Chicago Press, 2009), 77–83.

6. William B. Harlow, "Examinations," *Education* 8 (January 1888): 321–322.

7. *Annual Report of the School Committee, To the City of Portland, March 3, 1883* (Portland, ME: Ford & Rich, 1883), 60; and William J. Reese, *America's Public Schools: From the Common School to 'No Child Left Behind'* (Baltimore, MD: The Johns Hopkins University Press, 2011), 61–63, 76–77, 111.

8. John Swett, *Public Education in California: Its Origin and Development, With Personal Reminiscences of Half a Century* (New York: American Book Company, 1911), 40, 49–50, 60, 207; and John Swett, *American Public Schools: History and Pedagogics* (New York: American Book Company, 1900), 121–122.

9. Swett, *Public Education*, 41, 60–61, 67–72, 76, 82–83.

10. Swett, *Public Education*, 82, 86, 99, 108–113, 124–128; John Swett, "How I Became a School Master," *Pacific School & Home Journal* 1 no. 1 (1877): 10–11; and William G. Carr, *John Swett: The Biography of an Educational Pioneer* (Santa Ana, CA: Fine Arts Press, 1933), Chapter 4. For complaints about nepotism and patronage in Boston, read "Competitive Examinations," *Boston Daily Advertiser*, January 25, 1871.

11. Swett, *Public Education*, 122, 128–132, 198, 206.

12. Swett, *Public Education*, 141, 207–209, 213–218.

13. On Swett's rise to national prominence, see the untitled editorial, *New England Journal of Education* 9 (May 22, 1879): 328–329; and Swett, *Public Education*, 6–7.

14. John Swett, *Questions for Written Examinations: An Aid to Candidates for Teachers' Certificates, and A Hand-Book for Examiners and Teachers* (New York: Ivison, Blakeman, Taylor, and Company, 1872), 3–4. The book had steady sales, still attracting buyers in the early twentieth century. See Carr, *John Swett*, 124–125.

15. Swett, *Public Education*, 198, 238–239; John Swett, *Methods of Teaching: A Handbook of Principles, Directions, and Working Models for Common-School Teachers*

(New York: Harper & Brothers, 1880), 118; and *Annual Report of the Superintendent of the Public Schools of the City and County of San Francisco For the School and Fiscal Year Ending June 30, 1893* (San Francisco, CA: James H. Harry, 1893), 13.

16. See two articles by Mary M. Ide, "Written Examinations," *New England Journal of Education* 1 (May 1, 1875): 206–207; and "Written Examinations," *New England Journal of Education* 1 (May 8, 1875): 218–219.

17. "Local Matters," *Daily National Intelligencer* (District of Columbia), July 23, 1855; "Local Matters," *Daily National Intelligencer,* July 28, 1856; "The School Exhibition Last Evening," *Daily Evening Bulletin* (San Francisco), October 25, 1856; "Repetition of Union School Exhibition," *Daily Evening Bulletin,* October 28, 1856; "The Flower Queen Concert To-Night," *Daily Evening Bulletin,* May 15, 1857; and "The Festival at the Music Hall," *Boston Daily Advertiser,* July 27, 1859.

18. "The School Exhibition," *Daily State Register* (Des Moines), June 9, 1868; "The Third Ward School Exhibition," *Daily State Register,* June 14, 1868; "School Exhibition," *The Dakota Republican,* June 20, 1868; "Local Intelligence," *The Weekly Arizona Miner,* November 13, 1869; and "School Examination," *The Weekly Arizona Miner,* January 25, 1878.

19. "High School Examination," *Daily Evening Bulletin* (San Francisco), December 14, 1863; and "School Examination," *Daily Evening Bulletin,* May 31, 1869, where a writer compared the superficial "annual show days" (i.e. the exhibition) and the "real workings of our Educational system." Comparisons of the average scores of schools on admission tests were common. See, for example, "The High School Examination," *Public Ledger* (Philadelphia), July 12, 1858; and William J. Reese, *The Origins of the American High School* (New Haven, CT: Yale University Press, 1995), 142–161, on the competitive ethos. Complaints about teachers and pupils ignoring rules limiting homework or the number of exams were rife. Attempts to ban or severely restrict homework were also frequently resisted by ambitious parents, pupils, and teachers. See, for example, "School Census Total," *Chicago Daily Tribune,* July 21, 1892. Even when promotion tests were banned, they were sometimes still given; see *Fifty-First Annual Report of the Board of Education of the City of New York* (New York: Hall of the Board of Education, 1893), 116.

20. "Windsor County Teachers' Institute," *Vermont Chronicle* (Bellows Falls), October 11, 1848; "Teachers' Associations," *The Boston Daily Atlas,* June 13, 1851; N., "School Examinations," *New York Herald-Tribune,* December 22, 1874; and A Subscriber, "Topics for Educational Essays," *New England Journal of Education* 3 (May 13, 1876): 233.

21. *Eighteenth Annual Report of the Board of Directors of the St. Louis Public Schools, For the Year Ending August 1, 1872* (St. Louis, MO: Democrat Litho. and Printing Company, 1873), 155; B. A. Hinsdale, *Our Common Schools: A Fuller Statement of the Views Set Forth in the Pamphlet Entitled, "Our Common School*

Education," With Special Reference to the Reply of Superintendent A. J. Rickoff (Cleveland, OH: Cobb, Andrews, and Company, 1878), 40–41; untitled article by Dr. Samuel Willard, *The National Teacher's Monthly* 1 (November 1874): 9; *Thirty-Fourth Semi-Annual Report of the Superintendent of Public Schools of the City of Boston* (Boston: Rockwell and Churchill, 1878), 22; E. P. Peabody, "Some Defects of Our School System," *Journal of Education* 17 (January 4, 1883): 23; Orion C. Scott, "Educational Intelligence," *Journal of Education* (October 2, 1884): 220; C. N. Sims, "Examination and Education," *Nineteenth Century* 25 (June 1889): 2; W. H. Buchanan, "School Examinations," *Ohio Practical Farmer* 94 (July 7, 1898): 10; and Reese, *America's Public Schools*, 112–114.

22. *Twentieth Annual Report of the Trustees and Visitors of Common Schools, To the City Council of Cincinnati, for the School Year Ending June 30, 1848* (Cincinnati, OH: Printed at the Daily Times Office, 1848), 36. On the shift from oral to written exams, and ungraded to graded schools, read W. H. Morgan, "General Sketch of System," in *A History of the Schools of Cincinnati*, ed. John B. Shotwell (Cincinnati, OH: The School Life Company, 1902), 9–13.

23. *Twentieth Annual Report* (Cincinnati), 37–40.

24. *Twentieth Annual Report* (Cincinnati), 39, 41.

25. *Twenty Second Annual Report of the Trustees and Visitors of Common Schools, To the City Council of Cincinnati, for the School Year Ending June 30, 1851* (Cincinnati, OH: Printed at the Nonpareil Office, 1852), 28; *Twenty Third Annual Report of the Trustees and Visitors of Common Schools, To the City Council of Cincinnati, for the School Year Ending June 30, 1852* (Cincinnati, OH: From the Press of the Cincinnati Gazette Company, 1852), 21; *Twenty-Fourth Annual Report of the Trustees and Visitors of the Common Schools, To the City Council of Cincinnati, for the School Year Ending 30th June 1853* (Cincinnati, OH: From the Press of the Cincinnati Gazette Company, 1853), 40; and *Origins*, 53, 66.

26. *Twenty-Sixth Annual Report of the Trustees and Visitors of the Common Schools, To the City Council of Cincinnati, for the School Year Ending 30th June 1855* (Cincinnati, OH: Gazette Co. Steam Printing House, 1855), 71; *Twenty-Seventh Annual Report of the Trustees and Visitors of the Common Schools, To the City Council of Cincinnati, for the School Year Ending June 30th 1856* (Cincinnati, OH: Gazette Co. Steam Printing House, 1856), 11, 43–51; *Twenty-Eighth Annual Report for the School Year Ending July 6, 1857* (Cincinnati, OH: B. Frankland, Book and Job Printer, 1857), 42; and *Twenty-Ninth Annual Report for the School Year Ending June 30, 1858* (Cincinnati, OH: B. Frankland, Book and Job Printer, 1858), 24–31.

27. *Twenty-Eight Annual Report* (Cincinnati), 16, 69; and *Twenty-Ninth Annual Report* (Cincinnati), 81–108.

28. Pedagogue, "The Supervision of Schools," *The Cincinnati Daily Gazette* (June 17, 1872); and L. W. H., "The Tests of Scholarship," *The Cincinnati Commercial* (February 12, 1882). One early historian of Cincinnati noted that Rickoff

had a strong personality and his views on grading, examinations, statistics, and recordkeeping left a deep imprint on the system; see W. H. Venable, "Education in Cincinnati," in *History of Cincinnati and Hamilton County, Ohio* (Cincinnati, OH: S. B. Nelson & Co., 1894), 106.

29. "Local Matters," *Daily National Intelligencer,* July 23, 1855; and "Hold Up," *Journal of Education* 13 (June 16, 1881): 407.

30. "Boston Normal School," *Boston Daily Atlas,* October 23, 1852.

31. *Annual Report of the School Committee of the City of Boston* (Boston: George C. Rand & Avery, 1860), 16.

32. "City Affairs," *Boston Daily Advertiser,* March 13, 1861, on Philbrick's remarkable progress in grading the schools and assigning one teacher per class; *Annual Report of the School Committee of the City of Boston* (Boston: J. E. Farwell & Company, 1862), 102–104; *Annual Report of the School Committee of the City of Boston* (Boston: Rockwell & Churchill, 1872), 173–74; Reese, *Origins,* 127, 195; and Reese, *America's Public Schools,* 57–58.

33. *Boston School Committee Report* (1860), 53; *Annual Report of the School Committee of the City of Boston* (Boston: J. E. Farwell and Company, 1864), 46, 138–139; and *Annual Report of the School Committee of the City of Boston* (Boston: Rockwell & Churchill, 1874), 273–278.

34. *Annual Report of the School Committee of the City of Boston* (Boston: Alfred Mudge & Son, 1867), 159; and *Annual Report of the School Committee of the City of Boston* (Boston: Rockwell & Churchill, 1874), 275.

35. "The School Board," *Boston Daily Advertiser,* January 26, 1876. On the diploma exams for the grammar schools and high schools, see "The Supervision of the Schools of Boston," *Boston Daily Advertiser,* November 17, 1880; and, on the common grammar school admission test, *Annual Report of the School Committee of the City of Boston* (Boston: Rockwell and Churchill, 1883), 25–26. Michael B. Katz provides essential background on Philbrick's clash with the supervisors and bureaucratization of the system in *Class, Bureaucracy, and the Schools: The Illusion of Educational Change in America* (New York: Praeger Publishers, c. 1975), Chapter 2.

36. On the appointment of the inspectors in San Francisco, see *Thirtieth Annual Report of the Superintendent of Public Schools, For the School Year Ending June 30, 1883* (San Francisco, CA: George Spaulding & Co., 1883), 18; "Board of Education," *Daily Evening Bulletin,* March 21, 1883; and "The New Departure in Language Training," *Pacific Educational Journal* 1 (March 1887): 83. Committeemen debated whether to inspect the teachers through observing classrooms or testing their pupils in written exams. Various administrators in later reports called for the hiring of more inspectors, similar to Europe. In addition to the reports by the two inspectors who were ultimately hired, see the praise for their work in *Thirty-Fifth Annual Report of the Superintendent of Common Schools, of the City and County of San Francisco, For the Fiscal Year Ending June 30, 1888* (San Francisco, CA: W. M. Hinton & Co., 1888), 7–13. On

corruption in national politics, read Ari Hoogenboom, *Outlawing the Spoils: A History of the Civil Service Reform Movement 1865–1883* (Urbana: University of Illinois Press, c. 1968); and Bensel, *Yankee Leviathan*, 131–132, 299–300.

37. *In Memoriam. William Harvey Wells, Sketches of His Life and Character, Memorial Addresses and Proceedings and Resolutions of Public Bodies on the Occasion of His Death* (Chicago: Fergus Printing Company, 1887), n.p. (on biographical information), 3, 101; "Editorial Correspondence," *New England Journal of Education* 10 (November 13, 1879): 277; and Tyack, *One Best System*, 45–46.

38. W. H. Wells, *The Graded School: A Graded Course of Instruction for Public Schools: With Copious Practical Directions to Teachers, and Observations on Primary Schools, School Discipline, School Records, etc.* (New York: A. S. Barnes & Burr, 1862), 3, 31, 130–131; and Reese, *Origins*, 145.

39. Wells, *Graded School*, 153; and *In Memoriam*, n.p. Wells exaggerated how much uniformity in classifying pupils actually existed when he claimed: "Each of the successive grades has its appropriate work, plainly and sharply defined; and the standing of a class can at any time be tested by comparing it with a fixed and known standard." See *Tenth Annual Report of the Board of Education, For the Year Ending December 31, 1863* (Chicago: The Chicago Times Book and Job Printing House, 1864), 15.

40. "Meeting of the Board of Education," *Daily Cleveland Herald*, June 11, 1866; and *The Common Schools of Indianapolis..Annual Report of the Public Schools of the City of Indianapolis, For the School Year Ending September 1, 1866* (Indianapolis, IN: Douglass & Conner, Journal Office, Printers, 1867), 43–44; William J. Reese, "Education," in *The Encyclopedia of Indianapolis*, ed. David J. Bodenhamer and Robert G. Barrows (Bloomington & Indianapolis: Indiana University Press, 1994), 72–77; and Amy C. Schutt, "Abram Crum Shortridge," in *Encyclopedia of Indianapolis*, 1259.

41. "About Town," *The Quincy Whig*, June 16, 1874.

42. *Fifth Annual Report of the State Superintendent of Public Instruction, To The Governor of Nebraska, for the Year Ending December 31st, 1873* (Lincoln, NE: Journal Printing Company, 1873), 368, 371–372; and *Sixth Annual Report of the State Superintendent of Public Instruction, To The Governor of Nebraska, for the Year Ending December 31st, 1874* (Lincoln, NE: Journal Printing Company, 1874), 188.

43. *First Annual Report of the Public Schools of Portland, Oregon, For The Year Ending July 3, 1874* (Portland, OR: Swope & Taylor, 1874), 10; and *Fourth Annual Report of the City Superintendent of the Public Schools of the City of Portland, Oregon, For The Year Ending June 22, 1877* (Portland, OR: David Steel, Book and Job Printer, 1877), 16, 20. Also see Tyack, *One Best System*, 47–48.

44. *Fifteenth Annual Report of the Board of School Visitors, of Memphis City Schools, and Superintendent's Report For the Year 1866–67* (Memphis, TN: Memphis Daily Post Job Printing Establishment, 1867), xxx; *Annual Report of the Board of Education, of the Memphis City Schools, For 1868–69, With Appendix for 1868–69* (Memphis, TN: Hite and Corwine, n.d.), 52; on Nashville, "Southern

Colleges and Schools," *The Educational Journal of Virginia* 15 (September 1884): 387; and Potomac, "Correspondence of the Baltimore *Sun*," *The Sun* (Baltimore), May 28, 1863.

45. "Letter from F. M. Chrisman," *Morning Republican,* October 25, 1871; "School Examinations," *Arkansas Gazette,* April 3, 1872; "Public School Examination," *Little Rock Daily Republican,* May 19, 1872; "The City Public Schools," *Columbus-Enquirer Sun,* June 19, 1887; "Public School Examination," *Columbus-Enquirer Sun,* June 6, 1891; and *Report of the Chief Superintendent of the Public Schools, of New Orleans, to the State Board of Education* (New Orleans, LA: Printed by Seymour & Stevens, 1880), 8; *Report of the Chief Superintendent of the Public Schools of the City of New Orleans, La., to the State Board of Education* (n.p.: January 1886), 255–256, on the use of printed questions; and *Report of the Chief Superintendent of New Orleans, La., to the State Board of Education* (n.p.: January 1888), 255, on rules recently adopted on promotion exams. Also read James D. Anderson, *The Education of Blacks in the South, 1860–1935* (Chapel Hill: The University of North Carolina Press, 1988); and, on teachers, Ronald E. Butchart, *Schooling the Freed People: Teaching, Learning, and the Struggle for Black Freedom, 1861–1876* (Chapel Hill: The University of North Carolina Press, 2010).

46. See the following articles in the *Atlanta Constitution:* "List of Scholars," July 21, 1874; "Our Schools," October 10, 1875; "Public School Teachers," June 6, 1877; and "The Public Schools," June 8, 1881.

47. Reese, *Origins,* 142–143.

48. "School Supervision," *The Teacher, and Western Educational Magazine* 1 (May 1853): 138.

49. *Twenty-Ninth Annual Report* (Cincinnati), 24–26.

50. *Fifteenth Annual Report of the Board of Education for the Year Ending July 3, 1869* (Chicago: Church, Goodman and Donnelly, Printers, 1869), 170.

51. On examination etiquette and other rules, see G. Dallas Lind, "Appendix," in J. E. Sherrill, *The Normal Question Book: Containing Three Thousand Questions and Answers Taken from the Best Authorities on the Common School Branches* (Indianapolis, IN: Normal Publishing House, 1882), 427–429; Swett, *Questions,* 3–4; and *Eighteenth Annual Report of the Board of Education for the Year Ending June 28, 1872* (Chicago: Bryant, Walker & Craig, 1872), 156.

52. "An Idyl of Co-Education," *Cincinnati Daily Gazette,* January 14, 1879.

53. *Thirtieth Annual Report* (San Francisco), 21.

54. *Twenty-Second Annual Report of the Board of Education of the City and County of New-York* (New York: C. S. Westcott & Co., 1864), 48; *Discussion Before the Joint Committee on Studies, etc., of the Board of Education, Appointed February 19th, 1868, in Reference to Modifications of the Course of Studies, etc. 1868* (New York: William C. Bryant & Co., Printers, 1868); and *Annual Report of the Board of School Commissioners for the Year Ending August 31, 1873* (Milwaukee, WI: J. H. Yewdale & Sons, Printers, 1874), 32–34.

55. Louisville, "Editorial—Miscellany," *Indiana School Journal* 8 (July 1863): 220–221; and *Eighteenth Annual Report of the Superintendent of Common Schools, For the School Year Ending June 30th, 1871* (San Francisco, CA: Cubery & Company, 1871), 19–20.

56. "Public Schools," *Morning Oregonian,* February 27, 1875; "New Hampshire," *New England Journal of Education* 5 (April 26, 1877): 201; Junius, "Boston Letter," *New England Journal of Education* 16 (October 19, 1882): 249; *Thirty-Fourth Semi-Annual Report* (Boston), 22; and Peabody, "Some Defects," 23.

57. "Editor's Table," *Western Journal,* reprinted in *Journal of Education* 18 (December 6, 1883): 361; on oranges and peanuts, see S. Simon, "Chicago," *New England Journal of Education* 5 (February 1, 1877): 59. For some examples of articles on scores attached to names and schools, see the *Chicago Tribune:* "Meeting of the Board of Education," July 14, 1862; "High School Commencement," July 4, 1866; "Board of Education," April 29, 1868; and "Educational," June 27, 1874.

58. *Forty-Third Annual Report for the School Year Ending June 30, 1872* (Cincinnati, OH: Wilstach, Baldwin & Co., 1873), 44–48. On the printing of names of schools, pupils, and their scores, see "Local Affairs," *Public Ledger* (Philadelphia), July 7, 1860; "Candidates for the High School," *The Quincy Whig* (Illinois), July 8, 1872; A. L. Jackson, "Letter from Sacramento," *Elevator* (San Francisco), July 4, 1874; "The Windsor School," *Wisconsin State Journal* (Madison), May 20, 1879; and "Educational Department," *Daily Herald* (Grand Forks), April 30, 1882. Also see John S. Hart, *In the School-Room: Chapters in the Philosophy of Education* (Philadelphia: Eldredge & Brother, 1868), 61–63; Reese, *Origins,* 132, 147–148; and the outstanding study of meritocracy by David F. Labaree, *The Making of an American High School: The Credentials Market and the Central High School of Philadelphia, 1838–1939* (New Haven, CT: Yale University Press, 1988). To deter cheating, Hart and the teachers at Central High wrote separate exams for pupils.

59. Emerson E. White, *The Elements of Pedagogy* (New York: American Book Company, 1886), 193–194; and Reese, *America's Public Schools,* 31.

60. Swett, *American Public Schools,* 206–207, 219–230. On the fascinating subject of writing, see Tamara Plakins Thornton, *Handwriting in America: A Cultural History* (New Haven, CT: Yale University Press, 1996), which explores the place of copy books in instruction.

61. *Twenty-Sixth Annual Report* (Cincinnati), 78; *Twenty-Ninth Annual Report* (Cincinnati), 27–28; *Thirty-Eighth Annual Report for the School Year Ending June 30, 1867* (Cincinnati, OH: Times Steam Book and Printing Office, 1867), 154–160, on slate lessons; and *Forty-Fifth Annual Report for the School Year Ending August 31, 1874* (Cincinnati, OH: Wilstach, Baldwin & Co., 1875), 56–58.

62. "The Blackboard and Chalk," *American Educational Monthly* 2 (February 1865): 44.

63. "Concerning Oral Instruction," *New England Journal of Education,* reprinted in *The Educational Journal of Virginia* 12 (May 1881): 143; *Boston School Committee*

Report (1864), 106–107; *Annual Report of the School Committee of the City of Boston* (Boston: Rockwell and Churchill, 1874), 377–379; "The Question of Primary School Supervision," *Boston Morning Journal,* February 23, 1882; and *Annual Report of the School Committee of the City of Boston* (Boston: n.p., 1888), 30.

64. *Eighteenth Annual Report of the Board of Education, of the City and County of New York* (New York: Joseph Russell, Printer, 1860), 56; "Our Schools," *Atlanta Constitution,* October 10, 1875; and *Twenty-Eighth Annual Report of the Board of Education for the Year Ending July 31, 1882* (Chicago: George K. Hazlitt & Co., 1883), 42.

65. R. Heber Holbrook, *The New Method: Or School Expositions* (Indianapolis, IN: Normal Teacher Publishing House, 1881), 14–15; Thomas J. Morgan, *Studies in Pedagogy* (Boston: Silver, Burdett & Company, 1892), 247; and J. M. Greenwood, *Principles of Education Practically Applied* (New York: D. Appleton and Company, 1899), 47.

66. "The Spells," *The Idaho Avalanche,* July 28, 1883.

67. *Annual Report of the School Committee of the City of Boston* (Boston: Rockwell and Churchill, 1884), 11–12.

68. "The Modern School Teacher," *Educational Gazette,* reprinted in the *Daily Inter Ocean* (Chicago), May 5, 1892.

7. The Culture of Testing

1. On displays of needlework, drawings, and so forth, see "The Grand Public School Exhibition Today," *New York Herald,* November 22, 1858; "A Novel School Exhibition in Milford," *Boston Morning Journal,* April 3, 1885; "School Exhibition," *The Philadelphia Inquirer,* February 28, 1888; "The New York Trade Schools' Exhibition," *The Critic: A Weekly Review of Literature and the Arts* 22 (August 25, 1894): 126; and "Sewing Schools Exhibition," *New York Observer and Chronicle* 75 (March 11, 1897): 379–380; "The Public School Examinations," *Daily Evening Bulletin* (San Francisco), November 27, 1858; *Nineteenth Annual Report of the Board of Education, of the City and County of New-York* (New York: Joseph Russell, Printer, 1861), 39–40; *Annual Report of the City Superintendent of Schools to the Board of Education, of the City and County of New York* (New York: Cushing & Bardua, 1875), 91; *Fourteenth Annual Report of the Board of Education, For the Year Ending July 3, 1868* (Chicago: Church, Goodman, and Donnelly, Printers, 1868), 198–199; and *Fifty-Seventh Annual Report for the School Year Ending August 31, 1886* (Cincinnati, OH: Wilstach, Baldwin & Co., 1887), 86–87.

2. "Agricultural Matters," *Hartford Daily Courant,* March 2, 1870; Terre Haute *Express,* quoted in untitled article, *Territorial Enterprise* (Virginia City, Nevada), May 6, 1876; on violence, see "Particulars of the Killing of Two Young Men," *Albany Journal* (New York), January 11, 1869; "Georgia in Brief," *The Columbus Enquirer-Sun* (Columbus, GA), July 5, 1888; "Played the Crowd for Suckers," *Dallas Morning News,* April 5, 1891; and "Three

Killed and Fifteen Wounded," *New York Herald-Tribune*, February 29, 1896; on Lincoln and Booth, untitled article, *Memphis Daily Avalanche*, April 11, 1867; "Laughable," *Jamestown Journal* (New York), September 20, 1867; on fires, "Jute on Fire," *Evening Bulletin* (San Francisco), December 24, 1872; on catastrophes, untitled article, *The Pittsfield Sun* (Massachusetts), May 6, 1858; and "Public Hall Collapses," *Grand Forks Daily Herald*, April 28, 1888.

3. "Amusements," *Cincinnati Daily Gazette*, August 6, 1867; "Amusements," *Cincinnati Daily Gazette*, October 16, 1867; and "The Old School Exhibitions," *Atlanta Constitution*, reprinted in numerous newspapers. Other poems offered more nostalgia: "The Old Schools," in *Wheeling Register* (West Virginia), June 16, 1896; and "Speaking Pieces," *Idaho Statesman* (Boise), December 11, 1896; and "The Old Schoolhouse," *Dallas Morning News*, February 21, 1898.

4. Eugene Wood, "The Old Red School-House," *McClure's Magazine* 24 (February 1905): 392. The music for "School Days" was written by a German immigrant, Gus Edwards, and the lyrics by Will D. Cobb, born in Philadelphia. See Elisabeth Rider Montgomery, *The Story Behind Popular Songs* (New York: Dodd, Mead & Company, 1960), Chapter 6; Ian Whitcomb, "Gus Edwards," in *The New Grove Dictionary of American Music*, ed. H. Wiley Hitchcock and Stanley Sadie (New York: Macmillan, 1986), 2: 21; and William E. Studwell, *They Also Wrote: Evaluative Essays on Lesser-Known Popular American Songwriters Prior to the Rock Era* (Lanham, MD: The Scarecrow Press, 2000), 46, 63.

5. William J. Reese, *The Origins of the American High School* (New Haven, CT: Yale University Press, 1995), 1–4, 14–15, 239; and the biographical details in David H. Wallace, "The Art of John Rogers: 'So Real and So True'," *American Art Journal* 4 (November 1972): 59–60; and Wallace's excellent biography, *John Rogers: The People's Sculptor* (Middletown, CT: Wesleyan University Press, 1967), 3–18; Kimberly Orcutt, "Neoclassicism and the Artist's Ideal," in *John Rogers: American Stories*, ed. Kimberly Orcutt (New York: New-York Historical Society, 2010), 42; "Chronology," in *John Rogers: American Stories*, 216; and Mr. and Mrs. Chetwood Smith, *Rogers Groups: Thought & Wrought* (Boston: Charles E. Goodspeed & Co., 1934), 9.

6. Smith and Smith, *Rogers Groups*, 14–20, 38; Freeman Henry Morris Murray, *Emancipation and the Freed in American Sculpture* (Washington, DC: Press of Murray Brothers, 1916), 143; Michael Leja, "Sculpture for a Mass Market," in *John Rogers: American Stories*, 12–13; Melissa Dabakis, "John Rogers, Lilly Martin Spencer, and the Culture of Sentimentality," in *John Rogers: American Stories*, 77–95; "New York Art Notes," *Boston Daily Advertiser* (January 2, 1869); quotation from *Daily Miners' Journal* from David Jaffee, "John Rogers Takes His Place in the Parlor," in *John Rogers: American Stories*, 175; and Wallace, *John Rogers*, 18 (on exam "torture"), 35, 41, 60.

7. Smith and Smith, *Rogers Groups*, 62, 72; Paul and Meta Bleier, *John Rogers' Groups of Statuary* (N. Woodmere, NY: Paul & Meta Bleier, 1971), 54, 75;

Kimberly Orcutt, "Selling the Rogers Brand," *John Rogers: American Stories,* 163–164; and "The School Examination," *Frank Leslie's Illustrated Newspaper,* December 28, 1867. On retirement gifts, "Educational Notes," *Boston Daily Advertiser,* July 1, 1876.

8. Kimberly Orcutt, "The Rise and Fall—and Rise—of John Rogers," in *John Rogers: American Stories,* 181–195; and *Five Plays by Charles H. Hoyt,* ed. Douglas L. Hunt (Princeton, NJ: Princeton University Press, 1941), vii–x; and "Coming Attractions," *Morning Oregonian,* January 31, 1899. All subsequent references to Hoyt's play, "A Midnight Bell," are from Hunt, *Five Plays.* Though some lines of the play were occasionally revised, newspaper reviews reveal that the school exhibition scenes remained substantially the same.

9. Hoyt, "A Midnight Bell," in Hunt, *Five Plays,* 73.

10. Hoyt, "A Midnight Bell," 73–77.

11. Hoyt, "A Midnight Bell," 77; and "Where's the North Pole?" an 1896 lithograph advertising the play that depicts a student pointing to the sky. (Library of Congress Prints and Photographs Division, no. 7040).

12. "Bijou Theatre," *New York Times,* May 30, 1889; "A Midnight Bell," *Chicago Daily Tribune,* November 17, 1889; "Amusements This Evening," *The Daily Picayune* (New Orleans), December 21, 1896; and "At the Play," *Duluth Daily Tribune,* March 21, 1899.

13. "Examination at the Female College," *Milwaukee Daily Sentinel,* April 12, 1861; X.Y.Z., "Some Views in Regard to Exhibitions and Examinations," *Massachusetts Teacher* 17 (January 1864): 7; and "School Examination," *The Daily Cleveland Herald,* June 22, 1865.

14. *Eighteenth Annual Report of the Board of Directors of the St. Louis Public Schools, For the Year Ending August 1, 1872* (St. Louis, MO: Democrat Litho. and Printing Co., 1873), 155; and, for some examples of hyperbole, "Martha's Vineyard," *New York Tribune,* September 1, 1871; A. D. Mayo, "School Examination," *New England Journal of Education* 7 (April 18, 1878): 249; "Editor's Table," *Journal of Education* 18 (December 6, 1883): 361; and E. E. White, "The Art of Teaching," *Journal of Education* 20 (July 10, 1884): 55.

15. J. B. Peaslee, "Examinations and Transfers," *Journal of Education* 12 (November 5, 1885): 300. Also read "Educational Notes," *New York Tribune,* November 12, 1874; "The Percentage System in our Public Schools," *The Cincinnati Commercial,* May 28, 1881; "The Marking System for Examinations," *Themis* (Sacramento), February 17, 1894; and "Editor's Department," *The National Normal* 1 (October 1868): 34. On prominent national magazines: "The Murder of the Innocents: A Second Epistle to Dolorosus," *Atlantic Monthly* 4 (September 1859): 345–356; Charles Francis Adams, Jr., "Scientific Common-School Education," *Harper's New Monthly Magazine* 61 (November 1880): 934–942; and, in a critical though more moderate vein, William DeWitt Hyde, "School Examinations," *The Forum* 8 (May 1889): 305–313.

16. On fears of excessive training of the minds of infants and very young children, see Amariah Brigham, *Remarks on the Influence of Mental Cultivation and Mental Excitement Upon Health* (Boston: Marsh, Capen & Lyon, 1833), 54–56; and Maris A. Vinovskis, *Education, Society, and Economic Opportunity: A Historical Perspective on Persistent Issues* (New Haven, CT: Yale University Press, 1995), 33–36 (Chapter 2, written with Dean May); and Maris A. Vinovskis, *History and Educational Policymaking* (New Haven, CT: Yale University Press, 1999), 71–72. No one disputed the superior performance of girls. See "Our Schools," *Harper's New Monthly Magazine* 20 (March 1860): 551. In Groveland, Massachusetts, the school committee highlighted the "indisputable" superiority of female students. See *Twentieth Annual Report of the Board of Education, Together With the Twentieth Annual Report of the Secretary of the Board* (Boston: William White, Printer to the State, 1857), 11. On high schools, Reese, *Origins*, 197–207, 225–226, 236–241; the sensitive reading of the sources by Jane H. Hunter, *How Young Ladies Became Girls: The Victorian Origins of American Girlhood* (New Haven, CT: Yale University Press, 2002), 4, 169, 201–203, 210–221; and Gail Gaisin Glicksman, "Overstress Among American School Children, 1840–1920" (Ph.D. diss., University of Pennsylvania, 1997).

17. Girls always seemed to do better than boys, especially in reading. See, for example, *Twenty-Ninth Annual Report of the Board of Education of the City and County of New York* (New York: The New York Printing Company, 1871), 148; *Thirtieth Annual Report of the Board of Public Instruction of the City and County of New York* (New York: NY School Journal Print, 1872), chart before p. 207. Girls regularly outperformed boys in high school, according to numerous sources: see "Brevities," *The Chronicle & Constitutionalist* (Augusta, GA) (July 2, 1879); and "The Fair Sex," *Cincinnati Times and Chronicle*, July 12, 1871. On the futility of trying to ban or restrict homework, see, for New York City alone: *Nineteenth Annual Report*, 54–55; *Twenty-Fourth Annual Report of the Board of Education of the City and County of New York* (New York: Wm. C. Bryant & Co., 1866), 29–30; *Twenty-Ninth Annual Report*, 137; *Annual Report of the City Superintendent of Schools to the Board of Education of the City of New York* (New York: Cushing & Bardua, 1876), 13; *Thirty-Sixth Annual Report of the Board of Education of the City and County of New York* (New York: Hall of the Board of Education, 1878), 129; and Reese, *Origins*, 201–205. On special classes, read Robert L. Osgood, *For "Children Who Vary from the Normal Type": Special Education in Boston, 1838–1930* (Washington, DC: Gallaudet University Press, 2000), 37–39, 70–78. The percentage of pupils in Boston's ungraded classes grew from 2.7 percent in 1881 to 6.2 percent in 1900 (p. 77). On the spread of ability groups, special classes, and promotion policies, see the National Education Association, *Journal of Proceedings and Addresses* (Chicago: The University of Chicago Press, 1898), 422–448.

18. "Sudden Death of Mr. Hugh Miller," *The Charleston Daily Courier* (South Carolina), January 16, 1857; "The Abuses of Education," *Bangor Daily Whig*

and Courier, December 1, 1858; "Twenty-Five Years an Idiot," Cleveland *Plain Dealer*, reprinted in the *Boston Investigator*, November 23, 1859; "The High School Once More," *Cleveland Morning Herald*, February 27, 1871; and Alert, "Schools Vs. The Home," *The New Haven Evening Register*, February 10, 1883.

19. On Howe's warnings, *Thirty-First Annual Report of the Board of Education, Together With the Thirty-First Annual Report of the Secretary of the Board* (Boston: Wright and Potter, 1868), 9; "Nervous Wear of Teachers," *Journal of Education* 15 (May 11, 1882): 298; untitled editorial, *Boston Daily Advertiser*, May 25, 1867; "Brain and Body," *Troy Times*, reprinted in the *American Phrenological Journal* 28 (November 1858): 80; and "School Examinations," *The Phrenological Journal and Life Illustrated* 72 (May 1881): 271. On complaints about memorization, rote teaching, and written tests, see Reese, *Origins*, 134–141, 149; and William J. Reese, *America's Public Schools: From the Common School to "No Child Left Behind"* (Baltimore, MD: The Johns Hopkins University Press, 2011), 29–30, 33, 37–38, 42, 85–86, 138.

20. "John Jacob Astor, Jr.," *The Farmer's Cabinet* (Amherst, NH, February 27, 1868); "John Jacob Astor's Imbecile Son," *The Hawaiian Gazette* (Honolulu), April 8, 1868; "In General," *The Daily Constitution* (Middletown, Connecticut), June 3, 1873; "Five Weeks in a Trance," *New York Sun*, reprinted in *St. Louis Globe-Democrat*, January 31, 1881; "Saddest Scenes," *The Daily Inter Ocean* (Chicago), August 19, 1881; and "Death of a Child from Over-Study," *St. Louis Globe-Democrat*, March 5, 1883.

21. "Moloch in the School Room," *The Daily Cleveland Herald*, March 25, 1867; "Multiple News Items," *The Daily Cleveland Herald*, May 22, 1874; "Self Destruction," *St. Louis Globe-Democrat*, January 6, 1883; "State News," *Bangor Daily Whig & Courier*, March 31, 1884; on runaways and suicides, see "The Overworked School Girl Found," *New York Tribune*, September 22, 1884; and "Death of Laura Buchanan," *Denver Evening Post* (February 20, 1899). On cures, typical ads include "The Health of Growing Children," *The Kalamazoo Gazette*, April 5, 1890; "School Again," *Bangor Daily Whig & Courier*, September 5, 1891; and "Success," *Rocky Mountain News* (Denver), November 8, 1896. On the New York story, "Americanisms," *Norristown Herald*, reprinted in the *North American* (Philadelphia), November 29, 1881.

22. "Editor's Table," *Journal of Education* 19 (January 31, 1884): 73; and *Report of the Superintendent of Common Schools of the City and County of San Francisco For the Fiscal Year Ending June 30, 1891* (San Francisco, CA: W. M. Hinton & Co., 1891), 132. On teacher turnover, *Fourteenth Annual Report of the Board of Directors of the St. Louis Public Schools, For the Year Ending August 1, 1868* (St. Louis, MO: George Knapp & Co., 1869), 16; and *Thirtieth Annual Report* (New York), 230.

23. *Twenty-Second Annual Report of the Board of Education of the City and County of New York* (New York: C. S. Westcott, 1864), 84; "School Examination," *The Popular Science Monthly* 24 (November 1883): 133; and Jack K. Campbell,

Colonel Francis W. Parker: The Children's Crusader (New York: Teachers College Press, Columbia University, 1967), 142.

24. Yvette C. Rosser, "Francis Wayland Parker," in *Historical Dictionary of Education*, ed. Richard J. Altenbaugh (Westport, CT: Greenwood Press, 1999), 174–175; Charles F. Adams, Jr., *The New Departure in the Common Schools of Quincy and Other Papers on Educational Topics* (Boston: Estes and Lauriate, 1879), 36, on Parker's unprecedented authority; "Meeting of New-England School Superintendents," *New England Journal of Education* 5 (May 31, 1877): 262; the gentle critique of Parker's bombast by E. E. White, "A Few Hours With Educational Journals—Progress in Education," *Indiana School Journal*, reprinted in *The Educational Journal of Virginia* 15 (April 1884): 135–136; *Forty-Third Annual Report of the Board of Education: Together With the Forty-Third Annual Report of the Secretary of the Board* (Boston: Rank, Avery, & Co., 1880), 178–186, 198; Campbell, *Colonel Francis W. Parker*, 90–91; Reese, *America's Public Schools*, 91–92, 112, 116; and Francis W. Parker, "The Quincy Experiment," *The School Journal* 60 (April 28, 1900): 451.

25. "School Examination," *Popular Science Monthly*, 133–134; and *Forty-Sixth Annual Report of the Board of Commissioners of Public Schools, To the Mayor and City Council of Baltimore, For the Year Ending October 31, 1874* (Baltimore, MD: Kelly, Piet & Company, 1875), 26.

26. *Thirty-First Annual Report of the Board of Commissioners of Public Schools, To the Mayor and City Council of Baltimore* (Baltimore, MD: Bull & Tuttle, 1860), 15. In city after city, the least experienced, worst paid teachers instructed the largest number of pupils. See, for example, *Twenty-Fifth Annual Report of the Trustees and Visitors of the Common Schools of Cincinnati, for the School Year Ending 30th June 1854* (Cincinnati, OH: Ben Franklin Mammoth Steam Printing Establishment, 1854), 33.

27. *Annual Report of the School Committee of the City of Boston* (Boston: George C. Rand & Avery, 1856), 14; *Annual Report of the School Committee of the City of Boston* (Boston: George C. Rand & Avery, 1858), 32; and *Annual Report of the School Committee of the City of Boston* (Boston: Rockwell and Churchill, 1898), 49.

28. *Thirty-Sixth Annual Report of the Board of Commissioners of Public Schools, To The Mayor and City Council of Baltimore* (Baltimore, MD: Printed by James Young, 1865), 47, 62–63; *Fifty-Seventh Annual Report of the Board of Commissioners of Public Schools, To The Mayor and City Council of Baltimore, For the Year Ending December 31, 1885* (Baltimore, MD: Wm. J. C. Dulany & Co, n.d.), 63; *Thirtieth Annual Report of the Board of Education, for the Year Ending June 30, 1884* (Chicago: George K. Hazlitt & Co., 1885), 45–46; and William R. Johnson, "'Chanting Choristers': Simultaneous Recitation in Baltimore's Nineteenth-Century Primary Schools," *History of Education Quarterly* 34 (Spring 1994): 1–23. Concert recitations, forbidden by the rules, were common. See *Twenty-Second Annual Report of the Superintendent of Public Schools For the School Year Ending June 30, 1875* (San Francisco, CA: Spaulding and Barto, 1875), 90;

and *Thirty-Fifth Annual Report of the Board of Education of the City and County of New York* (New York: Hall of the Board of Education, 1877), 145–148.

29. John M. Gregory, *The Seven Laws of Teaching* (Boston: The Pilgrim Press, 1886), 34, 46; and *Thirty-Fourth Semi-Annual Report of the Superintendent of Public Schools* (Boston: Rockwell and Churchill, 1878), 18–19.

30. "Public School Idyl," *Puck* 24 (January 16, 1889): 349. On Procrustean beds, see "Faults of Our Schools," *Independent Statesman* (Concord, New Hampshire), September 9, 1875; and "Torture in Our Public Schools," *Daily Inter Ocean* (Chicago), January 29, 1887. On comparisons to stuffed geese and so forth, see "Common School System of Massachusetts," *New Englander and Yale Review* 13 (February 1855): 45; and Caroline B. LeRow, *The "Young Idea" or Common School Culture* (New York: Cassell & Company, Limited, 1888), 195–210.

31. Charles Dickens, *Hard Times* (Oxford: Oxford University Press, c. 1989), 1.

32. *Twenty-Sixth Annual Report of the Trustees and Visitors of Common Schools, to the City Council of Cincinnati for the School Year Ending 30th June 1855* (Cincinnati, OH: Gazette Co. Steam Printing House, 1855), 69–70; *Fifth Annual Report of the State Superintendent of Public Instruction, To The Governor of Nebraska, for the Year Ending December 31st, 1873* (Lincoln, NE: Journal Printing Company, 1873), 26; and *Annual Report of the City Superintendent of Schools, of the City of New York* (New York: Wm. C. Bryant & Co., 1858), 45, on "dull" teaching.

33. On unscrupulous salesmen, "The Examiner," *Old and New* 11 (February 1875): 212; and, regarding the mastering of textbooks, some examples from one city: *Fifteenth Annual Report of the Board of Directors of the St. Louis Public Schools, For the Year Ending August 1, 1869* (St. Louis, MO: Missouri Democrat Book and Job Printing House, 1870), 27–28; *Seventeenth Annual Report of the Board of Directors of the St. Louis Public Schools, For the Year Ending August 1, 1871* (St. Louis, MO: Plate, Olshausen & Co., 1872), 180–181; and *Twenty-Second Annual Report of the Board of Directors of the St. Louis Public Schools, For the Year Ending August 1, 1876* (St. Louis, MO: Slawson, Printer, 1877), 187–188. Also see W. H. Wells, *The Graded School: A Graded Course of Instruction for Public Schools: With Copious Practical Directions to Teachers, and Observations on Primary Schools, School Discipline, School Records, etc.* (New York: A. S. Barnes & Burr, 1862), 154–155. Since elementary school teachers often had little formal education, textbooks were widely seen as a necessary evil, rote instruction a regrettable reality.

34. John D. Philbrick, "The Proper Objects and Uses of School Examinations," *Massachusetts Teacher, and Journal of Home and School Education* 10 (December 1857): 564–565; and *Annual Report of the School Committee of the City of Boston* (Boston: Rockwell & Churchill, 1872), 174–175.

35. *California Teacher,* paraphrased in "Editor's Table," *New England Journal of Education* 18 (October 11, 1883): 223; and E. E. White, "Several Problems in Graded-School Management," *The Addresses and Journal of Proceedings of the*

National Education Association (Worcester, MA: Printed by Charles Hamilton, 1874), 257.

36. White, "Several Problems," 257–258; Reese, *Origins*, 137, 149; and *Thirtieth Annual Report of the Superintendent of Public Schools, For the School Year Ending June 30, 1883* (San Francisco, CA: George Spaulding & Co., 1883), 20.

37. "About Questions and Questioners," *New England Journal of Education* 4 (September 30, 1876): 138.

38. "Dr. White," *Proceedings of the Department of Superintendence of the National Education Association* (Washington, DC: Government Printing Office, Circular of Information No. 2, 1889), 252. Antebellum newspapers frequently discussed and advertised question books for religious instruction, for example, "American Sunday School Union," *The Sun* (Baltimore), May 27, 1839; and "Topical Question Book," *Salem Gazette* (Massachusetts), February 16, 1841. On the criticisms of the keys, see "Text-Books and School Studies," *The Massachusetts Teacher* 5 (August 1852): 240; and "Common School System of Massachusetts," 51.

39. "Slang Phrases," *Brooklyn Daily Eagle*, April 7, 1878. On the spread of the "information" and "knowledge revolution" of the nineteenth century, see Richard R. John, "Recasting the Information Infrastructure for the Industrial Age," in *A Nation Transformed: How Information Has Shaped the United States from Colonial Times to the Present*, ed. Alfred D. Chandler, Jr. and James W. Cortada (New York: Oxford University Press, 2000), 55–105.

40. P. L. Chrispell, *The Teachers' Pocket Manual: Containing an Outline, With the Definitions, of Arithmetic, Geography, History and Grammar* (Hackensack, NJ: William H. Bleeker, 1876), n.p.; W. J. King, *Treasury of Facts. A Cyclopedia of Natural and Mathematical Science With the Art and Science of Teaching* (New York: A. Lovell & Co., Publishers, 1884); and Josiah Hughes, *Hughes' Common School Branches in a Nutshell. Prepared for the Benefit of Teachers and Students* (Charleston, WV: Butler Printing Company, 1893), n.p.

41. Asa H. Craig, *The Question Book: A General Review of Common School Studies. For the Use of Teachers, and Those Intending to Teach* (Delafield, WI: The Rural Book and Pamphlet Press, 1872); Asa H. Craig, *The New Common School Question Book. A General Review of Common School Studies. To Be Used in Schools in Connection with Text Books* (Cleveland, OH: J.R. Holcomb & Co., 1887), 112; and William Hawley Smith, *Walks and Talks* (Chicago: A. Flanagan, Publisher, 1893), 80.

42. Lamont Stilwell, *The Practical Question Book: A Hand-Book of Practical Questions,* (Boston: The Educational Publishing Company, 1887); J. E. Sherrill, *The Normal Question Book: Containing Three Thousand Questions and Answers Taken from the Best Authorities on the Common School Branches* (Indianapolis, IN: Normal Publishing House, 1882); Mary F. Hendrick, *A Series of Questions in English and American Literature* (Syracuse, NY: Davis, Bardeen, & Co., 1880); and J. Dorman Steele, *Manual of Science for Teachers, Containing Answers to the Practical*

Questions and Problems in the Author's Scientific Text-Books (New York: American Book Company, 1888).

43. "Some New Books," *Springfield Republican* (Massachusetts) (October 14, 1885). Both Albert P. Southwick, who authored "dime question" books and B. A. Hathaway, who priced his volumes higher, also wrote similar volumes on pedagogy. See Albert P. Southwick, *A Quiz Manual of the Theory and Practice of Teaching* (New York: E. L. Kellogg, 1888); and B. A Hathaway, *1001 Questions and Answers on the Theory and Practice of Teaching* (Cleveland, OH: The Burrows Brothers Company, 1886).

44. A. C. Mason, *1000 Ways of 1000 Teachers* (Chicago: A. Flanagan, Publisher, 1881), 10; Albert Henry Thompson, *The Examiners' Companion, A General Review of Questions and Answers* (Chicago: n.p., 1887), n.p.; and, on Parker, Southwick, *Quiz Manual,* 34–35 and especially Dana Williams, *Questions on Theory and School Government for Use at Examinations* (York, PA: York Daily Printing, 1884), 3–29.

45. Untitled editorial, *Central School Journal* 9 (May 1886): 9; "Question Books With Answers," *Central School Journal* 9 (August 1886): 16; untitled editorial, *Central School Journal* 9 (December 1886): 10; and "One Thousand and One Questions," *Trübner's American, European and Oriental Literary Record* 6 (Numbers 7–8, 1885): 65.

46. Craig, *Question Book,* 25–36, 84–100; and Sherrill, *Normal Question Book,* 89–99, 142–157.

47. "Examinations and Promotions," *Ohio Educational Monthly,* quoted in *Journal of Education* 19 (March 13, 1884): 163; T. W. Bicknell, "Reply," *Journal of Education* 20 (October 9, 1884): 231; and "Letter from Dr. Ellis," *Journal of Education* 20 (October 23, 1884): 263.

48. Emerson E. White, *Promotions and Examinations in Graded Schools* (Washington, DC: Government Printing Office, U.S. Bureau of Education, Circular of Information, No. 7, 1891), 28–30. Newspapers throughout the country commented on the elimination of promotion exams in various cities and the use of a wider range of scores, grades, and evidence; for a small sampling, read "School Promotion Without 'Marking,'" *Springfield Republican* (Massachusetts), February 17, 1889; "Board of Education," *Wheeling Register* (West Virginia), April 17, 1885; untitled article, *Morning Oregonian* (Portland), October 18, 1889; and "The Written Examination," *Boston Morning Journal,* April 27, 1893. On resistance to change in high schools, see "High School Interests," *The New Haven Evening Register,* April 11, 1892; "Opposition From The High School," *Pawtucket Times,* February 3, 1900; and *Report of the Chief Superintendent of New Orleans, La., to the State Board of Education* (n.p.: January 1888), 255.

49. "Ohio Teachers," *The Cincinnati Commercial,* June 30, 1881; and "Ohio Educators at Put-In-Bay," *Journal of Education* 13 (July 14, 1881): 65.

50. On the teachers in San Francisco, read "School Examination," *Evening Bulletin,* September 9, 1881; S. H. White, "The Over-Study Humbug," *Milwaukee*

Daily Sentinel, December 4, 1876; "Concerning Sleep," *Providence Journal,* reprinted in *St. Louis Globe-Democrat,* July 9, 1877; "What Kills," *Teetotaler,* reprinted in *The Wisconsin State Register* (Portage), August 3, 1878; and *Thirtieth Annual Report* (Chicago), 52. On support for hard work and academic rigor, Reese, *Origins,* 202–204. Teachers also complained when undeserving pupils were promoted; see "Sympathy," *Plain Dealer* (Cleveland), March 23, 1894. On the Portland hearings, see untitled editorial, *Journal of Education* 19 (April 3, 1884): 216; and Thomas Tash, "New England Department," *Journal of Education* 19 (April 24, 1884): 268.

51. X., "The Marking System," *Massachusetts Teacher* 27 (December 1874): 470; *Thirty-Ninth Annual Report of the Board of Education, Together With the Thirty-Ninth Annual Report of the Secretary of the Board* (Boston: Wright and Potter, 1876), 78, 130; "Examinations," *Journal of Education* 17 (March 1, 1883): 131; and R. W. Stevenson, "City and Town Supervision of Schools," *The Journal of Proceedings and Addresses of the National Education Association* (Boston: J. E. Farwell & Co., 1885), 290–291. For a defense of written exams, see Conservative, "The Percentage System in the Public Schools," *The Cincinnati Commercial,* May 15, 1881.

52. XYZ, "Some Views," 7; "School Examination," *Evening Bulletin* (San Francisco, May 31, 1869); *Forty-Third Annual Report for the School Year Ending June 30, 1872* (Cincinnati, OH: Wilstach, Baldwin & Co, 1873), 82; *Annual Report of the Board of Education, of the Memphis City Schools, For 1869–1870* (Memphis, TN: Hite & Corwine, n.d.), 52; and "The Disappearance of the School-Master," *The Century Magazine* 23 (February 1882): 617–618.

53. "School Examinations and Reports," *The Massachusetts Teacher* 2 (November 1849): 323.

54. Henry Barnard, *Proceedings of the National Teachers' Association, Afterward the National Education Association* (Syracuse, NY: C. W. Bardeen, 1870), 253–257, which reprinted an 1860 committee report; Wells, *Graded School,* 132–133; and *Annual Report of the School Committee of the City of Boston* (Boston: Rockwell & Churchill, 1876), 8–9, on the dangers of comparing statistics across school districts; and, on corruption, Richard White, *Railroaded: The Transcontinentals and the Making of Modern America* (New York: W. W. Norton & Company, 2011).

55. *Annual Report of the City Superintendent . . . New York City* (1858), 50; *Thirty-Second Annual Report of the Board of Commissioners of Public Schools, to the Mayor and City Council of Baltimore* (Baltimore, MD: William M. Innes, 1861), 50–51; Letter, Committee on Rules, "To the Principal of the _____ School," (July 3, 1878), (Box 5); and "Circular No. 14, Office of the Superintendent," (April 1, 1889), (Box 9) (San Francisco Unified School District Collection, 1854–2005, San Francisco History Center, San Francisco Public Library) [hereafter SFUSDC] ; *Fifth Annual Report of the City Superintendent of the Public Schools of the City of Portland, Oregon, For the Year Ending June 27, 1878* (Portland, OR:

A. G. Walling, Printer and Bookbinder, 1878), 17; and *Eighth Annual Report of the City Superintendent of the Public Schools of the City of Portland, Oregon, For the Year Ending June 28, 1881* (Portland, OR: Printing and Publishing House of Himes the Printer, 1881), 32.

56. George A. Walton, "Examinations of Norfolk County Schools," in *Forty-Third Annual Report of the Board of Education: Together With the Forty-Third Annual Report of the Secretary of the Board* (Boston: Rand, Avery, & Co., 1880), 123–125, 132.

57. Walton, "Examinations," 124; and *Forty-Fourth Annual Report of the Board of Education: Together With the Forty-Fourth Annual Report of the Secretary of the Board* (Boston: Rand, Avery & Company, 1880), 79–80. The Norfolk report generated national attention, disputes over how to read the evidence, and heated exchanges between friends and critics of public education. For a small sampling of the sources, see "The Schools and the Prisons," *New York Times*, November 29, 1880; Adams, "Scientific Common-School Education," 934–942; Richard Grant White, "The Public-School Failure," *North American Review* 131 (December 1880): 537–551; John D. Philbrick, "The Success of the Free-School System," *North American Review* 132 (March 1881): 249–263; and John D. Philbrick, "Which is the True Ideal of the Public School?" *Education* 1 (January 1881): 305–306.

58. Administrators commonly assigned numbers to students to ensure more objective evaluations, especially in high-stakes tests, and they warned about the untrustworthiness of many statistics. See "Examination of Applicants for Admission to the High School," *Evening Bulletin* (San Francisco), June 3, 1861; "Examination in the Grammar School," *Morning Oregonian* (Portland), July 17, 1874; *Annual Report of the Superintendent of Public Schools, For the Year Ending October 15th, 1867* (San Francisco, CA: Joseph Winterburn & Co., 1867), 134–135; *Fortieth Annual Report for the School Year Ending June 30, 1869* (Cincinnati, OH: Gazette Printing, 1870), 46–47; and Reese, *Origins*, 147–148.

59. No author, "District Graded Schools," *Maine Journal of Education* 8 (February 1874): 55; H. S. Jones, "Educational Tests," *New England Journal of Education* 9 (March 20, 1879): 179; and, for a typical claim about improvement, *Thirty-Fifth Annual Report . . . New York* (1877), 112–118.

60. *Report of the Superintendent of Public Instruction*, in *Official Documents* (Harrisburg, PA: Edwin K. Meyers, State Printers, 1889), 2: 163; and James Denman, "To the Principals of the Public Schools," July 6, 1875 (Box 5 SFUSDC). On the spread of "useless examinations and the gathering of statistics" see "Inspection of Schools," *Boston Daily Advertiser*, June 15, 1887.

61. *Fourteenth Annual Report of the Board of Education of the City and County of New York* (New York: Wm. C. Byrant & Co., 1856), 33–34; and David B. Tyack, *The One Best System: A History of American Urban Education* (Cambridge, MA: Harvard University Press, 1974), 94–95.

62. On over-crowding, see "Chicago's Schools," *The Sunday Times* (Chicago), August 2, 1874; and "Needs School Room," *Chicago Daily Tribune*, June 7, 1894. Availability of seats strongly shaped premature promotions or retention in the same grade. See "Retarding Scholars," *The Philadelphia Inquirer*, May 14, 1890. On the gap between theory and practice in promotions, see P., "Our Primary Schools," *Boston Daily Advertiser*, February 11, 1882; "The Public Schools," *Boston Daily Advertiser*, February 22, 1882; *Thirty-First Annual Report of the School Board of the City of Milwaukee, For the Year Ending August 31, 1890* (Milwaukee, WI: Ed. Keogh, Printer, 1890), 36; and *Thirty-Second Annual Report of the School Board of the City of Milwaukee, For the Year Ending August 31, 1891* (Milwaukee, WI: Commercial Printing Co., 1891), 52, 64–65.

63. *Fifty-Ninth Annual Report of the Public Schools of Cincinnati, For the School Year Ending August 31, 1888* (Cincinnati, OH: The Ohio Valley Company, 1889), 42; John Taylor, "Circular 66," July 12, 1881 (Box 5, SFUSDC); and *Thirtieth Annual Report* (San Francisco), 21. Promotion rates varied depending on the perspectives, some said whim, of principals, superintendents, and teachers.

64. "Events in Council Bluffs," *Morning World-Herald* (Omaha) (November 2, 1891). Tensions between administrators and the school board over promotions in Baltimore were described in "Public Schools," *The Sun*, October 18, 1893; and, for the quotation from New Orleans, *Report of the Chief Superintendent of the Public Schools of the City of New Orleans, La., to the State Board of Education* (n.p.: January 1886), 255. In Atlanta, as in other cities, some students who failed to reach the minimum entrance exam score were admitted on probation; see "List of Scholars," *Atlanta Constitution*, July 21, 1874.

65. *Fifteenth Annual Report of the Superintendent of Public Schools, For the School Year Ending June 30th, 1868* (San Francisco: Printed by the John H. Carmony & Co., 1868), 60–61. On patronage and graft, see William A. Bullough, *The Blind Boss & His City: Christopher Augustine Buckley and Nineteenth-Century San Francisco* (Berkeley, CA: University of California Press, 1979), 130–133, 148–150. On opposition to high schools, see Reese, *Origins*, 43–44, 59–79.

66. *Fifty-Third Annual Report of the Board of Commissioners of Public Schools, to the Mayor and City Council of Baltimore* (Baltimore, MD: Printed by John B. Piet, 1882), 79; *Fifty-Fourth Annual Report of the Board of Commissioners of Public Schools, to the Mayor and City Council of Baltimore* (Baltimore, MD: King Brothers, n.d.), xxxvii; and *Thirty-First Annual Report of the Superintendent of Public Schools, For the School Year Ending June 30, 1884* (San Francisco, CA: W. A. Woodward & Co., 1884), 37.

67. James D. Anderson, *The Education of Blacks in the South, 1860–1935* (Chapel Hill: University of North Carolina Press, 1988); and, for evidence for Baltimore on African-American scores, *Fifty-Third Annual Report . . . Baltimore*, 59–60; and *Sixty-Third Annual Report of the Board of Commissioners of Public Schools, to the Mayor and City Council of Baltimore* (Baltimore, MD: John Cox,

1892), 109–110. Also see Reese, *Origins*, 230–35; and Reese, *America's Public Schools*, 43–44, 70–77.

68. *Thirtieth Annual Report of the Board of Public Instruction of the City and County of New York* (New York: NY School Journal Print, 1872), 210; *Eleventh Annual Report of the Superintendent of Public Schools of the City and County of San Francisco* (San Francisco: Magee Brothers, 1863), 47; Victor Low, *The Unimpressible Race: A Century of Educational Struggle By the Chinese in San Francisco* (San Francisco, CA: East/West Publishing Company, 1982), Chapters 1–4; and, for typical xenophobic comments, "Circular 86," (April 1, 1886), (Box 9) [SFUSDC]. On northern segregation, see Hillary J. Moss, *Schooling Citizens: The Struggle for African-American Education in Antebellum America* (Chicago: The University of Chicago Press, 2009); Davison M. Douglas, *Jim Crow Moves North: The Battle over Northern School Segregation, 1865–1954* (Cambridge: Cambridge University Press, 2005), Chapters 2–4; and Reese, *America's Public Schools*, 73–74.

Epilogue

1. *Thirty-Eighth Annual Report of the Board of Education for the Year Ending June 30, 1892* (Chicago: Hack and Anderson, 1893), 47; "Examinations and Promotions in Elementary Schools," National Education Association, *Journal of Proceedings and Addresses* (St. Paul, MN: Published by the Association, 1895), 295; "Dreams and Nightmares," *The Sunday Inter-Ocean* (Chicago), December 13, 1891; and Rene Bache, "Science in Dreamland," *Butte Weekly Miner*, May 5, 1898.

2. "Educational Matters," *The Knoxville Journal*, October 29, 1893; and L. E. Rector, "Secondary Schools and the Co-Ordination of Studies," *Education* 15 (January 1895): 285. Rector believed the Regents' exams in New York State proved his point.

3. "The Regents' System in New York," *Journal of Education* 45 (April 8, 1897): 224; and "Middle Atlantic States," *Journal of Education* 45 (May 13, 1897): 312. Also see William J. Reese, *The Origins of the American High School* (New Haven, CT: Yale University Press, 1995), 155, and Nancy Beadie, "From Student Markets to Credential Markets: The Creation of the Regents Examination System in New York State, 1864–1890," *History of Education Quarterly* 39 (Spring 1999): 1–30.

4. See the report by the committee chaired by Harris, "Report of the Subcommittee on Instruction and Discipline," National Education Association, *Journal of Proceedings and Addresses* (Chicago: The University of Chicago Press, 1897), 484–485, on the problems associated with high-stakes tests and the graded system; William J. Reese, "The Philosopher-King of St. Louis," in *Curriculum & Consequence: Herbert M. Kliebard and the Promise of Schooling*, ed. Barry M. Franklin (New York: Teachers College Press, 2000), 155–177;

Emerson E. White, *Promotions and Examinations in Graded Schools* (Washington, DC: U.S. Bureau of Education, Circular of Information, No. 7, 1891), 57 and Emerson E. White, *The Art of Teaching* (New York: American Book Company, 1901), 90–91.

5. "Defends His Pupils," *The Chicago Herald*, October 19, 1891; "Calls Schools Too Solemn," *The St. Albans Messenger* (Vermont), June 22, 1900; Francis W. Parker, "The Quincy Experiment," *The School Journal* 60 (April 28, 1900): 450; and William J. Reese, "When Wisdom Was Better Than Rubies: The Washington, D.C., Public Schools in the Nineteenth Century," in *Clio at the Table: Using History to Inform and Improve Education Policy*, eds. Kenneth K. Wong and Robert Rothman (New York: Peter Lang, 2009), 71–72.

6. *Sixty-First Annual Report of the Public Schools of Cincinnati For the School Year Ending August 31, 1890* (Cincinnati, OH: The Ohio Valley Company, 1891), 63–64; and *Annual Report of the School Committee of the City of Boston* (Boston: Rockwell and Churchill, 1893), 40.

7. "The Failure of the Examination," *Journal of Education* 46 (December 16, 1897): 364.

8. On local celebrations in Boston, see Lillian Whiting, "Life in Boston," *The Daily Inter-Ocean* (Chicago), May 2, 1896; "Mann's Good Work," *Boston Daily Advertiser*, May 4, 1896; and "Horace Mann," *Boston Daily Advertiser*, May 5, 1896.

9. Nelson Sizer, "Horace Mann: His Centenary, May 4, 1896," *The Phrenological Journal and Science of Health* 101 (June 1896): 50; *Troy Times*, quoted in "Horace Mann's Birthday," *Boston Daily Advertiser*, May 8, 1896; "A Vanished Type," *Morning Oregonian* (Portland), May 10, 1896; "The Day at Houston," *The Galveston Daily News* (Houston), May 2, 1896; and "The Day at Houston," *The Galveston Daily News*, May 3, 1896.

10. "Progress of Education," *The Milwaukee Sentinel*, October 25, 1896.

11. William T. Harris, *Horace Mann* (Syracuse, NY: C. W. Bardeen, 1896), 5, 8.

12. Theophilus Parsons, William Brigham, and J. I. T. Coolidge, "Address of the Sub-Committee," *Boston Daily Atlas*, April 23, 1846. Recall that Theophilus Parsons and Brigham were the respective chairs of the reading and writing examination committees; Coolidge was a member of Brigham's committee.

13. Horace Mann to Rev. S. J. May, July 4, 1845, in *Life of Horace Mann*, ed. Mary Peabody Mann (Washington, DC: National Education Association of the United States, c. 1937), 238; and *Reports of the Annual Visiting Committees of the Public Schools of the City of Boston, 1845* (Boston: J. H. Eastburn, City Printer, 1845), 18–19.

14. Numerous books examine different aspects of the history of testing in the twentieth century, including the rise of eugenics, scientific management, and other important themes. In addition to the numerous references to other scholars in the endnotes of previous chapters, see especially David B. Tyack, *The One Best System: A History of American Urban Education* (Cambridge,

MA: Harvard University Press, 1974), 198–216; Daniel J. Kevles, *In The Name of Eugenics: Genetics and the Uses of Human Heredity* (Cambridge, MA: Harvard University Press, c. 1995); Leila Zenderland, *Measuring Minds: Henry Herbert Goddard and the Origins of American Intelligence Testing* (Cambridge: Cambridge University Press, 1998); and Nicholas Lemann, *The Big Test: The Secret History of the American Meritocracy* (New York: Farrar, Strauss and Giroux, 1999). On important changes underway in statistical analysis before the early twentieth century, see, for example, Victor L. Hilts, *Statist and Statistician: Three Studies in the History of Nineteenth Century English Statistical Thought* (New York: Arno Press, 1981); and Victor L. Hilts, "Statistics and Social Science," in *Foundations of Scientific Method: The Nineteenth Century,* eds. Ronald N. Giere and Richard S. Westfall (Bloomington: Indiana University Press, 1973), 206–233. Also see a guide to the extensive literature on the subject in William J. Reese, *America's Public Schools: From the Common School to "No Child Left Behind"* (Baltimore, MD: The Johns Hopkins University Press, 2011), 345.

15. Fernanda Santos and Robert Gebeloff, "City Releases Ratings of 18,000 Teachers; Acknowledges Limitations of Data," *The New York Times,* February 25, 2012.

16. Jack Gillum and Marisol Bello, "When Test Scores Soared in D.C., Were the Gains Real?" *USA Today,* March 28, 2011; Kim Severson, "Systematic Cheating Is Found in Atlanta's School System," *The New York Times,* July 6, 2011; Michael Winerip, "Pennsylvania Joins the List of States Facing a School Cheating Scandal," *The New York Times,* August 1, 2011; Michael Winerip, "A New Leader Helps Heal Atlanta Schools, Scarred by Scandal," *The New York Times,* February 20, 2012; Trip Gabriel, "Cheats Find An Adversary in Technology," *The New York Times,* December 28, 2010; Sharon Otterman, "Under Bloomberg, a Sharp Rise in Accusations of Cheating by Educators," *The New York Times,* August 23, 2011; Jennifer Medina, "Warning Signs Long Ignored On New York's School Tests," *The New York Times,* October 11, 2010; and Diane Ravitch, "Waiting for a School Miracle," *The New York Times,* June 1, 2011, on bogus statistics.

17. Sam Dillon, "Overriding a Key Education Law," *The New York Times,* August 8, 2011. For a blistering critique of the excesses of standardized testing and the modern movement to privatize schools, read Diane Ravitch, *The Death and Life of the Great American School System: How Testing and Choice Are Undermining Education* (New York: Basic Books, 2010). On federal policy, also see Patrick J. McGuinn, *No Child Left Behind and the Transformation of Federal Education Policy, 1965–2005* (Lawrence: University Press of Kansas, 2006); Lee W. Anderson, *Congress and the Classroom: From the Cold War to "No Child Left Behind"* (University Park: The Pennsylvania State University Press, 2007); Maris A. Vinovskis, *From A Nation at Risk to No Child Left Behind* (New York: Teachers College Press, 2009); and a brief exploration of *No Child Left Behind* in Reese, *America's Public Schools,* 322–337. On new forms of assessment,

see Douglas N. Harris, *Value-Added Measures in Education: What Every Educator Needs to Know* (Cambridge, MA: Harvard Education Press, 2011); and Richard Pérez-Peña, "Trying to Find a Measure for How Well Colleges Do," *The New York Times*, April 8, 2012; David Brooks, "Testing the Teachers," *The New York Times*, April 20, 2012, on higher education trends.

18. Anna M. Phillips, "As Number of Gifted Children Soars, a Fight Brews for Slots in Kindergarten," *The New York Times*, April 14, 2012.

19. Educational Testing Services website: www.ets.org http://www.ets.org (accessed June 18, 2012).

Acknowledgments

Testing Wars in the Public Schools began as a study of promotion policies in urban schools in the twentieth century and became a history of the origins of standardized testing a century earlier. For the freedom that allowed me to find my way, I am grateful to a host of people and institutions. A generous grant from the Spencer Foundation helped me launch my research. It is one of the few major philanthropic organizations that funds basic educational research (to historians, no less), and it does so without intellectual or ideological strings attached. I am also indebted to the Graduate School and the Wisconsin Alumni Research Foundation of the University of Wisconsin–Madison for their financial support. In addition, timely and persistent help from research assistants helped smooth my path from start to finish. I hope that Robert Gross, Christine Hanzlik, Story Matkin-Rawn, Campbell Scribner, and Patricia Stovey know how much they taught me and how much I depended upon them.

For many years, numerous friends and colleagues with Job-like patience listened to me talk about my research. Neither they nor my graduate assistants are responsible for the shortcomings of my research and writing, but they deserve full credit for helping me improve every aspect of my work. For their time, encouragement, and rich conversations, I also tip my hat to many friends: Harvey Black, William Cronon, Peter Cunningham, Barry Franklin, Michael Fultz, Richard Halverson, Diana Hess, Carl Kaestle, Jennifer Ratner-Rosenhagen, John Rudolph, Karl Shoemaker, Jeremi Suri, Jim Sweet, Maris Vinovskis, and Jed Woodward. Richard Aldrich shared his unparalleled knowledge of educational policies in Great Britain. Robert Orsi helped me think more clearly about the parallel worlds of religious and educational history. Cogent advice from Jonathan Zimmerman proved invaluable. Mary Ann Dzuback, Erin Hardacher, Doug Harris, Adam Nelson, and John Rury also read the entire manuscript and offered constructive criticisms. By reading different versions of the manuscript, David McDonald, Margaret Nash, and Robert Gross went beyond the call of duty and friendship.

My editor, Elizabeth G. Knoll, has been a model of support, guidance, and professionalism. My sincerest thanks to her and to editorial assistant Joy Deng. Marianna Z. Vertullo, editorial services manager at Integrated Book Technology, kindly shepherded the manuscript through production, as did Leslie Ellen Jones, a superb copyeditor.

In addition, invited addresses at Beloit College, Binghamton University, Grand Valley State University, Indiana University at Bloomington, Seoul University, the University of New Hampshire, the University of Notre Dame, and my home institution on different occasions provided unparalleled opportunities to think out loud in different settings. A special thank you to Maureen Hallinan, Adam Laats, and Paul Murphy. I am especially grateful to John Bodnar, distinguished historian and director of the Institute for Advanced Study at Indiana University at Bloomington, for the opportunity to serve as a Visiting Scholar at that esteemed institution.

Librarians and archivists remain among steadfast friends of every historian. A special thank you to James Danky and Andy Kraushaar for their help in locating materials at the Wisconsin Historical Society. At the Rare Books and Manuscripts Department at the Boston Public Library, Sean Casey provided expert advice in utilizing the School Committee Archives Collection and other relevant sources. Materials located there are cited courtesy of the Trustees of the Boston Public Library/Rare Books. Tami J. Suzuki provided similar aid at the San Francisco History Center, and Susan Goldstein, City Archivist, granted permission to draw upon the materials in the San Francisco Unified School District Record Collection. Since my graduate school days, librarians at the Library of Congress have been unfailingly generous. For permission to cite letters from the Horace Mann Collection, microfilm edition, I am grateful to Elaine M. Grublin, head of reader services, Massachusetts Historical Society. Scott Sanders, Antioch College Archivist, kindly granted permission to cite materials from the Robert L. Straker Collection related to Horace Mann. Jack Dougherty of Trinity College, with the assistance of the staff at the Watkinson Library, located and provided an electronic copy of the controversial 1845 report on Boston's grammar schools.

A special thank you to Carole, for her love and enthusiasm for life. The book is dedicated to the memory of her remarkable parents, Lil and Ike Blemker, for their kindness and generosity to me and to so many of my friends.

Index

academies, 10, 16, passim
ACT, Inc., 232
achievement tests, 229, 231–232
Adams, William J., 68, 101
Adelphic Union, 84
African-Americans, 4, 18–19, 62, 80, 82–89, 96, 123–124, 149–150, 177, 218–220, 227–228. *See also* Boston; Abner Forbes; Samuel Gridley Howe; Smith School
Albany, New York, 31, 34
American Institute of Instruction, 55, 81
American Statistical Association, 137, 139
Andrews, Abraham, 47–48
Astor, John Jacob, 197
Atlanta, 177, 185, 230

Bacon, Francis, 28
Baltimore, 17–18, 25, 31, 176, 197, 201, 213, 218–219
Bangor, Maine, 198
Barnard, Henry, 38
Barney, H.H., 169
Barnum, P.T., 23
Barrett, Samuel, 120–121
Bartlett, Sidney, 114
Bates, Joshua, Jr., 68
Bicknell, Thomas W., 208–209
Bingham, Caleb, 14–16, 20, 27, 32, 62
Bishop, Nathan, 146, 149, 156

Boston: African-Americans, 62, 71, 76, 82–91, 123–124, 228; and written tests, 5, 40–41, passim; colonial education, 12, 38; corporal punishment, 48–49, 64–65, 67, 71, 75–83, 88, 92, 99, 104, 111–112, 142, passim; English grammar schools, 41–45, 70, 98–99, passim; English High School, 38, 41–42, 61, 131, 191; examination committees (1845), 40–41, 50–53, 91–97, passim; exhibitions, 39, 42–44, 87; Girls' High and Normal School, 171; Girls' High School, 41; Latin grammar school, 12, 38, 41–42, 53; masters (grammar schools), 41–43, 46–50, 58, 69, 85–87, 92–93, 104, 142, 171–172, 225; primary schools, 46, 147, 171–172, 185; School Committee, 38, 43, 50, 71–73, 122; superintendent, 58, 71, 94, 113, 141–146, 153, 170–173; teachers (grammar schools), 42, 46–47, 142; teachers (primary schools), 46, 171–172; truancy, 87, 152. *See also* Nathan Bishop; Abner Forbes; John D. Philbrick; Edwin P. Seaver; Smith School
Boston Phrenological Society, 55–57. *See also* Samuel Gridley Howe
Bowen, Francis, 74–75
Bowker, Albert, 115–117, 128, 144, 146. *See also* Lyman School

Brattleboro, Vermont, 25

Brewer, Thomas M., 102–104, 108–109

Brigham, William: and statistics, 56, 100, 110, 137–138, 178; Boston School Committee, 107, 129; writing school committee of 1845, 51–52, 56, 92–96, 102–103, 119, 124, 128–131, 140–141, 223

Brooks, Charles, 144–145, 150

Brownson, Orestes, 65

Burlington, Vermont, 33

Burton, Warren, 8–10, 11, 20, 24, 161

Busby, Richard, 77–78

Cambridge University, 4, 12, 59–60, 222

Capen, Aaron D., 80–81, 119, 123–124

Central High School (Philadelphia), 37, 183

charity schools, 10, 12, 14, 16–19, 21, 30–33, 59, 166, 178, 185

Charleston, South Carolina, 34

charter schools, 3

Chicago, 173–174, 179–180, 182–183,185–186, 189, 197, 201, 210, 216, 221. See also William Harvey Wells

Chinese-Americans, 219–220

Cincinnati, 37, 167–170, 179, 183–185, 189, 195–198, 203, 217, 222. See also John Hancock; John B. Peaslee; Andrew J. Rickoff; Emerson E. White

Clarke, Marilla, 168

Clay, Henry, 32–33

Cleveland, 194, 196

Codman, John, 153–154

College Board, 232

Columbus, Georgia, 177

Columbus, Ohio, 211

Combe, George, 55, 67, 86, 98, 125

Concord, Vermont, 33

Cook County Normal School, 199

corporal punishment, 48–50, 60, 67, 74–83, 99, 111–112. See also Boston; Aaron D. Capen; Barnum Field; Abner Forbes; Leonard Withington

Council Bluffs, Iowa, 217

Cowper, William, 26–28

Craig, Asa H., 206, 208

Crawford, T.H., 213

Dale, William J., 109

Dartmouth College, 14–16

Democratic Party, 58, 146

Des Moines, 166

Dewey, John, 3. See also progressive education

Dickens, Charles, 49, 202–203

Dickinson, J.W., 214

disputations, 11

Douglass, Frederick, 19

Dowd, John, 211

Easton, Hosea, 85–86

Educational Testing Service, 232

Edwards, H.H., 168

Ellis, S.A., 209

Emerson, Frederick: and African-American education, 83–90, 149; and grammar masters, 89–90, 94, 109, 117, 122–126, 138–139, 142, 144–145, 148–149; and statistics, 138–139; background, 87–88; mathematics textbooks, 72, 104, 134, 140–141, 146; opponent of Horace Mann and Samuel Gridley Howe, 72, 83, 86–89, 103, 110, 119–121, 124–125, 129–130, 132, 138–139, 145, 226; professional achievements, 72, 88, 104; scandal, 148; service on Boston School Committee, 89, 108–109, 120–121

Emerson, George B., 61–63, 74, 76, 91, 148, 153, 178

emulation, 22, 26–30, 37, 40, 73–74, 169, 197. See also written examinations

Erie, Pennsylvania, 215

exhibitions: and nostalgia, 189–193, 209; characteristics, 14–15, 178, passim; colonial America, 12; criticism of, 13, 21–27; decline of, 158, 161, 165–166, 188–190, 228; defense of, 23–24, 27–29, passim; European origins,

11–13; in Boston, 44–45; in the South, 23; influence upon teaching, 8–9, 22, 25–26; popularity, 2, 10–12, 22, 28–29, 37, 165–166, passim

Fairbank, Josiah, 124
Field, Barnum: and Horace Mann, 81–82, 94, 101, 121; and Samuel Gridley Howe, 130; background, 81–82; death, 149; defense of corporal punishment, 81–82, 90, 119–123; grammar school master, 88, 121–123, 140, 142; textbook author, 85, 134
Fillmore, Millard, 18
Forbes, Abner: and Horace Mann, 94; background, 83; grammar school master, 62, 82–87, 96, 119, 123, 140; views on corporal punishment, 82, 89–91, 119. *See also* Smith School
Fowle, William B.: and Horace Mann, 91–92, 94–95, 100, 125–126; apprenticeship, 62; author and publisher, 62–63; background, 62; persistence of rote teaching, 156; preparation of 1845 exams, 91–92, 95, 133, 156
Franklin, Benjamin, 27, 39

Garrison, William Lloyd, 83–85
geography instruction, 2, 134–135, 140, 206, 208, 219. *See also* Barnum Field
Georgetown, DC, 18
Gillan, S.Y., 225–226
Goldsmith, Oliver, 191
grade retention, 216–219
Graves, H.A., 70, 113–118. *See also* Albert Bowker; Lyman School
Greenwood, James M., 186
Gregory, John M., 201–202
Guilford, Nathan, 169
Guy Fawkes Day, 11

Hagerstown, Maryland, 21
Hague, William, 108–109
Hall, Samuel R., 27
Hancock, John, 184

Harlow, William B., 160
Harris, John, 48, 149
Harris, William T., 150, 167, 222, 226
Hart, John S., 183
Hartford, Connecticut, 34, 116, 189
Hathaway, B.A., 207–208
high school, 5, 25, 34, 36–37, 59, 61, 131, 162–164, 166, 171, 177–178, 181–183, 191, 196, 198, 209, 217–219
Hillard, George S., 144–145, 150–151
history instruction, 2, 133–135, 140, 168, 201, 208
Houston, Texas, 225
Howe, Julia Ward, 57–58, 111, 120
Howe, Samuel Gridley: and African-Americans, 131, 149, 218; and Barnum Field, 81–82, 120, 130; and grammar masters of Boston, 54, 58–59, 67; and phrenology, 54–55, 111, 195–197; and statistics, 56–57, 110, 128, 130–138, 178; background, 53; European influences upon, 54–59, 146, 178, 226; friendship with Horace Mann, 52–58, 63–67, 76, 91, 103, 119–120; loses nomination to Boston School Committee, 129, 144, 159; opponent of Frederick Emerson, 72, 119–121, 226; reading school committee of 1845, 40, 52–53, 130–143, 183, 197, 211, 218, 223–229; school for the blind, 53, 72, 131; views on corporal punishment, 76. *See also* Horace Mann
Howland, George, 210
Hoyt, Charles H., 190, 192–194, 198
Hyde Park, Illinois, 1–2

Indianapolis, 174–175
infant schools, 12
intelligence tests, 229, 231–232
Irish immigrants, 49, 151–153

Jersey City, 222
Jerusalem, Illinois, 189
Jones, H.S., 158–160, 215

Kansas City, Missouri, 186
Kaplan, 232
Keillor, Garrison, 3
Kennedy, Ted, 3
Kiddle, Henry, 181, 188–189, 213, 219
King, Rufus, 169
King, S.W., 176, 182
Knoxville, 221

Lancaster, Joseph, 30–32. *See also* charity
    schools
Lane, Albert G., 221
Leath, J.T., 176
Leavitt, Joshua, 75, 101, 106, 112–113,
    121–122
Lexington, Kentucky, 31
Little Rock, 177
Longfellow, Henry Wadsworth, 73
Loring, Edward G., 121, 151–152
Louisville, 176, 181
Lyman School (Boston), 70, 100, 115–
    118, 132, 144. *See also* Albert Bowker

Maldon, Massachusetts, 20
Mallon, Bernard, 177
Mann, Horace: and 1845 examina-
    tion, 51–52, passim; and Barnum
    Field, 81–82, and grammar masters
    of Boston, 52–54, 58–68, 75–76, 78,
    224–225; and phrenology, 54–55,
    111, 195; and statistics, 56–57, 61,
    103, 110–111, 130–132, 159, 178; and
    teaching, 58, 60–62, 136; background,
    53–54; centenary of birth, 224–225;
    European influences upon, 54–60;
    friendship with George Combe, 55,
    67, 75–76; friendship with Samuel
    Gridley Howe, 52–59, 63, 65–67, 71,
    91, 103, 119–120; opponent of Fred-
    erick Emerson, 87–88, 226; *Seventh
    Report*, 59–67, 75, 80, 91, 99, 119,
    133, 146–147, 149, 225; views on cor-
    poral punishment, 60, 76–77; views
    on temperance, 89. *See also* Samuel
    Gridley Howe

Mason, A.C., 207
Mason, Lowell, 47
mathematics instruction, 2, 139–141,
    168, 187, 201, 208. *See also* Frederick
    Emerson
May, Samuel J., 96–97, 127–128
May Day, 11, 18–19, 162, 165
McCleary, S.F., 40
McKeen, Joseph, 216
Medfield, Massachusetts, 37
Memphis, 176, 212–213
Milwaukee, 181, 210, 216
Minns, George W., 88–89
Mitchell, W.Z., 176
Montez, Lola, 148

Nashville, Tennessee, 176
National Education Association, 158,
    204, 211, 221
Neale, Rollin H.: and statistics, 56;
    background, 52; European travel,
    57; reading school committee of
    1845, 40, 95, 102, 115–116, 128–132,
    146–148; Smith School examination,
    123–124
Nell, William Cooper, 85
New England, 20, 31, 35–36, 98
New Haven, 21–22, 36, 116
New Orleans, 32–33, 177, 217
New York City, 16–19, 22, 24, 30–31, 33,
    38–40, 181, 185, 188, 196, 213, 216,
    219, 230. *See also* Henry Kiddle
Nichols-Wellington, Leah, 47–48
Nightingale, A.F., 175–176
No Child Left Behind, 3, 231
Norcross, Loring, 89
Norfolk County, Massachusetts, exami-
    nations, 200, 213–214
normal schools, 58, 60–62, 73, 147–149,
    223
Norristown, Pennsylvania, 20
Northwest Territory, 174

O'Connor, Joseph, 180, 204–205
Odin, John, Jr., 66, 102, 113–114

Omaha, 175–176
over-study, 195–198, 209, 211, 220–221

Parker, Charles I., 1–2, 6–7
Parker, Francis W., 3, 199–200, 207,
209, 211, 214, 223. *See also* progressive
education
Parsons, Theophilus: background, 52,
137, 144; European travel, 57; reading
school committee of 1845, 40, 95,
102, 108, 114–123, 128–132; truancy
report, 152
Peaslee, John B., 195
Peirce, Cyrus, 126
Pelton, John C., 214
Pestalozzi, Johann, 62. *See also* progres-
sive education
Philadelphia, 16, 18, 30, 37, 183
Philbrick, John D., 147, 156, 171–173,
201, 203–204, 224
phrenology, 54–56, 111, 195–198. *See
also* George Combe; Samuel Gridley
Howe; Horace Mann
Pickard, J.L., 179, 189
Pope, Alexander, 82
Pope Day, 11
Portland, Maine, 210–211
Portland, Oregon, 176, 182, 213, 225
Portsmouth, New Hampshire, 31, 34,
182
Pottsville, Pennsylvania, 215
Poughkeepsie, New York, 31
Powell, William B., 223
Princeton Review, 232
progressive education, 3, 188, 194, 199–
200, 203, 207, 211, 214, 223–224. *See
also* John Dewey; Francis W. Parker;
Johann Pestalozzi
promotion standards, 215–219, 221

Quincy, Illinois, 175
Quincy, Josiah, 45
Quincy, Josiah, Jr., 51, 67, 73, 93–94,
113, 129, 143–146
Quincy, Massachusetts, 200, 226

Quincy School, 147, 154, 171, 204,
224–225
Quintilian, 27–28
quiz books, 2, 205–208, 232

reading instruction, 63, 135–136
Regents' examinations, 222
Rickoff, Andrew J., 169–170, 174, 179,
184, 203
Rochester, New York, 19, 209
Rogers, John, 190–194, 198
Roxbury, 116, 130, 138, 226

Saint Nicholas Day, 11
Salem, Massachusetts, 32
San Francisco, 162–166, 180–181, 184,
188, 204–205, 210, 214–215, 217–220.
See also Joseph O'Connor; John Swett
Seaver, Edwin P., 185, 187, 223–224
Shepard, William, 92
Sherrill, J.E., 206–208
Shortridge, Abram C., 174–175
Smith, Adam, 28, 159–160
Smith School (Boston), 62, 71, 76, 80,
82–91, 96, 123–124, 149–150, 153,
227. *See also* African-Americans; Abner
Forbes; Rollin H. Neale
Smyth, Anson, 194
Southern states, 23, 31, 176, 219
Spurzheim, Joseph, 55
standardized tests, 2, 5, 29, 132, 229–
230. *See also* written examinations
Stark, Joshua, 181
statistics: and record keeping, 212–215;
and written examinations, 4, 131,
211; European influence, 56–57, 111,
178; popularity, 1–2, 10, 61, 103,
110–111, 120–121, 139, 157–159, 178,
passim; limitations of, 129, 136–139,
152–154, 182, 211–215, 220, 226–227.
See also William Brigham; Samuel
Gridley Howe; Horace Mann; written
examinations
Steele, J. Dorman, 207
Sterling, Massachusetts, 29

St. Louis, 167, 178, 194

Streeter, Sebastian, 72, 113–116, 120, 129, 144

Sumner, Charles, 64, 73, 100, 118

Sunday schools, 12, 59

Sutton, William S., 225

Swan, William D., 94

Swett, John, 161–167, 170, 173, 180, 182, 184, 205. *See also* San Francisco

Swift, Jonathan, 13

Syracuse, New York, 160

Tash, Thomas, 161

Taylor, Zachary, 18

test prep, 3, 205–208, 232

Thompson, Albert Henry, 207

Toledo, 211

Trenton, 29–30

U.S. Bureau of Education, 6, 173, 209

Vanderbilt, John, 17

Walker, Cornelius, 149

Walker, David, 85

Walton, George A., 213–214

Washington, DC, 18, 165, 223

Webster, Daniel, 28, 224

Wells, Samuel Adams, 45–46, 50

Wells, William Harvey, 173–174, 176

Whig Party, 51, 58, 71, 129, 141, 143, 167, 228

White, Emerson E., 183–184, 204, 217, 222–223

Wigglesworth, Edward, 72–73, 81, 114

Windship, Charles Williams, 39

Winerip, Michael, 230

Withington, Leonard, 73–75, 98, 101

Worcester, Joseph Emerson, 85, 133–134

Wordsworth, William, 145

writing instruction, 32–33, 39, 45, 158, 160, 162, 172, 175–176, 183–187, 201

written examinations: cheating, 95–96, 115–117, 160, 175, 179–181, 222, 226, 230; criticisms, 5, 158, 194–205, 207–209, 221; defense of, 200, 209–212, 221–224; European influence, 4, 59–60, 146; influence upon teaching, 2, 4, 156, 194–212, 228; rules and procedures, 104, 132, 137, 169–170, 173–180, 214; spread of, 1–2, 10, 143, 151, 155–161, passim; teaching to the test, 5, 203–208, 220–222; test preparation, 3, 160, 164, 179–180, 197–198, 205–208. *See also* Boston; emulation; Regents' examinations; statistics

Young, Alexander, 94, 114, 118–119

Young Ladies Academy of Philadelphia, 30

TESTING WARS IN THE PUBLIC SCHOOLS

William J. Reese

Testing Wars in the Public Schools

A Forgotten History

HARVARD UNIVERSITY PRESS

Cambridge, Massachusetts, and London, England   2013

Library of Congress Cataloging-in-Publication Data

Reese, William J., 1951–
    Testing wars in the public schools : a forgotten history / William J. Reese.
        p. cm.
    Includes bibliographical references and index.
    ISBN 978-0-674-07304-3
    1. Educational tests and measurements—United States—History—19th
century.   2. Public schools—United States—History—19th century.   I. Title.
    LB3051.R3553 2013
        371.26097309034   2012033665

To the memory of Lil and Ike Blemker

Contents

Introduction *1*

1 Festivals of Learning *8*

2 A-Putting Down Sin *38*

3 Screwing Machines *69*

4 A Pile of Thunder-Bolts *98*

5 Thanatopsis and Square Roots *127*

6 Chewing Pencil Tops *158*

7 The Culture of Testing *188*

Epilogue *221*

Notes *235*

Acknowledgments *291*

Index *293*